The Exemplary Middle School

William M. Alexander
University of Florida

Paul S. George
University of Florida

Holt, Rinehart and Winston, Inc.
New York Chicago San Francisco Philadelphia
Montreal Toronto London Sydney Tokyo

Library of Congress Cataloging in Publication Data

Alexander, William Marvin
  The exemplary middle school.

  1. Middle schools. I. George, Paul S., joint
author. II. Title.
LB1623.A43   373.2'36   80–27086
ISBN 0–03–052301–X

Printed in the United States of America
Published simultaneously in Canada
1 2 3 4   038   9 8

Holt, Rinehart and Winston
The Dryden Press
Saunders College Publishing

Preface

This book is intended as a basic textbook for students in the field of middle school education. It is relatively comprehensive in scope in that it defines the middle school concept, describes in detail the characteristics of exemplary middle schools and illustrates the implementation of these characteristics in practice. We have prepared the book so as to be of significant and specific help both to the beginner in middle school education and the practitioner seeking explanations and alternatives for schools in the middle.

We ourselves have long been directly and deeply involved in the search for better education of children in the middle school years. This search has really lasted throughout the twentieth century, with the junior high school developing early and becoming the dominant school between elementary and high school during the 1920 to 1960 period. Dissatisfactions with the junior high school and also with the still common K8–4 plan of organization without a middle school, led one of the authors and other educators to propose early in the 1960's the alternative organization now commonly called "middle school." As explained in chapter 1, the middle school concept has caught on very widely since 1960, with some 5000 schools now using this organization (usually but not always three or more years including grades 6 and 7). As consultants to school districts and faculties, and as trainers of middle school personnel, we have been very actively involved in the search for effective middle schools which would help achieve the long sought goal of educational continuity from early childhood through adolescence, linking elementary and secondary education with a dynamic program for children in the middle.

Although the middle school movement of the 1960's and 1970's has encompassed the development of some 5000 middle school units, these schools do not uniformly exhibit the characteristics educators have come to agree upon as essential for effective education in the middle of a child's school career. Perhaps the movement has been a bandwagon; the reasons for establishing the schools at times has been primarily social, economic and/or political rather than educational. In chapter 1 we examine the movement in detail, and call attention to the gap between the consensus-based characteristics of middle schools and the actual practices. This book is a major attempt by the authors to bridge the gap of theory and practice to the end of a significant increase in the number of exemplary schools and of exemplary practices in schools.

The authors believe that most books on the middle school published since *The Emergent Middle School* (Holt, Rinehart and Winston, 1968) have lacked adequate illustrative practices. In order to help our readers relate theory and practice and understand how practices can be developed and used to apply theory, we were eager to have many illustrations of exemplary practices and schools. Using our experience and knowledge, the recommendations of other middle school educators and the literature of middle school education, we selected some 75 schools throughout the United States as being representative of exemplary practices. We asked the principals of these schools early in 1979 to send us materials explaining their schools which we could use in the preparation of this book, and were pleased with the wealth of materials provided by many of these schools. Excerpts and references to these materials and schools are interspersed throughout the text at relevant points. Early in 1980 we asked the schools whose materials we had used to complete a form giving us specific data in summary form, for inclusion in the appendix of this book; thus our appendix is an incomplete but, we think, useful directory of exemplary middle schools. We regret the impossibility of including all good middle schools in the original survey, as well as our failure to hear from a few schools we contacted.

The organization and content of the text are based on the definition of the middle school and its essential characteristics presented in chapter 1. This chapter summarizes the information available on the characteristics of middle school students, traces the development of alternative organizations in the middle of children's school careers and states goals and characteristics of the middle school. It ends with a statement on "How Fares the Middle School Movement?" Chapter 2 is devoted to the planning process, since the planning process before the establishment of a new school organization as well as the continued, detailed operations of effective planning is a great determinant of the success of the middle school. The chapter stresses the frequently overlooked steps of analyzing community and student needs, securing and maintaining community cooperation and developing the school-home partnership. Chapter 3 deals with the curriculum of the middle school, its planning, and, especially, its various domains and elements. Alternative curriculum designs are considered, and extensive illustrations are given of the various curriculum elements. The somewhat unique feature of the teacher's role in guidance of middle school children is explained in chapter 4, with extended illustrations of the advisor/advisee relationship increasingly common in good middle schools. Another almost unique feature of the middle school as it should be, an interdisciplinary team organization which bridges the somewhat self-contained classroom of earlier elementary education and the departmentalized organization of the high school, is considered in chapter 5. Again, illustrations are drawn from many middle schools. Chapter 6 describes alternative methods of student grouping in the middle school, with particular attention to alternatives to age-grade grouping, especially types of multiage grouping. A major section of this chapter is devoted to "Mainstreaming: Grouping Exceptional Students in the Middle School." In chapter 7 we give attention to the problems of time and space which we have found to be very critical in the middle school, especially since so many middle schools have inherited the buildings of predecessor organizations and sometimes maintain their schedules, too. Schedules and floor plans of many middle schools illustrate this chapter. The authors' concern for providing readers with specific, sometimes how-to-do-it, materials is true in chapter 8, too, on instruction. Prospective and inservice middle school teachers are given extended analyses of different instructional systems, with major attention to total class, small group, individualized and teamed instruction. Chapter 9 turns attention to the critical matter of leadership roles in the middle school, and also the related one of staff development. Principles and practices are related to the roles of middle school principals and other status leaders, and to special leadership roles including those of faculty and staff, students, parents and other citizens and persons from outside the school community. The final chapter, 10, deals with evaluation, both of student progress and of the school itself. Much use is made in this chapter, too, of illustrative materials and of the programs of exemplary middle schools.

The authors consider our use of illustrative materials a unique feature of this book, and we and our readers are indebted to the schools involved for providing these materials. Readers may also find the directory of schools in the appendix and the index references useful in identifying schools and practices. Our section at the end of each chapter on "Additional Suggestions for Further Study" should provide useful additional references for students and instructors and other readers.

Particular attention is called to the inclusion in these lists of bibliographic information about doctoral dissertations dealing with middle school education; these studies are providing significant resources for further implementation of middle school theory and desired practices.

We are grateful to all the personnel of the middle and other schools in which we have worked as teachers and consultants for the stimulus given our thinking and writing about middle school education. We are also influenced by and are grateful for the challenge and other contributions of hundreds of students in our middle school teacher education courses. Especially we wish to thank again the principals and other personnel of the exemplary middle schools cited in this text for their invaluable assistance. Appreciation is also expressed to Martha Marsh for her most helpful compilation of sources from which our end-of-chapter reading suggestions are drawn.

Gainesville, Florida   W. M. A.
February, 1981   P. S. G.

Contents

Chapter 2   Planning an Exemplary Middle School   25

Chapter 3   The Middle School Curriculum   46

Chapter 4   Providing Teacher Guidance   87

Chapter 5   Interdisciplinary Team Organization   113

Chapter 6   Alternative Methods of Student Grouping   141

Chapter 7   Organizing Time and Space in the Middle School   172

Chapter 8   Instruction   217

Chapter 9   Leadership Roles and Staff Development in the Exemplary Middle School   258

Chapter 1

The Middle School Concept and Movement

This book is about schools in the middle of the school ladder. This first chapter is devoted to defining the middle school, explaining its focus, emergence, and growing popularity, and describing briefly the characteristic features of exemplary middle schools, those middle schools that the authors would like to see available for each American child of middle school age. We also note the progress attained by the middle school movement thus far, and indicate our judgment as to its continuing success.

What Is a Middle School?

In American usage, a middle school is a school in the middle of the school ladder, kindergarten through high school. In some foreign countries "middle school" denotes a school in the middle of the entire educational structure, elementary school through college or university. In the United States, the term itself was used very rarely prior to the early 1960's when educators began to use it with increasing frequency.

These new schools, or, more accurately, the new concepts of a school in the middle were conceived in part as bridges from elementary to secondary education, from the childhood level served by the elementary school to the adolescent level served by the high school. A widely cited definition of the middle school first appearing in the 1968 edition of the *Emergent Middle School* is germane:

> . . . a school providing a program planned for a range of older children, preadolescents, and early adolescents that builds upon the elementary school program for earlier childhood and in turn is built upon by the high school's program for adolescence.[1]

The concept of a bridging school is not enough, however, because children of middle school age have their unique characteristics and needs which cannot be subordinated to the impact of the elementary school nor to the demands of the high school. An effective middle school must not only build upon the program of earlier childhood and anticipate the program of secondary education to follow, but it must be directly concerned with the here-and-now problems and interests of its students. Furthermore, the middle school should not be envisioned as a passive link in the chain of education below the college and university, but rather as a dynamic force in improving education.

Definitions of the middle school should, and generally do, give much emphasis to the role of the school in providing for continuous educational progress of students. For example, leaders in one school district planned for its new middle schools in a summer seminar which adopted and promoted the following policy:

> The central goal of the middle schools in Alachua County is to assist students in moving forward continuously at their own rates of learning without undue breaks from one level to another. In the best educational program, students should move upward on an inclined plane rather than through a series of graded steps. Thus, the middle school should take each student as he is and help him move forward successfully on a continuum of learning into the high school.[2]

It is especially important for children moving into adolescence to make some of their own decisions, educational and otherwise, and so this seminar also described the middle school as "a transitional school seeking to help students who have been largely dependent on adults to become more self-directed," and suggested curriculum options as significant means of making choices:

> In the elementary school, the students have no choice of subjects, whereas in the high school they may make several choices. The middle school helps the students to develop leisure-time, career and other special interests so that they may choose widely from the many courses and activities available in the high school.[3]

Because of the dominance of the graded school organization, the definitions of any school level—elementary, middle, junior high, high school—inevitably indicate the grades included. Early discussions of middle school organizations in the 1960's gave extended attention to this topic, and it remains one for consideration in most middle school conferences and planning groups. Educators generally agree that grades 6 through 8 should be included, but difference of opinion comes as to whether grade 5 should also be in the middle school, and as to whether grades 7 and 8 could constitute a two-year middle school. Also, what about grade 9, and so on. If there must be a very specific grade definition, the one used in a national survey (1967–68) of middle schools and consistently followed for comparison purposes in later surveys, seems adequate:

> . . . a school which combines into one organization and facility certain school years (usually grades 5–8 or 6–8) which have in the past usually been separated in elementary and secondary schools under such plans as the 6–3–3, 6–2–4, and 6–6. . . . and having at least three grades and not more than five and including grades 6 and 7.[4]

Thus, we believe that an adequate concept of the middle school must view it as a bridging school, but one that affects, as well as is affected by, the schools above and below; as a school that is focused on the educational needs of learners who are usually in transition from childhood to adolescence; and as a school which therefore generally provides a program of three to five years in the middle of the school ladder below the college and university. More briefly, we define a middle school as a school *of some three to five years between the elementary and high school focused on the educational needs of students in these in-between years and designed to promote continuous educational progress for all concerned.*

Focus: The Middle School Student

A recent position paper from the Missouri Middle School Association states especially well the rationale of middle schools:

> The heart of the middle school is the learner. The child's uniqueness must always be considered. The arteries that feed the heart are the staff members and parents. We must be sensitive to the special needs and abilities of the ''in-betweenager'' and build on a program which will allow for the intellectual, social, physical and emotional growth of each child according to that child's capabilities. The goal of schools in the middle should be to provide for each student the opportunity to become self-directing and self-sustaining in a friendly, positive and encouraging atmosphere.[5]

Indeed it is the uniqueness of the ''in-between'' years that led many educators to favor the creation of a school to serve students in transition from childhood to adolescence. The lack of an adequate term to designate this period caused an early leader, Donald H. Eichhorn, to coin the terms ''transescent'' to designate the individual, and ''transescence'' the period of development:

> Transesence: the stage of development which begins prior to the onset of puberty and extends through the early stages of adolescence. Since puberty does not occur for all precisely at the same chronological age in human development, the transescent designation is based on the many physical, social, emotional, and intel-

lectual changes that appear prior to the puberty cycle to the time in which the body gains a practical degree of stabilization over these complex pubescent changes.[6]

Knowledge About the Age Group

Although Eichhorn's term, transescence, was viewed as controversial, it was used by the authors of the most complete review of knowledge about this age group available in 1980, *Toward Adolescence: The Middle School Years,* a yearbook of the National Society for the Study of Education (NSSE). The yearbook editor, Mauritz Johnson, observed that "only time will tell if this controversial word is destined to disappear or to become widely accepted in the literature pertaining to this age group."[7] This yearbook brings together data and insights from many fields to focus on the age group of about ten to fourteen, the middle school years, and is an invaluable reference for persons interested in middle school education. The present authors heartily recommend that persons preparing for or engaged in middle school education have specific studies in human growth and development with special focus on the middle school years, and with full attention to the growing body of knowledge about the age group.[8] In this book we can merely summarize major aspects of this knowledge and suggest sources for readers' further study.

Unfortunately, knowledge about emerging adolescents has been both inadequate and somewhat ignored in the past. Lipsitz introduced her chapter on "The Age Group," of the NSSE 1980 Yearbook with the observation (citing her earlier research review, *Growing Up Forgotten,* for the Ford Foundation) that "we are less informed about this stage of development than about any other among minors in America."[9] But the tremendous importance of the group and its possible past neglect and its present acute problems are highlighted by data she summarized elsewhere in 1979 on the social cost of neglect of early adolescence:

The social cost of our society's ambivalent attitude toward early adolescence is becoming more apparent daily. Seventh graders are most likely to be the victims of violence in school. The reported incidence of gonorrhea in adolescents aged 10–14 increased 10 percent between 1964 and 1975, nearly twice the increase of reported cases in 15–19 year olds. Drug abuse peaks during early adolescence. Girls 15 and under are the only age group for whom the birth rate is not decreasing. The onset of alcohol abuse occurs at around age 12. The rate of running away has doubled in the past decade, and the average age of runaways is 14. Fifteen and under is the only age group experiencing an increase in the rate of first admissions to mental hospitals. Juvenile crime appears to "blossom" around age 14. The average age of children in foster care is 12.

Continuing, however, she also cautioned that "in our tendency to generalize troubled characteristics to the entire age group, we forget that those who are troubled young people represent only a small percentage of young adolescents, the vast majority of whom manage to negotiate this time of significant growth and change remarkably well."[10]

Present knowledge of the middle school years suggests that the most outstanding characteristics of the entire population of middle schoolers is that of extreme variability, for the range of development on each trait is great. The ten to fourteen year-old group, the years most usually involved, includes older children, preadolescents, emerging and early adolescents and adolescents. It is this range in development which involves a large area of knowledge and makes extremely difficult the use of any one term to include all of the boys and girls of middle school age. It is the same type of problem, albeit more extensive, as comes from equating adolescence with high school, since some high school students are really still preadolescent. Although the term "transescence" is very useful, it too is somewhat inaccurate, for some children in middle schools are not yet in transition from childhood to adolescence and some have already completed the transition and arrived at adolescence. Similarly, the term "transitional" is descriptive but not all-inclusive. Maybe use of "middle school students" is more accurate! Each of the terms later childhood, preadolescence, emerging adolescence and early adolescence describes definite and large groups of the middle school population, but each is not inclusive. To use all these terms in a single reference is tedious. So we ourselves are inclined to use these terms somewhat interchangeably, and mostly to talk about boys and girls, learners, or students in the middle school or of middle school age, and sometimes just to abbreviate the reference to "middle schoolers."

Regardless of what we call these students, there are common developmental tasks that each one will encounter, or is currently encountering, or has just encountered. Usually a middle-schooler will become involved with most if not all of these tasks while in the middle school, but not necessarily at the same time. Thornburg's designation of seven developmental tasks is a useful one to note as we turn to a brief identification of some major characteristics of the age group:

1. *Becoming aware of increased physical changes*
2. *Organizing knowledge and concepts into problem-solving strategies*
3. *Learning new social/sex roles*
4. *Recognizing one's identification with stereotypy*
5. *Developing friendships with others*
6. *Gaining a sense of independence*
7. *Developing a sense of morality and values*[11]

Physical Characteristics

The most dramatic change in the human life span, puberty, is accompanied by a full range of physical changes in girls and boys. Physical growth over the three to five years of movement from childhood to adolescence is probably the greatest of the human experiences: increased height and weight, increased body breadth and depth and increased muscular strength. But individuals grow at different rates and times, and the question "Am I normal?" is an engrossing one as adolescence nears, especially with regard to the development of the sexual characteristics.

With the improvements in nutrition and disease control of the past century, puberty has been arriving earlier and earlier. Many of today's girls are physically capable of bearing children by age thirteen, and many of today's boys can probably father children by age fourteen or fifteen. The fact of young teen-age parentage constitutes a major problem in our society. Today's middle school provides sex education whether or not teachers provide the instruction! Program planning for the school must recognize the realities of the inevitable physical development of middle schoolers. At the same time it must recognize the variations between girls and boys and within each sex as to the readiness and need for such instruction.

The physical growth patterns also may involve lack of coordination of bone and muscle development, with the bones quite susceptible to damage in intense activities such as sports competition. There are also the tendencies during the periods of great growth, toward restlessness, overexertion, and fatigue. Middle school students need frequent opportunities for physical movement, and for the rest and change of activity. They also need help in diet, nutrition, personal hygiene, and coping with such physical problems as menstruation, growing beards, changing voices, and outgrowing clothes. The opportunity for personal counseling on such matters is unparalleled, but physical development is only a part of the cycle that eventually turns the adolescent away from adult to peer approval.

Intellectual Characteristics

Until the late 1970's, middle school educators had been somewhat guided by Piaget's classification of the stages of intellectual development. His work[12] assigned the beginnings of formal intellectual operations (that is, from reliance on concrete to use of abstract relationships) to about age eleven and thus to the approximate age group served by the middle school. Piagetan theory has frequently been used as the justification for curriculum and instruction changes in the middle school toward more emphasis on complex intellectual tasks. Recent research on brain growth seriously challenges any such marked emphasis for children ages twelve to fourteen since there is evidence of a brain growth plateau during these years.[13] Toepfer stated this challenge quite clearly in the following paragraph:

> The problem for middle grades seems to reside in the nature of educational programming offered during the age 12–14 years span. Clearly, achievement and growth during the age 10–12 period seem to confirm that emerging adolescents have the capacity to learn new and higher level thinking skills along with facts and information at that time. However, the fact of the plateau period of brain growth during the following age 12–14 years period and the classic mental age growth studies . . . indicate that youngsters cannot continue to grow and develop new and higher level cognitive, thinking skills during the brain growth experienced between age 10–12 years and (the plateau period of ages 12–14).

Further citing data concerning the "turn-off" in achievement of learning in grades 7 and 8, Toepfer commented that "such startling figures must cause middle grades educators to be careful that they are not challenging learners at an unachievable level of difficulty during the plateau period within the age 12–14 years interval."[14]

As Toepfer pointed out, the new brain growth data do not constitute a dictum to eliminate formal intellectual operations in the middle school. In addition to creating a need for continued research, these data also suggest that "each middle school (should) establish the degree to which students in that school are ready to initiate formal operations learning with any kind of predictable success."[15] The danger of over challenging children during brain growth plateau periods is very real, and middle school educators must be concerned with developing the broader curriculum we describe in chapter 3, with its inclusion of the curriculum domain of personal development. As to cognitive development, Epstein and Toepfer recommended that "education in the middle grades must develop a readiness for development of new cognitive skills during the brain growth period between ages 14 and 16."[16]

Whether or not middle school learners are more able to deal with abstractions than their younger selves, their added years of exposure to the world through school, television, movies, reading and relations with adults mean that they have greater stores of information, and usually greater curiosity for more. Today's average middle schooler is not only larger and more mature physically than his grandparents at the same age, he also knows far more. Data compiled and reported by Van Hoose indicate an average of about 35 hours per week of television viewing by the emerging adolescent, with the peak level at about the twelfth year.[17] Most twelve-year-old children have seen more of the world through television and movies and perhaps travel than their grandparents did in a lifetime, but they also have a range of social, economic, and political problems to confront and solve that were not solved and in fact were in some cases produced by previous generations. Middle school curriculum planners must recognize the variations in previous experience, knowledge, and potential for critical thinking and problem solving of their students, and provide correspondingly varied learning opportunities.

Social/Emotional Characteristics

Physical and mental changes in middle-schoolers are clearly reflected and even accentuated in the social and emotional domain. They are becoming increasingly aware of their own selves and of relationships with other individuals. Not only is "Who Am I?" a persistent question, but also "Who Do You Think I Am?" dominates much reflection and many relationships. For many children the self-concept becomes very low when at home and school comments are frequent and sharp about the children's awkwardness, terrific appetite, pimples, and/or ignorance. It is not surprising that the child who was happily tied to a mother's apron strings last year is staying farther away from them this year, as prepubescence or puberty intervenes.

Furthermore, the evidence is clear that the movement toward adolescence is one toward greater independence, greater freedom from the authority of adults, including parents and teachers. This change does not happen overnight—none does—but gradually, with many backs and forths from dependence to independence, the transescent is becoming self-directing. In the process he increasingly turns to the peer group for approval and encouragement, and away from the former authority. Parents and teachers who were once the ever-omnipotent center of a child's life are shocked, hurt, and perhaps angry when their omnipotence ceases.

The emerging adolescent is also finding a peculiarly different relationship with members of the opposite sex. Physical contact produces new reactions, and sometimes only one partner is affected. Beware when both sexes are titillated! Establishing a new and wholesome relationship with the opposite sex becomes a very significant developmental task. Along with this relationship the middle schooler must also learn to adopt a role as a girl or boy, possibly by accepting a relatively stereotyped one or perhaps resisting this and becoming for a time the "odd ball" of the class. With changing conceptions of sex roles today, transescents need much help in understanding current roles and conflicts, and determining appropriate behavior for themselves, for it is truly the arrival of felt sexuality in transescence that makes it the unique and challenging period of human development it is.

The facts of puberty, the changes in mental outlook, the turning to peers, and the phenomena of sexuality make the middle school years a period of tremendous emotional turmoil. Ideals are high for many, and the breakdown of an ideal or a hero or heroine can be disastrous. Interests are many but mostly short-lived, and the school is challenged to provide a variety of worthwhile activities to stimulate each child to explore and latch on to an interest that is desirable and persistent. Our discussion in chapter 3 of special interests activities and other aspects of the personal domain of the middle school curriculum is intended to emphasize and illustrate the scope and significance of the interests and values developing goals of middle school education. Their reviews of brain growth data underlie Epstein and Toepfer's emphasis on the same domain:

> The holistic education of the emerging adolescent will also require a greater emphasis upon learning experiences based as closely as possible upon youngsters' interest centers during this plateau period. The development of positive self-concepts during this period will require the definition and exploration of student interests through valuing experiences if the learner is to know who he or she really is as well as whom he or she would like to become.[18]

Middle school educators should also follow with great interest research on the right and left brain hemispheres. But Chall and Mirsky's summary of the educational implications of present knowledge about the brain calls for more research and great caution, and especially for collaboration of neuroscientists and educators:

> No simple inferences for what and how schools should teach the various curriculum areas can be drawn from the knowledge that the left hemisphere specializes more in analytic and/or sequential processing, such as language, while the right tends to specialize in parallel processing, more characteristic of spatial learn-

ing. . . . Since the application of the neurosciences to education is still relatively new, it must therefore be approached with caution as well as with the excitement that comes from viewing old problems in a new light.[19]

Tears, giggles, crushes and tantrums, all are common in adolescence and all begin to appear in prepubescence. The peaks and valleys of emotional development during the middle school years indicate an exciting period—and indeed to observe, work with and enjoy youngsters at this age is exciting, but also fatiguing for both the teacher and the taught.

Focus on the Middle School Student: Summary

The foregoing section has only briefly identified some of the most salient characteristics of middle school learners, and it is hoped that interested readers will use additional sources (such as those suggested here and at the end of the chapter) for further information. The point of greatest significance is that the middle school must be uniquely planned, staffed and operated to provide a program that is truly focused on the rapidly moving and changing learners in transition from childhood to adolescence. We have enumerated some of the characteristics and emphasized some implications for the middle school. But in truth this entire book is devoted to implications of the focus on middle school students, for the authors see the exemplary middle school as one whose facility, organization, curriculum plan, student services, instruction, indeed every aspect, is developed and utilized to serve the needs and characteristics of its unique population. The chief implications of our knowledge about middle school age learners are that they need a school focused on their needs, the exemplary middle school, and that educators, with the help of researchers in related fields, must keep searching out these needs and best means of their satisfaction.

Alternative Organizations

A complete history, yet to be written, of the middle school movement in the United States would need to include the development of graded schools and districts, and the establishment and reorganization in time of various schools serving children between ten and fourteen. When graded schools became common in the latter part of the nineteenth century the tendency was to make the elementary (grammar school) one of grades 1 through 8, with the high school usually including grades 9 through 12. There were many other organizations, including twelve-year schools, six-year high schools, seven-grade elementary and four-year high schools in some Southern states, and others. But by 1920 about four out of every five high school graduates had gone through an eight-grade elementary school and a four-year high school.

Even before 1920 a new organization, the junior high school, had arisen and had been recommended by various national committees, with great impetus given its establishment by the Commission on the Reorganization of Secondary Education in its 1918 report:

We, therefore, recommend a reorganization of the school system whereby the first six years shall be devoted to elementary education designed to meet the needs of pupils approximately 6 to 12 years of age, and the second six years to secondary education designed to meet the needs of pupils approximately 12 to 18 years of age.

The six years to be devoted to secondary education may well be divided into two periods which may be designated as the junior and senior periods.[20]

The junior high caught on, in part because the increasing school enrollment following World War I in the 1920's required new facilities. The moving of two grades into the new junior high school organization (not necessarily the new building) was an economical solution. The 6–3–3 organization became widely adopted, so that by 1960 the situation of forty years earlier had been reversed, with now about four out of five high school graduates having gone through the 6–3–3 organization rather than the 8–4 one.

By 1960 the junior high school had achieved some of the goals set for it in various pronouncements early in the century. One of the earliest proposals was to bring down college preparatory subjects to grades 7 and 8 in order to prepare students better over a longer period of time for college, making for ''better economy of time,'' since many argued that grades 7 and 8 in the elementary school were repetitive and wasteful. Another, later, argument for the junior high school was related to the high rate of dropout at the end of grade 8; the argument was that many students who left school at the end of the elementary school would stay through grade 9 in the junior high school. Both arguments were generally upheld by the development of the junior high school: mathematics, science and foreign language courses were brought into grades 7 and 8, and the dropout rate at the end of grade 8 did reduce. True, some educators felt that the junior high school too readily adopted the college preparatory aim and thereby neglected the needs of the noncollege-going population, and compulsory attendance laws and other social developments did result in more universal secondary education regardless of school organization. But we believe the junior high school made a very positive contribution toward relieving the rather sterile elementary curriculum for older students and toward keeping more students interested in formal education.

Throughout the past century the elementary school has provided the program of schooling for many transescents in grades 5 through 8. Even today we have many eight-grade elementary schools and senior elementary schools (corresponding in grade organization to middle schools). Most fifth and sixth graders are enrolled in elementary schools. Proponents of both the junior high school beginning in the 1920's and later, and the middle school beginning in the 1960's have questioned the appropriateness of the usual elementary school organization, even the traditional facility, for emerging adolescents.

Another argument for the junior high school, later to be sounded again for the new middle school, was that a transitional program was needed to bridge the gap between elementary and high school. The other argument common to both movements was that of the need for a program especially geared to the needs of young or emerging adolescents. The junior high school movement needs to be examined in detail to determine how these goals were attempted and what success was achieved.[21] Our own judgment is that any categorical assessment of success or failure is both impossible and unwise. Without doubt many junior high schools have served a very much needed transitional function in their communities. Equally unequivocally, we can state that many junior high schools became in time almost duplicate copies of their senior high schools in terms of credit and grading systems, methods of teaching, time schedules and student activities, so that sixth graders in June became high school students in September without adequate readiness or maturity. It was these schools that were cited in the 1960's for the failure of the junior high school to serve a transitional function, and as the reason for establishing a new transitional school in the middle.

As to the focus of the junior high school on the needs and interests of transescents, again we can make no categorical judgments. Junior high schools, in general, have made commendable and successful efforts to meet many preadolescent needs and interests. A wider curriculum than that of the elementary school has been provided, with some types of student activities introduced into the program. Counseling services, better libraries, a greater variety of teachers, association with more students came with junior high schools. And yet critics of the junior high schools of the 1960's could say with justification that some schools had curtailed activities and electives because of the public pressures for better academic programs (the very argument for junior highs originally); and that the effect of departmentalization of curriculum and instruction with an inflexible, fixed period schedule was to eliminate teacher counseling, individualization, and independent study.

Perhaps the most significant and indisputable fact about the alternative organizations for schooling of children ages ten through fourteen is that no single pattern for them had been as fully accepted and widely implemented as has the elementary school for younger children and the high school for older ones. In addition to the elementary and junior high schools which were the dominant schools for the ten to fourteen year-olds in 1960, there were intermediate schools, a few so-called middle schools, senior elementary schools, six-year high schools, two-year junior high schools (now frequently middle schools, grades 7 through 8), plus a myriad of schools and "centers" with the grades included varying from year to year. The time was ripe in 1960 for a new plan for the education of transescents to be tried, and it is not surprising that proposals for a new middle school were listened to with interest and widely, if not always wisely, implemented.

Emergence of the Middle School

Paul Woodring's 1965 comment in his influential *Saturday Review* section on education that "it now appears that the 6–3–3 plan, with its junior high school, is on the way out"[22] seemed then an exaggeration of the facts, for the middle school movement was barely on its way in. However, a proposal for a general reorganization of schools in the middle had been made at the Cornell Junior High School Conference in 1963.[23] At least one school (Williamsville, New York) represented at the Conference was in the process of construction and planning for a middle school program, and certainly there were a good many senior elementary schools, grade 6 through 8 junior high schools, and even many grade 7 through 9 junior high schools throughout the country that exemplified a substantial number of characteristics of the middle school as defined in the proposal. For example, Superintendent Carl Streams of the Upper St. Clair School District, Pennsylvania, had received permission in 1959 from the Pennsylvania State Department of Public Instruction to develop a grade 6 through 8 organization, which was subsequently planned by a faculty and administration led by Donald H. Eichhorn, with the Fort Couch Middle School program going into operation in 1962–63. Much earlier the organization of different elementary and secondary school districts in Illinois had caused some elementary school districts to establish grade 6 through 8 junior high schools, that were much more like elementary schools than the standard junior high schools. For example, Skokie Junior High School in Winnetka, Illinois, even in the 1940's had modular scheduling, interdisciplinary teaming and units, core-type curriculum plans, activities of a great variety called "enterprises," advisory systems, many exploratory, short-term "survey" courses, and much individualized instruction. Thus, there were several good prototypes for the new middle school, but few people knew about them. A period of promotion and dissemination of the middle school concept during the 1960's was essential to the full emergence of the movement. Even as late as 1968 when a course was introduced at the University of Florida on middle school education, "The Emergent Middle School," it was difficult to provide an adequate bibliography of titles including the term middle school; only a decade later the comprehensive course bibliography ran over 30 pages.

The emergence of the middle school at least in terms of grade organization and title can be readily documented, due to several national surveys that have been conducted. The most complete ones by Alexander (1967–68) and Brooks (1977–78) make possible a comparison of the status of middle schools in several particulars.[24] The accompanying table shows the tremendous growth in numbers of the middle school. Both surveys used the organizational definition cited earlier in this chapter of a school having not more than five grades and not less than three and including grades 6 and 7. Further details of the growth of middle schools in the 1960's and 1970's can be found in these surveys and comparisons and also in three other less comprehensive but useful surveys.[25]

What we can clearly conclude from the surveys and our general observation and review of current literature and school publications, is that the middle school has become very popular, its numbers having increased at least fourfold even in the past ten to twelve years. Our best guess is that there were at least 5000 middle schools as defined in this chapter and in the surveys cited, in operation in the United States as of 1980, as compared with

Table 1.1 / Number of Middle Schools by State*

STATE	1967	1977	STATE	1967	1977
Alabama	15	76	Montana	0	3
Alaska	0	6	Nebraska	3	0
Arizona	14	38	Nevada	0	11
Arkansas	4	29	New Hampshire	0	21
California	131	229	New Jersey	91	113
Colorado	4	49	New Mexico	7	21
Connecticut	25	72	New York	92	236
Delaware	2	22	North Carolina	8	98
Dist. of Columbia	0	0	North Dakota	1	1
Florida	10	149	Ohio	3	221
Georgia	24	119	Oklahoma	0	49
Hawaii	0	37	Oregon	30	42
Idaho	0	15	Pennsylvania	25	175
Illinois	142	261	Rhode Island	3	17
Indiana	31	102	South Carolina	6	126
Iowa	3	67	South Dakota	1	12
Kansas	0	31	Tennessee	3	40
Kentucky	4	36	Texas	252	480
Louisiana	2	84	Utah	0	12
Maine	3	66	Vermont	0	12
Maryland	13	55	Virginia	0	132
Massachusetts	10	128	Washington	22	70
Michigan	97	232	West Virginia	0	28
Minnesota	1	38	Wisconsin	21	100
Mississippi	3	40	Wyoming	0	3
Missouri	5	56			
			TOTAL	1,101	4,060

* From Brooks and Edwards, *The Middle School in Transition*, p. 3. The 1967 data are from the Alexander survey, the 1977 data from the Brooks survey.

not more than 100 in 1960! We turn now to the more complex and subjective questions and answers regarding why they grew so rapidly in number and whether they are really the middle schools their proponents hoped for.

Goals of the Middle School Movement

Early publications regarding the middle school proposed or inferred its goals. The Cornell proposal (1963) argued that "experimentation with a new middle school . . . should serve several purposes," with the following cited:

1. *It would give this unit a status of its own, rather than a "junior" classification.*
2. *It would facilitate the introduction in grades 5 and 6 of some specialization and team teaching in staffing patterns.*

3. *It would also facilitate the reorganization of teacher education sorely needed to provide teachers competent for the middle school; since existing patterns of neither elementary nor secondary teacher training would suffice, a new pattern would have to be developed.*
4. *A clearly defined middle unit should more easily have the other characteristics already described as desirable, than the typical junior high school: (1) a well-articulated 12- to 14-year system of education; (2) preparation for, even transition to, adolescence; (3) continued general education; and (4) abundant opportunities for exploration of interests, individualization of instruction, a flexible curriculum, and emphasis on values.*[26]

Eichhorn's school experience and graduate study convinced him that a new organization in the middle was essential; he especially found lacking the provisions of the traditional junior high school program for the unique needs of transescents. Hence he, too, proposed (1966) an attack on the root of the problem:

More and more professional literature is offering evidence that the junior high school concept is being seriously challenged. Usually, however, the suggested remedies take the form of treating the ills of the present structure rather than proposing an attack at the root causes of the problem. Substantiated assumptions of this study indicate that the root of the problem be attacked—through an altered school district organizational pattern—that an elementary unit of grades kindergarten through five, a middle school grouping of grades six through eight, and a high school unit of grades nine through twelve, be initiated.[27]

The authors of *The Emergent Middle School* (1968) cited the following "three principal lines of justification which have major implications for the program of the emergent middle school":

1. *To provide a program especially adapted to the wide range of individual differences and special needs of the "in-between-ager."*
2. *To create a school ladder arrangement that promotes continuity of education from school entrance to exit.*
3. *To facilitate through a new organization, the introduction of the needed innovations in curriculum and instruction.*[28]

In his book published the following year (1969) Theodore Moss decried the lack of a set of goals for the burgeoning middle schools and also proposed middle school goals that included most program features being generally recommended for the middle schools: provisions for health and physical education, and for mental health with special attention to sex education; learning situations and instructional strategies geared to the transescent; continuous educational guidance, with much use of teacher guidance; a well-articulated program, nursery through grade 12; and activities related to the interests and needs of middle school students.[29]

Unfortunately, the national surveys revealed that the actual reasons for establishing individual schools were in some cases considerably different from the general goals cited by these writers in the 1960's. As shown in Table 1.2, the most frequently cited reason by middle school principals

Table 1.2 / Reasons for Establishing Middle Schools*

| | PERCENT | |
REASON	1967	1977
To eliminate crowded conditions in other schools	58.2	47.7
To provide a program specifically designed for children in this age group	44.6	68.3
To bridge the elementary and high school better	40.0	62.7
To provide more specialization in grades 5 and/or 6	30.0	20.1
To remedy the weakness of the junior high school	24.5	36.0
To move grade 9 into the high school	24.5	29.2
To try out various innovations	23.6	22.9
To utilize a new school building	20.9	18.7
To use plans which have been successfully implemented in other school systems	12.7	13.4
To aid desegregation	6.5	14.2

* The 1967 data are from the Alexander survey, 1967–68, and the 1977 data from the Brooks survey, 1977.

queried in 1967 was "To eliminate crowded conditions in other schools" although the second most frequent does conform to the proponents' goals: "To provide a program specifically designed for students in this age group." The ranking of these two reasons was reversed in 1977. Some of the other reasons conform to the accepted rationale, but others are largely pragmatic. Vars and Lounsbury, long associated with the junior high school movement but more fundamentally interested in the education of emerging and early adolescents than in a single structure, commented in 1978 regarding the causes or goals of the middle school movement, that:

> The need for additional facilities to relieve overcrowding, consolidation as residential patterns shifted, and the elimination of racial segregation through court-ordered integration plans—all have contributed more to the prodigious growth of the movement than any purported advantages.[30]

Neither the surveys, especially the later one, nor our observation of the establishment of many middle schools fully confirm the foregoing statement. In numerous instances immediate social factors have precipitated a reorganization that became the opportunity to create a new and better school program. Even if more middle schools were established originally for reasons other than program improvement, the more important question is whether today's schools, however established, are trying to be or become good middle schools. We turn shortly to facts and conjecture as to the status of the middle school movement.

In addition to the publication of suggested goals for the middle school such as cited above, many individual schools and school districts and even state organizations have developed their own statements of the goals of middle school education. Most statements we have seen emphasize much the same points: focus on the needs and interests of middle schoolers, transition from childhood to adolescence with a program of continuous progress education, and a broad and flexible curriculum, with appropriate instructional, guidance, and administrative support and implementation. Perhaps the most significant set of goals comes from a 1977 report of its Committee on Future Goals and Directions to the National Middle School Association, subsequently adopted by the Association. The Committee noted that it has "opted for the priority of meeting the needs of middle age children wherever found, not just for establishing middle schools," and took the following position on goals for the movement:

> We recognized the absence of any universal definition of the middle school and of middle school goals, and indeed would tend to reject any set of standards which prescribed specific goals. At the same time we felt that the NMSA should stand for certain priority goals, and hoped this would influence members to incorporate these goals into their own school statements:
>
> 1. *Every student should be well known as a person by at least one adult in the school who accepts responsibility for his/her guidance.*
> 2. *Every student should be helped to achieve optimum mastery of the skills of continued learning together with a commitment to their use and improvement.*
> 3. *Every student should have ample experiences designed to develop decision-making and problem-solving skills.*
> 4. *Every student should acquire a functional body of fundamental knowledge.*
> 5. *Every student should have opportunities to explore and develop interests in aesthetic, leisure, career, and other aspects of life.*[31]

We ourselves accept wholeheartedly this conception of the rationale of middle school education, and heartily recommend that it be widely studied, expanded and otherwise revised if needed, and implemented in the continuing establishment and improvement of American middle schools.

Characteristics of an Exemplary Middle School

The literature of middle school education of the past decade or so has been replete with discussions and lists of essential characteristics of good middle schools, and in general there has been increasing unanimity as to the characteristics. Several of these lists are presented before turning to our own.

The Montebello, California, Unified School District, in its *The Golden Age of Education* (1969) outlined the desirable program characteristics of the three major grade level divisions of the K4–4–4 plan of organization, and specified the following characteristics of the "intermediate school":

1. *Team Teaching*
2. *Non-Gradedness*
3. *Flexible Scheduling*
4. *Transition Pattern (from single disciplines to interdisciplinary approaches)*
5. *School Structure (school within a school possibility)*
6. *Measurable Objectives*

7. *Instructional Learning Center (Student)*
8. *Instructional Resource Center (Teacher)*
9. *Individualized Instruction*
10. *Exploration*
11. *Pupil Personnel Services Center*
12. *Innovation*
13. *Administration Team*
14. *Auxiliary Personnel*[32]

In 1973 Georgiady and Romano proposed these characteristics of the middle school, stated as criteria for determining, "Do You Have A Middle School?"

1. *Is Continuous Progress Provided For?*
2. *Is a Multimaterial Approach Used?*
3. *Are Class Schedules Flexible?*
4. *Are Appropriate Social Experiences Provided For?*
5. *Is There an Appropriate Program of Physical Experiences and Intramural Activities?*
6. *Is Team Teaching Used?*
7. *Is Planned Gradualism Provided For?*
8. *Are Exploratory and Enrichment Studies Provided For?*
9. *Are There Adequate and Appropriate Guidance Services?*
10. *Is There Provision for Independent Study?*
11. *Is There Provision for Basic Skill Repair and Extension?*
12. *Are There Activities for Creative Experiences?*
13. *Is There Full Provision for Evaluation?*
14. *Does the Program Emphasize Community Relations?*
15. *Are There Adequate Provisions for Student Services?*
16. *Is There Sufficient Attention to Auxiliary Staffing?*[33]

Enough consensus was developing by the mid-1970's for an ASCD Working Group on the Emerging Adolescent Learner to declare that the middle school have the following ten characteristics:

1. *A unique program adapted to the needs of the pre- and early adolescent learner.*
2. *The widest possible range of intellectual, social and physical experiences.*
3. *Opportunities for exploration and development of fundamental skills needed by all while making allowances for individual learning patterns. It should maintain an atmosphere of basic respect for individual differences.*
4. *A climate that enables students to develop abilities, find facts, weigh evidence, draw conclusions, determine values, and that keeps their minds open to the new facts.*
5. *Staff members who recognize and understand the student's needs, interests, backgrounds, motivations, goals, as well as stresses, strains, frustrations, and fears.*
6. *A smooth educational transition between the elementary school and the high school while allowing for the physical and emotional changes taking place due to transescence.*
7. *An environment where the child, not the program, is most important and where the opportunity to succeed is ensured for all students.*

8. *Guidance in the development of mental processes and attitudes needed for constructive citizenship and the development of lifelong competencies and appreciations needed for effective use of leisure.*
9. *Competent instructional personnel who will strive to understand the students whom they serve and develop professional competencies which are both unique and applicable to the transcent student.*
10. *Facilities and time which allow students and teachers an opportunity to achieve the goals of the program to their fullest capabilities.*[34]

We ourselves have also developed and expounded in previous publications and elsewhere our own research, observations, and conclusions as to the characteristics of good, really exemplary, middle schools. Our lists have probably included most all of the various points on the foregoing lists and other ones because there is now near consensus on the desirable characteristics of middle schools. For the purpose of this book we have set up twelve essential characteristics or elements of exemplary middle schools, and organized our material so as to develop fully each element, in most cases by a chapter. The twelve essential characteristics, in abbreviated form, and in the order of our corresponding chapters are as follows:

1. A statement of philosophy and school goals that is based on knowledge of the educational needs of boys and girls of middle school age and is used in school program planning and evaluation. (Chapter 1)
2. A system for school planning and evaluation which is specifically designed for the middle school level and which involves all concerned in the school community. (Chapter 2)
3. A curriculum plan for the middle school population that provides for their continuous progress, basic learning skills, use of organized knowledge, personal development activities, and other curriculum goals as locally determined. (Chapter 3)
4. A program of guidance which assures the availability of help for each student from a faculty member well-known to the student. (Chapter 4)
5. An interdisciplinary teacher organization which provides for team planning, teaching, and evaluation, and for appropriate interdisciplinary units. (Chapter 5)
6. Use of methods of student grouping for instruction which facilitate multiage and other instructional arrangements to maximize continuous progress. (Chapter 6)
7. Block scheduling and other time arrangements to facilitate flexible and efficient use of time. (Chapter 7)
8. Planning and use of physical facilities to provide the flexible and varied program required for middle schoolers. (Chapter 7)
9. Instruction which utilizes a balanced variety of effective strategies and techniques to achieve continuous progress of each learner toward appropriate instructional objectives. (Chapter 8)
10. Appropriate roles for the various individuals and groups required for

continued and dynamic leadership in the middle school, with a continuing program of staff development and renewal focused on the unique problems of middle school personnel. (Chapter 9)

11. A plan for evaluation of student progress and of the school itself to assure the achievement of the goals of the school. (Chapter 10)

12. Participation with other schools and with community groups in the continuing study of the middle school population and of society as a whole, to be responsive to changing needs and conditions of the future. (Epilogue)

Summing up, an exemplary middle school is one so planned, organized and operated as to be a model for all persons interested in middle school education, with full recognition that no one school will exhibit to perfection all if any of the above characteristics. But an exemplary middle school tries and tries hard, with some success, to meet such criteria. All middle schools, we think, should be or become exemplary.

How Fares the Middle School Movement?

The national surveys already referred to in this chapter provide one objective basis for assessing the progress of the middle school movement. Comparison of the survey reports of 1967–68 and 1977–78 reveals that the one great change was in the number of middle schools identified: from 1101 in the first survey to 4060 a decade later. Supplementing these data are other series of events in the 1960's and 1970's that attest to widespread interest and involvement in the middle school movement: the establishment of the National Middle School Association and of many state associations and leagues, the extensive efforts now underway to establish or improve teacher education and certification for middle school education, the extensive publications previously noted and the plethora of middle school institutes, seminars and conferences.

The slowness of progress is in the programs, not the numbers of middle schools. Certain program features usually advocated for middle schools were widely lacking in both 1967–68 and 1977–78. About 90 percent of the schools continued strict chronological age grade grouping, and 79–85 percent, varying by grade, of the schools reported that they did not use a team teaching arrangement. But perhaps progress along these lines is just very slow, for there was little evidence of any nongraded schools in 1967, and over 90 percent of the schools then had no interdisciplinary teaming. However, many middle schools now have an interdisciplinary faculty organization, even if there is relatively little teaming in actual instruction. There was little change in required and elective subjects offered, and in the number of schools having interscholastic athletics, about half at the time of both surveys.

However, these surveys may have failed to get data on some even more significant matters, such as teacher guidance services, involvement of parents and community in the school program, opportunities for individualized instruction, and independent study, use of varied instructional materials and techniques appropriate to middle schoolers, emphasis on basic skills, variety of recreational, cultural, and career-related activities for development of student interests, and the commitment of its personnel to the middle school concept. We do not have, but do need, adequate data on such questions as these, but the authors' observations of middle schools throughout the United States indicate that there has been marked improvement on all of these criteria during the past decade.

The fact is that fifteen to twenty years in the life of an institution such as middle schools is a very short period. It can even be that the almost landslide movement into this organization has restricted the careful evaluation and planning and replanning sorely needed with new organizations and institutions. The numbers of schools are now stabilizing, and educators can make real middle schools out of their grade organizations; if not, the middle school of 1980 may be replaced by some other school in the middle by the year 2000, or even earlier.

Probably the greatest problem and need of the middle school movement is the lack of personnel trained for and committed to the education of transescents. Many, probably most, of the personnel working in some 5000 middle schools of today did not originally choose to work at that level. They have learned almost all they know about middle school education through limited inservice education, and their experience, either or both possibly mediocre. Fortunately there are many persons in service who are highly committed and well trained, and they offer our greatest hope for bringing about more complete commitment to middle school education. Not to be overlooked, too, is the fact that many middle school age students are taught in elementary and junior high schools by some teachers, who however trained and certified, are competent and committed to effective education for the age group. The middle school movement may well fare best when distinctions and competition between upper or senior elementary schools, middle schools, intermediate schools, junior high schools, and six-year high schools, can be minimized, with greater sharing of resources and programs for the development and operation of exemplary schools for transescents, wherever housed.

ADDITIONAL SUGGESTIONS FOR FURTHER STUDY

A.   Books

George, Paul S., Editor, *The Middle School: A Look Ahead.* Fairborn, Ohio: National Middle School Association, Inc., 1977.

Leeper, Robert, Editor, *Middle School in the Making.* Washington, D.C.: Association for Supervision and Curriculum Development, 1974.

Romano, Louis G. and Others, Editors, *The Middle School: Selected Readings on an Emerging School Program*. Chicago, Illinois: Nelson-Hall Company, 1973.

Storen, Helen F., *The Disadvantaged Early Adolescent: More Effective Teaching*. New York: McGraw-Hill, Inc. 1968.

B. Periodicals

Alexander, William M. and Williams, Emmett L., "Schools for the Middle School Years," *Educational Leadership,* 23, 217–23 (December 1965).

Eichhorn, Donald H., "Middle School: The Beauty of Diversity," *Middle School Journal,* 8, 3, 18–9 (February 1977).

George, Paul. "Florida's Junior High and Middle Schools: How Do They Compare?" *Middle School Journal,* 8, 10–1, 23 (February 1977).

Havighurst, Robert J., "The Middle School Child in Contemporary Society," *Theory Into Practice,* 7, 120–2 (June 1968).

Howell, Bruce. "A Strategy for Furthering the Middle School Movement," *Middle School Journal,* 8, 6–7 (November 1977).

Mead, Margaret, "Early Adolescence in the United States," *The Bulletin of the National Association of Secondary School Principals,* 49, 5–10 (April 1965).

"Middle School Status in Ten States," *National Elementary Principal,* 51, 67–77 (November 1971).

Sinks, Thomas A. and Others. "What's Happening to Middle Schools in the Upper Midwest?" *Clearing House,* 55, 145–51 (January 1978).

Thompson, Loren J., "Benchmarks for the Middle School," *Theory Into Practice,* 15, 153–5 (April 1976).

Toepfer, C. F., Jr. "Challenge to Middle School Education: Preventing Regression to the Mean," *Middle School Journal,* 7, 18–22 (September 1976).

Van Til, William, "Junior High School or Middle School?" *Contemporary Education,* 41, 222–31 (April 1970).

C. ERIC

Eichhorn, Donald H., *Middle School Challenges: Are We Meeting Them?* Paper presented at the National Middle School Conference, Pittsburgh, Pennsylvania, November, 1978. (ERIC No. ED 165–269)

Gore, Ethel V., *A Descriptive Study of Organizational, Curriculum and Staff Utilization Patterns of Selected New England Middle Schools,* Paper presented at the Canadian School Trustees' Association Congress on Education, Toronto, Ontario, June, 1978. (ERIC No. ED 161–136)

D. Dissertations and Dissertation Abstracts

Barton, Ronald Rex, "A Historical Study of the Organization and Development of the Junior High and Middle School Movement 1920–1975," *Dissertation Abstracts,* 37 (November 1976) 2682–A.

Blight, John, "Identifying the Unique Characteristics of the Emergent Middle School," *Dissertation Abstracts,* 35 (August 1975) 794–A.

Cave, Burton B., "A Comparison of Organizational, Curricular Practices and Innovational Factors Between Schools Named Junior High Schools and Those Named Middle Schools Within the Rocky Mountain Region," *Dissertation Abstracts,* 36 (January 1976) 4143–4–A.

Decoste, Lee F., "Junior High School and Middle School: A Comparison of Problems Students Experience," *Dissertation Abstracts,* 36 (July 1975) 62–A.

Draud, Jon E., "The Effects of Organizational Structure of Middle Schools and Junior High Schools on the Attitudes of Teachers and Students Toward the School," *Dissertation Abstracts,* 39 (February 1979) 4620–A.

Dubel, Thomas Trenton, Sr., "A Descriptive Study of Organizational, Curriculum, and Staff Utilization Patterns of Selected Middle Schools," *Dissertation Abstracts,* 37 (October 1976) 1903–A.

Gross, Bernard M., "An Analysis of the Present and Perceived Purposes, Functions, and Characteristics of the Middle School," *Dissertation Abstracts,* 33 (July 1972) 141–2–A.

Hunsaker, Johanna Steggert, "A Comparison of the Organizational Climates of Selected Middle Schools and Junior High Schools," *Dissertation Abstracts,* 39 (December 1978) 3502–A.

Miller, W. Barry, "Achievement of Ninth Grade Students in Science Curricula Emphasizing Concrete and Formal Reasoning," Unpublished doctoral dissertation, The University of Florida, 1980.

Unruh, Clarence G., "A Study of Junior High Schools and Middle Schools with Reference to Philosophy, Function, Curriculum, Personnel, and Activities Programs," *Dissertation Abstracts,* 36 (October 1975) 1975–A.

FOOTNOTES

1. William M. Alexander and others, *The Emergent Middle School* (New York: Holt, Rinehart & Winston, Inc., 1968), p. 5.
2. Summer Seminar, *Report of the Middle School Task Team* (Gainesville, Florida: Alachua County Schools, 1972), p. 7.
3. Summer Seminar, pp. 6 and 7.
4. William M. Alexander, *A Survey of Organizational Patterns of Reorganized Middle Schools,* Final Report, USOE Project 7-D-026 (Gainesville, Florida: University of Florida, July, 1968), p. 1.
5. Thomas E. Moeller, President, Missouri Middle School Association, "Missouri Middle Schools Position Paper," mimeographed, March 10, 1978, p. 4.
6. Donald H. Eichhorn, *The Middle School* (New York: The Center for Applied Research in Education, Inc., 1966), p. 3.
7. Mauritz Johnson, Ed., *Toward Adolescence: The Middle School Years,* Seventy-ninth Yearbook of the National Society for the Study of Education, Part I (Chicago: University of Chicago Press, 1980), p. xii.
8. Additional useful sources include: Mary Compton, Ed., *A Source Book for the Middle School* (Athens, Ga.: Educational Associates, Inc., 1978); Joan Lipsitz, *Growing Up Forgotten: A Review of Research and Programs Concerning Early Adolescence* (Lexington, Mass.: D.C. Heath & Co., 1977); Geneva D. Haertel, "Literature Review of Early Adolescence and Implications for Programming," Appendix C in National Science Foundation, Directorate for Science Education, *Early Adolescence: Perspectives and Recommendations to the National Science Foundation* (Washington, D.C.: U.S. Government Printing Office, September, 1978); and Herschel D. Thornburg, Guest Editor, "Early Adolescence," *The High School Journal,* 63, entire issue (March 1980).
9. Joan Lipsitz, "The Age Group," Chapter 2 in Johnson, Ed., *Toward Adolescence,* p. 7.
10. Joan Lipsitz, "Growing Up Forgotten—Must They?", *Middle School Journal,* 10, 3 (February 1979).

11. Thornburg, "Early Adolescents: Their Developmental Characteristics," p. 216.
12. See Robert B. Sund, *Piaget for Educators* (Columbus, Ohio: Charles E. Merrill, 1976).
13. See Herman T. Epstein, "Growth Spurts during Brain Development: Implications for Educational Policy and Practice," Chapter X in Jeanne S. Chall and Allan F. Mirsky, Eds., *Education and the Brain,* Seventy-seventh Yearbook of the National Society for the Study of Education, Part II (Chicago: University of Chicago Press, 1978). Also see Herman T. Epstein and Conrad F. Toepfer, Jr., "A Neuroscience Basis for Reorganizing Middle Grades Education," *Educational Leadership,* 35, 656–660 (May 1978).
14. Conrad F. Toepfer, Jr., "Brain Growth Periodization Data: Some Suggestions for Reorganizing Middle Grades Education," *The High School Journal,* 63, 224–226 (March 1980).
15. Toepfer, "Brain Growth Periodization Data," p. 226. Also see regarding the need for research, Toepfer and Jean Marari's Chapter (XIV) on "School-based Research" in Johnson, Ed., *Toward Adolescence.*
16. Epstein and Toepfer, "A Neuroscience Basis," p. 658.
17. John J. Van Hoose, "The Impact of Television Usage on Emerging Adolescents," *The High School Journal,* 63, 240 (March 1980).
18. Epstein and Toepfer, "A Neuroscience Basis," p. 658.
19. Chall and Mirsky, "The Implications for Education," Chapter 12 in *Education and The Brain,* pp. 374–375.
20. Commission on the Reorganization of Secondary Education, *Cardinal Principles of Secondary Education,* Bulletin 1918, No. 35 (Washington, D.C.: U.S. Bureau of Education, 1918), pp. 12–13.
21. See William Van Til, Gordon F. Vars, and John H. Lounsbury, *Modern Education for the Junior High School Years,* 2nd ed. (Indianapolis: The Bobbs-Merrill Co., Inc., 1967), Unit One, for an excellent history of junior high schools. Other relevant sources include James B. Conant, *Education in the Junior High School Years: A Memorandum to School Boards* (Princeton, N.J.: Educational Testing Service, 1960); John H. Lounsbury and Jean V. Marani, *The Junior High School We Saw* (Washington, D.C.: Association for Supervision and Curriculum Development, 1964); John H. Lounsbury and Gordon F. Vars, *A Curriculum for the Middle School Years* (New York: Harper & Row, 1978), Chapter 2; and Samuel Popper, *The American Middle School: An Organizational Analysis* (Waltham, Mass.: Blaisdell Pub. Co., 1967).
22. See Paul Woodring, "The New Intermediate School," *Saturday Review,* 48, 77 (October 16, 1965).
23. See William M. Alexander, "The Junior High School: A Changing View," *NASSP Bulletin,* 48, 15–24 (March 1964) for this proposal. Also see for an appraisal of the junior high school and its problems this earlier article by the Director of the Cornell Junior High School Project: Mauritz Johnson, "School in the Middle—Junior High School: Education's Problem Child," *Saturday Review,* 45:40–42, 56 (July 21, 1962).
24. See Alexander, *A Survey . . .* (July, 1968), and Kenneth Brooks and Francine Edwards, *The Middle School in Transition: A Research Report on the Status of the Middle School Movement* (Lexington, Kentucky: College of Education, University of Kentucky, 1978). Also see for further comparison of the two surveys, William M. Alexander, "How Fares the Middle School Movement?", *Middle School Journal,* 9, 3, 19–21 (August 1978), and Kenneth Brooks, "The

Middle School—A National Survey,'' *Middle School Journal,* Part I, 9, 6–7 (February 1978) and Part II, 9, 6–7 (May 1978).

25.   See William A. Cuff, ''Middle Schools on the March,'' *NASSP Bulletin* 51, 82–86 (February 1967); Ronald P. Kealy, ''The Middle School Movement, 1960–1970,'' *The National Elementary Principal,* 51, 20–25 (November 1971); and Mary Compton, ''The Middle School: A Status Report,'' *Middle School Journal,* 7, 3–5 (June 1976). The studies by Kealy and Compton, each of whom had participated as research assistants in the 1967–68 survey, used the same definitions and methods as it and the 1977–78 one. These several studies also revealed the growing popularity of the term ''middle school'' as a part of the school's name, and the tendency for there to be about 60 percent of the schools having grades 6 to 8, and 25 to 30 percent with grades 5 to 8, and a scattering of other organizations.

26.   Alexander, ''The Junior High School: A Changing View,'' p. 22.

27.   Eichhorn, p. 104.

28.   Alexander and others, p. 11.

29.   Theodore C. Moss, *Middle School* (Boston: Houghton Mifflin Co., 1969), pp. 20–21.

30.   Lounsbury and Vars, p. 21.

31.   ''Report of the NMSA Committee on Future Goals and Directions,'' *Middle School Journal,* 8: 16 (November 1977).

32.   Montebello Unified School District, *Program Characteristics for the Golden Age of Education.* Montebello, California: The District, March, 1969.

33.   Nicholas P. Georgiady and Louis G. Romano, ''Do You Have A Middle School?'' *Educational Leadership,* 31, 238–41 (December 1973).

34.   Thomas E. Gatewood and Charles A. Dilg, *The Middle School We Need.* A Report from the ASCD Working Group on the Emerging Adolescent. (Washington, D.C.: Association for Supervision and Curriculum Development, 1975), p. 10.

Chapter **2**

Planning an Exemplary Middle School

America's approximately 5000 middle schools and all of the other schools that serve learners of middle school age have been planned in many different ways; some have been planned systematically, some through an adoptive process only, and some spasmodically and ineffectually. However the schools may have been planned originally, it is rarely too late to improve them. Conversely, it is nearly always possible for even well-planned, good schools and other institutions to deteriorate in an absence of continued planning for the future. Hence this chapter states and illustrates principles and steps of planning exemplary middle schools, both originally and thereafter, even remedially.

First, we emphasize our faith in the importance of planning at the individual school level. Granted that planning by the state and the school district is essential for financing and maintenance of public schools, and that planning by the individual teacher is essential to good instruction at every level, it is the individual school that provides the learning environment and opportunities which make or do not make for good schooling. Goodlad's extensive research and experience in the study of schools led him to the view "that the single school falls nicely between the depersonalized, complex, amorphous school system and the somewhat intimidated, impotent, individual teacher."[1] In Goodlad's later, comprehensive "Study of Schooling," data were collected and analyzed to determine what went on in 38 schools based on the belief that "studying what goes on in schools holds more promise for understanding schools (and, therefore, for being in a position to improve them) than studying what comes out of schools."[2]

We unreservedly accept for implementation in the middle school Goodlad's first postulate for school improvement:

> First, the optimal unit for educational change is the single unit school with its pupils, teachers, principal—those who live there every day—as primary participants. The interactions of these people, the language they use, the traditions they uphold, the beliefs to which they subscribe, and so forth make up the culture of the school. It is not necessarily a healthy ecosystem, but it exists, often with surprising tenacity.[3]

Especially because of this tenacity which works to inhibit change, it is very important to establish as sound a system of planning as possible whenever established, hopefully early in the life of the institution. We assume that the primary planning unit is the school faculty, although various other groups and individuals are utilized in the planning process. As shown in Table 2.1, surveys of the middle school movement identified some decline in the perceived influence of system-wide administrators in decisions to establish a middle school from 1967 to 1977. The influence of most other decision-influencing individuals and groups—principal, teachers, parents, and especially the local board of education—was perceived by larger percentages of principals as more influential in 1977 than in 1967. Apparently participation in the decisions to establish middle schools has been widening; this is encouraging, but it also emphasizes the need for all concerned in the decision to be involved in a systematic planning and decision-making process.

Although numerous planning models are possible, we ourselves have found useful a basic problem-solving process we refer to as the IDEAS process, described in the following section.

Table 2.1* / Person(s) Involved and Most Influential in Deciding to Establish a Middle School

	PERCENT INVOLVED		MOST
GROUPS	1967	1977	INFLUENTIAL
Principal	69.1	75.0	27.9
Teachers	46.3	62.6	20.3
Parents	21.8	34.2	5.4
Accrediting Bodies	2.7	9.8	1.3
State Department of Education	10.9	23.6	3.0
Survey of Outside Agency	6.4	4.7	0.3
System-Level Administration	78.3	56.2	19.9
Local Board of Education	11.8	67.3	18.2

* From Kenneth Brooks and Francine Edwards, *The Middle School in Transition: Research Report on the Status of the Middle School Movement* (Lexington, Ky.: College of Education, University of Kentucky, 1978), p. 6. (1967 data from Alexander Survey, 1967–68).

Using the *IDEAS* Process in Planning Middle Schools

The *IDEAS* process, developed and named by one of the authors in connection with school improvement programs in several school districts, is shown sequentially in Figure 2.1. Each of its phases is illustrated below with reference to school improvement through planning a middle school.

Figure 2.1 / The *IDEAS* Process of School Improvement

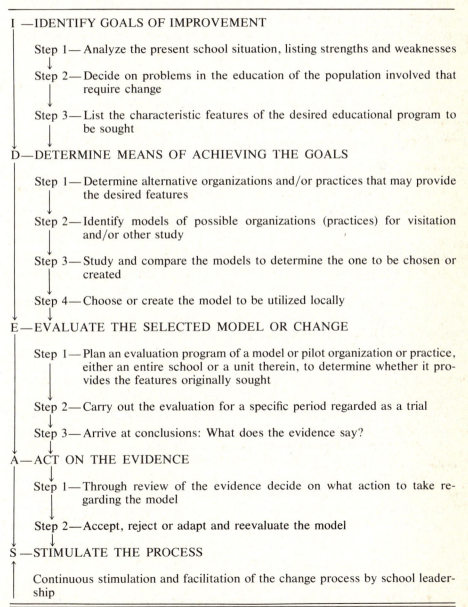

I —IDENTIFY GOALS OF IMPROVEMENT

Step 1— Analyze the present school situation, listing strengths and weaknesses

Step 2— Decide on problems in the education of the population involved that require change

Step 3— List the characteristic features of the desired educational program to be sought

D—DETERMINE MEANS OF ACHIEVING THE GOALS

Step 1— Determine alternative organizations and/or practices that may provide the desired features

Step 2— Identify models of possible organizations (practices) for visitation and/or other study

Step 3— Study and compare the models to determine the one to be chosen or created

Step 4— Choose or create the model to be utilized locally

E—EVALUATE THE SELECTED MODEL OR CHANGE

Step 1— Plan an evaluation program of a model or pilot organization or practice, either an entire school or a unit therein, to determine whether it provides the features originally sought

Step 2— Carry out the evaluation for a specific period regarded as a trial

Step 3— Arrive at conclusions: What does the evidence say?

A—ACT ON THE EVIDENCE

Step 1— Through review of the evidence decide on what action to take regarding the model

Step 2— Accept, reject or adapt and reevaluate the model

S —STIMULATE THE PROCESS

Continuous stimulation and facilitation of the change process by school leadership

Identifying Goals of Planning

Original planning of a middle school involves development of a statement of school goals, but even earlier there must be identified the dissatisfaction with the existing structure, or the new conditions or other problems which precipitated the planning process. That is, what is the new middle school to do that is not being done adequately already? Why plan a middle school? This is the question to be answered, with the answer(s) really constituting the major goal(s) of planning. The Shelburne, Vermont, district answered the question "Why A Middle School Organization?" very succinctly and appropriately, we think, in this statement for its patrons, of the transitional function of the middle school:

> At this particular time in the evolution of the best possible schools for Shelburne, Vermont, there is a need to help children to adapt to an increasingly specialized secondary educational program and at the same time not lose those special qualities of childhood to which each has a right.

More specific goals for planning encompass all features of a middle school; thus most chapters of this book indicate some desirable steps in planning for the respective elements of the middle school, just as the present chapter deals with steps in the planning process itself. And once the elements of curriculum, personnel, plant, and others, have been planned for a particular school, and the school is in operation, new problems and needs require planning for new elements or changes in old elements. Thus in addition to the continuing goal of maintenance and renewal through evaluation of the school (see chapter 9) there are usually specific planning projects in process.

Discussion of "Why the Middle School?" is to be expected wherever one exists or is proposed. It is a very significant question because the answers arrived at rightly set the goals of the school and its planning. Although we gave our own answers to this question in chapter 1, it should again be emphasized in this discussion of the planning process that the focus of the middle school must be on the education of children in the middle of the school ladder. Hence inevitably it is the shortcomings of existing schools, their failure to provide well for these children, that precipitate change to the middle school. These shortcomings may lie, as we saw in chapter 1, in the building facilities or even in segregated schools, but the remedy of a new organization creates the opportunity for improvement. For the success of the new organization, it is essential that the real motives for the reorganization be clarified and disclosed.[4] Once the change is made, it is the failures and successes of the new organization in achieving its original purposes, and others which develop, that keep the planning process operating to search out always better programs, personnel, and facilities.

Determining Means of Achieving the Goals

By the time the purposes of reorganization are determined and before planning proceeds very far, efficiency requires the development of some organization for planning. Two features seem essential: (1) a planning group representing the major interests involved—community; prospective students and their parents; school faculties most concerned; district administration; (2) an individual qualified to guide and coordinate the investigative and planning activities needs to be designated as the responsible chairman or director. With responsibility so fixed, planning can proceed much more expeditiously in preparation of the recommendations to the appropriate authorities, usually the school board.

If the goal of planning is to establish and/or maintain a school which serves adequately the educational needs of middle schoolers, the planning group first determines alternative school organizations that promise to serve these needs. Since it is usually some one organization that is already considered deficient, a junior high school or an extended elementary school or a six-year secondary school, the existing organization is eliminated from consideration. The search is for another, typically some form of middle school. But middle schools, indeed all schools, vary widely in quality, and so some models are sought that have been determined as successful or at least very promising. A brochure on the Montgomery Middle School, El Cajon, California, reported that "much care, planning and research have gone into developing Montgomery, its curriculum, and the selection of its staff" and asserts that "as a result, an educational environment exists that will meet the needs of that unique individual . . . the middle schooler." The result is further described in this paragraph:

Montgomery Middle School is neither an elementary school nor a junior high school. It is an educational facility designed to meet the unique needs of preadolescent and early adolescent students. Montgomery's curriculum and facilities are designed to provide educational programs which gradually bridge the gap between student dependency in elementary school and self-sufficiency in high school.

To us this statement may sound more like a goal than an achievement, but the significant point is that the planning group had arrived at the plan for this school through "care, planning and research."

The search for models usually involves identifying schools and programs for visitation and study. A substitute for such visitation, or perhaps better, a guide for study, identification, and visitation is such a book as this, or a collection of case descriptions like those we procured for reference in this book. Our appendix presents a summary of information about most of the schools we identified as exemplary schools, and could be a point of reference for planning groups interested in identifying schools for extended study.

Some planning groups or established school faculties choose to affiliate with some center or league for middle school development. Thus the Webster Transitional School in the Cedarburg, Wisconsin, School District, replacing in 1973 the Cedarburg Junior High School, adopted the pattern of Individually Guided Education (IGE) used in the Cedarburg elementary schools, with appropriate modifications for the grade 6 through 8 population of the new middle school. The IGE/Secondary system is described as follows:

It is a system of nine interrelated components with related mechanisms and strategies for attaining educational objectives. Individually Guided Secondary Education offers distinctive administrative arrangements, organizations for instruction and advisement, ways of organizing curriculum, and patterns of adapting instruction to meet individual student needs and societal demands. It incorporates coordinated strategies for the continuous evaluation, refinement, and renewal of the school's total educational program; and it stimulates, as well as requires continuous staff development and also innovations related to all components.[5]

The nine components in this popular system are:

1. Administrative arrangements
2. Organization for instruction and advisement
3. Curriculum
4. Arranging instruction for the individual student
5. Evaluation for instructional decision making
6. Home-school relations
7. Community learning and work experiences
8. Internal and external supportive arrangements
9. Continuing research and development

These components are comparable to the essential elements of an exemplary middle school that we listed in chapter 1 and are expanding throughout this book, although our list is designed specifically and only for the middle schools, as were some other lists presented in chapter 1.

The study of exemplary middle schools, whether through such models as Individually Guided Education or visitation of individual schools or review of published descriptions, is necessary in both continued and original planning. If the Xville Middle School faculty or its steering committee or its lay advisory council is dissatisfied with the curriculum or the facility or organization of its school, one of its best sources of information about alternative curriculums, facilities, or organizations may be other schools reliably reported to have better ones. But the planning group develops its own model for tryout after critically reviewing alternative models and/or other schools.

Evaluating the Selected Model of Change

Once the alternative models, patterns or programs that are possible have been reviewed, the planning group must make its selection of the model or pattern or program to try out. Frequently after extensive study of various models and visits to various schools, the planning group develops its own model. This creation, whether it be an entire school, or a phase of schooling to be substituted in an ongoing program, really becomes a hypothesis for testing. That is, the planning group in proposing a particular solution to the educational problems they had tackled, is saying that "if this new model (or school organization and program) is used, the previous problems (dissatis-factions) will be lessened or solved.'' Such a hypothesis, more precisely stated to yield criteria for testing out the model or program, becomes the basis for a systematic evaluation of the new organization.

Relatively few districts have gone about the establishment of middle schools through the establishment of pilot schools, although this procedure would conform best to the scientific planning process we are describing. However, the following excerpt from an early handbook of the Briarcliff Manor Middle School, Briarcliff Manor, New York, describes a two-year study and tryout process that is not uncommon:

> In the Fall of 1969 teachers interested in becoming a part of the middle school met regularly to explore the most recent professional literature on middle schools. In early 1970, Mr. Van Hoven was appointed principal and pursued this planning with the prospective faculty members during the Spring.
>
> In the Summer of 1970 about one half of the middle school staff met for two weeks with Mr. Van Hoven to establish specific objectives for the middle school and to outline organizational plans and operational procedures. The report produced by this group has continued to serve as a guide for all further planning.
>
> As the 1970–71 school year began every effort was made to create a feeling that the middle school already existed. Students from all three grades were brought together periodically and staff meetings involving teachers from all three grades were held regularly. It was not until the new high school was completed, however, that the school could begin to function as a separate operation.
>
> *The Spring of 1971 provided a short period in which to try out new scheduling and other operational procedures so they could be assessed systematically and improved where needed.* These improvements are reflected in the contents of this handbook.[6]

In large urban districts an individual school which has an especially unique program may come to be a model, or perhaps the pioneer, in a comprehensive reorganization. Indeed it is the lack of such a model or pioneer, or lack of its acceptance that prevents many large districts from moving to a new organization. In Milwaukee a transition to the middle school got under way in 1972, with various committee reports prepared and considered prior to the decision to move transitionally toward the middle school organizational structure in September, 1979, with full reorganization to a grade six through eight middle school in 1980–81. During these planning years Milwaukee's Steuben Junior High School was changed to a middle school using the IGE/Secondary Model of the University of Wisconsin R & D Center described earlier in connection with the Webster School, and served as one model for the transition. Three other middle schools were also created in 1978–79, with all former junior high schools operating as grade 7 through 8 schools in 1979–80 with grade 6 added in 1980–81. Throughout the transition years studies and innovations were intended to prepare the way for middle schools.

In other districts the evaluation of the pilot school or of specific phases of a middle school program vary from extensive controlled experimental studies to loosely organized observations and reviews yielding recommendations for the new schools or new program phases. Further information regarding such school and program evaluations is presented in chapter 10. The important principle for present purposes is that a specific plan for change is tried out before general adoption. Furthermore, subsequent changes are also dictated by experience in the continuing evaluation of programs as initiated. Mullen's dictum in a bulletin for Georgia educators is highly relevant: "There will be greater success (in instituting middle school programs) if the middle school program is kept open to revision and reconsideration if experience indicates that changes would be desirable."[7]

Acting on the Evidence

The ultimate aim of the IDEAS process is the implementation of change arrived at through a scientific problem-solving process. Once problems and parallel goals for planning have been identified, possible means of achieving the goals determined, and promising means evaluated, action decisions are needed to implement the findings or evidence. Implementation can mean adoption of proven solutions; or elimination from further consideration of the change tried out, or, most usually, modification of the change and further tryout. The nature of this action process is illustrated by the opening statement in *A Description of Webster Transitional School, 1977–78:*

This working paper is the first chapter of an exciting story that we hope will continue for many years. It describes the major features of the program of Webster Transitional School for the 1977–78 school year. A considerable amount of information regarding students' achievements and attitudes was gathered during 1977–78 also, but it is not included herein. This information enables the personnel of Webster Transitional School to gain a first approximation of the effectiveness of their total educational program as it is described in this paper. With similar data gathered during the 1978–79 school year, a beginning basis for the Webster teachers and students to set realistic goals for the 1979–80 school year became possible. Furthermore, any planned changes in the program of the school can be described and also evaluated.[8]

Stimulating the Process

Throughout the problem-solving process there is urgent need for its stimulation and facilitation by appropriate leadership and resources. There is probably no substitute for a dynamic administrator who works unceasingly and effectively to bring together the individuals and resources for study and action. Faculty members also play essential roles in their commitment to good schooling, and parents and community members can block or expedite change. Time for study and action, funds for visitation and workshops and consultants, the freedom to experiment and even to fail—all these are essential, too.

Several specific illustrations of how steps in the planning process are stimulated appear in subsequent sections of this chapter. Each section deals with an aspect of planning an exemplary middle school considered critical by the authors, but to which a later chapter is not devoted in this book. Each of these aspects is best related to such a planning process as IDEAS to ensure sound, continued planning and evaluation.

Analyzing Community and Student Needs

Plans for the new middle school should be based on some specific information about the population of middle schoolers to be served as well as on the characteristics in general of the age group. Among questions for which planners need answers are these:

- How many students of what ages and grades are to be served?
- What are the characteristics of the school community to be served? Socioeconomic status? Mobility/stability? Racial, religious, cultural backgrounds?
- What is the age/grade distribution of the population? What factors explain any unusual age variations (e.g., overage students?)
- What data as to the distribution of mental ability are available? What do they show?
- What data as to academic achievement, especially reading levels, are available? What do they show?
- What generalizations can be made from available data regarding previous students in this school community as to such factors as: Continuation in high school? College attendance? Career choices?

Additional insight regarding the needs of the school community and the student population may be gained from examination of data that are available or can be gathered on such items as these:

- Occupations of the parents of students who attend the school
- Attitudes of parents toward schooling
- Stability of families
- Presence of both parents in the home

The availability of community resources is also a major factor to be considered in planning the educational program. School planners need to know what is available for the middle schoolers in such resources as: churches; community libraries and museums; recreational facilities and parks; music and art centers; television; radio; theaters; clubs, organizations, and community-sponsored athletic, and other activities for the age group.

More specific information as to individual students and their families is essential and usually gathered as students enter the school or as their records are transferred. On the basis of the preliminary and general data available for planning in advance, many decisions such as the following are made that usually need to be checked annually as particular populations begin and continue the school year: grouping for instruction; arrangements for special education programs and students; and special opportunities for work-study, talented and gifted, and other programs.

Securing and Maintaining Community Cooperation

The history of educational innovations is replete with lessons as to the necessity of community cooperation. Although the middle school seems to be surviving well, individual schools can have disastrous reversals if they neglect these lessons. Clearly the best step toward community cooperation is community involvement, and numerous approaches are possible. First of all, the decision to have a middle school is itself one in which as widespread participation as possible is desirable. Board of education leadership and representation plus lay advisory council involvement frequently suffices if there is adequate opportunity for community members to be informed and to be able to supply input for the official deliberations.

Many school districts planning middle schools have named community representatives to the planning committees, and frequently these members bring needed skills to the planning process. They also may be very helpful in the significant and continuing task of *community information*. Most techniques for this task are illustrated in the following report of its provisions for keeping the school community informed from the Brookhaven Middle School of Decatur, Alabama:

The central office has acted in the area of public affairs. They have had newspaper articles published continually prior to and after the opening of the middle school. Visits were made by the middle school administrators to the elementary schools to prepare the children for the transition. The administrators also presented P.T.A. and civic club programs to explain the middle school concept. A booklet on the middle school was published and included with a newspaper issue. System-wide inservice meetings kept the staff informed about concepts and procedures relating to the middle school. Parent visitations to the suites, open house, and informal coffees were held to familiarize parents with the total school program. Through the medias of newspaper and radio, booklets and programs were presented to the public informing them of the current philosophy and objectives of the middle school.

In some districts the information to the community is quite comprehensive as to the rationale and nature of the middle school. A long article on the Rupert A. Nock Middle School of Newburyport, Massachusetts, appearing in several area newspapers the year after the school opened, emphasized that this was to be an "authentic" middle school and explained its various features, concluding as follows:

The people of Newburyport deserve an outstanding school for their children. In the Rupert A. Nock Middle School, they have it.

A release from the principal of the Amory, Mississippi, Middle School, indicated the self-analysis to be made by school people and thereby invited community feedback on such questions as these:

Do we have enough open houses each year? Should they be altered to be more informal so that parents would feel free merely to drop by, if for nothing more than to say they like the experiences being given their children?

Do we take advantage of telling parents about the good things their children do, or do we only contact the home after something bad has occurred?

Does our school stand out in the community? Is it noticed, or are its doors closed to the public too much?

Are parents happily involved in day-to-day activities?

What about the impressions we give when away from school at the club, church, beauty-barber shop?

Middle schools with community education programs may also use these as opportunities to inform the participants about the school and to secure assistance; for example, a statement supplied by the Griffin Middle School in Cobb County, Georgia, notes that the Community School Director "assumes a facilitative role related to the day school instructional program," and indicates services performed for the school such as coordinating a volunteer program.

Developing the School-Home Partnership

A close relationship of home and school is a perennial requisite of good schools. It is at the end of elementary schooling that parents have traditionally quit coming to the PTA, and in other possibly more significant ways withdrawn from the partnership. Frequently discouraged by their children of middle school and high school age from intervening in school problems and increasingly less confident of their own roles in the partnership, and perhaps too seldom consulted by their children's teachers, parents need much incentive, opportunity and help in working for the total education of middle schoolers.

Parents can surely be welcomed into the school and its program by such a parent information folder as distributed by the Cobb County, Georgia, Schools, or such a brochure as one entitled "Facts for Parents" distributed by the Poway Unified School District, Poway, California, along with handout material in both districts for each individual school. For example, a folder, "Welcome to Twin Peaks Middle School" in the Poway District, includes brief explanations of such items as "The Middle School Concept," "Activities," "A Well-Rounded Program," and "Special Assistance." Parents of children in the A.G. Currie Intermediate School of Tustin, California, may be individually invited to observe demonstration lessons. The invitation form includes the explanation that after the demonstration the parent will have a chance to discuss it with the teacher and the principals "while enjoying treats prepared by our Home Ec classes"; it also has a return slip.

Parent participation in school projects is also effective in bringing parents and teachers together in common efforts. At the Farnsworth Middle School of Guilderland, New York, a Saturday work day for parents was utilized to construct an "Adventure Playground," also using some donated equipment to provide for students' free time "a new adventure in learning by helping them use their imagination, skill and physical ability." A "P.T.A. Communique" from this school reported on these activities also involving parents: bowling tournament, variety show, parent effectiveness training program, school open house, health fair, scholarship fund, and snow sculpture. One brochure invites parent volunteers in classrooms, the art center, the library, the learning disabilities program and as secretary, tutor and/or friend.

The major objective of the home-school partnership is, of course, the optimum learning of the students concerned. A section of the pamphlet given parents at the Farnsworth Middle School is "Suggestions to Parents for Helping Your Youngster to be Productive in School" and includes seven "tips," the first five dealing specifically with study habits, and the sixth this interesting point: "(6) Encourage your child to participate in other activities which the child can balance with the demands of school." The last item (7) is one of invitation and instructions about calls to the school if problems arise.

Various types of organizations of parents are utilized by middle schools. The usual PTA organization affiliated with the state and national Congress of Parents and Teachers is widely used, but many middle schools have developed their own variants. The MacDonald Middle School of East Lansing, Michigan, has a Middle School Council with all families served by the school considered members; the objective of the Council according to its by-laws is "to facilitate a close relationship between the home and school so that parents and teachers may lend mutual support in the training and education of the children they serve." A parent in the L'Anse Creuse School District, near Detroit, Michigan, wrote about the role of parents in parent area councils and also extolled the membership of parents in middle school associations:

It is important that parents take part in Middle School Conferences for the same reasons that professional educators attend conferences. Through conferences we learn to do better that which we are already doing and how to do that which we do not do at all.[9]

She also noted the parents' role in parent advisory councils, school district publications, curriculum development and other school functions.

Additional types of community, parent, and/or lay councils, variously entitled and organized, are widely used to assist in the leadership and operation of school districts and individual schools. We defer further consideration of these organizations to our chapter on leadership, chapter 9.

Stating the School's Philosophy and Goals

Although much of the school's philosophy and most of its goals may well be implied from the original rationale for its planning, that is, from the goals for planning discussed early in this chapter, a specific statement of philosophy and goals of a school is critical in its original and continued planning. We would expect the original statement to be prepared by the members of whatever group is responsible for planning the school, but would hope that this group could soon include, after initial establishment, as many representatives of the faculty as possible. The continued planning for the school, once it is established, will necessarily be led by the faculty, with help from other individuals as needed and available. And the original statement needs periodic review by the faculty and advisory councils to keep it relevant and current, and to make modifications in goals and/or program as discrepancies are found.

The authors examined many statements of philosophy for middle schools, and many lists of school goals. We like best those statements which give heavy emphasis to the middle school as one for aiding the growth and development of children in the in-between years, and in fact we find this emphasis increasingly common. Note, for example, this very brief statement of philosophy from the Azalea Middle School of St. Petersburg, Florida:

Because we recognize the uniqueness of the transition from childhood to adolescence in a rapidly changing world, we will endeavor to provide an atmosphere which will help each student feel adequate as an individual. We believe the student should have the opportunity to experience self-discovery through a flexible curriculum. We, the faculty at Azalea Middle School, believe that we are able to combine our many and varied talents and experiences to realize each student's potential.

Accompanying this statement of philosophy in a 1978 handout for parents and students was this succinct statement of goals of the school:

1. *To help pupils develop skills which enable them to collect and critically evaluate information with emphasis on how to learn.*
2. *To build positive self-concepts.*
3. *To offer a flexible and adaptable program providing pupils with a wide range of educational and social experiences.*
4. *To provide each student not only with the mastery of basic skills but also with the means of accepting aesthetic and moral values.*
5. *To help each pupil work with others and in so doing to respect others as well as himself.*
6. *To provide an atmosphere which evolves around the nature of the student rather than around the subject matter and to emphasize special student interests.*

A more extended statement entitled, "MacDonald Middle School Philosophy" from the MacDonald Middle School of East Lansing, Michigan, deals with several aspects of the school's philosophy and program and concludes:

Regardless of the organizational structure, the ultimate goal of the MacDonald Middle School is in human relationships. Humanizing education can be accomplished when each person involved in the process recognizes and cares about the needs of each individual student. It is the goal of the middle school to help transescents meet and effectively deal with the challenges confronting them. *Thus, all personnel—students, teachers, administration, parents, community members, and other school related personnel—have responsibilities toward this end.*

The transitional function of the middle school is emphasized in these excerpts from a statement of the philosophy of the Andrews, Texas, Middle School:

> The school will endeavor to assist each student in making the necessary transition from the elementary level to the high school program . . . The Middle School Curriculum must be built on, and be a continuation of, the elementary program and provide experiences and activities that will help prepare the Middle School student for the more specialized curriculum of the high school. The curriculum of the Middle School must be integrated with both the elementary and secondary so that there will be continuous progressive educational growth.

The statements of goals from the various exemplary middle schools vary in length and specificity, but in general tend to include much the same points as illustrated by the statement above from Azalea Middle School. We ourselves favor those statements which lead easily to the definition of curriculum domains (see chapter 3) and to curriculum planning of subgoals and eventual instructional objectives. Thus, inclusion of goals related to basic skills, personal development, organized knowledge and special interests can be interpreted into curriculum language and plans less easily than goals equated with subject areas but more easily than goals stated as specific attitudes and emotional behavior. The chief criterion to be observed, however, is that of the serious involvement and commitment of the persons most concerned in the local school—the professional staff, students and parents. The goals they develop and use, and revise from time to time, on the basis of experience and evaluation, chosen in the light of social conditions and knowledge of the age group involved—these are the goals which should be the bases of school planning.

Implementing the Goals

Planning for implementation of the goals of the organization embraces the entire planning system. In addition to the process and the aspects of planning we have already considered and to those to which we next turn, there are these especially comprehensive and significant aspects to be planned: the school's curriculum, the school plant, personnel recruitment and training, instructional organization and schedule, the guidance program, roles of leadership, and the evaluation program. Since this book includes a chapter or major section on each of these matters, we do not give them further space in this chapter. We turn instead to three other very critical aspects of middle school planning before and after initial establishment: planning with other middle schools; planning with the schools above and below; and maintaining continuing orientation and information programs.

Relating to Other Middle Schools

In many small communities there is only one middle school (and one elementary and one high school). Also, occasionally in the large organization a middle school is the exceptional child being used as a pilot or temporarily. But increasingly urban districts are transforming their school organizations so that there are multiple middle schools. In each of these situations there may be a problem of identity: the lone middle school is an only child in the organization, with no peers or siblings to share problems and successes with; at the other extreme, with a complete, large family of middle schools each one may have some problem of individual identification. Perhaps the ideal organization is that of a small community or a small parochial or other private school system in which there is one elementary, one middle and one high school, each with its own identity yet closely associated with each other; here there really is not an only child problem since there are three well identified and related units of the organization. Each unit may of course identify schools at its level elsewhere for the sharing of resources and problems.

In the District

Several solutions are available to solve the identity problems in a school district. The lone middle school in a large unit has perhaps the most difficult situation, and cannot long exist satisfactorily unless it is clearly identified as a pilot or alternative school, with clearly established arrangements for its experimentation and dissemination of ideas. Such a school, as we noted early in this chapter and as illustrated in the Milwaukee transitional program, can serve a very significant purpose in the process of determining an improved organization or improved features of an existing organization. Lacking such a status, the lone middle school in larger districts may well identify with other organizations serving students of middle school age, and work out the best available plans for dealing with common problems despite the differing organizations. But in a hypothetical situation wherein there is strong support from one faction of parents and school personnel for a middle school type program and from another faction for a junior high school type program, sharing and cooperation seem unrealistic. Leadership has the task here of trying to bring the factions together, at least to work out plans for evaluation of the respective approaches or perhaps of developing guidelines for common curriculum areas. And perhaps it is good to have strongly held views that conflict in a school district; airing these views, and attempting to resolve them may help to keep school personnel working effectively to maintain superior programs. We believe that friendly competition among schools can be good.

But competition needs to be for purposes that are understood and in accordance with guidelines which protect learners from malpractice. Cooperation is the strongest approach to identity, and the one we believe most likely to bring about the needed recognition and strengthening of middle school education. In a sense, competition and cooperation can flourish together in a school district. Given multiple middle schools (or elementary or high schools) should not the school district make it attractive for the personnel of each school to develop unique programs within a general framework of guidelines for good education? Such a policy is suggested in the following statement from the Milwaukee Plan for the transition to middle schools:

> It is imperative that local school staff, parents, pupils, central office personnel, and community residents continue to be actively involved in the ongoing planning of the transition to a middle school program. It is suggested that, while there is a general plan for the middle school, each school develop a program within the context of that general plan that best meets the needs of the early adolescent pupils attending that school.[10]

For competition and cooperation to flourish together, shared decision making is needed, and the Milwaukee Plan includes an excellent section on ''Shared Decision Making As It Relates to the Middle School Program,'' a topic discussed further in this book as leadership roles are examined (chapter 9).

There must also be frequent opportunities for middle school personnel to plan, share, work, and perhaps play together. Among such opportunities provided by exemplary middle schools are these:

1. Middle school steering committees, hub groups, councils, representing the schools within a district and coordinating planning for the middle schools
2. Special committees, set up by the steering committee or the central administration, usually on an *ad hoc* basis, to work out plans for particular purposes and problems, such as marking and reporting systems
3. Curriculum planning groups, perhaps including the entire teaching staff of the middle school, to develop guidelines by subjects or other curriculum domains
4. Preschool and postschool conferences for stimulation and dissemination of ideas, involving speakers, discussion, and study groups
5. Demonstrations or exhibits hosted by individual middle schools, perhaps on a rotating basis
6. Self-study programs and other evaluation approaches (see chapter 10) involving interchange and exchange of visitation and reviewing
7. ''Open House'' for personnel from other schools, including middle schools, frequently introduced or followed by a social period
8. Recreational activities sponsored by the middle schools for their personnel, perhaps open to other levels as well, and sometimes combined with workshops and other inservice activities

In the State

The idea of sharing between middle schools in a state (and through sharing, the achievement of greater identity) has stimulated the development of leagues or associations of middle schools widely in the United States. So far as the authors know, the Florida League of Middle Schools was the first such organization. Created in 1972, the Florida League was to serve the following purposes:

1. To facilitate continuing curriculum improvement, inservice education, school planning and other phases of middle school education
2. To serve as a clearinghouse for exchange of ideas, materials and personnel needed for middle school development
3. To assist in developing plans for evaluation of middle schools in Florida
4. To help secure and maintain support of agencies and groups in the state interested in educational improvement
5. To represent the middle schools in professional and public discussions of educational programs and problems

The Florida League's membership is primarily of individual middle schools, each of whose personnel is thereby eligible for attending its conferences, serving on its committees, and other usual membership privileges. In addition, membership is open to school districts, teacher education institutions, state department of education and other agencies, and individuals. In 1980 the Florida League had over 200 schools as members. Its annual sessions have been attended by as many as 1200 persons.

Other states subsequently also developed leagues with similar organizations and programs, and some states have set up associations with memberships on an individual basis. The total number of state leagues and associations for middle schools as of 1980 was forty-one.

In the Nation

The need for identity of middle schools and middle school educators led to the establishment in 1974 of the National Middle School Association (NMSA). This organization publishes the *Middle School Journal,* and occasional special publications such as the *Middle School: A Look Ahead* (Paul George, editor; 1977). The national conferences have been increasingly well attended, and the association also sponsors special institutes and seminars.

In addition, many middle school educators maintain membership in organizations they had been affiliated with before NMSA was established, such as the various classroom teachers organizations, and the respective organizations for counselors, librarians, and other special personnel, and for elementary principals (National Association for Elementary Principals— NAEP), and secondary principals (National Association of Secondary School Principals— NASSP) and for all interested in curriculum and supervision (Association for Supervision and Curriculum Development— ASCD). Of these various organizations other than NMSA, ASCD has probably produced and sold the largest number of publications on the middle school through its *Educational Leadership* and its separate pamphlets including *Middle School in the Making* (1974) and *The Middle School We Need* (1975) and videotapes *Designing a Middle School for Early Adolescents* (1977) and *Profile of A Middle School* (1979).

Relating to the Schools Below and Above

As a school in the middle, the middle school has unique opportunities and responsibilities to relate to the elementary school below and the high school above. Indeed, as we have noted repeatedly, its major function is generally believed to be in this role of transition from childhood to adolescence and correspondingly from elementary to high school. Note these examples of statements of philosophy in addition to similar ones cited earlier. From the Goddard School of Littleton, Colorado, this statement:

> The philosophy of Goddard School is based on the premise that the middle school is an integral part of the District Six educational program and that the Goddard program must be developed so that middle school students can follow a K-12 program of study without experiencing any gaps between the elementary school and the middle school or between the middle school and the high school.

And from the Tipton Community Schools, Tipton, Iowa:

> The Tipton Middle School exists for the purpose of maintaining growth in basic skills and to provide a smooth transition from the closely supervised atmosphere of the elementary school to the free atmosphere of the senior high. To function successfully in senior high the student must learn, while in the middle school, to handle responsibility, to make wise decisions, to develop good peer relationships, and to respect authority.

Unfortunately our review of school practices, even of those of our exemplary middle schools, yields too few tangible examples of specific practices for articulation or continuity that really tie together well the elementary and middle school and even fewer examples relating to middle school/high school ties. The authors' impression is that administrators, in fact educators in general, agree heartily that educational continuity should be aided by the middle school organization, but that they have generally been too busy establishing middle schools and trying to make them good to really work at the continuity problem. We believe that this problem is initially one for school leadership, especially school district leadership, and that it is one of the major challenges to be faced ahead. The following suggestions are offered as a summary of means for securing continuous educational progress through middle school education:

1. Work for better education in the middle school years, not just for the middle school.
2. Use community and/or parent advisory groups in planning and evaluating educational goals, organizations, processes and products for all levels.
3. Involve representatives of elementary and high schools in planning and evaluating middle schools.
4. Develop student evaluation and reporting systems which facilitate educational continuity.
5. Use interschool movement of teachers and students as feasible.

6. Get and utilize openly feedback from the school above, and make feedback available to the school below.
7. Maintain continuous orientation programs at each school level for faculties of other levels, and for students and parents.
8. Organize staff development programs that cut across levels.
9. Develop curriculum continuums in the learning skills and make them available to all teachers concerned.
10. Plan vertically for increasing student self-direction, especially through independent study, on a K-12 basis.

Maintaining Continuing Orientation and Information Services

The last aspect of planning the exemplary middle school emphasized in this chapter is that of planning to maintain a continuing service for orientation and information about the middle school. Some of the fine press releases and bulletins the authors have seen were obviously developed for one-time use in the original opening of a new middle school. However useful they may be for the public and members of the school community when the school opens, there will be many other new parents, students and citizens to be informed for another year, and another year, and on as long as the school exists. Although the concept of the middle school may eventually be understood so that there is not continually a need for its explanation, ''eventual'' is a long time off because the majority of parents for an indefinite period ahead will not have had children attending a middle school, especially an exemplary middle school. And so we would contend that whatever techniques and devices are planned for initial orientation activities should be designed for reuse, and that whoever serves as the information services leader maintain a continuing flow of information about the middle school. Many of the suggestions made in this chapter in regard to relationships of the middle school with students, parents, community and other schools may be applicable to the continuing orientation and information service.

Perhaps the most critical service is that pertaining to the feeder elementary school(s)' faculty, students and parents. A teacher of grade five in the feeder elementary school may have much more to do with the expectations and attitudes of incoming sixth graders than any other person. Hence priority in orientation and information services should go to the teachers of prospective middle school students. Plans for these teachers and other personnel of the elementary school, to visit the middle school and to talk with middle school faculty and counselors are most important. Similarly, the students themselves and their parents need much help in understanding the new school for their children. They know about an elementary and a high school, but what, they say, is a middle school? The best answers that can be developed to this question—in print, on tape, in pictures, by school visits and by word of mouth—are needed for the continuing orientation of all persons in the school and community who have not themselves been involved in middle school education, and this is the vast majority of the population in most American communities in 1980. Ignorance of its nature and purposes is perhaps the worst enemy of effective middle school education. Careful planning and execution of the information services of the school and its district should make the middle school an increasingly understood, popular, and successful community institution.

ADDITIONAL SUGGESTIONS FOR FURTHER STUDY

A. Books

Alexander, William M. and Others, *The Emergent Middle School*, 2nd enlarged edition. New York: Holt, Rinehart and Winston, 1969.

Brandt, Ronald S. Editor, *Partners: Parents and Schools*. Alexandria, Va.: Association for Supervision and Curriculum Development, 1979.

Davies, Don, Editor, *Schools Where Parents Make A Difference*. Boston: Institute for Responsive Education, 1976.

Deal, Terrence and Robert Nolan, *Alternative Schools: Ideologies, Realities, Guidelines*. Chicago: Nelson Hall, 1978.

George, Paul S., Editor, *The Middle School: A Look Ahead*. Fairborn, Ohio: National Middle School Association, Inc., 1977.

Goodlad, John I. and Associates, *Curriculum Inquiry: The Story of Curriculum Practice*. New York: McGraw Hill Book Co., 1979.

Leeper, Robert, Editor, *Middle School in the Making*. Washington, D.C.: Association for Supervision and Curriculum Development, 1974.

Lounsbury, John H. and Vars, Gordon, F., *A Curriculum for the Middle School Years*. New York: Harper & Row, 1978.

B. Periodicals

Alexander, William M., et al, "Community-Home-School Cooperation in Middle School Goals," *Journal of North Carolina League of Middle/Junior High Schools,* Monograph No. 1 (1980).

Brown, Willard V., "Implementing a Climate for Learning," *Middle School Journal,* 7, 8–9 (March 1976).

Harmon, Stanley J., "The Systems Approach to the Management of a Middle School Planning Task Force," *Middle School Journal,* 7, 14–7 (March 1976).

Hanson, Neil G., "Changing the Junior High School to a Middle School," *NASSP Bulletin,* 63, 66–72 (May 1979).

McDonald, William G. and Tierno, Mark J., "From Junior High to Middle School: The Story of One Conversion," *Middle School Journal,* 10, 20–3 (February 1979).

McGee, Jerry C. and Blackburn, Jack E., "Administration of the Middle School Program," *Theory Into Practice,* 18, 39–44 (February 1979).

Mitchell, Roland, "How to Start a Middle School," *National Elementary School Principal,* 58, 46–8 (June 1979).

C. ERIC
Bondi, Joseph, *Guidelines for Developing and Sustaining Good Middle School Programs,* Paper presented at the Annual Conference of the National Middle School Association, Denver, Colorado, November 1977. (ERIC No. ED 150 745)

D. Dissertations and Dissertation Abstracts
Golembiewski, Leonard K., "Development of Strategies for the Superintendent in the Design and Initiation of a Non-Graded Middle School Program," *Dissertation Abstracts,* 34 (February 1974) 4697–A.
Weaver, Roosevelt Rivers, "The Preparation and Planning for the Opening of a New Middle School in East Orange, New Jersey," *Dissertation Abstracts,* 36 (March 1976) 5732–A.
Youngberg, Robert Stanley, "Perceptions of Parents' Role in Curriculum Development at the Middle and Junior High Level," *Dissertation Abstracts,* 36 (September 1976) 1286–A.

FOOTNOTES

1. John I. Goodlad, *The Dynamics of Educational Change: Toward Responsive Schools* (New York: McGraw-Hill Book Co., 1975), p. 173.
2. John I. Goodlad, Kenneth A. Sirotnik, and Bette C. Overman, "An Overview of 'A Study of Schooling,'" *Phi Delta Kappan,* 61:178 (November 1979). This is the first of a series of four articles in this journal—the other three in December 1979, and January and February 1980, reporting on the study.
3. Goodlad, p. 175.
4. See for expansion of this point and other implementation steps, Paul S. George, "Ten Steps Toward Implementing Middle Schools," *NASSP Bulletin,* 61, 93–100 (September 1977).
5. Herbert J. Klausmeier and John C. Daresch, *A Description of Webster Transitional School 1977–78* (Madison, Wisconsin: Wisconsin Research and Development Center for Individualized Schooling, April 1979), p. 3.
6. *Community Handbook,* Briarcliff Manor Middle School, Briarcliff Manor, New York, Mimeographed, September 1971. Italics supplied.
7. David J. Mullen, "The Middle School—Promise or Fad?" in David J. Mullen, ed., *Middle Schools* (Athens, Georgia: University of Georgia, Fall 1972), p. 50.
8. Klausmeier and Daresh, p. v.
9. Pauline P. Pavlick, "Parent Involvement—Two Views: A Parent," *Middle School Journal,* 9:5 (May 1978).
10. Milwaukee Public Schools, *The Plan for the Two-Year Transition to the Middle School* (Milwaukee, Wisconsin: The Schools, March 1979), p. 2.

Chapter 3

The Middle School Curriculum

A very comprehensive characteristic of the exemplary middle school is its curriculum, that is, the program of planned learning opportunities for its students. This should be uniquely and effectively set to provide for the continuous progress of each child enrolled. This chapter describes briefly the processes of planning such a curriculum, alternative designs, and the nature and scope of learning opportunities in major domains of the curriculum.

Planning an Exemplary Middle School Curriculum

Curriculum planners for the new middle school must choose whether to develop a new program for the new school or to adopt the programs of predecessor schools for the grades, ages and levels involved, or to make some combination of new and old programs. The fact is that old rather than new programs have predominated in the early and possibly the continuing development of the middle school movement. The first comprehensive survey of middle schools concluded that the aims of the reorganization movement as of 1968 had not been reflected in program change:

Aims generally stated, both in the literature and by the respondents for the schools in the sample, such as "to remedy the weaknesses of the junior high school'' and ''to provide a program specifically designed for this age group'' are not generally reflected in the curriculum plan and instructional organization of the schools surveyed. The program of studies is generally comparable to that of these grades in predecessor organizations, with a relatively sparse offering of elective and other curriculum opportunities, especially for grades 5 and 6. Instructional organization for grade 5 is most frequently similar to that of the elementary school, with the departmentalization pattern of the junior high school introduced even here and becoming the predominant organization in the other grades.[1]

Five years later, an active participant in the middle school movement, James DiVirgilio, asked ''Why the Middle School Curriculum Vacuum?'' and noted this observation:

The changes that have been made in middle schools are in such areas as clubs, athletics, socials, and general school environment. . . . Currently the practice is to continue curriculum programs as they existed in the elementary fifth and sixth grades and the junior high seventh and eighth grades and to incorporate these programs into a middle school setting. This being so, it is apparent to educators interested in middle school growth that more effort is needed in projecting and organizing a curriculum that will enhance the further development of young people of middle school age.[2]

In their report of a ''modified replication'' a decade later of the Alexander study, Brooks and Edwards concluded that ''it can be safely stated that most middle school students in those schools sampled spend their day in a disciplinary, nonteamed organizational format, the same format likely dominant in junior high schools and high schools.''[3]

Although the present authors suspect that the somewhat negative survey findings were partially due to lack of understanding of the terminology, we are certain that guidelines for planning the curriculum needed will not come from surveys of most frequent practice in today's middle schools. Better curriculums can be derived from practices in our more exemplary middle schools and from the judgment of middle school educators as to what ought to be. Accordingly, we turn to the processes of planning considered most productive in developing new, appropriate curriculum plans and to the plans themselves.

Curriculum Planning at the School Level

As we stated in the previous chapter, the essential locus of planning for the middle school is in the individual school. Much as external agencies and groups may facilitate and guide school planners, it is the vision and industry of the latter that determine whether the school develops a program that is unique and effective for its student body. Difficult as it is to plan and operate at the same time, it can be and is being done. A handout on ''Curriculum Development'' from the principal of the Marshall, Minnesota, Middle School reviewed some experience in the first years of curriculum planning at this school and insightfully reported:

Six years later we have come to the realization that curriculum work is very difficult. It takes cooperation and time, and it seems to be never ending. It does seem worth the struggle, and we are coming to terms with the total process.

Three levels of planning within the individual school are essential: schoolwide; team and other small groups; individual faculty members and their students and parents. For schoolwide planning, the total faculty must of course make those critical decisions within their power which relate to basic goals, the general design of the curriculum, the policies of student progress and grouping, and faculty development and inservice education for curriculum and instructional improvement. Especially in faculties too large for extended and interested participation in discussion of details of such matters, responsibility for their exploration and development, and in some matters decision making and implementation, is typically vested in some type of representative curriculum council.

One model for planning at the school level is the Program Improvement Council (PIC) recommended in the Individually Guided Education (IGE) program as assisted by the Kettering Foundation IDEA Program:

> A Program Improvement Council, known as the PIC, has a membership of the principal and Learning Community (team) leaders. The Council's job is to resolve problems affecting two or more Learning Communities and to establish school-wide policies.[4]

A school bulletin at the Spring Hill Middle School, High Springs, Florida, reporting the establishment of a PIC there early in the school's history, noted that "the primary function of the PIC is to establish communication lines between the various teams and the administration" and suggested the following possible contributions of the organization:

1. Discuss ways to improve the use of shared school facilities
2. Coordinate curriculum development and inservice education
3. Define the roles of support systems to make for their more efficient use
4. Resolve problems involving two or more units
5. Coordinate use of outside consultants and special staff members
6. Present projects from teachers in their respective units when expenditure of funds is required

The meetings were open to all members of the faculty, with the PIC itself representing the teams ("Learning Communities," as termed by IDEA) and the administration.

An organization with a similar purpose for the Webster Transitional School, Cedarburg, Wisconsin, utilizing IGE in connection with the Wisconsin Research and Development Center, was described as follows:

> *Faculty Advisory Committee.* The Faculty Advisory Committee is composed of one member from each academic team, two members of the allied arts team, a member of the supportive services team, student representative (optional), and the three members of the leadership team (principal, dean of students, and instructional consultant). It meets weekly. It shares decision making with all members of

the professional staff on matters related to the daily operation of the school. Emphasis is on involving the staff in policy making rather than on the diffusion of information. The committee organizes and holds inservice meetings and also general faculty meetings.[5]

Such councils are variously called, in addition to the terms just used, "curriculum council," "council on instruction," "steering committee," "coordinating council," and other names. Their work generally includes consideration of these essential elements of curriculum planning specified in a description of the work of the Caloosa Middle School Curriculum Council of Lee County, Florida:

1. Curriculum development, articulation, and evaluation as these relate to pupil needs and achievement.
2. Instructional strategies and all areas related to these.
3. Inservice needs and activities as related to staff and program development.
4. Instructional supplies and equipment together with budgetary recommendations to support these needs in all departmental operations.[6]

Plans and materials developed by such schoolwide groups are essential to the successful implementation of the individual school's role in curriculum development. It is in their deliberations, consideration of goals, content and strategies, compromises and recommendations that each school can develop a unique but effective program related to the needs of its students and the resources of its faculty and plant and community. But the curriculum council cannot succeed without the careful input of ideas and implementation of program by teacher teams and individual faculty members.

Planning by Teaching Teams and Other Small Groups

Chapter 5 of this text is completely devoted to interdisciplinary team organization, and gives much attention to the planning activities of teams. The development and the implementation of the curriculum for the students in their team are the central functions of team planning, although their successful discharge involves such matters as scheduling, budgeting and pupil personnel decisions as well as content and instructional strategies. We simply cannot overemphasize the great importance of the cooperative planning of each team in the school and of the planning between teams accomplished in large part by the schoolwide council. Chapter 9 gives especial consideration to the leadership role of the team leader, who is a very critical person in a very critical organization!

   In addition to the teaching team organization, other curriculum planning groups are employed in middle schools. The subject department, the basic element in curriculum and instruction in the junior high school and other secondary school organizations, is still utilized in some middle schools, and in these schools planning for the program in each curriculum area is accomplished within the departments. Even when there is a full-fledged team organization, there is definitely need for teachers specializing in a particular subject area to work together periodically to plan for the scope and sequence of learning opportunities within the area, to share materials and to select new materials for requisition, and to react to and possibly select from curriculum materials developed and distributed by external agencies and groups. There may also be need from time to time to organize special committees or other groups to work out tentative solutions to curriculum problems that cut across teams and subjects and even schools, such as special developments in the community, state or nation demanding curriculum recognition, for example, festivals, fairs, contests and so forth.

Planning by Individual Teachers

We describe in chapter 5 the responsibilities of individual team members for planning as members of the team and as teachers of specific student groups and individuals, and in chapter 8 we deal with many instructional tasks, including the planning of instruction. Here we simply note that the middle school teacher is no less responsible than teachers at any other level for detailed and effective planning. Team teaching and planning make it possible for teachers to share problems and plans, but also create the obligation for each team member to do her or his share of the individual homework required for effective teaching.

Planning by External Agencies and Groups

The curriculum plan of any school at any level is almost inevitably the result of planning by many groups outside the school as well as those inside we have considered: state board and department of education; state committees on programs of studies, textbooks, and special curriculum areas; professional organizations; various special interests with materials and plans to advance their missions; and the school district curriculum organization. The latter is not fully external to the individual school, but it serves all schools in the district. The city or county curriculum council and curriculum staff can be a most effective aid to the individual school, and is certainly the first resource to be consulted in the school's own planning. Districts differ widely of course as to the extent of centralization, and in some large, centralized districts curriculum planning may be primarily at the district level with only immediate and sometimes relatively insignificant matters settled within the school and classroom. In some districts with a long tradition of individual school initiative and in those with little resources at the district level, planning may be almost entirely at the local school level.

The pattern which seems most promising for exemplary middle schools and their districts is one in which the district provides these types of services for individual school planning:

1. A general framework of goals for the schools of the district, with an indication of specific state and local curriculum requirements and expecta-

tions and of the areas in which local schools have the freedom to develop unique programs.

2. Consultative and coordinating assistance in curriculum planning and materials for all curriculum areas and especially in regard to special areas such as industrial arts wherein the individual school may have only one faculty member

3. The organization and maintenance of district-wide councils or leagues to give optimum opportunity for sharing and planning between schools both at the same and at different levels. Such district-wide leadership is essential to the fulfillment of the basic transitional function of the middle school as stated very clearly in the ''Philosophy of Education'' material distributed by the Goddard School of Littleton, Colorado:

> The philosophy of Goddard School is based on the premise that the middle school is an integral part of the District Six educational program and that the Goddard program must be developed so that middle school students can follow a K-12 program of study without experiencing any gaps between the elementary school and the middle school or between the middle school and the high school. All important as this function is to the middle school it cannot be achieved by the middle school alone; the active involvement of district leadership and the elementary and high schools as well as the middle school is essential.

The district may also organize groups of citizens for participation in curriculum decisions or assist local schools in involving parents and other citizens. The Kirkwood, Missouri, Schools, for example, operate three Curriculum Policy Committees—one at the elementary, one at the middle and a third at the high school level. These Committees, according to a flier inviting citizens to join, have these functions:

> Help to coordinate curriculum offerings between the high school, middle school and elementary divisions
> Analyze course offerings to ensure they meet student needs
> Recommend curriculum improvements to the district administration
> Study student activity programs and make suggestions for improvement
> Involve R-7 (the district) citizens, students and staff members in curriculum planning, selection and evaluation

The foregoing seems a good list of the functions a school district curriculum organization should discharge provided there is full representation of local schools and ample feedback from the schools. We turn now to alternative curriculum designs to be considered in curriculum planning at the district and school levels.

Alternative Curriculum Designs—a Continuum

The curriculum plans of most middle and other schools too frequently are developed or adopted without conscious attention by the planners to the design, pattern or framework of the curriculum. Yet it is the inflexibility of some designs that cause the many problems in the school's attempt to deal effectively with curriculum pressures, especially those of the great individual differences of learners. Careful consideration of alternative curriculum designs is needed with conscious decision to employ the most appropriate design for each major aspect of the curriculum plan. Although full treatment of principles and practices of curriculum designing is beyond the scope of this book,[7] we do note in this section some major design models that can be considered in planning the curriculum of a middle school. We see these models as being on a continuum of structure, with the most highly structured at the left and the least structured at the right (See Figure 3.1).

The Separate Subjects Design

The traditional and dominant curriculum design at all levels of education is one of disciplines, major organizations of knowledge and subjects, derived for school instruction from the disciplines. Although significant departures from the subject organization occurred in the elementary school early in this century, the secondary schools have characteristically maintained the subject pattern, departing from it at first and still most frequently only to introduce various extracurricular activities to meet better the interests and needs of adolescents. The middle schools generally have adopted the subject design for most of their program, but made many combinations with other designs. And as in the elementary school, the subjects in the middle school program of studies tend to be broad fields, such as social studies, rather than separate subjects, such as history and geography.

While fully recognizing the importance of the organized knowledge content within the broad fields and other cognitive areas, middle school planners need to avoid the stereotyped program of studies, instructional organization, and schedule of many junior high schools. Indeed, it was in part to gain flexibility for the varied population that the middle school was first espoused. Language arts, social studies, science and mathematics are constants in all middle school curriculum plans, but their provision does not enforce on the middle school the period-per-day class in each broad field, developed and taught without attention to the other fields. Subjects and activities may well be organized separately, but in the exemplary middle school the activities are curricular, a significant part of the program and of the faculty's assignments. So are the teacher guidance responsibilities in the advisor-advisee programs described in chapter 4. Thus the hope and, to some extent, the practice is that the advantages of a knowledge-based subject organization can be used without it usurping the entire curriculum.

Core, Block and Interdisciplinary Designs

Designs that utilize subject matter within and across subject lines to focus on some other organizing center such as personal and social problems, have long been used in the middle school years. Units of work including materials

Most Structure →

Least Structure →

SEPARATE SUBJECTS	CORE, BLOCK, AND INTERDISCIPLINARY	INDIVIDUAL NEEDS, INTERESTS & PROGRESS	DOMAINS AND OTHER GOAL CENTERED
Basic Decisions:	Basic Decisions:	Basic Decisions:	Basic Decisions:
What subjects? When?	What areas in core, etc., and what areas separate?	What areas to be planned on individual design basis?	How do students, parents and faculty work together in defining goals and domains?
What relative emphasis—how much time per subject?	In combined area units, what factors decide scope and sequence?	What factors determine student choices?	Which school programs should serve each goal?
What principles for selecting content within each subject?	What options for teachers as to objectives?	How can teachers plan with individual students?	How can new programs be created as needed?
What options for students?	What options for students in unit activities?	How is progress determined within each area?	How can existing programs be discontinued?
What opportunities to cross subject lines?		How can learning opportunities be created as new needs and interests arise?	

Figure 3.1 / Continuum of Alternate Curriculum Designs

from social studies, language arts, fine arts and perhaps mathematics and science, have been widely used in elementary schools, including grades 6 through 8 as earlier organized in many communities and still so provided in some districts. The core program, generally including language arts and social studies and in some instances other subject fields, was attempted in many high schools beginning in the 1930's, and was most widely provided in a block-time program in junior high schools, especially in grades 7 and 8. Called by various terms—core, block, unified studies, basic education and others—the core was widely seen as an improvement in the junior high school program that might meet better the needs and interests of early adolescents. Had it fully succeeded, the middle school reorganization might not have occurred or been so popular.

But the reemphasis on subject organization of the post-Sputnik era of the late 1950's and 1960's caused many junior highs to abandon any design other than a strict subject one. With the advent of the middle school as in part a reaction against extreme subject departmentalization in the junior high school, the opportunity again existed to use some type of core, block or interdisciplinary design. Although interdisciplinary teaming does not automatically result in a core program or even in the teaching of interdisciplinary units, it has been regarded as a desirable one for the middle school because of all the reasons we explain in chapter 5. The interdisciplinary team organization, with appropriate use of interdisciplinary units, is probably the most widespread form of core in current middle school education. Some middle schools however, maintain block time and partial self-contained programs, especially in the former elementary grades, that can follow essentially the core design as described and recommended by two of its leading proponents, John H. Lounsbury and Gordon F. Vars. The following excerpt of their description of the core component of the middle school curriculum summarizes the core design and the case for this design:

A major portion of the common learnings should be provided through a core program, most simply described as a problem-centered block-time program. At its best, core provides students with a direct and continuing opportunity to examine in depth both personal and social problems that have meaning to them. It also provides a situation in which a teacher can know a limited number of students well enough to offer the advisement or counseling most of them need so badly during the transition years, and in the process they can learn essential human relations and communication skills.

Most, but not all, of the content and skills traditionally taught in English, social studies, and science classes may be taught in core, where they become tools to be utilized in the process of inquiry. Art and music, so often relegated to a peripheral role, also become important sources and tools in an inquiry process which knows no subject matter limitations.[8]

The present authors believe that the advisement function recommended for core teachers is better provided in the middle school by the advisor/advisee plan described and illustrated in chapter 4. This plan can involve more members of the faculty, with each member presumably having fewer advisees than in the core teacher guidance pattern. We also believe there are highly significant advantages in the team arrangement regarding such matters as planning for individual students, setting schedules, and involving teachers in special areas: these could not exist in a one-teacher core pattern and might be less effective in a two- or three-teacher pattern than the usual four- or more teacher team. Nevertheless, we fully agree with the major goal of focusing material from certain related subjects on the personal and social problems that serve as the designing centers in both core and interdisciplinary units. In fact, contentwise there is no real distinction between the two.

We do not believe that any informed and experienced middle school educator would argue that the entire curriculum design should be core; certainly not Lounsbury and Vars, who propose it as one of three components. However, self-contained classrooms in the elementary school do offer the possibility, once regarded as advantageous, of a one-teacher core pattern embracing the total curriculum. And a middle school team or core organization which leaves the team or core teachers responsible for planning and guiding all special interest and exploratory experiences for their students could have the same possibilities. We simply believe that the complexities of knowledge and culture today make desirable, if not necessary, the utilization of special competencies usually beyond those of interdisciplinary and core teachers.

Designs Focusing on Individual Needs, Interests and Progress

No educator we know seriously advocates a middle school curriculum of a completely elective nature, nor is any public middle school likely to provide one. But there are two quite different influences and developments in current curriculum development that conceivably could result in an almost totally individualized curriculum offering. On the one hand there is the considerable use of various systems of individualized instruction and continuous progress. Whether these systems are, in the language of Lounsbury and Vars, "single-sequence, variable-rate," "multiple-sequence, variable-rate," or "variable-sequence, variable-rate" approaches, they all assume a considerable variation in the rate of progress through the system by individual students, and the latter two approaches assume a variation in the scope of the curriculum as well. Since these systems are most frequently provided in skills subjects, especially reading and mathematics, the difference in student experiences is usually related to learning ability and style rather than interest. However, multiple sequences in science and social studies through learning activity packets and other materials providing for variable progress may be based on the interest factor.

Individual interests are especially the basis of such curriculum specialties of the middle school as special interest activities, exploratory courses in the fine and applied arts and other fields, minicourses in various subject fields and outside of any field, and independent study. The greatest contribution middle school curriculum has made, many educators believe, is to provide these learning opportunities for students in the middle. We doubt if any school could long and successfully maintain a curriculum based wholly on individual needs and interests, but programs for students' continuous progress are desirable indeed. These programs cannot be only of the sequential learning type characterized by programmed instruction and various self-drilling features that have dominated skills instruction. An adequate curriculum for the middle school must offer many opportunities for individual choice and many opportunities to meet individual needs, each opportunity providing so far as possible for sequential experiences that ensure continuous progress. These many and varied opportunities must be as wide in their range as schooling can provide.

Domains and Other Goal-Centered Design Plans

We believe the curriculum plan should be designed around major educational goals, and that an array of learning opportunities related to each goal is best thought of as the *domain* set by the goal. Thus, we see personal development as a very major goal of the middle school, and suggest various curriculum opportunities as being most closely related thereto. Health and physical education, guidance and counseling, affective development activities and interest-exploring and developing activities and courses should be classified as within the personal development domain of the curriculum so that planning and evaluation for this goal has a clear focus and convenient base.

We recommend that study and planning of the middle school curriculum be based on a statement of major educational goals of the middle school, with each major goal defining a domain of related learning opportunities. Each domain may include traditional subjects or significant aspects of such subjects, interdisciplinary units or aspects thereof and many types of activities only casually if at all related to the subject design. These separate but related learning opportunities are indicated by the subgoals of the domain. Our suggested design is presented in the rest of this chapter in relation to the three educational goals seen as dominating the curriculum of the middle school and defining its domains:

- Personal Development
- Skills of Communication and Learning
- Major Knowledge Areas[9]

Although there are overlappings between these goals and their domains, it is expected that any middle school can fruitfully set up and evaluate its program in relation to these broad, inclusive domains. Each school, too, can add or substitute domains if indicated by its goals and certainly it can work out problems of overlapping and omissions by its faculty's own analysis and classification of learning opportunities.

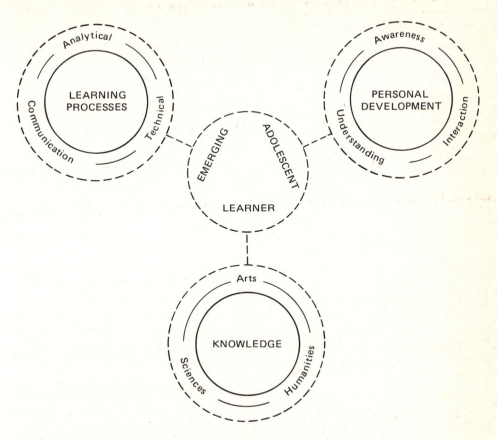

Figure 3.2 / Emerging Adolescent Curriculum.

(From Donald Eichhorn, "The Emerging Adolescent School of the Future—Now," in J. Galen Saylor, ed., *The School of the Future—Now,* 1972, p. 41. Reprinted with permission of the Association for Supervision and Curriculum Development and Donald H. Eichhorn. Copyright © 1972 by the Association for Supervision and Curriculum Development. All rights reserved.)

A similar design has been developed by Donald E. Eichhorn and utilized in the middle schools of the Upper St. Clair School District in Pennsylvania. Figure 3.2 from Eichhorn's description presents the three domains of Learning Processes, Personal Development and Knowledge. Eichhorn's full explanation of the design provides for a somewhat different classification than ours within the domains, but his design is a useful model for analysis and planning purposes in any middle school. Both of these designs are based on the principles Eichhorn so well stated:

The characteristics and needs of the emerging adolescent learners are central to school program development.

There are three fundamental curriculum needs. These include the acquisition of learning processes necessary for self-education; the actualization of self through self awareness, understanding, and interaction; and the active involvement of the learner with knowledge as it relates to the various aspects of man's heritage and contribution.[10]

Domain of Personal Development

Exemplary middle schools provide many services and opportunities to assist their students in optimum development as unique and well adjusted, healthy personalities. Subgoals of the school program for this major goal include:

1. Offering advice and guidance and other assistance with personal, educational, social and other problems
2. Assisting students in the development of attitudes, values and moral judgment
3. Providing programs for the development of physical fitness and health
4. Assisting each student to explore and develop worthwhile interests

Learning opportunities for each of these subgoals are described in the following sections.

Guidance and Special Services

Exemplary middle schools may be expected to have such advisor/advisee programs as we describe in chapter 4. This organizational plan provides for each student to have one adult to whom the student can turn for help on many types of problems, and it also provides a setting in which students can learn about school services outside their own school group. The advisory group may also be expected to help students achieve some maturity in their decision making which will decrease reliance on others for help but also increase selectivity in the choice of other confidants and advisors. Futhermore, the advisory relationship is an excellent basis for referrals of students to the special services available in and out of the school.

As we note in chapter 4, the use of teacher advisors in no way reduces the need for trained school counselors, but it does make possible a more effective channeling of counseling services. In many middle schools the school counselor works closely with the faculty teams. The following statement from the district plan for middle schools in Milwaukee describes this arrangement and explains the role of counselors:

> The prime concern of the counselors shall be in the realm of accentuating the positive development of student potential, assisting in the development of a positive self-concept, enabling students to develop effective ways of relating to others, developing their problem-solving and decision-making competencies, and fostering the career development of each student. As an integral part of the middle school educational environment, the counselors shall be a part of the teaching teams and shall work with the teams in determining the needs of the students assigned to the team and shall work with the teams to resolve situations internal to that group.[11]

Ideally the middle school student should have access to various other special services as needed: psychological, medical, social work and exceptional child education. And indeed many of these services are provided. For example, the Milwaukee plan cited above proposed that at least one school psychologist and one social worker be assigned to each middle school. Nurse and other medical services are widely available through cooperative arrangements with health departments. Special provisions for many exceptional education programs are available in the middle school or in some other facility of the district. Counselors are challenged in many situations to be so well informed about the referral services available as to use them all wisely and effectively for the students. There are also those less fortunate situations where schools simply do not have such resources, and school personnel have to investigate providers of services to be found among themselves and also in other community institutions, including the home.

Guidance and other special services are generally considered as being "received" by students without the active role associated with learning. We would call attention to the fact that the aim of many, perhaps all, of the types of services involved is to help the individual become his own problem solver to the extent possible. The involvement of the learner in his problem-solving activities, whether they be in learning, physical and mental health, family relationships, work outside school or other areas, should be sought through learning opportunities to be planned and evaluated as other aspects of the curriculum.

Affective Development

The most critical of all middle school goals is considered to be that of aiding a population of ever-changing individuals in the development of desirable attitudes, values, and moral judgments. These are the aspects of personality we are grouping under the general heading of affective development. The development of interests and problem-solving skills is relevant but so important and sufficiently different that we classify these subgoals elsewhere. We accept as a good definition of the affective development area the following statement of desirable student characteristics from the Stoughton, Wisconsin, Middle School:

1. *Have a positive self-image*
2. *Enjoy being alive*
3. *Respect the rights, views and ideas of others*
4. *Know their own strengths and weaknesses*
5. *Cope with problems by practicing self-discipline*
6. *Set realistic goals and put forth their best effort in all things done*
7. *Develop a sense of morals*
8. *Are able to pursue their own interests effectively.*

We like, too, a statement from the Poway Unified School District in California dealing more specifically with the values subgoal:

Every person develops a value system of his own. The core of this system contains those values held common by all Americans. Other values, however, will differ according to the racial, religious, or cultural group to which the individual belongs. The strength of America depends upon our ability to maintain the strength of the common core of universally accepted values, and yet leaves room for individual values which differ from the core. It is vital that teachers provide opportunities for pupils to become aware of their own values, to examine them for consistency and worth and to compare them with values held by others. The result will be deep and understanding faith in the commonly held values of our people.

Unfortunately, statements of affective goals like these are more numerous than descriptions of implementing practices, although both of the school districts cited do have quite specific programs for these goals. In Poway much responsibility for affective outcomes is given to the core-like Basic Education program of two or three hours daily, while at Stoughton the responsibility is primarily that of the Multi-Level Block (four-teacher team).

Observation of exemplary middle schools as well as the review of their materials indicates that the learning opportunities for the development of affective outcomes are best planned and evaluated in the following three categories:

Advisory Groups. As described in chapter 4, it is the A/A or advisory or homebase group, however organized and entitled to embrace the teacher guidance function, in which most faith is placed for the values clarification and moral judgment outcomes. Here also is much opportunity for the discussion of issues in and out of school, the exercise of student initiative and responsibility in conducting the affairs of the group and the management of behavior and discipline. Our later chapter deals fully with the operation of the advisory group program as a very significant part of the middle school curriculum.

Instructional Groups. Every class, small group and other instructional group in the middle school is a learning opportunity for the development of affective outcomes. Students acquire attitudes toward themselves as well as teachers, classes and school, in these groups. Agreement of the faculty on desired outcomes and general means of their achievement is an important step in effective use of instructional groups for these affective goals. Among the characteristics of instructional groups which seem to be seeking desirable affective as well as cognitive outcomes are these:

1. Controversial, attitudinal, and other affective-type questions and discussion are permitted, even encouraged and pursued whenever the teacher sees the possibility of making a positive contribution to affective development.
2. The feelings and values of students are respected by the teacher and their respect by students is expected.
3. Students are consulted for assistance in planning and evaluating as appropriate, with frequent opportunity to give feedback about their feelings toward the group and the curriculum.
4. The distinctions between fact and opinion and feeling are clarified wherever useful.
5. Praise is given wherever deserved, and blame is minimized.

Individual Relationships. The most critical situation for the development of feelings and values seems to be in that of the relationships of the individual student with other individuals. The teacher who is able to be empathetic and supportive with all students is likely to help their own feelings of self-worth and thus to influence their attitudes toward school, curriculum, and the teacher. It is in the teacher-student conversations, privately and, perhaps more significantly, publicly, that feelings, values and judgments get stimulated and even exposed. And so it is that each teacher-student contact is an opportunity for affective learning, and a potentially significant item in the curriculum had by students.

Exploration and Development of Interests

Middle schools are generally continuing and expanding the exploratory program regarded by many educators as the most significant contribution of the junior high school, one unfortunately contracted when pressures such as the post-Sputnik ones came to give greater priority and time to the traditional academic subjects. Without a ninth grade and its usual dominance by the high school program of studies and the college preparatory function, the middle school may and does provide a wide variety of exploratory experiences. In some middle schools all of these experiences are called "exploratories," but other schools differentiate the more formal ones as courses and others as activities, and still other schools may call them all "electives." Some schools make some experiences, usually the more formal ones, required and the others electives. Although we prefer for each school to use the classification and nomenclature best suited to its program, we think a three-way classification may be best for this description: (1) exploratory courses; (2) special interest activities; and (3) seminars and independent study.

Exploratory Courses. The characteristic exploratory courses of the junior high were art, music, home economics and industrial arts, and these four in some form are prominent in middle school offerings too. These areas are frequently grouped as "Unified Arts." With typing and perhaps a broader business course, and drama and speech, and even health and physical education, and other courses, they may be termed "Related Arts." The original intent of the exploratory program was to have relatively brief, introductory courses for beginners, with longer, more intensive courses available another year for those interested. This philosophy is stated as follows in a description of the Unified Arts program of the Marshall, Michigan, Middle School:

At Marshall Middle School, all students, grades five through eight, are required to take courses within the Unified Arts block. The emphasis at the earlier ages is on basic orientation to tools, safety, and procedures, and, by exposing students to each subject area, students are prepared for making choices later in their middle school years where more complex courses and projects are offered.

Thus, art in grades 5 and 6 is a four-weeks unit, in grade 7, five weeks, and grade 8, ten weeks. The courses in home economics, general music, crafts and woodworking follow the same general pattern.

The Unified Arts approach may also be designed to promote teaming and an interdisciplinary design within these fields. Thus a description of this approach at Hightstown Intermediate School in New Jersey, where art, home economics and industrial arts were grouped together physically and in instruction, emphasized the unification of these courses:

> Since the main thrust behind the Unified Arts approach is to unify the special subjects area, no attempt is made toward grade distinction. Students receive only one grade for their participation in the Unified Arts program. An interdisciplinary approach to learning employs a combination of subjects involving students in integral thought patterns.[12]

Another approach, illustrated by the Ballston Spa, New York, Middle School Humanities Program utilizes the time traditionally allotted to music, art, industrial arts, home economics and study hall, and provides in this block a wider range of activities as follows: Block Printing, Children's TV, Clothing, Colonial Ballston, Copper Foil, Craft Design, Creative Painting, Crocheting and Knitting, Drama, Food Exploration, Graphics, Guitar, Home Decoration, Lamp or Pet Cage Construction, Musicals, Power Mechanics, TV News, Tutoring, Tutoring Projects and Tye-dying Macrame.

The exploratory areas have great potential for helping middle school students to identify their own interests (and disinterests), to appreciate fine and applied arts, and to develop some rudimentary concepts and skills in the areas concerned. Art is an area for the student to try out his or her expressive tastes, and to learn a few approaches to appreciating others' art expressions. Crafts provide another outlet, one that can become a significant leisure activity. Homemaking (or home economics) may be less exploratory than practical, but many individuals do find interests here for further development. Industrial arts also emphasizes the practical aspects of home living, but it too can stimulate many interests, traditionally those of boys. Music has usually emphasized performance but the general music course is intended to develop appreciation. Many students have already discovered interests in musical performance, and so the music program provides band and chorus opportunities. Speech and drama, less frequently provided, give still further opportunities for testing out one's interests and abilities, and going farther as indicated. Typing and any business courses are also more practical than exploratory, although there is definitely the opportunity for the interested student to plan career studies in this area as well as to improve typing and other skills later as interested.

Career education emphases and support have stimulated more exploratory programs in the practical arts. For example, the Practical Arts course at Noe Middle School, Louisville, Kentucky, exposes students in the sixth grade to an overview of twelve of the standard career clusters, with additional recycling possible later as students are interested. At North Marion

Middle School in Ocala, Florida, students follow a "wheel" schedule in grade 6 rotating through each of the following programs for about five weeks each: Agriculture, Business Education, Construction, Graphic Communication, Home Economics, Manufacturing, Power and Transportation.

Foreign languages are also commonly offered on an exploratory basis. Unfortunately, if the student determines interest in a particular language by an introductory exploratory course in grade 6, there may be nothing further available until high school. Other "electives" as they are frequently called, especially for eighth graders, include special science, mathematics, language arts and social studies courses, with these most frequently being either remedial or for academically talented students (see "Seminars" below). To the extent that such courses are introductory and are followed in high school by additional related courses, they further enrich the exploratory offering.

Special Interest Activities. Variously called "classes," "activities," "minicourses," "electives" and other terms, the learning opportunities which we are classifying as special interest activities have the following distinguishing characteristics:

1. Student initiative in organizing, selecting, planning and conducting is encouraged.
2. The activity meets much less frequently and for a shorter term than the traditional exploratory courses (although some middle schools do not differentiate between the latter and the activities, giving less time to General Music, for example, than in the usual six- to eighteen-week course, and perhaps more time to the guitar activity than the typical middle school having the usual exploratory course in Music).
3. Teacher responsibility for an activity is a part of the teacher's assignment, but teachers have much freedom in proposing and planning the particular activities they guide.
4. The students' participation is voluntary and no grades are given by teachers; however, the teacher advisor does help students make choices of appropriate activities.
5. Students throughout a middle school may choose activities so that these activities are not organized by grades or ability levels or other factors toward homogeneity. In some schools the activities are organized within teams; if the teams are heterogeneous, the activity groups are likely to be also.

Examination of the descriptions of various such activity programs indicates many interesting titles and examples. At the Rupert A. Nock Middle School in Newburyport, Massachusetts, it is a SPARK program: "The program is based on *S*ervice, *P*articipation, *A*ctivity, *R*ecreation and *K*nowledge, and in keeping with its purpose, it will be referred to as the SPARK program." The basic principles of the program, as stated in a bulletin for parents and others, further explain and illustrate the goals and nature of this special interest activity program:

1. The SPARK program offerings are student initiated.
2. The SPARK program is established to develop a student's role as a cooperative, successful and well-adjusted group member.
3. The SPARK program offers a natural outlet for the curiosity, interest and talents of the students.
4. The SPARK program is to help students to develop positive interests and activities for leisure time.
5. The SPARK program is a necessary creativity outlet for students to meet the adjustment needs for the transitional period between childhood and adolescence.

Separate lists of activities available for one quarter for grades 5–6 and grades 7–8 students in each of the three houses of the school, showed that each student has more than forty activities from which to choose.

Similarly, the Louisville, Colorado, Middle School provides a SEARCH program—*S*tudents *E*ducational *A*ctivities in *R*esearch and *C*reative *H*obbies, and uses PALS (*P*ersons *A*ssisting *L*ouisville *M*iddle *S*chool) in operating the program. During one quarter, twenty-four activities were offered on Mondays, twenty-eight on Tuesdays and twenty-three on Wednesdays. Activities open to all students in grades 5 through 8 included the following: Silent Study, A Bank, School Services, New Games, Liquid Embroidery, Country Carvings, Ping Pong, Crewel, Minute Mysteries, String Program, All About Horses, Indoor Games, Outdoor Games, Puppetry, Soccer, Sign Language, Creative Writing and Guitar, with many other activities restricted to one, two or three grades.

At Oak Park Middle School, Decatur, Alabama, the program is one of minicourses of four to six weeks duration, with some variation in the number of days each minicourse meets. The total listing of such activities issued by the school for one year is a very comprehensive one, including some usual exploratory courses as described above. The list may be useful to readers in indicating the range of possible special interest activities. It is to be noted that not all these would be taught in any given school term but that the list might "serve as a guide for students and teachers in setting up exploratory offerings in the future":

    I. ACADEMIC ACTIVITIES: Banking; World-Wide Folktales and Superstitions; Classic Books; Geometric Designs; Geometric Line Design or String Art; Geometric Mobiles; Math for Fun; Plant Collections; Pleasure Reading; Reading for Pleasure; Speed Math; Small Mammal Survey of Fields and Woods.

    II. ART AND CRAFT RELATED ACTIVITIES: Basic Drawing; Basket Weaving; Bottlecrafts; Bread Dough Artistry; Ceramics; Christmas Crafts in Felt; Christmas Decorations; Copper Tooling; Craftsticks; Decorative Painting; Decoupage; Float Painting and Other Oddities; Flower Arranging; Flower Making; Gingham Flowers; Graphics; Handicrafts; Linoleum Block Printing; Macrame; Number Painting; Papier Mâché; Polydom; Tuilling; Rice Mosaics or Seed Mosaics; Rock Art; Scrap Art; String Art; Surform Sculpturing; Tie Dye; Transfer Art; Water Color; Wood Carving.

    III. COMMUNICATIONS: One-Act Plays; Plays and Skits; Spanish (conversational); Teen Talk.

IV. GAMES: Beginning Bridge; Advanced Bridge; Chess; Checkers; Science Games; Scrabble.

V. HOBBIES: Ghost Stories; Home Decorating; Horses, Horses, Horses; Hot Air Balloon; Model Airplanes; Model Rocketry; Movie History; Pen Pals; Photography; Small Engine Repair; Soap Box Derby; Stamp Collecting; Whittling, Lanyard Weaving, and other related crafts.

VI. MUSIC: Band (Beginning); Band (Concert); Band (Intermediate); Chorus (6th grade); Chorus (7th, 8th); Guitar; Group Singing; Music Theory (Beginning).

VII. NEEDLEWORK: Cover Your Racquet (Tennis); Crewel; Crochet; Cross-stitch; Decorate Your Denims; Embroidery for Fun; Knit and Crochet; Knitting; Macrame; Needlepoint; Patchwork Pillows; Simple Sewing Crafts and Creativity.

VIII. PERSONAL IMPROVEMENT: Bicycle Safety; Careers; Charm; Hand-writing; Human Relations; Lettering (Calligraphy); Medical Self Help; Motorcycle Safety; Penmanship; Safety Sanity; Shorthand; Slimnastics; Travel; Typing.

IX. PHYSICAL ACTIVITIES: Archery; Basketball; Baton; Bowling; Camping; Cheerleading; Drills and Ceremonies; Flag Football; Junior Football; Gymnastics; Softball; Volleyball; Snorkeling; Swimming; Rhythms and Games; Tennis.

Seminars and Independent Study. Any class can be termed a seminar although we prefer to reserve the use of the term for an instructional group in which the students have primary responsibility for investigations and creative activities culminating in their exchange and critique of papers and other products. Such a seminar is probably most frequently organized for more able students. For example, the Esperanza Middle School in Lexington Park, Maryland, assigns students identified as academically talented to one of four reading groups which rotate each nine weeks between four teachers who provide for a seminar experience. Seminar activities include film making, school newspaper, novels, and science fiction, involving approximately ninety-five students. This school also provides extensive independent study opportunities, and a peer-aide program for eighth grade students. The latter program includes guiding parents visiting the school, counseling sixth grade students about their work, presenting plays and discussions with elementary school students, and orienting incoming students to the middle school.

Independent study can be made available through any type of group instructional organization: classes, teams, seminars and special groups. Teachers can guide students who are interested and have rudimentary study skills to do independent study projects in lieu of part or all of the regularly assigned work in regular classes. We accept as the definition of independent study the following one developed originally in a survey of practices in secondary schools, including junior high schools, and applicable, we believe, to the middle school:

Independent study is considered by us to be learning activity largely motivated by the learner's own aims to learn and largely rewarded in terms of its intrinsic values. Such activity . . . utilizes the services of teachers and other professional personnel primarily as resources for the learner.[13]

Independent study projects that are in lieu of regular classes or of major assignments therein are frequently formalized by contracts or other written agreements covering such items as prerequisites, if any: description of the project and its goals; estimate of time involved; statement of student tasks; and specifics as to teacher role, conferences and other responsibilities. The distinguishing characteristic is the student's motivation and self-direction. Note the following statement in a bulletin on "Independent Study" from the Rupert A. Nock Middle School:

> To be effective, independent study must be a part of, not apart from, the regular program. Its emphasis should be on creative, meaningful research that will stretch and strengthen the minds of students. Properly conducted it will help pupils grow in self-correction, self-analysis, and self-direction.
> . . . The pupil must develop self-discipline and make generalizations and comparisons. Self-control, time management, and decision-making are not taught by lecturing or completing questions in a workbook, but by allowing the pupil the freedom to develop these traits by experiencing them.

The University Middle School of the University of Northern Colorado, Greeley, uses an Independent Activity Period, with students choosing each six weeks either an independent study activity, a workshop or intramurals. A sample sign-up sheet included as workshops the following, plus basketball as the intramural option, and independent study as arranged with one of several designated teachers: Leather Work, Backpacking, Macrame and Rocket Building.

Health and Physical Education

The dominance of physical growth and development and related characteristics in the life of the middle school child demands that the program of health and physical education be carefully planned and implemented. We see these significant aspects: health education, including sex education; physical education; intramurals.

Health Education. Although aspects of health education may be treated in physical education, science, homemaking and other classes, the great need for instruction in this area suggests separate classes with qualified instructors and adequate instructional materials needed. A school coordinator of the program, with planning and advisory groups representing various related school areas and the parents and community, should help to develop and maintain an effective program. Typical content for the health program includes: hygiene and personal care; nutrition; tobacco, alcohol and drugs; communicable diseases; mental health; community health services; consumer health; chronic diseases; first aid and safety education.

Sex education is provided in various ways. Although its provision has been and may remain controversial in some communities, the need for emerging adolescents to understand their changing bodies and the specifics of human sexuality is critical. Teenage pregnancies and venereal disease have become national problems, and there is also the related problem of changing life styles and mores as to marriage and the family. For certain, any specific course, unit, assembly or other approach to sex education had best be carefully planned with, and sponsored by, parent representatives along with representatives of the health professions, family and church. Concentrated programs involving medical and other community representatives, along with a definite unit in the health program, and related instruction as appropriate in science, physical education and other subjects, seem a good combination.

Physical Education. Frequent physical movement is characteristic of the middle school student. The greater care given to regular body-building exercise, the better for proper direction of the growing body. The physical education program characteristically includes a program of physical movement and exercise; lifetime recreational activities; and sports activities. The instructional program aims at a balance between these aspects. For example, an Aberdeen, Maryland, Middle School printed brochure on the physical education program explains the program as follows:

Sixth grade students will receive developmental skill instruction. The seventh and eighth grade program requires that each student participate in one dance activity, two individual sports, two team sports, and one fitness activity. In addition to this, seventh and eighth grade students will select numerous activities in keeping with their individual interests.

The list of activities at Aberdeen is extensive:

- *Archery, I,II*
- *Badminton*
- *Cross Country, I,II*
- *Cycling, I,II*
- *Fencing*
- *First Aid*
- *Golf*
- *Gymnastics—apparatus tumbling and floor exercise*
- *Handball*
- *Low organization & foreign games*
- *Orienteering*
- *Paddleball*
- *Physical Fitness Activities*
- *Recreational Games—bowling, horseshoes, deck tennis, ping-pong, shuffleboard*
- *Self-Defense*
- *Swimming*
- *Target Tennis*
- *Track and Field*
- *Weight Training—Conditioning*
- *Wrestling*

- *Aerobic Dance*
- *Creative Dance*
- *Folk and Square Dance*
- *Modern Dance*
- *Basketball, I,II*
- *Field Hockey, I,II*
- *Floor Hockey*
- *Flag Football*
- *Lacrosse*
- *Soccer I, II*
- *Speedball*
- *Softball I, II*
- *Team Handball*
- *Volleyball I,II*[14]

Intramurals. Although many middle schools provide interscholastic athletics, as did their junior high predecessors, this practice is decidedly controversial, and is vigorously opposed by many educators and parents. The major basis of opposition is the belief that children of middle school age should not be involved in competitive contact athletics. There is also the model of some athletics-dominated high schools and even the junior highs that many wish to avoid. Relevant, too, is the widespread desire for the middle school to be a unique institution focused on the needs of its own population rather than modeling itself after a higher level. But to us the most significant argument is that all the students in the middle school need to have experience in sports, experience that is appropriate for their physical status and that can yield feelings of satisfaction to many children who would never make the varsity team. The possible physical damage of inappropriate activities must be avoided.

The evidence against interscholastic athletics and for intramurals in the middle school is impressive. An excellent review of the issue by Romano and Timmers concluded with this comment in which the present authors fully concur:

> Middle school people who really are concerned for what is best for their students increasingly are looking for a quiet burial for interscholastic athletic programs with their overcompetitiveness and overorganization of these youngsters. They are trying in their middle schools to offer a program of intramural sports and strong physical education programs for both boys and girls, with teachers who understand and are dedicated to the best interests of these transescents.[15]

Intramurals are organized in various ways in middle schools—by grades, teams, periods, and other ways. Where there is a team organization, and we hope this will become universal, it is a very natural outgrowth of the team organization to have various types of sports contests within and between teams. The intramurals may be organized by the physical education teachers and certainly should operate under their supervision, but with much interest and support from all members of the faculty.

Domain of Communication and Learning Skills

The most commonly understood goal of public schools has been the development of basic communication and learning skills. We use this compound term to refer both to specific communication skills, such as speaking and listening, and specific learning skills, such as reading. We also recognize that communication skills are usually also skills of learning, and vice versa. For convenience, the major skills areas are identified here in the following categories: (1) reading and related study skills; (2) speaking, questioning, and listening skills; (3) writing skills; (4) quantitative skills; (5) use of major learning tools; (6) problem-solving and other higher intellectual processes.

In the 1970's, a perennial call for a return to the basics in the public schools again raised the question of "What is basic?" To most critics, stimulated by the disclosure of declining test scores and rising school costs, the basics probably are the traditional 3 R's of reading, writing and arithmetic. The movement to reemphasize or at least to explain more fully these areas, also at times has brought a return of such characteristics of traditional education as increased homework and memorization and a tendency to designate any content that seems important as "basic skills." Foshay's analysis of the basics controversy involved his classification of the 3 R's as "coping skills," in which he also included "emotional development, physical realization, intellectual functioning, social growth, aesthetic encounters, and spiritual awareness." In addition to these coping skills, Foshay included as basics, "citizenship, morality or character, and a valid view of self," and he warned "leave one out, and the student's ability to survive is impaired."[16]

The present authors also believe that the middle school has many "basic skills" to teach—all of the goals and related opportunities cited in this chapter. We also believe that basic skills and essential knowledge can be and indeed usually should be taught and learned differently. Skills include those behaviors which can be performed somewhat identically both at different times by the same individual and by different individuals; they are learned through repeated, directed performance; and their competent performance is of importance to every individual. The particular skills with which we are concerned here are those that the middle school student must be or become able to perform in order to communicate with other people and to continue learning. Thus the domain of these skills includes aspects of several knowledge areas, especially language arts and mathematics, and it is perhaps difficult for the teachers concerned to remember to distinguish between the specific skills and the concepts of these areas. Yet a major weakness of teaching is the failure to make this distinction, having students attempt to acquire concepts and understandings by a stepwise approach developed for teaching skills. In this section we are concerned only with the communication and learning skills, to us basic skills, both as aspects of subjects and independent of the subject organization.

Reading and Related Study Skills

Reading, generally taught directly in the junior high school as remedial instruction for students lacking adequate skills for the junior high textbooks, has had a much more significant place in the curriculum of the middle school. During the late 1970's, with the national clamor for better reading, this place became even more dominant.

Some middle schools follow a basic reading program with a commercial reading series, using a special grouping for reading within the team arrangement or a separate schedule outside the team organization. Three-level programs are also utilized, as described below in a curriculum description of the language arts program of two teams at the Boyce Middle School, Upper St. Clair, Pennsylvania:

Students are placed on three reading strands—corrective, developmental, and enrichment. On each of these strands, comprehension of ideas is developed through the mastery of such subskills as main ideas, specific details, sequences, comparisons, cause and effect relationships, assessment of character traits, and predictions of outcomes. Materials appropriate to the reading level of each strand have been selected for the implementation of these objectives.

In addition, a unit designed to increase the reading rate of students has been included in this instructional level. The students are also instructed in methods of adjusting rate, to purpose and in study skills.

The reading program at Boyce includes several skills that are usually designated as study skills: note taking, outlining, book reporting, library skills, dictionary skills and reading for pleasure.

In some middle schools the reading program is considered wholly developmental; note the description of the North Marion Middle School program in Citra, Florida:

Based on the philosophy that everyone has reading skills which may be improved, all students participate in an individualized reading program for a minimum of nine weeks each year. This is a developmental not a remediation program.

This program utilizes a specially equipped laboratory and a special reading teacher for each grade. Pretests lead to an individual prescription, with daily evaluations. Most laboratory time is spent in individual activities, but at least one day a week is a group experience. Posttests are given at the end of the nine weeks and most students have two nine-week sessions each year.

Indicative of the great interest in reading in the middle school is the schoolwide reading period, called at the A.G. Currie Intermediate School in Tustin, California, a "Read-In" program:

In keeping with the trend of "back to basics," the Currie staff is implementing a "Read-In." The Read-In is a regularly scheduled daily occurrence. It is a 20-minute period during which everyone on campus (students and staff) reads.

The purpose of the program is multi-faceted. The primary objective is to increase the joy of reading. A second goal is to increase reading skills, such as comprehension and vocabulary. Results of last year's Read-In showed a marked improvement in overall reading scores.

Continuums of reading skills have been developed within many school districts to aid in the diagnosis of reading levels and the planning of instruction. The classification of reading skills in the continuum for middle school years at the Poway Unified School District in California indicates the breadth of the combined reading-language arts program: word identification skills; structural analysis; word meaning; comprehension skills; types of literature; literary devices; critical evaluation; study skills; organizing information; outlining; reading rate; and reading for personal/social development. Study skills in this continuum include:

- Locating information: dictionary, encyclopedia, atlas, almanac, graphic materials, library and library aids; parts of a book, index, glossary, etc.; reference material; Thesaurus
- Synthesizing
- Skimming

Speaking, Questioning and Listening Skills

Although questioning rarely appears in statements of objectives and written curriculum plans, as a learning skill it is of first-rank importance. Oral questioning is a very frequent learning activity, and the quality of this learning is directly related to the quality of the questions asked. Exercises in middle school language arts classes sometimes do include question formulation and refinement, and some teachers frequently do correct poorly phrased questions; but more attention seems needed. Speaking and listening skills are much more likely than questioning skills to be stipulated in the curriculum plans and their objectives, and to be implemented in classroom situations. The following statement of "Goals in Listening" in a description of the seventh grade language arts program of Nipher Middle School, Kirkwood, Missouri, is representative of the goals and nature of instruction in listening skills:

1. *The ability to follow oral directions.*
2. *The ability to summarize ideas and draw conclusions from group discussions.*
3. *The ability to evaluate the accuracy and relative importance of what is heard on radio, television, lectures, and reports.*
4. *The ability to distinguish between relevant and irrelevant material.*
5. *The ability to identify the main theme of an orally presented paragraph.*

Also representative is the statement in the same material on Goals in Speaking for the sixth grade (similar goals for speaking and listening are included for each middle school year):

A. *Demonstrate self-confidence and poise in a variety of speaking situations.*
B. *Organize content for a clearly defined purpose.*
C. *Speak from notes or an outline.*
D. *Get and maintain listeners' attention.*
E. *Participate in group and panel discussions.*
F. *Give adequate oral directions.*
G. *Use appropriate pitch, stress, and juncture as meaning signals in spoken language*
H. *Participate in skits, plays and readings.*

Despite the tendency of such lists and curriculum opportunities to overemphasize the formal speech-making skills, the inclusion of specific instruction in speech, both conversational and formal, seems highly desirable for middle school children. Speech and especially dramatics are of high interest appeal to many middle school students, and should have a significant place in the language arts program, both in regular classroom instruction and optional, special interest activities.

Writing Skills

Writing, both by hand and by machine, is a highly important skill of communication, and its use for note-taking and preservation, record-keeping and composition is significant in learning. Middle schools teach spelling to help in both reading and writing, composition in various forms, and, less frequently, handwriting and typing to facilitate achievement of the communication and learning goals. The writing program is generally an important phase of the language arts (or English) program, and an excellent opportunity for students to synthesize and utilize many of their learnings in other phases of language arts such as spelling, reading, literature and grammar. Our observation indicates wide variation in the time and attention given to writing, with perhaps too much of what time and attention are given going to formal papers and too little to systematic exercises for the development of writing skills. A checklist of writing skills developed in Marion County, Florida, for grades 6–10 is specific and comprehensive: (The student will—)

- *Compose grammatically correct sentences.*
- *Organize objects and information into logical groupings and orders.*
- *Write a paragraph expressing ideas clearly.*
- *Write for the purpose of supplying necessary information.*
- *Write letters and messages using commonly accepted formats.*
- *Fill out common forms.*
- *Spell correctly.*
- *Punctuate correctly.*
- *Capitalize correctly.*
- *Write legibly.*

Each of these skills appears in Level I, II, and III lists and each is further broken down to include more specific objectives.

Writing is also taught through laboratory approaches and creative writing classes, minicourses and activities. The laboratory approach in which a special teacher is available to help students with acute writing problems can be combined with the reading laboratory. For example, a creative writing minicourse described as follows is offered in the Andrews, Texas, Middle School:

Say It With Words—An opportunity for creative writing will be provided in this unit. Poetry, short stories, and other types of writing will be attempted.

Quantitative Skills

It is difficult indeed to separate skills and knowledge in the mathematics field. For general communication purposes one needs enough understanding of some basic mathematics terms and processes to be literate in their use. This involves mathematical knowledge. Sometimes one also needs the mental agility in quantitative relationships to solve a percentage or other commonplace problem. This involves mathematical skill. For continued learning one needs the same plus skills in using tables and other presentations of quantitative data, in interpreting graphs and pictorials using quantitative data or relationships, and in projecting such data and relationships. We have to conclude that the citizen needs both the understanding of basic mathematics concepts and the skill to handle quantitative data and problems, and that his mathematics education must include both, probably taught somewhat integrally. Thus we are really dealing here with the mathematics program as a whole.

Only reading has equalled or surpassed mathematics in public interest and concern in recent decades. The so-called ''new'' mathematics movement, stimulated by several post-Sputnik national curriculum projects such as the School Mathematics Study Group (SMSG), forced parental interest as children brought home new materials and terminology. More recently this movement has been under reassessment and continuing modifications are being made. Probably the most pervasive development has been the use of various systems of individual progress plans and materials, many of them commercially produced but some developed at least initially within a particular school or district.

Mathematics is a discipline with much clearer sequential aspects than other fields, and the answers to problems, and the processes to solve them are generally more precise and certain than elsewhere. Hence it is possible to have such systematic mathematics programs as stated in this description from the Ballston Spa, New York, Middle School:

> Our mathematics program is based on three hundred specific mathematics behavioral objectives. Each objective has been placed in one of five categories: integers, rationale, reals, sets or measurement and geography. In all categories but one, the objectives are divided into three sections for a total of fourteen sections. Within the fourteen sections which are listed under the five categories, the objectives are arranged on the basis of difficulty and necessary prerequisites in both its own and the other sections.

In the implementation of such a program, testing on an objective yields a prescription for the student, with the student's subsequent work again tested to determine further progress. Each student has an individual record monitored by a teacher. The program is common for all students, but each progresses individually. This pattern seems very desirable in middle school mathematics.

The mathematics cumulative record card of the Kirkwood, Missouri, Middle Schools shown in Table 3.1 is illustrative of the scope and sequence of mathematics in the middle school and also of an individualized progress system. The record is to show the student what topics have been included each year and how they are included, at an introductory, instructional (worked with in depth), or competency level (mastery).

Using Major Learning Tools

Middle schools today, as all other educational institutions, have access to many learning tools of great potential for learners. Printed tools, books and

Table 3.1* /

```
Kirkwood Middle Schools
MATHEMATICS CUMULATIVE RECORD CARD              NAME_____

    Code:  ☑  Introductory Level
           ☒  Instructional Level
           ■  Competency Level

    CONCEPTS:
```

Year in School	6	7	Math 8 Algebra
School Year			
Teacher's Name			

WHOLE NUMBERS	6	7	8
Addition with regrouping			
Subtraction with regrouping			
Multiplication with 2-digit factors			
Division with 1-digit divisors			
2-digit divisors			
Place Value through millions			
Rounding through millions			
Find averages			
Prime numbers			
Greatest common factor			
Least common multiple			
Word problems			
Use of properties			
Commutative			
Associative			
Distributive			
Exponents			

FRACTIONS / MIXED NUMBERS	6	7	8
Fractions			
Find equivalents			
Compare and order			
Addition (unlike denominators)			
Subtraction (unlike denominators)			
Multiplication			
Division			
Mixed Numbers			
Fractions ⟷ Mixed Numbers			
Addition with regrouping			
Subtraction with regrouping			
Multiplication			
Division			
Work Problems			
Exponents			

DECIMALS	6	7	8
Place Value through millionths			
Read and write through millionths			
Compare and order			
Round off			
Addition and subtraction			
Multiplication			
Division			
Mult. & Divide by powers of ten			
Fractions ⟷ Decimals			
Terminating and repeating			
Exponents			
Word problems			
Scientific Notation			

MEASUREMENT	6	7	8
Telling time			
Money (making change)			
English			
Linear: nearest 1/2"			
nearest 1/4"			
nearest 1/8"			
Weight			
Volume			
Metric			
Prefixes			
Linear: meter			
centimeter			
millimeter			
Weight			
Volume			

GEOMETRY	6	7	8
Points, lines, segments			
Rays, angles, planes			
Identify plane figures			
Symmetry			
Constructions/compass and			
straightedge			
Identify and measure angles			
Parallel and perpendicular lines			
Related angles			
Polygons			
Classification			
Perimenter			
Area			
Triangles			
Congruent			
Construction			
Proofs			
Similar			
Construction			
Calculations			
Word problems			
Pythagorean Theorem			
Inscribed and circumscribed			
Circles			
Characteristics			
Circumference			
Area			
Solid Figures			
Identify			
Volume			
Surface Area			

all other printed publications, remain the most widely targeted learning aids, and create the entire field of reading. The past few decades have brought a plethora of other learning tools: visual ones ranging from maps and charts to films, the great auditory ones of telephone and radio, the once revolutionary audiovisuals of sound movies and television, and today the computer. And so the Media Center becomes an all-important facility of the middle school, and the use of its resources and of other learning resources in the community and elsewhere the needed focus of lifelong learning skills.

Middle schools approach the teaching of these various tools in many

Table 3.1 (cont.) /

NAME _____

RATIO AND PROPORTION	6	7	8
Write ratios and proportions			
Find equal ratios			
Find missing number in proportions			
Word problems			
Scale drawings			
PERCENT			
Percent ⟶ fractions			
Percent ⟷ decimals			
Find percent of a number			
Find percent one number is of another			
Find a number when a percent of it is unknown			
Word problems			
INTEGERS			
Number line			
Compare and order			
Addition and subtraction			
Multiplication and division			
Absolute value			
Expressions with exponents			
Word problems			
GRAPHING (read, interpret, construct)			
Bar graph			
Line graph			
Circle graph			
Coordinate graphing			
Cartesian products			
Graphing points in all four quadrants			
Graph linear equations and pairs of equations			
Slope and slope-intercept forms of equations			
SETS			
Sets, set notation			
Venn diagrams			
IRRATIONAL NUMBERS			
Perfect squares			
Square roots			
Finding square roots by averaging and tables			
Pythagorean Theorem			
Word problems			
BASES OTHER THAN TEN			
Place Value			
Convert to base ten			
Addition and subtraction			

CLOCK ARITHMETIC	6	7	8
Convert to a ten clock			
Addition and subtraction			
Multiplication and division			
PROBABILITY			
Single event			
Compound event			
Sample spaces			
Word problems			
EXPRESSIONS: EQUATIONS			
Missing addends			
Missing minuends			
Missing factors			
Missing dividends			
Simplify expressions			
Whole numbers			
Fractions			
Decimals			
Integers			
Grouping symbols			
Order of operations			

STANDARDIZED TEST DATA

Test	Date	Concepts	Computation	Applications

ALGEBRA PLACEMENT

Test	Date	Score	Recommended

COMMENTS:

* From Kirkwood, Missouri, Schools

ways. At Lincoln Middle School in Gainesville, Florida, a series of learning stations has been developed for use in an intensive instructional sequence on learning tools including the items shown in the accompanying student checklist (Table 3.2). Each student's checklist serves as a record kept on file in Lincoln's Media Center during his or her attendance, and is forwarded to the student's high school English department upon transfer.

Most middle schools use some type of introduction to the library/media center facility, and may involve language arts and/or other teachers in such series as above or in occasional special sessions. Instructional teams and individual teachers also develop their own sessions for introduction of stu-

Table 3.2* / Student Checklist—Information Retrieval Skills

NAME _____
TEAM _____

ASSIGNED	REFERENCE CENTERS	COMPLETED	ASSIGNED	CARD CATALOG	COMPLETED
	Encyclopedias are about Everything			Which Word do You Look Up	
	Inside Encyclopedias			Information on Catalog Cards	
	An Atlas Is . . .			Author, Title & Subject	
	Unabridged Dictionary			Cross Reference and Analytic Cards	
	The World Almanac			Using Audio-Visual Materials	
	Atlas: Where in the World			Call Numbers	
	Subject Area Dictionaries				
	Specialized Encyclopedias			**DEWEY DECIMAL SYSTEM**	
	National Geographic Index			Main Classes	
	Florida Handbook			Using Signs in the Media Center	
	Vertical File			Arrangement of Books on the Shelves	
	Guinness Book of World Records			Dewey Decimal Hunt	
	Biographical Dictionaries			Reader's Guide to Periodical Literature	
	Quotations			Super Search	
	Careers: It's Your Choice			Public Library	
	Thesaurus				
	Review of Reference Works				

* From Lincoln Middle School, Gainesville, Florida

dents to their textbooks, learning packets, and learning stations and other learning resource centers. The important principle is that there is a systematic program of instruction in the use of each major tool, with the program frequently itself individualized in terms of sequential steps for learning the use of such an aid as the card catalog.

Television is a great educational tool for which schools have assumed minimal responsibility. Direct instruction over educational and closed-circuit channels continues in some school districts, but it has not had the popularity early advocates predicted. Some middle school teachers arrange to utilize appropriate telecasts when scheduled during an instructional period, or by assignments to students for out-of-school viewing. Despite widespread recognition of the great potential of television in education and of the many hours spent by the average middle schooler viewing television, community-home-school cooperation in this field awaits great expansion to bring about adequate usage of the resource. The use of videotapes and other recordings offers increased opportunities.

Some few middle schools do have computer terminals by special arrangements for use in research projects and experiments with computer-based instruction. Current developments in the use of microcomputers may be paralleled with more opportunities for teaching about and with computers as major tools of learning for the future. Undoubtedly the computer makes increasingly possible readier access to great bodies of information, and citizens will increasingly need to know how to retrieve and utilize information on demand. Whether computer-centered, electronic technology will actually be the ''fourth revolution'' (after the revolutions of schools, written word, and printing), as some have predicted,[17] remains to be seen. However, our experience with other major mechanical innovations such as television and pocket calculators suggests that use of computers by individuals will become commonplace and that the earlier instruction in their use, the better.

Problem Solving and Other Higher Intellectual Processes

As we noted in chapter 1, recent brain growth data indicate a plateau in ages twelve through fourteen that probably influences a very slow beginning for most students. However, of formal operations the middle school should undoubtedly include some opportunities for students ready for limited problem solving, evaluation of ideas, critical thinking and related processes. At the same time it must be recognized that most children do not become capable of these formal operations in the middle school. Epstein and Toepfer's review of the brain growth data and of learning programs in the middle school led them to these recommendations:

Thus, middle school programs must: (a) discontinue the mass introduction of novel cognitive skills to middle grade students who do not have such readiness; (b) present new cognitive information at the existing skill level of students; and (c) work to mature existing cognitive skills of middle grade learners.[18]

To these ends and to aid the development of positive self-concepts, these authors would restructure the middle school program to include a large component of opportunities for experience and practice of skills such as "community service projects in which students learn through working with the elderly in nursing homes, with children in day care centers, and in community and natural resources reclamation projects."[19]

Problem solving and the related processes are sought in some of the activities of the advisory group (see chapter 4). They can also be included as objectives for some students in some social studies and science programs, as well as of interdisciplinary units. Problem solving as an activity in mathematics may be developed in such ways as to emphasize correct processes rather than correct answers. Special interest activity groups, frequently involving more student initiative and management than regular instructional programs, may also give opportunities for students to work out individual and group problems.

The goal, problem solving, needs to be viewed as central in the total instructional program, grades K-12. Curriculum planning groups can plan advisory group activities, interdisciplinary units and specific instruction in the broad knowledge areas at appropriate levels so as to provide many opportunities for developing the conceptual background and interests for the problem solving and other higher intellectual skills to be learned and practiced as intellectual maturities permit.

Domain of Major Knowledge Areas

From one-half to two-thirds of the instructional time in the middle school is typically allotted for instruction in the major knowledge areas of language arts, mathematics, science and social studies. Much of this ought to be and is used by teachers for learning opportunities in the other domains, especially that of communication and learning skills. Undoubtedly the majority of scheduled instruction in language arts, almost all of that in mathematics, and smaller portions of that in science and social studies are focused on the learner becoming more competent in communication and in continued learning. But the learner also needs knowledge about the environment, physical and social, and of the cultural heritage to provide a substantive base for communication and further learning. This section describes how this need for knowledge is approached in the four major areas universally included in the middle school curriculum.

Language Arts

The predominant goals and learning opportunities of the language arts program relate to the learning and communication skills just considered. In addition to learning opportunities in reading and other study skills, speaking and listening, and writing, the language arts program usually includes specific instruction in grammar and spelling. Both of these areas are almost inextricably mixed with the skills areas as we defined them, but separate study materials and time allocations do have to be made for spelling and grammar, or perhaps English usage. Both spelling and grammar can be and are taught in part through vocabularies and composition within the subject matter under study in science, social studies, or literature materials. For sequential development, however, research-based spelling and grammar usage guides are usually considered essential, with the teachers' and students' own lists from current instruction used as supplementary guides.

One area of the language arts program is not skills based—literature. Unfortunately, because of the press of the skills components, especially in a "back-to-the-basics" period, literature may be neglected or taught almost as a skills subject itself—a good way to dull student appetites for reading! Among ways of organizing the literature component in the middle school are these: use of anthologies of literary selections on a class basis; studies of a few complete pieces of literature; independent reading of many sources; study of selected readings of a particular type (e.g., poetry); use of several pieces of literature related to some central theme, from either language arts or a cross-disciplinary approach; minicourses or short units on many different types and pieces of literature, perhaps with some options for student selection of the minicourses and readings therein; and combinations of these approaches. The present authors especially like those approaches which aim toward building student interests in continued reading. Hence we find provocative a listing of minicourses in the Andrews, Texas, Middle School which includes the following, for example: Independent Reading; Mythology; The Odyssey; Safari through the Animal World; The Sporting World; The American Dream; The Diary of Anne Frank; Mark Twain; With Sword and Shield; the Fifth Dimension (science fiction); Johnny Tremain; American Folktales; The Bible as Literature; Whodunit; It's a Small World; Heroes of the Old West. Surely almost every student can find and further develop an interest here.

We believe that the end results of independent reading will be much more significant interest and knowledge development than will come from programs of literature focused on such topics as these gleaned from an examination of some middle school program descriptions: figures of speech; identification of literary types; interpretation of footnotes in literary selections; definition of literary terms such as "theme"; marking of end rhyme. Important as these matters may be, students can learn about them after they become really interested in literature, just as they can learn many rules of grammar after they sense the need for rules.

Mathematics

As we noted in the earlier discussion of Quantitative Skills, it is difficult and probably unwise to separate the teaching of mathematical skills and concepts at the middle school level. Certainly the skills are learned more readily when the concepts are understood, and the intent of mathematics instruction is to maintain the integral relationship of concept and operation. Hence we shall give little more space to mathematics in this section, but certainly recommend its full allocation of time in the curriculum for all of the purposes and program aspects considered earlier. We would emphasize the hope, too, that mathematics would be related to knowledge in other areas since so many concepts in science and social studies do have mathematical relationships and frequently require use of quantitative skills; for example, the whole area of taxation involves both social studies and mathematics concepts and skills.

Science

In science, too, both the knowledge and the skills domains have claims. As we noted earlier, problem solving is a central objective in much science teaching. A curriculum description of the Marshall, Michigan, Middle School includes among skills "to be developed or re-enforced in the science curriculum," the following: problem solving and critical thinking; communication skills (reading, vocabulary development, speaking and discussion, writing and library skills); and mathematical skills (twenty-three items listed). Knowledge outcomes are generally quite specifically defined, but the curriculum and instructional plans for their attainment are much more flexible and comprehensive than the premiddle school science readers of the elementary school and general science taught without a laboratory of the junior high school. Note, for example, some of the instructional guidelines developed by the Stoughton, Wisconsin, Middle School:

1. *Teachers will teach science to heterogeneous groups . . .*
2. *Basic skill development will be an integral part of the science program . . .*
3. *Occasional enrichment excursions will be provided for students such as photography, scuba diving, the energy crisis, energy and other subjects, in addition to the Earth Science theme.*
4. *Learning modes will include lecture, lab, research, small group projects or contracts when utilizing the science program.*
9. *The scientific method will be emphasized in the teaching of the Environmental Science program. These are the major categories: observation, prediction, application, extrapolation, synthesis and evaluation.*
10. *An attitude survey will be attached to each pre- and post-test to measure affectively the motivation of the students toward science.*
11. *Students' knowledge and interests will increase as the Earth Science program, eighth grade curriculum; Life Science curriculum, seventh grade or the environment curriculum for sixth grade is taught, as shown by assessment instruments.*
12. *Inter-block communication will be increased for the science program by implementing periodic meetings, in an effort to coordinate and share common ideas.*

Various national curriculum development projects have influenced the development of science in the middle schools. A program description from the Ballston Spa, New York, Middle School, for example, reported the use of certain units in grade 6 as follows:

The units offered were: Rocks and Charts (earth science), Heating and Cooling (physics), and Small Things (Life science). The three above units are ESS (Elementary Science Study) that we have had much success with. The science teachers prepare instructional units of their own to use in addition to the purchased programs.

The grade 7 program includes an ISCS (Intermediate Science Curriculum Study) unit on physics, and grade 8 an ISCS chemistry unit, with the possibility for students who progress rapidly going on to the third level of ISCS, including short units from many science areas. A program description from the White Brook Middle School in Easthampton, Massachusetts, describes use of the ISCS program in grades 7 and 8, too, and use of the SCIS Program in grades 5 and 6:

The Science Curriculum Improvement Study consists of two series of related and sequential units. One unit in life science, and one in physical science are paired for each of six levels. Taking advantage of the natural curiosity of children, SCIS presents a wide variety of phenomena for classroom exploration and investigation. At each of the six levels numerous inquiry-oriented activities help children accumulate experiences and ideas which advance their thinking from the concrete to the abstract, and enable them to relate scientific concepts to the everyday world.

Science in the middle school is usually a graded, sequential ordering of units of content, with life science units seemingly most common in grade 7 and earth science in either or both grades 6 and 8, and other subject matter emphases coming in any grade. The listing of units in the science continuum of the Azalea Middle School, St. Petersburg, Florida, for example, is as follows:

Grade Six: Introduction (scientific method, etc.); Meteorology; Electricity; Astronomy; Geology; Environmental Studies.
Grade Seven: Introduction; Cells; Microscopic Organisms; Organismal Processes; Life—Past, Present, and Future; The Human Body; Environmental Studies.
Grade Eight: Introduction; Matter; Energy; Environmental Studies.

But electives, special interest activities, and minicourses also are used to achieve science objectives. In addition to its basic science program utilizing national project and other materials in such a sequence as described above, the Graveraet Middle School, Marquette, Michigan, offers the following electives in science: Photography; Advanced Photography; Pebble Puppies (geologic features of Michigan's Upper Peninsula); Planting; Recreational Safety and Outdoor Education (RSOE) and Substance Abuse. The Andrews, Texas, Middle School uses a minicourse approach in science similar to the one described earlier in language arts:

The minicourse curriculum has injected "new life" into our science program. We still teach the basic subjects required by state law, but we do it in a much different way. Our minicourses are six weeks' minicourses that span the subjects from astronomy to zoology. The minicourse curriculum allows the teacher to select what courses he or she will teach. This allows the teacher to teach in areas of high interest and strengths.

Course descriptions from Andrews include the following minicourse titles:

- *Anatomy (the only minicourse required of all students—12 weeks)*
- *Chemistry*
- *Ecology*
- *Rocks and Minerals*
- *Historical Geology*
- *Micro-Biology*
- *Oceanography*
- *Pathology*
- *Petroleum Science*
- *Physiology*
- *Psychology*
- *Physical Geology*
- *Genetics*
- *History of Science*
- *Laboratory Techniques*
- *Meteorology*
- *Space Science*
- *Zoology*
- *Astronomy*

Social Studies

As the other major knowledge areas at this level, social studies has considerable responsibility within the other domains. Values clarification exercises are frequently used in social studies periods, and social studies content can provoke consideration of many ethical and moral questions.

In addition to such personal development possibilities, social studies provides the opportunities for development of many skills of communication and continued learning. For example, a comprehensive curriculum workbook developed by teachers in the Nipher and North Middle Schools, Kirkwood, Missouri, included the following in a list of skills to be taught in grade 7 social studies:

- *Reading for information*
- *Observation*
- *Recall*
- *Classification*
- *Analysis*
- *Evaluation*
- *Group discussion and interaction*
- *Making written reports*
- *Using the library*
- *Making oral reports*
- *Interviewing*
- *Role playing*
- *Advanced map skills*
- *Decision making*
- *Study skills processes*
- *Interpreting polar projection maps*
- *Interpreting latitude and longitude*
- *Evaluating qualifications of author*
- *Separating relevant and unrelated ideas*
- *Bibliographies*

Perhaps more than any other knowledge area, social studies provides the subject matter base for many interdisciplinary or core units. It is relatively easy to identify literature related to social studies themes, movements and eras. Also, along with science, social studies provides the context for practicing and acquiring all of the skills of learning and communication we presented earlier in this chapter and illustrated in the preceding paragraph.

But social studies is more than a vehicle for teaching values, literature and learning skills. There is a great body of knowledge indispensable to successful membership in the human society, and much of this knowledge is embodied in the various plans of social studies curriculum scope and sequence used in American middle schools. The plans we have examined indicate a considerable agreement in practice only on the content of grade 8, American history. Some illustrations of the variety of plans especially for other grades, as abstracted from curriculum materials supplied the authors, follow.

In Cobb County, Georgia, the middle schools provide two courses in grade 6: Geography Skills and Georgia Studies (two quarters); in grade 7, the course is "Cultures of the World" with focus on various cultural regions; and grade 8, American history, chronologically organized. The MacDonald Middle School of East Lansing, Michigan, offers three basic units in grade 6: (1) people and the traits they share; (2) society and interacting groups; and (3) people and their political systems. Grade 7 is World Studies, with a content similar to that of Cobb County, plus miscellaneous units such as education for consumerism, human sexuality and careers. Grade 8 is American history with general citizenship objectives emphasized. The grade 6 program of Alton U. Farnsworth Middle School, Guilderland, New York, lists the same three units as the MacDonald School, and also these: Social Scientists; Cities and the People Who Build Them; Societies and Interacting Groups; Economics and their use of Resources; and Nations and Their Changing Boundaries. The grade 7 program includes four units (fifteen to twenty-three weeks) relating to state geography, history and culture, and four units (fourteen to twenty-two weeks) on early United States history (through the formation of the U.S. government). In grade 8 the chronological organization of American history is continued and concluded. The Shelburne, Vermont, Middle School includes a somewhat diverse organization of units in grade 6: Mapping Skills; Analysis of a Newspaper; U.S. Government; Human Relations; Specific Behavior Science; Value Clarification. Grade 7 combines study of local and distant areas: Basic Fundamentals (map study especially); Champlain Valley; Europe, Africa, and Asia; Urban Study; and Current Events. The grade 8 program is the familiar chronological study of American history.

We ourselves believe that it is quite desirable for middle schools to have differing social studies and other programs. They are influenced by many factors which vary from state to state, community to community and school to school: local traditions, state and district regulations; programs of the schools which precede and follow; social philosophies and values; and others. But common emphases on core values of democracy are also needed and found.

Interdisciplinary, Core and Other Organizations of Knowledge

The knowledge domain in the middle school is not completely confined to the four major subject fields just discussed. Interdisciplinary and core teaching and scheduling arrangements facilitate combinations and interdisciplinary units that draw knowledge from various disciplines. Illustrative of the frequent combination of language arts and social studies, CLASS (Combined Language Arts and Social Studies) is a three-period block in grade 7 at Wayside Middle School, Saginaw, Texas. The main event of the year is the Pioneer Fair, with a museum, a pictorial of Texas History, a medicine show and an exhibit room. A description of the presentation of two units taught in the Alief, Texas, Middle School, "Free Enterprise" and "Archaeological Dig," cited "the advantages of teaching specific skills and content by involving students in interesting activities and projects which require the interrelation of many disciplines as well as organizational and social skills." It is such advantages that in part cause the authors to devote chapter 5 to the interdisciplinary team organization we believe essential to the success of a middle school.

Organizations of knowledge can also be made in fields other than the established ones—witness career education, consumer education, humanities, "the related arts," "the unified arts" as examples in the middle school program. Illustrative of how such organizations may draw on the usual knowledge areas is a program in consumer education of the Newburyport, Massachusetts, Schools, that centers in science. For the middle school, the program description ("Product Testing") suggests the following:

> At the middle school level, each team member will be encouraged to participate to some degree once the activity has emerged from the science class, e.g.
> 1. *Math*—interpretation and display of numerical data, graphing, statistics, unit pricing, geometric display and packaging design. (Similar suggestions follow for language arts, social studies, art, and music.)

We should also recognize again that the various fields we have discussed in connection with the domains of personal development and continued learning skills have significant knowledge components, and that middle school curriculum planners can and do draw from fields usually considered college level, for example, philosophy, psychology and anthropology. Flexibility and creativity in curriculum planning at the school, team, and teacher levels, along with reasonable resources of teachers' own knowledge, and school and community materials and personnel, can make the domain of knowledge an exciting, motivating pathway to further learning by middle school students.

ADDITIONAL SUGGESTIONS FOR FURTHER STUDY

A. Books

Alexander, William M. and Others, *The Emergent Middle School*, 2nd enlarged edition. New York: Holt, Rinehart and Winston, 1969.

Curtis, Thomas E. and Bidwell, Wilma W., *Curriculum and Instruction for Emerging Adolescents*, Reading, Mass.: Addison-Wesley Publishing Company, 1977.

Eichhorn, Donald H., *The Middle School*, New York: The Center for Applied Research in Education, Inc., 1966.

Goodlad, John I. and Associates, *Curriculum Inquiry: The Story of Curriculum Practice*, New York: McGraw Hill Book Co., 1979.

Moss, Theodore C., *Middle School*, Boston: Houghton Mifflin Company, 1969.

Saylor, J. Galen, Alexander, William M., and Lewis, Arthur J., *Curriculum Planning for Better Teaching and Learning*. New York: Holt, Rinehart and Winston, Inc., 1981.

B. Periodicals

Acklen, Leila and Garner, Art, "Incorporating Moral Education in the Middle School," *Middle School Journal*, 8, 6–7 (May 1977).

Alexander, William M. et al, "Community-Home-School Cooperation for Middle School Goals," *Journal of North Carolina League of Middle Schools*, 1980, 19–28 (1980).

Beane, James A., "The Case for Core in the Middle School," *Middle School Journal*, 6, 33–4, 38 (Summer 1975).

Dilg, Charles A., "Curriculum Planning as It Relates to the School in the Middle," *Middle School Journal*, 10, 16–7 (February 1979).

Vaupel, Carl F., Jr., "The Wonderful World of the Mini-Course Program," *Middle School Journal*, 7, 6–7 (June 1976).

Waltz, Thomas F., "Exploratory Teaming: An Interdisciplinary Approach to the Fine and Practical Arts," *Middle School Journal*, 7, 18–9 (June 1976).

Wiles, Jon W., "Developmental Staging—In Pursuit of Comprehensive Curriculum Planning," *Middle School Journal*, 6, 6–10 (Spring 1975).

C. Dissertations and Dissertation Abstracts

Bishop, Wilma Jean, "A Study to Determine Alternative Approaches for Administering a Curriculum for Adolescents, Ages 12–14," *Dissertation Abstracts*, 39 (October 1978) 2116–A.

Cavanagh, Darol M., "A Curriculum Design Deduced from a Model of the Middle School Child," *Dissertation Abstracts*, 36 (August 1975) 679–A.

Kuhlmann, Sandra Ellen Muse, "The Emerging Middle School Language Arts Program," *Dissertation Abstracts*, 39 (October 1978) 2034–A.

Lonsdale, Helen Coulter, "The Implications of Jean Piaget's Theory of Cognitive Development Stages for Middle/Junior High School Career Education Curriculum," *Dissertation Abstracts*, 37 (May 1977) 6928–A.

Ritz, John Michael, "Unified Arts: An Integrative Approach to Curriculum Design for the Art, Home Economics, and Industrial Arts Subject Areas in the Middle Grades," *Dissertation Abstracts*, 38 (October 1977) 1863–A.

Smith, Donald Floyd, "A Study of the Middle School Arts Program As Perceived by Middle School Experts and Middle School Arts Teachers," *Dissertation Abstracts*, 37 (August 1976) 855–6–A.

Smith, Robert Pleas, Jr., "A Case Study in Middle School Staff and Curriculum Development and its Impact on Student Attitudes and Achievement," *Dissertation Abstracts*, 37 (April 1977) 6203–A.

Youngberg, Robert Stanley, "Perceptions of Parents' Role in Curriculum Development at the Middle and Junior High School Level," *Dissertation Abstracts*, 36 (September 1975) 1286–A.

FOOTNOTES

1. William M. Alexander, *A Survey of Organizational Patterns of Reorganized Middle School*, USOE Cooperative Research Project No. 7–D–026. Gainesville, Florida: University of Florida, July 1968. p. 34.
2. James DiVirgilio, "Why the Middle School Curriculum Vacuum?", *Educational Leadership*, 31, 225 (December 1973).

3. Kenneth Brooks and Francine Edwards, *The Middle School in Transition: A Research Report on the Status of the Middle School Movement*, (Lexington, Kentucky: College of Education, University of Kentucky, 1978), p. 12.

4. Billy B. Reeves, *Implementation Guide, /I/D/E/A Change Program for Individually Guided Education. Ages 10–15*, (Dayton, Ohio: Institute for Development of Educational Activities, Inc., 1974), p. 16.

5. Herbert J. Klausmeier and John G. Daresh, *A Description of Webster Transitional School, 1977–78* (Madison, Wisconsin: Wisconsin Research and Development Center for Individualized Schooling, April 1979), p. 5.

6. Special State Committee on the Middle School, *The Development of Middle Schools in Florida* (Tallahassee: Florida Department of Education, n.d.), p. 61.

7. See for relevant and comprehensive sources, John H. Lounsbury and Gordon F. Vars, *A Curriculum for the Middle School Years*, (New York: Harper and Row, 1978), Chapters 4–7; and J. Galen Saylor, William M. Alexander, and Arthur J. Lewis, *Curriculum Planning for Better Teaching and Learning* (New York: Holt, Rinehart and Winston, Inc., 1981), Chapter 5.

8. Lounsbury and Vars, p. 46.

9. See William M. Alexander, Emmett L. Williams, Mary Compton, Vynce A. Hines, and Dan Prescott, *The Emergent Middle School*, (New York: Holt, Rinehart and Winston, Inc., 1968), for an early development of this design for middle schools.

10. Donald E. Eichhorn, "The Emerging Adolescent School of the Future—Now," in J. Galen Saylor, ed., *The School of the Future—Now*, (Washington, D.C.: Association for Supervision and Curriculum Development, 1972), p. 42.

11. Office of the Superintendent, Milwaukee Public Schools, *The Plan for the Two Year Transition to the Middle School*, (Milwaukee: The Schools, March 1979), p. 48.

12. J.D. Angelhelone, "Unified Arts: A Realistic Approach to Learning Thru Team Teaching at the Middle School Level," *Dissemination Services on the Middle Grades*, 5, 4 (January 1974).

13. William M. Alexander, Vynce A. Hines, and Associates, *Independent Study in Secondary Schools*, (New York: Holt, Rinehart and Winston, Inc., 1967), p. 12.

14. Aberdeen Middle School, *Physical Education* (Aberdeen, Maryland: The School, n.d.,) p. 5.

15. Louis G. Romano and Nicholas Timmers, "Middle School Athletics—Intramurals or Interscholastic," *Middle School Journal*, 9, 16 (May 1978). Also see for a comprehensive review with excellent documentation of the case against interscholastics, C. Kenneth McEwin, "Competitive Sports in the Middle School—A Closer Look," *Journal of the North Carolina League of Middle/Junior High Schools*, 1979, 16–19, and for an extended bibliography of related sources, Paul S. George and Christopher Rampachek, "Interscholastic Athletics and Early Adolescents: An Annotated Bibliography," *Middle School Journal*, 10, 20–21 (May 1979).

16. Arthur W. Foshay, "Editorial: It Could Work Better," *Educational Leadership*, 36, 164 (December 1978).

17. See Evan Jenkins, "Computers Programed for a Revolution," *New York Times*, April 30, 1978, p. EDUC 13.

18. Herman T. Epstein and Conrad F. Toepfer, Jr., "A Neuroscience Basis for Reorganizing Middle Grades Education," *Educational Leadership*, 35, 658 (May 1978).

19. Eptstein and Toepfer, p. 660.

4

Providing Teacher Guidance

Guidance and Counseling in the Middle School

The position of counselor continues in middle schools much the same role as in junior high schools. The counselor is a student service person working in a myriad of ways to help in personal, educational, social and other affairs of the students. Counselors are generally assigned duties that border on administration, with almost always too many students! We consider their services sufficiently common in middle school and other levels and sufficiently well treated in the literature of guidance and counseling to focus our attention on the unique aspects of guidance and counseling in the middle school: teacher guidance. In the description of teacher guidance services which follows, we indicate various helping roles for school counselors, but the primary focus is on the guidance activities of teachers as they work with individuals and small groups.

The Teacher-Student Relationship in the Middle School

Middle school educators often identify the teacher-student relationship in the middle school as the starting point of the entire program, proclaiming the middle school to be specially suited to the characteristics of this age learner. Among the list of characteristics which determine the uniqueness of the transescent, the need for a particular kind of teacher-student relationship is almost always placed at the top. Written philosophies from individual middle schools consistently strive to highlight the student-centered nature of the program, implying a concern for each student and a commitment to firm teacher-student bonds. The teacher-student relationship in the middle school, is however, different from the elementary school or high school model.

In the early years of the elementary school, the teacher-student affiliation has, perhaps, more significance than at any other time in the educational program. Young children, moving for the first time from the home to the public institution of the school, require a relationship with the adult teacher which very closely parallels the association experienced between parent and child. This relationship, in the past, took on the exclusive character of the parent-child affiliation, and was formalized by the legal system as in the Latin phrase "in loco parentis." Teachers were expected to assume the care of young children, in at least a quasi-parental way, when the child came to school. Indeed, many of the activities of teachers in kindergarten and the primary school years today can hardly be distinguished from those of parents. Young pupils, many educators believe, need an exclusive connection with one adult as they complete the move from the home to school, today as in years past. Following a decade or two of practices which weakened this association between the elementary school teacher and her pupils, many teachers and parents seem ready for a return to the conditions which permitted the strong relationship to develop. Even if such a reestablishment of the exclusive relationship experiences between teacher and student in the elementary school did not transpire, many would agree that this is the way it has always been, and still is, in the majority of elementary schools in this country. Some would argue that the practices which weakened the teacher-student relationship existed in only a few schools in only a few states, and never affected the majority of elementary schools.

Six-year-old children need a great deal more guidance and supervision than do high school students. The American high school has never acknowledged an obligation to establish formal teacher-student relationships. Not that high school educators were or are unconcerned about the nature of the relationships between teachers and students; they are, of course. Such relationships have, however, usually arisen from common subject matter interests, extracurricular pursuits, similar personality or style and so on, rather than from an attempt on the part of the school to mandate such affiliations. Students who are close to the legal age of adulthood have been presumed to have the maturity to choose their own friends from among the professional adults in the school.

The middle school must find a way to weave together these two disparate patterns of teacher-student relationship, to assist students in moving from the exclusive association with one adult to the situation in which the student is equally responsible for establishing and maintaining the rapport.[1] Most middle school students are beyond the need for the self-contained classroom and the relationships it provided, but are not yet ready to be completely on their own in a large school. The middle school attempts to help students move from one type of relationship to the other, while providing its own special brand of teacher-student affiliation along the way.

The teacher-student relationship in the middle school is often characterized by the term "advisor." Each middle school student is seen as needing to reach out and explore the world of adults, while maintaining a type of interpersonal haven until a new level of maturity permits him to function as a high school student. Middle school students are allowed to leave the sheltered atmosphere of an exclusive relationship with one adult behind, but are guarded from the impersonal anonymity of the large high school. Exemplary middle schools attempt to see to it that every middle school student interacts with more than one, and perhaps as many as a half dozen, adults during a day or week, while maintaining a special connection with one. Each student has a teacher in the school who will know them better and care about them more than most other adults in the school. Every student will have a teacher who considers himself to be the school expert on that particular child. In this way the middle school continues to supply a unique educational experience while providing for a smooth transition from the elementary to the high school.

The middle school attempts to precipitate the student into just manageable difficulty. Extricating the student from the exclusive one-to-one situation of the early elementary years, the middle school encourages the development of meaningful contacts with several teachers. In the midst of these multiple contacts, however, the middle school permits the student to retain the refuge of one special teacher. Slowly but steadily the middle school student moves from dependency toward independence.

Many lists of objectives for education written to guide program development have, somewhere close to the top, an enthusiastic commitment to objectives which can best be summarized as affective. The middle school program for older children and early adolescents takes this commitment seriously, as every school philosophy proudly proclaims; and while there is a great deal more to affective education than the teacher-student guidance program, it is the position of the authors that such a program is the hub of affective education in the middle school.[2]

As defined here, the focal point of the teacher-student guidance program is what has come to be known as the advisor-advisee program. Although known by different names in different places (homebase, small group, fourth R, homeroom), the faculty of almost every school that takes this commitment seriously is familiar with this term or recognizes its meaning immediately. Hence, for the remainder of this chapter, the teacher-student guidance program and the advisor-advisee program should be considered as one and the same, and the terms will be used interchangeably.

Purposes of the Advisor-Advisee Program

The fundamental purpose of the advisor-advisee program, regardless of its design in any particular school, is to promote involvement between a teacher and the students involved in the advisory group. Every student needs to have a relationship with at least one adult in the school which is characterized by warmth, concern, openness and understanding. Such a program focuses on what has been called the "fourth R," relationships: interpersonal relationships which produce growth for both people involved. Good middle schools cannot be places where teacher and students pass by each other without recognition or attachment, like the stereotypical ships in the night.

Teachers need this type of involvement with students no less than the students do. While mature, stable adults, teachers still need to be involved with students who show that they respect and care for them. But more directly, from the teacher's perspective, the most relevant personal reason for the advisor-advisee program is that in a school of a thousand or more students, or on a team where the teacher meets as many as 150 students per day, it is often almost impossible to develop the kind of relationships with students that allow teachers to make a significant difference in their lives. Since most teachers really do seem to have a deeply felt need to make a significantly positive difference in the lives of their students, and the daily demands of the classroom often seem to make this difficult or impossible, the advisor-advisee program provides the teacher with an opportunity to get to know some manageable number of students in a meaningful way.

Education for personal and interpersonal competence is a closely related objective of the advisor-advisee program. Middle school students need models of effective interpersonal communication. They need an adult to whom they can look for assistance in their attempts to achieve success in school and out, an adult who is their school friend without being a peer. Middle school students do not arrive at the school door feeling as good about themselves as they might, or as able to use themselves as effectively as they should. The advisor-advisee program provides a forum for the exploration of these issues, and an adult who is committed to helping each advisee grow stronger and more positive about himself.

The advisor-advisee program also attempts to offer an opportunity for social and emotional education. Students in the middle school are, perhaps, more concerned about social group difficulties than they are at any other time of their lives. The need for acceptance and approval by their peers is matched in its strength only by the frequent inadequacy of their efforts to secure this peer support. Consumed by the unquenchable need to belong, they are seemingly less able to satisfy this need than almost any other.

Perhaps for the first time in their lives, middle school students are able to think about and analyze their emotions in a semisophisticated fashion. Sometimes experiencing amazing arrays of emotions in incredibly brief periods of time, middle school students need continuing assistance in comprehending, analyzing and accepting the emotional components of their lives.

Middle school students require aid in getting to know themselves, as well as the teacher. They need constant support in the struggle to master the requirements of successful living with peers, within and beyond the classroom and the school.[3]

In a society characterized by Vance Packard as "a nation of strangers," students need a sense of community now more than ever.[4] With the demise of the neighborhood school, the attempt to build a "home base" within the school takes on considerably more meaning. Middle school students are simply too immature to function well as complete individuals in an anonymous, amorphous institution of from five hundred to one thousand or more people. The advisor-advisee program continues, where the homeroom left off, to work for an educational milieu in which students and teachers feel part of a group which students experience as supportive, safe and familiar. This atmosphere is simply impossible on the level of the total school, and it is often difficult to achieve in even the most reasonably sized interdisciplinary teams.

The advisor-advisee program can also be a significant source of civic education. Since the advisor-advisee group is usually the substitute for the homeroom or synonymous with it, decisions about student council representation, intramural competition and a host of related school issues can be discussed in a situation where the democratic process can be brought to a level that middle school students are capable of understanding. In schools where multiage grouping exists in the advisor-advisee groups, it is also possible that exposure to more mature moral reasoning over a period of several years will produce growth in this dimension that would otherwise not have occurred. The advisor-advisee group becomes somewhat of a model democracy in microcosm.

The advisor-advisee program is a source of guidance for the student, different from that available from the school counselor. While the guidance provided by the student's advisor will never replace that of the school counselor, it is a crucially important supplement to it. Teachers who not only act as advisors to students, but who also teach those same students at least once each day, and possibly more often, have a knowledge of and a relationship with those students that school counselors, burdened as they are by a plethora of other duties, can never hope to have. Consequently, the advisor is likely to be aware of conditions in a student's life in or out of school which may influence his behavior and need to be handled. The advisor, as team teacher, will be well acquainted with the student's academic performance in every class. This knowledge of the students' lives, combined with the relationship which grows from the advisor-advisee program, and the repeated contact which they have with the students during each day, is likely to make the advisor the first source of guidance.

Teachers in middle schools report that their students turn to them for guidance in increasing increments under circumstances fed by an effective advisor-advisee program, if, for no other reason, because the student's needs for guidance are often immediate and situation specific. Such needs must be dealt with at the time they occur. Waiting for an appointment with a counselor who may have more than 500 other students to deal with, or for a small group counseling session, is often ineffective and counterproductive. Teachers can provide on-the-spot assistance.

Middle schools with effective advisor-advisee programs often report that classroom and school discipline situations improve as a result of the programs. Students who feel safe, accepted, and an important part of the school, are much less likely to be disruptive. On numerous occasions, teachers have told the authors that students who have a place, time and person to assist them in "centering" themselves, a situation which encourages the appropriate expression of feelings of frustration, hurt and sorrow, are much less likely to be found ventilating these feelings in regular classrooms. Teachers who know students well, and who have developed friendly relationships with them, are more able to deal effectively with them in regular classroom situations, and to be a source of support and information to other teachers in the school when their advisees are involved in classroom discipline problems. The advisor-advisee group is, furthermore, a unique opportunity to teach the behaviors that students no longer seem to come to school already possessing, but which are essential to a productive school atmosphere. Teamwide advisor-advisee units which focus on issues like theft, responsibility, rules and so on, are excellent advisor-advisee activities that have productive consequences for individual classrooms.

Finally, the advisor-advisee group time is often used effectively as the organizational and informational hub of each team, and of the school. Announcements are made there. Field trips are organized around the advisor-advisee group as the unit of responsibility during travel. School activities and projects, intramurals and other unifying operations are appropriately assigned to the advisor-advisee group. This is not only because it is efficient to do so, but because friendships form when people perform common day-to-day activities with each other as well as when they are involved in discussions which promote self-disclosure. Adults develop friendships with people they work with, study with, play bridge with, go to church with and so on. Students and teachers become closer to each other as they participate in (and sometimes endure) the daily rituals and activities of the school.

Alternative Designs for Teacher-Student Guidance Programs

Middle school teacher-student guidance programs are of essentially two varieties, those that involve a daily meeting of the teacher with the same students and those that have a more variable schedule. The programs that emphasize a daily meeting involving the same teacher and group of students tend to emphasize the sense of community, of groupness, that emerges, while those that do not involve a daily group meeting tend to stress the one-to-one relationship betwen the teacher and one student. Each has its advantages.

Daily Large Group Programs

A daily advisor-advisee program has been functioning in the middle schools of Alachua County, Florida, for well over five years. The advisor-advisee programs at Spring Hill, Mebane and Lincoln Middle Schools are held the first thing in the morning for about thirty minutes. Every certified teacher in the school has a group of advisees, and at Spring Hill even the school counselor has a group. As soon as the student arrives at school, the first experience is the advisor-advisee program. Homeroom and advisory responsibilities are combined, so that after the morning announcements and homeroom business teachers are left with about fifteen to twenty minutes for advisor-advisee activities. The four middle schools in Dothan, Alabama, proceed similarly.

At Stroudsburg Middle School, Stroudsburg, Pennsylvania, the daily advisor-advisee program adds up to about forty-five minutes, half an hour at the beginning of the day, and fifteen minutes at the end of the day. Homeroom and advisor-advisee activities are combined here, too. At Stroudsburg, however, the morning time is divided into formal and informal time, giving teachers a chance to meet informally with students as they drift in to school first thing in the morning. Then when everyone has arrived, a formal advisor-advisee time is available. The quarter hour at the end of the day is also intended as a formal advisor-advisee time, which is probably followed by another unscheduled informal advisor-advisee time, as students leave school for home.

At Marshall Middle School, Marshall, Minnesota, the advisor-advisee program begins during the daily homeroom period, but extends in one way or another throughout the entire day. Teachers meet all their advisees in homeroom, but thereafter meet with each one on a weekly basis during a scheduled independent study time, during unscheduled time before school or at lunch time.

One-on-One Programs

At Rusk Middle School, in Nacogdoches, Texas, a seven-period day permits the teachers in the school to have one planning period and one period of advisor-advisee time. Since the school is organized in interdisciplinary teams with common planning and advisor-advisee times, each team has its advisor-advisee period at a different time of the day. In addition, students on the teams are involved in physical education and unified arts during the time that teachers have the planning and advisor-advisee time. As a consequence, there is no attempt to build a sense of groupness as in the programs described immediately above. Instead, teachers are free to use the advisor-advisee time to focus on building strong one-to-one relationships with each of their advisees. Students are drawn out of either physical education or unified arts on whatever basis the advisor requires, but usually the teacher will work with one or two students at a time. This time is also scheduled for parent conferences, in which the teacher is assisted by the counselor. A unique feature of this program is the effort of the school administration to secure the endorsement of the local chamber of commerce for the release of parents from work to attend a conference at the school.

Many middle schools, particularly those that follow this kind of schedule, use the advisor-advisee time for planning and conducting parent-student-teacher conferences. At Westbrook Junior High School, Omaha, Nebraska, the advisor assists in the conduct of such conferences on a quarterly basis as a substitute for the traditional report card. At Chaska Middle School, Chaska, Minnesota, the faculty has found that the conduct of such conferences, through the advisor-advisee program, has provided a ground swell of parent support for that aspect of the program and for most other components of the school. Brookings Middle School, Brookings, South Dakota, was the first middle school in that state and the first such school to use the advisory program for developmental parent-student-teacher conferences as well. As they are called at Brookings Middle, the "triad" conferences are held at the end of the first quarter, for the purpose of setting the student on a firm foundation for the remainder of the school year.

An advisor-advisee program with very special features has been operating in the middle schools of Marion County, Florida, for nearly a decade. In what is called the "small group guidance" program at North Marion Middle School, Citra, Florida, for example, only the academic team teachers have advisees. Each team teacher has about forty advisees from the team. In much the same way as Rusk Middle in Nacogdoches, the teachers at North Marion are organized in teams and operate on a seven-period day. This means that here, too, the teachers have a planning period and an advisor-advisee period which happens at different times during the day, depending on the team one is on.

At North Marion, however, each teacher has a double planning period on Mondays, when all of the teacher's advisees go to physical education class. Then on Tuesday, during the time for advisor-advisee, most of each teacher's students go to physical education and only nine or ten remain in the classroom for the small group. On Wednesday, ten more students remain with the teacher while the majority are at physical education, and the same thing happens on Thursday and Friday. By the end of the week, then, the teacher has had a double planning period on Monday, and from Tuesday through Friday has seen each of his or her advisees in a very small group situation for an hour. Each student has had four periods of physical education and one period of small group guidance with their teacher.

The North Marion model allows teachers to experience relationships with a large number of students, but meet with them in unusually small groups. It also allows teachers to plan one activity for the week and repeat it Tuesday through Friday. The program has lasted ten years, and whenever an innovation manages to survive, even flourish, for that period of time, we believe there must be a substantial advantage. The staff at North Marion point to the double planning period each Monday, to one period each Tuesday through Friday during which the teacher has a very small group of students, and the lack of need for a new daily preparation as factors which make this program easy for and popular with teachers.

A number of middle schools have experimented with an advisory program, without committing the school to a daily experience. At Noe Middle School, Louisville, Kentucky, the advisor-advisee program occurs on a regular and frequent basis, but the scheduling is left to each individual team. Teachers on the team schedule the advisor-advisee time within the allotted but slightly expanded block of time for the basic subjects. Noe's teachers have committed themselves to a program that provides balance between the advisor-advisee program and the rest of the academic effort, and the principal and counselors help teachers follow through. Many of the other middle schools that have established advisor-advisee programs on a less than daily basis have decided to do so on an alternating basis with the unified arts area. At Coan Middle School, Atlanta, Georgia, for example, students have an advisory period twice a month for forty-five minutes, in addition to the fifteen minutes homeroom period that occurs on a daily basis. At Lenoir Middle School, Lenoir, North Carolina, students have an advisor-advisee period three times per week alternating with a music program which involves all students. At Boyce Middle School, Upper St. Clair, Pennsylvania, students have advisor-advisee programs twice a week, alternating with an elective class that meets the other three days. Some schools expand the homeroom period when necessary, or on a regular basis, providing the opportunity for the advisor-advisee time, but not requiring it on a daily basis.

Teacher Roles

The advisory role of the middle school teacher is complex and multifaceted, and since advisor-advisee programs tend to vary at least slightly from school to school, the roles teachers fill also vary. Many schools take great care in spelling out to teachers, students and parents exactly what the roles played by the advisor in a specific school are likely to be. Combining the role descriptions of advisors provided by Marshall, Coan, Noe and Louisville Middle Schools, the authors summarize below potential duties and responsibilities for advisors.

Summary of Role Descriptions

The Advisor Is the Academic Expert on Each of His Advisees. As such the advisor:

- Assists the student in the planning of exploratory, extracurricular, independent study and other academic choice activities. The advisor keeps a record of electives chosen by each advisee
- Communicates information about facilities, materials and personnel to students and parents
- Maintains and utilizes cumulative records, personal profile sheets and other information-gathering options
- Prepares report cards

- Assists students in studying and learning how to study
- Assists students in the process of developing and clarifying special interests and aptitudes
- Will be able to identify and take into account any physical handicaps the student may have
- Will be able to identify and take into account reading level of the student, and the mental and chronological ages of the student
- Contributes to the understanding of other staff members of the academic strengths, weaknesses, problems and interests of each student
- Controls the student's overall academic schedule, assisting in decisions as to whom the student will study with, at what times, and in what groupings. The advisor will assist in determining the degree of responsible independence each student can assume, and what learning styles seem appropriate
- Prepares for and participates in parent conferences with reference to the student's academic progress

The Advisor Is the School Advocate and Guide for Each Student. As such the advisor:

- Attempts to build a relationship with each student that is characterized by caring, trust and honesty
- Is, in general, an available buffer between student, general faculty, administration, parent and community
- Attempts to see that each student acquires an increasingly positive self-image during his enrollment time at the school
- Knows each student and his background as thoroughly as possible
- Contributes to and supports the school guidance program
- Contributes to the other staff members' understanding of the personal strengths, weaknesses, problems and interests of each advisee
- Maintains an attendance record of each of the advisees
- Is responsible for parent-school communication, and for participating in and planning for parent conferences concerning the personality and behavior of the advisee

The Advisor Is the Person Most Directly Responsible for the Social and Emotional Education of His Advisees, and for Assisting in the Social and Emotional Maturation of Each Advisee. As such the advisor:

- Attempts to create a sense of belonging and responsibility through participation in homebase activities
- Conducts activities during the advisor-advisee program which focus on increasing the social skills of advisees and on growth in personal and interpersonal understanding
- Assists students in clarifying their values and in developing more mature reasoning abilities

- Places increased emphasis on prevention of problems in the lives of the students
- Participates in outings, field trips and after-school activities which promote opportunities for emotional and social education
- Helps students learn to work in a group and to realize the need for getting along with others in order to meet individual and groups needs
- Assists students in the appreciation of individual differences
- Helps students develop appropriate attitudes toward competition and co-operation as the advisor-advisee group participates as a group in intra-school programs

Conducting an Advisor-Advisee Group

Designing a Program

Conducting a successful advisor-advisee group, from a teacher's point of view, depends in large measure upon how the program is designed at the school level. If the program is designed primarily as a daily meeting of the teacher with the same group of advisees, the advisor proceeds differently than if the program is designed to focus sharply on the development of strong one-to-one relationships between the teacher and each of the advisees. It is also important to remember that both practical objectives, group feeling and individual relationships are important parts of each design, but that each fosters one of the objectives more easily than the other. In the daily group, teachers must work harder to build strong relationships with students, since their time is obligated to a group. In the situations where teachers do not meet with the same students on a daily basis, it is much more difficult to develop a sense of community, but easier to establish meaningful one-to-one relationships with students.

On the assumption that it is more difficult (but no less valuable) to function effectively in an advisor-advisee program which operates on the daily group design, and that many of the strategies a teacher pursues in this format can also be adapted to the one-on-one design, this section will focus on suggestions for successful operation of the daily program. It should be stressed, however, that the authors do not prefer one type of advisor-advisee program over another. Experience has not yet been broad enough to indicate whether either design (daily group or one-on-one) is superior.

Faced with the task of meeting with a group of advisees on a daily basis, for about a half hour each time, many teachers are initially quite apprehensive about beginning. Although almost every teacher in junior high school or middle school wants to be effective in this role, few feel confident in pursuing it without some special training. In addition, teachers who are hard pressed to complete all the other assignments they are given in a new school situation often see the daily advisor-advisee group as an additional preparation they could do without, a burden they would rather not assume even if they believe themselves to be capable. Under these circumstances, it is important for teachers to see that they are not being asked to replace the school counselor, and that it is possible to operate an advisor-advisee group on a daily basis without rigorous preparations each night.

Teachers are not expected to be counselors or psychiatrists. Some districts, simply because of inexperience, have made the mistake of expecting teachers and middle school students to spend each day in intense encounter-like sensitivity sessions, and as a consequence, have had to endure a great deal of frustration from teachers, students and parents. Teachers are not trained to conduct this type of activity, students are not ready for it and parents will not support it. Advisor-advisee programs that insist on this type of format must expect to encounter serious difficulties in operation.

Teachers are required, in their advisory role, only to be themselves. They are invited to display the same kind of characteristics that are found in good friendships, good teaching and helping relationships in general. They must be able to accept the student and what he is experiencing and communicate that understanding clearly, without becoming a part of the problem or situation themselves to the extent that they need help too. They must be able to communicate clearly to the student, so that what they say matches what they think and feel inside. Teachers must exhibit, to the degree possible and appropriate, the characteristics of unconditional positive regard, empathy and honesty in their interactions with their advisees. They are not asked to possess advanced training in psychology or psychiatry, but merely to be a helping adult school friend to the students they have in their advisor-advisee group.[5]

Teachers need to develop plans for a schedule for their advisor-advisee program, plans which do not require continued daily replanning. Middle school students seem to accept a planned schedule of advisor-advisee activities quite readily, and are much less likely to balk at participating in an activity if it is what "we always do on Tuesdays." Middle school students are often not, contrary to what an inexperienced lay person might believe, ready to talk about themselves and eager to engage in self-disclosing discussion without a great deal of help. So a daily or weekly schedule helps. Teachers who are the most successful with advisor-advisee programs in exemplary middle schools almost always have a schedule which, while flexible, does provide structure and stability to the program and security to the students.

The advisor-advisee activity schedule should be well balanced, and it should proceed from a set of overall goals. Even though some middle schools provide teachers with a set of objectives for the advisor-advisee program on a school-wide basis, the most effective advisors seem to give the program considerable additional thought, and design their own activities on the basis of the goals which they have established, perhaps with their students, for their individual groups. Most advisory group activities are of the type which can be done one day a week for the entire year, or for a week or so at a time without being repeated the remainder of the year. Beginning the year and the program with a schedule, modified by appropriate student input, will make the advisor-advisee time much more effective and much easier for the remainder of the year.[6]

The activities that the advisor chooses to include in the program will have a great effect on the success of the program. Advisors need to balance their advisor-advisee schedule with activities that require little or no daily planning, mixed in with some that do require additional thought and planning. Activities which happen regularly without extra effort on the teacher's part will prevent the teacher from becoming exhausted, and occasional things which do require new teacher effort will keep the program from becoming too stultifying by injecting fresh and invigorating approaches.

Weekly Activities

Many teachers in exemplary middle schools, after five to ten years of experience in the advisor-advisee program, have developed a number of activities which students enjoy but which are relatively easy for the teacher to arrange. Here are just a few that the authors have observed being used on a once-a-week basis:

"It's Your Day!"

Each Monday the teacher and the advisor-advisee group focus their attention on a different member of the group. Students, given pump-priming help by the teacher, ask the student of the day questions about his/her favorite teachers, subjects, foods, colors; questions about home and leisure time and so forth. All of the discussion is focused on getting acquainted in an in-depth way with one student, "stroking" that student, showing him or her that they are important enough for the entire group to spend the whole advisor-advisee period listening to. Books on values clarification, guidance and personal development are full of sample questions and discussion topics appropriate for this kind of activity. It should be easy to see that this activity and others like it can be used in the one-on-one situation as well.

Using this activity one day a week with, say twenty-eight advisees, will consume at least 20 percent of the total advisor-advisee time for the year with almost no additional preparation.

"USSR"

Many teachers, teams and whole schools use an activity called Uninterrupted Sustained Silent Reading. When used in conjunction with the advisor-advisee program, the teacher and all the advisees spend the greater part of the advisor-advisee time reading silently and individually. At Lincoln Middle School, in Gainesville, Florida, the students and teachers are involved in USSR on Tuesdays and Thursdays, during the advisor-advisee period. The only real preparation required of teachers is to see that each student has something to read; which for nonreaders may mean magazines to look at, if nothing else. When used on a school-wide basis, everyone reads, even principals, secretaries and custodians; visitors are simply not permitted. When teachers choose to do this individually it must be planned carefully at the outset and the rules must be firmly in place, but after that it will, on a once-a-week basis, account for another 20 percent of the advisor-advisee time for the year.

"USSW"

Many teachers have discovered that students will write about themselves in ways that they will not discuss verbally, with or without a group. Using a period each week in the advisor-advisee group to engage in journal writing is a very effective and appropriate use of student time together. There are several ways in which this can be done, apparently with equal success in middle school. Teachers can read and respond in writing to what the student produces, or they can choose not to do either. Some teachers have found that giving students the option to invite the teacher to read and respond or not is an effective practice.

"Academic Advisory"

Since the teacher-advisor is as concerned as much with the academic success of each of his advisees as he is with their social and emotional maturation, if not more so, it is entirely appropriate and probably necessary for some of the advisory time to be used in an academic way. In what might seem like a glorified study hall at first, the advisor encourages all of the advisees to bring their problem work to the advisor-advisee group with them on, say, each Wednesday. During the advisor-advisee time the advisor circulates from one student to another, gathering information about one student, encouraging another, counseling with a third, working with as many as possible during the time allotted. Short units on topics like "How to study" or "How to take standardized achievement tests" are very appropriate, and can even be done on a rotating basis throughout the team's advisor-advisee groups. Each teacher-advisor can design a part of the team's unit to teach to each other's advisor-advisee group. To do so would mean that a month's worth of advisor-advisee time would be used very effectively with the preparation that went into only one week. Certainly many other topics can serve as themes of guidance units that teachers can cooperatively develop and work with in the advisor-advisee program.

Indoor/Outdoor Games

There are many games which advisors can introduce into the advisor-advisee time; games which are fun for students, which can be used to teach the group skills these students so desperately need and which require very little preparation time from the teacher. Games like chess, checkers, the "Ungame,'' math puzzles, brain teasers and other similar things allow teachers to move quietly from one student to another, and attend to a game in which a group is involved whenever it seems necessary or appropriate.

It is important to make an observation about the nature of the process of friendship and its nurture. As was cited earlier, people become close to one another as they participate in other things, rather than directly requesting that another person become one's friend. These games are the sort of situation in which common interests become shared and friendships develop. It is not a waste of time.

"Story Time"

It is absolutely amazing how well middle school students will become involved in listening to the teacher or to other students read aloud, if it is a story that is relevant to them. One very productive advisor-advisee time, therefore, is when the teacher does just that, selects and reads a story aloud to the students. Done on a once-a-week basis, or for every day until the story is finished, this activity requires no more preparation than that involved in selecting a story and glancing at it prior to reading it so that one knows where the best dividing points are. Teachers who read stories to their students that contain values clarification issues and moral dilemmas report that talking about how a fictional character in a story handled a problem is relatively easy for middle school students, and consequently often much more successful for teachers. Reading a story during the first four days of the week, then involving students in a discussion of the issues on the last day is another commonly successful approach.

"Career Explo"

Another activity that fits with the nature of middle school students, and which requires just a little more teacher preparation than the preceding ideas, is the practice of devoting one advisor-advisee day a week to an investigation of adults and what careers they follow. All the teacher really has to do, and sometimes enlisting the students as assistants makes it even less, is to identify and select the adults in the community who are willing to come to the class and talk about what they do and the significance it has for them. One good evening on the telephone or a Saturday in the car should allow a teacher to line up enough classroom visitors to last half the school year on a once weekly basis. This sort of activity can also be done on a weekly basis once or twice a year.

Orientations

Teachers soon discover that a significant amount of their advisor-advisee time will often be consumed by activities which can best be described as orientation. Some schools schedule the first day of the year as nothing more than advisor-advisee time, used in large part to introduce students to the school as it is organized for them that year, to explain course and class choices and to get acquainted with the team and its processes. Throughout the year a teacher can expect that a number of advisor-advisee periods will be used to orient students to state and national assessment and testing programs, dental and physical examinations and treatments and so on. Obviously, there is often very little a teacher has to do to prepare for such activities that would not have to be done anyway, in some other context.

Occasional Activities

The above activities are simply samples of activities that can be used on a regular basis and which require little or no planning time on the part of the teacher. Teachers who build such activities into an advisor-advisee schedule will find that the burden of planning that they anticipated does not materialize to the extent they had expected. They may then find themselves willing to invest a little more of their time in planning activities which add a special flavor to the advisor-advisee group life. Here are a few activities that teachers have found to be worth the extra effort required:

Holiday Celebrations

Even in districts that sharply restrict the activities that can be conducted in the observance of religious holidays, or where teachers are concerned about the rights of religious minorities, there are literally dozens of secular holidays which can be a great deal of fun and which can produce both learning and community building opportunities. There are enough American patriotic holidays to fill the calendar, and one creative teacher known to the authors is a member of the Millard Fillmore Society and regularly involves his students in the conduct of Millard Fillmore Week, which includes the celebration of a birthday and a great deal of other ''camp'' activity highly attractive to middle school students. Using a week to decorate the windows of a classroom, or to collect and display memorabilia associated with the lives of the students in the advisor-advisee group are just two examples of appropriate uses of the holiday periods.

"Magic Circle"

Using the advisory time for small group discussions that focus on feelings and other affectively oriented topics is quite appropriate and to be encouraged. Such activities, conducted in low-risk fashion on a once weekly basis, require very little preparation on the part of teachers. There are any number of helpful books now available (which simply did not exist a few years ago) and these books contain an absolute plethora of activities that are workable in an advisor-advisee group.

It is important enough to bear repeating, however, that many middle school students find these sort of activities highly threatening and participate with great reluctance and no little difficulty. It has been recommended to the authors by teachers we respect that such activities be moved into the advisor-advisee program only with careful planning and with a great deal of preparation of the students. Individual teachers may find it easier, but many have found that by the spring of the year, students are ready for this sort of activity; not often earlier.

Community Help Projects

There are always projects in any community that need doing, for which there are few if any volunteers. A quick check with the service clubs in your home town and a contact or two with some homes for the aging or the handicapped will turn up enough projects for an advisory group to do for years. This type of activity gives students a sense of contribution as well as helping to develop an advisor-advisee spirit that does a great deal to foster the feeling that "we are proud of us."

School Help Projects

The same situation exists for the school. One middle school known to the authors has, throughout the school year, a rotating Pride Week project. Each advisor-advisee group in the school has one week of the year to conduct activities or plan projects which have as their goal the fostering of pride in the school. An advisor-advisee group might, for example, redo the hallway bulletin boards or clean up and repaint a particularly unsightly part of the building.

Field Trips

While few schools are scheduled in a way that permits advisor-advisee groups to take regular field trips to places around the community, it is possible to use the advisor-advisee group as the organizing center for such trips when taken by a whole team or part of a school. Walks to a local fast-food restaurant for a special lunch or breakfast are often popular in schools that are located near such spots.

Current Events

Advisor-advisee time is a very good time to be used to discuss current events, particularly if they are scheduled at the beginning of the day. Such an activity does require more preparation than other activities commonly do, but in schools where there is a geat deal of stress on the basic skills of reading and mathematics, this becomes one very valid justification for the inclusion of the advisor-advisee time in the schedule of the day.

All of the above activities are just samples of the many different types of activities which are both possible and appropriate for the advisor-advisee period. The important thing to remember is that teachers succeed best when they are able to design a schedule of activities, a schedule that is composed primarily of activities that require a minimum of extra planning on the part of the teachers involved.

Teachers who have had success with the advisory role in the middle school offer a number of additional suggestions for teachers and others who are new to or are considering the adoption of such a program. The advisor should be sure to have a balance in the type of activity that is offered to the students during the advisor-advisee time. Seventeen straight days, let alone seventeen straight weeks, of having one's values clarified is very likely to be an unsuccessful advisor-advisee activity. Having the goals of the program clearly in mind as a teacher, and explaining the purpose of the advisor-advisee program to the students will be a very important part of the beginning of the program. Orienting parents to the activities conducted in each advisor-advisee group is an important step toward gathering parent support for the program. Sharing oneself in appropriate ways with the students at the beginning and throughout the year, adopting a nonmoralizing attitude in which the teacher keeps from projecting what is believed to be correct onto student behavior, and doing lots of listening, are all correlates of success in the operation of individual advisor-advisee groups.

Requirements for Successful School-Wide Advisor-Advisee Programs

The advisor-advisee program is possibly the most attractive part of the entire middle school concept, but it seems to be the most difficult thing to implement successfully, and to carry out effectively over a period of years. Many middle schools have begun with such programs only to find the idea scrapped after a year, sometimes in several months or even weeks. Schools which have managed to achieve some success with advisor-advisee programs report having learned a number of important lessons about doing it well. Here are some of the suggestions that have emerged from the last decade of experimentation and innovation.

First, and of crucial importance, is the provision of staff development in advance of and accompanying the implementation of the program. Because the role of teacher as affective guide is an attractive and appealing one, it can sometimes seduce teachers into thinking that they are better prepared than they really are. Often supervisors, administrators and curriculum support people forget how much skill is required to operate such efforts effectively, and as a consequence, provide significantly less staff development than is necessary. Ironically, there is probably more staff development required for an effectively functioning advisor-advisee program than any other aspect of the middle school.

Organizing the program so that the maximum number of faculty members participate, leading to groups which are as small as possible, is equally important. If a school is so understaffed that advisors are asked to work with a daily group of thirty-five to forty students, it is probably better to postpone the program until the numbers can be reduced. Sometimes certain faculty members are excused from having an advisor-advisee group in exchange for a school duty such as hall or cafeteria supervision. When this occurs, some of the best advisors (e.g., coaches) are lost to the program, groups are larger, and the morale of the other teachers in the program suffers because of the subtle message which says that the advisor-advisee responsibility is really a lower priority than officially announced.

The authors believe that if a faculty values a progam, it will find its way into the schedule of that school in a way that announces the significance attached to the activity. When school staff say that "Oh, yes, we act as advisors all day long," or "We do it in social studies," it is likely that there is actually very little of the type of activity described in this chapter being conducted in the school. Or when the comment "We schedule it when necessary" appears, it is usually safe to guess that the need for the program appears very seldom. Schools which hope to develop any semblance of group feeling among their students need to think seriously about scheduling the activity on a daily basis. Schools that aim at the development of that special one-to-one relationship need to remember that this activity takes as much or more time to conduct.

There are some factors to consider in the realm of when the advisor-advisee time is scheduled. Practice seems to be confirming the place of the advisor-advisee time at the beginning of the school day as best. When slated for the last time of the day, it is usually a reflection of the fact that it was barely scheduled on a daily basis at all, and enjoys the lowest priority of any regularly scheduled activity. Few schools have been able to maintain the health of the advisor-advisee programs scheduled then, since the message which teachers and students perceive is that this is probably just one more of the stream of innovations which will come and go. It is probably better to postpone an advisor-advisee program than to schedule it at the end of the day. While obviously something has to be scheduled then, one of the required aspects of the curriculum is likely to suffer less in this slot than will the advisor-advisee program.

Scheduling an advisor-advisee time at some other time of the day other than the first or last times of the day seems to depend for its success on how and why it is done. Filling a half hour before or after lunch, as a scheduling convenience, usually fails because students are either hungry or lethargic, depending on which schedule they have, and are in no mood to participate in advisor-advisee activities. It also conveys the only partly hidden message that placing the program thus was a device to fill the schedule and not really all that important; and teachers and students usually act accordingly. When schools are fortunate enough to have a regular period of the school day for the program, it does not seem to matter if a particular team has its advisor-advisee time during any special segment, as long as it is clear that this is an important piece of the school day and deserves equal treatment by teachers and students alike.

The length of time devoted to the advisory period is important too. For programs where teachers meet daily with the same group of students, thirty minutes seems about right. Three quarters of an hour is too long for most of the activity that one would expect to be conducted during advisor-advisee programs, and less than twenty minutes seems too short and is likely to turn into a homeroom time where little else than attendance taking and announcements are accomplished.

It is becoming increasingly clear that teachers must be given a considerable amount of freedom in terms of the model of advisor which they attempt to emulate. Originally, many schools attempted to have each teacher follow a model which was almost identical to the Rogerian or client-centered therapy process, which should not be surprising since many of the people who were implementing the programs saw guidance in the traditional sense as the heart of the program. In a very short time following the beginning of those early programs, however, educators involved discovered that their expectations for teacher behavior were often incorrect. Given sharply restricted in-service education budgets which prevented teachers from receiving the type of intense training that might have made at least a portion of them capable of and comfortable with the Rogerian model, supervisors realized that it was impossible to achieve this goal. What is more, they came to realize that the goal was not really appropriate.

Just as there is no one right way to teach, there is no right way to operate an advisory group. So long as teachers have a stated goal and can demonstrate that they are making progress toward that goal with their advisees, they may make the most progress when permitted to pursue that goal in ways that are most comfortable for them. Many teachers are very comfortable with and effective when using a great deal of their advisory time for small group affective discussion; but many are not. It is important to the success of the program that teachers see themselves as free to pursue their own activities in a mode that feels safe. It is, nonetheless, also important that teachers receive enough guidance in alternative methods of working with an advisor-advisee group that they actively pursue at least one model, and do not respond to the freedom to be themselves by doing less than they might, merely substituting more of what they always do in a regular class for their advisor-advisee activities.

Many times, in schools newly opened or reorganized as middle schools, the temptation is to move to an advisor-advisee program as the first step in implementing the new concept. This temptation is not difficult to understand: everyone knows and accepts the need for such a program, and organization and implementation seem simple. No so. Schools which do not change from a departmentalized format, for example, but do implement an advisor-advisee program, will find themselves involved in a situation where teachers and students are together for that time, but may never see each other again during the day. Under such circumstances, the advisor-advisee program will work much less effectively, because of the absence of repeated face-to-face contact between advisors and their advisees, which they would normally receive during class later in the day. If teachers have students in their advisory groups whom they do not have in other classes, and the advisor-advisee group activity is not graded (as it should not be), there is often considerably more reluctance to participate fully in the activities of the group. Planners who fear the conflict that they believe will surround a change from departmentalized organization of teachers to an interdisciplinary framework, and who instead implement an advisor-advisee program in the hopes that this will satisfy the reorganization requirements, are often disappointed in the results, which usually include a failing advisor-advisee program.

The mutual support which the advisor-advisee program and the interdisciplinary organization of teachers offer to each other is another example of the synergism which operates in the middle school program. Implementing one part of the program without the others results in a loss of efficiency and effectiveness of considerable proportions. As the heart of the middle school program, the interdisciplinary team organization model, when present, will make the advisor-advisee program much more likely to succeed.

There are a number of other factors which contribute to the success of an advisor-advisee program. Some schools, such as Noe Middle School, Louisville, Kentucky, have found that preparing a handbook for teachers which explains the purposes of the program, offers suggestions for organizing one's group, and contains a package of effective advisor-advisee activities, is a very helpful project. Others have found that keeping the same advisor and advisees together over a period of years is an effective practice. A considerable number of schools have used a parent orientation process at the beginning of every year, and found that to be very helpful. Parents can be remarkably receptive to the advisor-advisee program if they are given the information they need to understand it.

Counselors play an important role, perhaps the most important, in the success or failure of the advisor-advisee program. When counselors see their role as including the success of the advisor-advisee program, they act in ways which provide support and enthusiasm to teachers. They become the school's team leader for guidance, acting as if the teachers were, in a sense, in their advisor-advisee group. When counselors mistakenly view the advisor-advisee program as a rebuke, perhaps as a result of the failure attributed to their counseling efforts by others, they react defensively and act in ways which undercut and lessen the chances for a successful activity. Counselors must be given the responsibility for the success of the advisor-advisee program, and the freedom to accomplish the task. When counselors are used as assistant administrators, they will not have the time to fill other roles.

Nothing is more important, however, to the success of the advisor-advisee program than the understanding and support of the school principal and other administrators. When administrators are enthusiastically in favor of a program and are willing to put themselves forward in support of it, the chances for success are good. When they are not, teachers will soon get the message, and those who really are uncomfortable with the program will begin to lobby against it with the principal, will neglect their own advisor-advisee groups and generally seek to erode support for the program among other faculty members. Principals must be willing to treat teachers in the same way that they want teachers to respond to students. That is, they must explain the goals of the program, show the teachers how they may succeed, encourage them to try and let them know that the program is an important part of their day, and that it is not an option.

The advisor-advisee program, properly organized and implemented, can be a bright place in the day of everyone involved. Implemented incorrectly, it can be a glaring failure and a barrier to further progress. Educators who wish to implement the program but who cannot do so without risking its success, should consider postponing the program. The advisor-advisee program is an excellent addition to the interdisciplinary team foundation, but it ought not be built in the absence of that foundation without extreme care.

Recent Research on the Advisory Program

During the spring of 1979, an evaluation of the advisory program at Lincoln Middle School was conducted by a research team from the University of Florida, as a part of a larger assessment of the affective components of the Lincoln program.[7] A stratified random sampling procedure was used so that only one third of the 900 students were required to evaluate any one aspect of the program, yet the results were generalizable to all students within the school. The evaluation team worked with the principal and the faculty Program Improvement Council to specify the program's goals and objectives; they then developed instruments reflecting these goals and objectives. The instruments for both students and teachers were reviewed by a committee of teachers and modified as appropriate. To maximize the amount of information available to the school staff, the student data were analyzed by race, sex, team and grade. The teacher data were analyzed only by team. The design was such that the anonymity of all respondents was maintained.

Students were asked questions which examined their relationship with and perceptions of their advisor-teachers and the related activities. The teachers were asked questions on the centrality of advisor-advisee programs to a middle school experience and the amount of teacher preparation required for an effective effort. In brief, all students:

1. Perceived their advisory teachers as caring for them, and for the other students in their group
2. Thought their group helped in their understanding of other people
3. Differentiated between academic and personal problems. They indicated they would turn first to their advisor for help in solving an academic problem, but would also seek out the guidance counselor for assistance with a personal problem

4. Felt the advisor-advisee group provided skills for problem solving
5. Differentiated between most important and favorite activities: the most important AA activities were USSR (silent reading) and study hall; while favorite activities were talking with a friend, and free time
6. Frequently listed the advisor-teacher as their favorite teacher or the teacher they knew best
7. Agreed that their advisor-teachers were fair

Only a few significant differences emerged when the student data were analyzed by race, sex, team and grade. These differences were:

1. Blacks were more likely than whites to believe that their advisors cared about them and other students; helped them understand other people; and helped them learn how to solve problems.
2. Females were more likely than males to believe that the advisory group helped them learn how to solve problems; they also identified more strongly with Lincoln Middle School than did the males.
3. There were no differences in responses among students by grade.
4. The only question on which there was a team difference was: ''I feel like an outsider in my group.'' While a majority of students indicated a strong sense of belonging to their group, some of the students on three of the teams were less positive on this item than were students on the other three teams.

The teacher findings were:

1. Overwhelming endorsement for the advisory concept for middle schools
2. Belief that teachers were prepared to function in the advisor role, although about one third of the teachers felt that they needed more training for this role
3. Indicated that they had long-range goals for their advisory groups
4. Perceived the guidance counselor as playing an active role in the program
5. Half of the teachers indicated they prepared special activities for advisor-advisee time
6. Slightly less than half of the teachers reported having a value clarification activity at least once a week

An evaluation such as this provides useful information about a program to a faculty. Strengths and weaknesses are highlighted and directions derived for staff and program development. For instance, the advisory program was seen as an integral part of the school's program by both faculty and students. Of some concern, however, might be the less positive ratings given by the white male students; perhaps efforts should be made to identify and address their special needs. Although the teachers at Lincoln say that value clarification is important, neither they nor their students ranked it highly. This may reflect the fact that a significant minority of the teachers failed to include activities of this nature in their groups. Since many of the teachers expressed a need for additional training, value clarification and related activities might be a focus of an inservice education program at this particular school.

One of the concerns of program specialists referred to earlier in this chapter, has been the role of the guidance counselor in an advisor-advisee program. Data collected in this evaluation indicated that both teachers and students perceived the guidance counselor as playing an important role in the school's program. The advisor-advisee program has not eliminated the need for a counselor. There are so many other duties that counselors must perform in a middle school (for example, staffing students into special programs, guiding new students, assisting in quasi-administrative duties and crisis intervention) that even the idea of eliminating or reducing their presence is unthinkable.

It is important to note that all students, regardless of grade level, felt an integral part of the school and their advisory group. Failure to find grade level differences is probably a reflection of the impact of multiage grouping at Lincoln, but additional information would need to be collected to insure this interpretation.

Teachers at Lincoln Middle School should be very pleased with the results of this evaluation. A critical step in developing an effective integrated school is for students to perceive their teachers as being fair and caring about them as individuals. This evaluation indicated that Lincoln had met this condition.

Another study of the advisor-advisee program at Lincoln Middle School was prompted by the Bell-Nathaniel and Damico study, and by some chance remarks made by some high school teachers, who, at a district teacher's meeting, observed that students from Lincoln were more mature and easier to teach when they reached ninth grade than were students from several other schools in the district.[8]

After gathering considerable data from both questionnaires and interviews, Doda's analysis confirmed and extended the conclusions of the study by Bell-Nathaniel and Damico. Among the significant conclusions were the following:

1. *Ninth grade students in Gainesville, Florida, high schools, felt good about their interpersonal relationships at school, and attributed some of their successes in this area to the advisor-advisee program at the middle school.*
2. *Students in the study felt that they understood themselves well and attributed this, in part, to the opportunities provided in the advisory program, particularly the extended relationship with a teacher who cared about them, and the chance to talk about personal matters with peers.*
3. *What might be called school survival skills appeared to be an area of weakness. Solving problems, using school time wisely, and meeting deadlines were perceived as unresolved difficulties by a significant portion of the students.*
4. *There were no special activities that students pointed to as having been particularly helpful. A caring advisor and a special peer group were cited much more frequently as having been helpful.*
5. *Males seem less prepared and less successful than females; black males in particular.*
6. *There was a small portion of youngsters who believed that the advisory program was of no help or value at all. They tended to remark, "We did nothing in A.A."*[9]

Comprehensively, this study came to the same positive conclusions about the advisory program at Lincoln Middle School as did the first one. While such studies are encouraging, there are still too few well-designed studies of these programs to permit more than modest speculations about the ultimate value of the advisor-advisee program, from the point of view of educational research. More of this type of research needs to be conducted, and we hope that these studies are indicative of future efforts.

ADDITIONAL SUGGESTIONS FOR FURTHER STUDY

A.   Books
Johnson, Mauritz, ed., *Toward Adolescence: The Middle School Years*, Seventy-ninth Yearbook of the National Society for the Study of Education, Part I. Chicago: University of Chicago Press, 1980, Sections One and Two.

B.   Periodicals
Bohlinger, Tom, "Middle School Guidance: Problems in Comprehensiveness and Implementation," *Middle School Journal*, 7,7,22–3 (December 1976).
Bohlinger, Tom, "Implementing a Comprehensive Guidance Program in the Middle School," *NASSP Bulletin*, 61, 65–73 (September 1977).
Cole, Claire and Hassall, Cherie, "Individual and Group Activities Class," *Middle School Journal*, 6, 63 (Winter 1975).
Driggers, R. Kim, Carr, Frances, and Swick, Kevin J., "A Learner-Centered Middle School Guidance Program," *Middle School Journal*, 6, 31–2 (Summer 1975).
Lewis, Katheryn Coor, "Developmental Group Counseling for Transteens," *Middle School Journal*, 7, 4–5, 16 (December 1976).
Pappas, John G. and Miller, Gary M. "Middle School Principals' Perceptions of Their Counselors," *Middle School Journal*, 7, 6, 22 (December 1976).
Ryan, Mary K., "Middle School/Junior High School Counselors' Corner," *Elementary School Guidance and Counseling*, 7, 48–50 (October 1972).
Ryan, Mary K. and Reynolds, Carol, "The Unique Role of the Middle/Junior High School Counselor," *Elementary School Guidance and Counseling*, 8, 216–8 (March 1974).

C.   Dissertations and Dissertation Abstracts
Scouller, John Deans III, "Guidance Needs of Middle School Educable Mentally Retarded and Gifted Children," Unpublished doctoral dissertation, The University of Florida, 1975.

FOOTNOTES

1.   Nancy M. Doda, "Teacher to Teacher," *Middle School Journal*, 7, 8 (September 1976).
2.   Thomas E. Gatewood, "Towards a Self-Identity: The Middle School and the Affective Needs of the Emerging Adolescent," *Middle School Journal*, 6, 25–30 (Summer 1975).

3. Thomas E. Gatewood and Charles A. Dilg, *The Middle School We Need*. A Report from the A.S.C.D. Working Group on the Early Adolescent Learner. (Washington, D.C.: Association for Supervision and Curriculum Development, 1975), pp. 14–17.

4. Vance Packard, *A Nation of Strangers* (Palo Alto, Calif.: Pacific Books, 1974).

5. See Keigh H. Hubel, *The Teacher-Advisor System* (Dubuque, Iowa: Kendall Hunt Publishing Company, 1974).

6. Nancy Doda, "Teacher to Teacher," *Middle School Journal,* 8, 8–9, (May 1977).

7. Associate Professors Afesa Bell-Nathaniel and Sandra B. Damico, along with their students Charles Green, Wendy McClosky and Nancy McCowan conducted the study. The assistance of Professors Damico and Bell-Nathaniel is gratefully acknowledged for providing a summary of the research.

8. N.M. Doda, "Advisor-Advisee and High School Preparation: An Evaluation Report on Student Perceptions," Gainesville, Florida: The University of Florida, Mimeographed, December, 1979.

9. Doda, p. 35.

Chapter 5

Interdisciplinary Team Organization

The organization of the faculty for instruction is a fundamental task of all schools. The interdisciplinary organization of teachers is both the most distinguishing feature of the middle school, and the keystone of its structure. In the presence of a stable interdisciplinary team organization, other components of the program function much more smoothly. In its absence they operate with considerably more difficulty, if they exist at all.

Organizing the Faculty for Instruction

The characteristics and needs of the learner have always been central factors in the selection of appropriate strategies for organizing faculty for instruction. In the elementary school the belief in a need for an almost exclusive relationship between the teacher and the student has preserved the self-contained classroom as the predominant mode of faculty organization throughout most of the existence of formal education in America. Some educators predict a resurgence of confidence in the self-contained classroom for the primary school years of the 1980's. Pupils leaving the home at earlier and earlier ages continue to need a strong relationship with one nonparent adult, to ease the transition from home to public school. One good way for this relationship to develop properly is for the teacher and student to spend the maximum amount of time together that the school day allows: the self-contained classroom.

In the primary school self-contained classroom each teacher works with a group of students, planning and managing an instructional program almost entirely alone. With the possible exception of a few specialists in art, music or physical education, the world of knowledge is presented to students in a manner decided primarily by the classroom teacher. It is this teacher, working alone, who decides what will be taught, to whom, by what methods, under what circumstances; one teacher working alone presents the whole world of knowledge to a small group of students. One might, of course, debate the merits of such a process, but that the self-contained classroom has been, is, and most likely will continue to be the predominant mode of primary school teacher organization is much less debatable.

At the high school, faculty have rarely been obligated to develop relationships with students in ways similar to the primary school teacher. Students who are driving, working and in many other ways demonstrating their young adulthood do not need and will reject that type of student-teacher relationship. Seventeen- and eighteen-year-olds ought to be encouraged to identify their own adult friendship choices from among the faculty on the basis of similar personality styles, common subject matter interests and the like. Teacher-student friendship is important to high school teachers and students but it has been, and probably should continue to be, based on mutual choice.

High school educators, steeped in the knowledge of particular disciplines, have historically argued that the sophistication of the subject matter at that level prohibits teachers from crossing disciplinary lines with ease. Released from a major commitment to student relationships, the high school has maintained a steady focus on organizing in a way which facilitates the delivery of what they are committed to, the academic disciplines. As a result, the pattern of teacher organization in high schools has almost always been the department, a group of teachers representing the same subject. Instead of one teacher generalist presenting the whole world of knowledge to a specific small group of children, the high school teacher is usually responsible for an even smaller part (for example, American history) of one of many areas (for example, social studies) of the world of knowledge. Instead of working alone, the teacher often works with other teachers, but with the common focus being the subject area.

The goal of the middle school is to contribute to the articulation between the elementary school and the high school by providing a program that ties the two together in a smooth and continuous way, while at the same time providing a unique experience for the education of older children and early adolescents; a middle way between the elementary school self-contained classroom and the high school department. This middle way has come to be known as interdisciplinary team organization, and the authors believe that the time for debate about the appropriateness of the interdisciplinary team organization as the cornerstone of the exemplary middle school should be over. The need for planned gradualism as the key to articulation (identified a decade or more ago) remains, and is met, in the exemplary middle school, through the interdisciplinary team organization.

Team Organization and Team Teaching

There is, currently, a considerable amount of misunderstanding and confusion about the meaning of terms used to describe the organization for instruction in middle schools. Numerous terms are commonly used: team teaching, interdisciplinary, intradisciplinary, multidisciplinary, cross-curriculum and several others. The two most often cited both use the term interdisciplinary: interdisciplinary team teaching and interdisciplinary team organization. The difference and the confusion comes from the words "teaching" and "organization."

Fifteen years ago, in one of the few books ever written on the topic of teaming, Shaplin defined team teaching as "a type of instructional organization, involving teaching personnel and the students assigned to them, in which two or more teachers are given responsibility, working together, for all or a significant part of the instruction of the same group of students."[1] With a few slight adjustments, this definition still works well for the exemplary middle school.

One modification has to do with the terms identified above, since a popular misconception of team teaching grows from an emphasis on the word "teaching." This misconception identified team teaching as basically a hierarchical graduation of faculty members' roles and titles wherein a master teacher has major responsibilities for planning and presenting lessons to large groups of students, who are then dispersed to small seminar-size groups, led by presumably less competent faculty, for discussion and review of the lesson presented by the master teacher. Quite naturally, the impression gained is one in which the essence of teaming is expressed in the act of instruction. Such a model may work well for high schools and colleges. It rarely plays a major role in the exemplary middle school.

By contrast, the term "organization" focuses on the structural requirements of the team. It highlights factors other than a particular style of large and small group instruction. Interdisciplinary team organization, the concept preferred by the authors, fits comfortably with Shaplin's definition cited earlier, but goes further. In this text, the authors use the term interdisciplinary team organization to define "a way of organizing the faculty so that a group of teachers share: (1) the responsibility for planning, teaching, and evaluating curriculum and instruction in more than one academic area; (2) the same group of students; (3) the same schedule; and (4) the same area of the building." These four factors are the necessary and sufficient elements of interdisciplinary teacher organization. When all four are present nothing else is needed; when one or more elements is missing, the team organization is less than complete. Interdisciplinary team teaching is not a critical element of the exemplary middle school; interdisciplinary team organization is.

Alternative Types of Interdisciplinary Team Organization

Although interdisciplinary team organization is essential to the exemplary middle school, it should not be assumed that there is only one acceptable model of such organization. The authors' study of exemplary middle schools reveals that there are a variety of ways of organizing teachers in an interdisciplinary fashion. They vary in regard to size, roles and responsibilities of teachers, student composition, teacher autonomy and the way time is structured for the team. All of these variations, however, fully satisfy the four conditions of the definition set forth above. While it is impossible, in practice, to separate the method of organizing the faculty for instruction from the method of grouping students for instruction, in order to be able to clearly distinguish the essence of interdisciplinary team organization, the discussion of student grouping will be delayed for the most part until chapter 6.

Interdisciplinary team organization in the exemplary middle school varies considerably in the number of teachers and students who comprise a separate team. The range of size commonly encountered extends from teams of two teachers and 50–75 students to teams of six teachers with 150–190 students. None of the exemplary middle schools described here has teams of two teachers as the model for the entire school, and very few schools have teams of more than five teachers. A number of exemplary middle schools have teams of varying sizes.

Graveraet Middle School, Marquette, Michigan, for example, has teams of varied sizes, with teams of two, three and four teachers with appropriate numbers of students. West Middle School, Aurora, Colorado, has teams of two, four and five teachers, and MacDonald Middle School, East Lansing, Michigan, has teams of two, three and four teachers each.

Nipher Middle School, Kirkwood, Missouri, is an excellent example of a school that offers a variety of team designs. Sixth-grade students, and parents, are given this choice (within the limits of staff flexibility): a modified self-contained classroom where one teacher will be responsible for teaching students the four basic subjects; a two-teacher team where one teacher is responsible for language arts and social studies, and another for math and science; a four-teacher team, students heterogeneously grouped, each teacher responsible for one subject; and, a two-teacher combined sixth- and seventh-grade team, multiage grouped, offering a two-year curriculum with a great deal of individualized instruction and student self-direction. Seventh-grade students at Nipher have the same options, with the exception of the self-contained classroom, and eighth graders are all assigned to four-teacher teams. Nipher designs its teacher teams on the basis of student maturity, allowing for the greatest flexibility in the sixth grade and gradually moving toward the large four-teacher team for all students in the eighth grade.

Kinawa Middle School, Okomos, Michigan, has a special method for organizing the faculty, in an essentially interdisciplinary way, but with opportunities for other emphases as well. For most of its history (opened in 1969), the faculty at Kinawa have been organized into three different types of learning environments. As at Nipher, parents, students and teachers are given considerable latitude in choosing which academic environment they prefer.

The "Sixth, Seventh, and Eight Grade Block Program" at Kinawa offers a highly individualized situation in which sixth, seventh, and eighth graders focus on developing responsibility in individual decision making concerning the use of time, space, materials and human resources in the learning process. A school publication describes the process:

Each student will be scheduled to meet personally with a learning facilitator once each week to determine weekly goals, objectives and activities. These sessions will also be used to discuss the progress on completion of the previous week's plan. All students are presented with minimal academic expectations for their grade level. All instruction will be accomplished in small groups, seldom larger than one learning facilitator to six students, and most instruction will be accomplished on a one-to-one tutorial basis. Student decisions about learning fall within school district and middle school policy and program. Each student will maintain a folder which will contain weekly plans. These will be open to a student's parents at any time.

A second academic atmosphere at Kinawa is represented by a grade level "Interdisciplinary Block" for the seventh and eighth grades. These seventh- and eighth-grade blocks function much like the standard four-teacher interdisciplinary team described in this chapter. The remainder of the teachers and students operate within a type of nonstructure called "self-contained by subject." Here each teacher functions autonomously, offering a variety of expectations and an array of teaching styles for the students, a situation similar in some ways to a loose knit departmentalized setup.

The organization of teachers at Kinawa offers the maximum choice to everyone involved. It offers a situation that recognizes value in each person's preference for a learning environment. And, it permits the design of a variety of alternatives which are possible without a prohibitive amount of staff development time and expense. This offers some explanation for Kinawa's successful long-term operation.

Often the variance in the size of the team stems from the existence of unequal numbers of students in schools using chronological age-graded grouping. A school may, for example, have an unusually large group of seventh graders compared to the numbers in the sixth or eighth grades, making it impossible to have teams of equal size. It may also be the design of the building that dictates the size of teams within the school. It may be that the middle school inherited an old junior or senior high school building not designed for team organization. The building may have little or no pattern to the way in which regular classrooms are grouped; for example, three classrooms together on one end of the hall, two at the other end, four in the center. The possibilities for grouping classrooms offered by older buildings seem infinite, while regularity seems almost nonexistent. School principals often demonstrate considerable creativity in making the most of their buildings, and varied team sizes is a common response.

For whatever reasons the size of a team varies, it is the number of teachers on a team that usually sets limits on the number of different subjects each teacher teaches. And almost always, the four basic subjects (language arts, social studies, science, math) are included, regardless of the number of teachers on the team. When two teachers form a team, as they do at Graveraet, West and MacDonald Schools, most often each teacher takes the major responsibility for planning and teaching at least two of the four basic academic subjects. Frequently the teachers divide their responsibilities on the basis of personal preferences, desire for collaboration or perceived subject matter compatibilty as well as certification requirements.

Here is how it looks at MacDonald and West:

MacDonald

Team 6–1	(2) Teacher 1:	math, science, social studies
	Teacher 2:	math, science, language arts
Team 6–2	(2) Teacher 1:	language arts, social studies
	Teacher 2:	math, science
Team 6–3	(2) Teacher 1:	math, science
	Teacher 2:	language arts, social studies
Team 6–7–8	(2) Teacher 1:	math, science
	Teacher 2:	language arts, social studies
Team 7–1	(2) Teacher 1:	language arts, social studies
	Teacher 2:	math, science
Team 8–1	(4) Teacher 1:	language arts
	Teacher 2:	math
	Teacher 3:	social studies
	Teacher 4:	science
Team 8–2	(2) Teacher 1:	language arts, social studies
	Teacher 2:	math, science

West

Team 6–0	(2) Teacher 1:	science, math
	Teacher 2:	language arts, social studies
Team 6–1	(2) Teacher 1:	language arts, math
	Teacher 2:	science, social studies
Team 6–2	(2) Teacher 1:	math, science
	Teacher 2:	language arts, social studies
Team 7–0	(5) Teacher 1:	science
	Teacher 2:	language arts
	Teacher 3:	language arts, reading
	Teacher 4:	math
	Teacher 5:	social studies
Team 8–0	(2) Teacher 1:	language arts, social studies
	Teacher 2:	math, science

Team 8–1   (4) Teacher 1: math
            Teacher 2: science
            Teacher 3: language arts
            Teacher 4: social studies

The most frequent combinations for two-teacher teams, quite possibly a common holdover from the days of the core curriculum in the junior and senior high schools, are social studies-language arts and math-science. But there are other possibilities, of course. One team at MacDonald (6–1) chose to share math and science and to assume individual responsibility for language arts and social studies. A team at West (also 6–1) divided it differently: language arts-math and science-social studies. Interestingly, none of the two-teacher teams at these schools opted to share all four of the basic academic subjects in a way that included each person teaching all of the four. There are certainly many schools where this is done.

A number of middle schools have teams composed of three teachers. At Griffin Middle School, Smyrna, Georgia, and in two new middle schools in Dothan, Alabama (based partially on the model at Griffin), the three-teacher team is the norm. When a team of three teachers is assigned to teach the four basics (as is almost always the case) several possibilities for teaching responsibilities exist. Three teachers usually share the responsibilities for four subjects one of two ways: by having all three teachers teach all four subjects; or, by having each teacher responsible for one subject, separately, while all three combine to teach the fourth.

Which path is chosen often depends on the number of elementary or secondary trained teachers on the team. In the sixth-grade teams, where elementary trained teachers predominate, the pattern often displays the three teachers commonly planning and teaching all four subjects in a coordinated and collaborative way. In the seventh-grade teams, teaching responsibilities seem split rather evenly between teams in which all teachers teach all subjects, and those in which each teaches two subjects, one separately and one in common. In the eighth-grade teams, it is the latter method which predominates.

In many teams of three teachers at the eighth-grade level, the teachers often plan and teach collaboratively those subjects that require their combined efforts to do well. An eighth-grade team might, for example, be composed of three secondary trained teachers, with certification in language arts, social studies and math, but not in science. Frequently, these teachers will choose to share the responsibility for science and teach the others individually. By pooling their expertise, they develop a science program that is respectable and maintain their individual specialties in the other areas. Schools which have opted for the three-teacher team have discovered that, by necessity, it produces a great deal of team planning in comparison with any other size team.

Teams composed of four teachers are by far the most common, probably because the basic academic curriculum is most commonly thought of as having four distinct elements. Even in schools which would describe themselves as far from being exemplary, the four-teacher unit is usually present. The four-teacher team organization is standard, but of course, not necessarily better than other possibilities.

The four-teacher situation usually finds one teacher having special responsibility for one subject area. Each teacher is a resource person for one of the four basic areas, with state certification or college preparation, or both, in that particular area. This special responsibility can be handled, however, in several different ways. Each of these different ways is acceptable in terms of the definition of team organization.

The most common division of responsibilities on the four-teacher team assigns almost total responsibility for one subject area to each teacher. At Fairview Middle School, Tallahassee, Florida, the team's math teacher plans and teachs all the math. The social studies, science and mathematics teachers each also plan and teach their individual subjects to the students on the team. Because they meet together regularly, however, teachers using this approach are likely to be aware of what is happening in the other academic areas, and may contribute suggestions for improvements even though their formal responsibilities do not extend to teaching these other subjects.

A second, less frequently found method for assigning teacher responsibilities on four-teacher teams often follows the model known as Individually Guided Education (IGE), developed by the Institute for the Development of Educational Activities (IDEA), a creation of the Kettering Foundation.[2] This model usually identifies resource people in each of the special areas, but expands their teaching responsibilities to all four subjects.

At Spring Hill Middle School, High Springs, Florida, teachers have followed the IGE model for a decade. Each team has a resource teacher in each of the four areas. It is the task of the resource person in math, for example, to take the major role in planning the mathematics instruction for the students on the team. This may involve many things: selecting objectives from the scope and sequence outlined in county and school curriculum guides; suggesting instructional activities; designing evaluative instruments; gathering materials and being certain that resources are ready; and many other activities. But when the math unit is ready to teach, all members of the team are involved in the instruction.

All four teachers teach math, but all four teachers are not likely to be teaching for identical math objectives. The teacher on the team least comfortable with teaching math may, for instance, end up teaching remedial long division for six weeks, while two other teachers have different instructional assignments and the math resource teacher has the task of teaching the prealgebra unit. The process is the same in the other three areas. All teachers on the team are involved in the planning and instruction of each unit, but in different ways. The same basic process is followed, with some differences, at Oregon Middle School, Oregon, Wisconsin, Glen Ridge Middle

School, Glenn Ridge, New Jersey and Trotwood-Madison Middle School, Trotwood, Ohio.

A third possibility exists for the four-teacher team, but because of several persistent problems, it is often only partially implemented, even in exemplary middle schools. It is possible for the teachers to integrate the four subjects into truly interdisciplinary units, thematic curriculum plans that weave together the several disciplines into coherent wholes. Several middle schools identify such possibilities in what they describe as core programs. Montgomery Middle School, El Cajon, California, requires that sixth graders experience a core program three periods a day, and seventh and eighth graders are involved in a two-period core. The core program is also a fundamental part of the interdisciplinary curriculum at Noe Middle School, Louisville, Kentucky. Typically, core at these schools and others, involves the integration of language arts and social studies programs under the direction of one or two teachers on the team, but it may involve entire teams and up to four subjects.

Other schools develop and teach thematic units without the formal designation of something like core. At Farnsworth Middle School, Guilderland, New York, teams taught these units: TETE (Total Education for the Total Environment), an interdisciplinary approach to the environment study on which all four basic subjects were involved; Anthropology (also involving all four subjects); Flow Charts (math and science); Earth Day (entire seventh grade); Drugs; and others. At Graveraet Middle School, Marquette, Michigan, this process produced thematic units like World War II, the Human Body, Japan, The Bicentennial, Russia and a grade-wide one on Camping. Beck Middle School, Cherry Hill, New Jersey, seems an example of the outstandingly thorough and balanced use of truly interdisciplinary units.

Thematic interdisciplinary units like those just described appear more or less frequently in almost all good middle school programs. However, few, if any, middle schools (no matter how exemplary) seem to be able to sustain the use of thematic units as the curriculum of the basic instructional program for a majority of the day over a long period of several years or more. This mode of teacher assignment on interdisciplinary teams remains largely at an aspirational rather than the actual level.

A number of exemplary middle schools find themselves at the other end of the range in terms of size of team, with five-teacher teams relatively frequent and teams of six and seven teachers less frequent. Teams composed of eight to twelve teachers are much less frequent and often seem to work out to be total grade label groups which then break into smaller, informal subject-oriented groups composed of teachers in the same discipline who often do a great deal of actual team teaching. The large teams (over six teachers) tend to subdivide, with each subdivision acting like a miniature subject-oriented department.

Teams of five teachers usually resemble the four-teacher team in that they assign one subject to each teacher for both planning and teaching. The extra member usually comes, as at Glen Ridge, New Jersey, Middle School, from the separation of reading from language arts, due to increased emphasis on reading skills now found in almost every school. At Glen Ridge this works out to about forty-five minutes per day in each of the five subjects.

Lincoln Middle School, Gainesville, Florida, is different from this pattern, using four teachers to teach five basic subjects. Having separated reading from the remainder of the language arts program, the Lincoln staff found themselves still heavily committed to other aspects of their program (advisor-advisee and exploratory courses). This commitment resulted in a four-person academic team where one teacher has the responsibility for language arts, one for reading, one for math and one teacher for both science and social studies. This means at Lincoln that students receive a half year of science and a half year of social studies.

Based on the definition of team organization offered earlier, all of the above descriptions are appropriate. In the exemplary middle school, interdisciplinary team organization seems to mean, most often, groups of from two to five teachers who share responsibility for planning and sometimes teaching curriculum and instruction in more than one academic area to the same group of students, with the same schedule, in the same part of the building. Teachers almost always represent a strength in one particular subject and they may teach only this subject to all the students on the team. Or, they may teach two, three or four different subjects in various collaborative arrangements with their team members. Frequently in some schools, and occasionally in almost all schools, teachers from various academic perspectives will combine their areas in thematic units. All of these efforts fall in the range of interdisciplinary team organization, and while some are more extensive in the actual amount of teaming done by the teachers, the greatest benefits of the interdisciplinary team organization accrue to both teachers and students in all of the various models described here.

Roles and Responsibilities of Teams and Their Members

The Team

The roles and responsibilities of team members vary, depending upon the model of team organization followed. Most exemplary middle schools, however, avoid complex hierarchical arrangements designating master teachers, regular teachers and other less qualified members, and instead are much more likely to use a model that assumes a much greater degree of equality of expertise on the team. Team leaders are often chosen and relied upon, but rarely given enough extra perquisites to make the tasks worthwhile simply in exchange for these extras. Most often team leaders serve because they feel a sense of professional duty, or because they need the challenge of extra responsibility and the consequent opportunities for personal and professional growth. Almost always, team leaders work longer and harder than even they had believed possible.

What must teams, once organized, accomplish? When teams meet, what concerns are central? What decisions must be made? Members of a team in the exemplary middle school participate in decisions on many of the following: scheduling of classes and teacher assignments; student schedules; patterns of student grouping for instruction within the team; selection and development of curriculum plans and supportive materials; correlation of curriculum plans from different subject areas to insure maximum effectiveness; space allocation; budget disbursement; use of blocks of time for planning and instruction; team teaching; selection of new staff members; parent contacts; placing students in special programs; orientation of new students; evaluation and inservice staff development of team members; cooperation with special area teachers. Some teacher responsibilities are more important than others, and few decisions can be made without taking the whole school into account.

Teaching Responsibilities. In many exemplary middle schools the team decides on the teaching responsibilities for each member. The team must decide how many subjects each teacher will teach and what those subjects will be. Once the teams have been established, with the principal seeing to it that certification and related problems are resolved, the teams can be given the responsibility for staff-subject assignments.

Arranging the Physical Environment. Having been assigned the full complement of rooms or space in an appropriate area, the team must decide how these rooms should be used. Will space be assigned to individual teachers, in pairs, or some other combination? Will the space be assigned for the year, on a more temporary basis, or not at all? Will there be a planning room where each teacher will have a small space?

Structuring Academic Class Time. In most exemplary middle schools teams are responsible for relatively large blocks of time to be devoted to instruction in the subjects for which the team has been given responsibility. Typically the team is notified as to when their students will have certain activities such as lunch, physical education and exploratory courses. Teams then decide what subjects will be taught at what times, and often how much time will be devoted to each subject or how frequently the subject will be studied each week. The teams are responsible for establishing, evaluating and reestablishing a daily schedule for subjects, teachers and students.

Grouping Students. Often teams have some autonomy in the issue of student grouping for instruction within the team. The team will have to decide whether students will be grouped according to ability, and, if so, how they will be grouped. Some teams group heterogeneously in all classes, others group by ability for reading or math, or both. Teams frequently attempt to have social studies, science and exploratory classes grouped without reference to ability. Typically, however, teams that find it necessary to group students according to ability for one or two subjects find it difficult to regroup heterogeneously for the other classes.

Scheduling Students. Principals of exemplary middle schools usually discover that teams can often do an outstanding job of scheduling students on their teams for their academic classes. Teachers quickly establish a method for assigning students to special programs like Title I reading and then parcel out students to different sections of academic subjects within the team. Teaming makes it possible for teachers to possess knowledge of students that enables them to decide which students should be grouped, which ones should be separated. Teachers also find it frequently necessary to change a student's schedule, and when the team has this responsibility the task can be accomplished much more efficiently. Having teachers make decisions about who studies what, with whom, at what time also relieves the administrators of a tremendously time-consuming burden. This way teachers appreciate having an important role to play in the decisions that have a daily effect on their lives, and administrators, sometimes counselors, are free for duties that they would otherwise be unable to perform.

One teacher from an exemplary middle school, experienced in the process of scheduling students, describes the approach that works in her school:

During pre-planning, each team of teachers (usually four academic teachers and three support teachers) sits as a group to ''hand schedule'' reading, math, language arts, and science/social studies (we offer a half year of each). Our first considerations are to those classes or programs with the least flexibility; classes for emotionally handicapped, educably mentally retarded, learning disabled and gifted students are scheduled first. These classes may only be offered two or three of the four possible times and therefore must be scheduled initially. Teachers of these specific classes present the teams with their time requirement for each individual student. Programs such as Title I and other compensatory classes are offered throughout the day and can be scheduled as are the regular academic classes.

Once these restrictive considerations are negotiated, the team teachers then continue by scheduling their own academics. Each team has the option of grouping homogeneously for one or two classes. For instance, if reading and math are to be ability grouped by a specific team, those classes would be scheduled first. Reading and math levels for each student would be determined (results from standardized tests), the students grouped, and then assigned to a class section. A student might be high in reading and low in math, so he/she would fall in a high reading class and a lower math class. Classes do not rotate as complete sections from one teacher to another. Students will have a new group of classmates in each class with only a few students following similar schedules.

Classes which are randomly grouped are scheduled last. In this case, numbers of students are balanced to give each class an appropriate load.

Changes from day to day can be made at the team's discretion. Our administrators leave the responsibility of this process up to the teams, with the team leader reporting back all difficulties or problems, and final decisions regarding grouping.

Our exploratory program rotates every twelve weeks and students may select the classes they want to take. Each student makes a first, second and third choice. From this selection, the homeroom or advisory teacher assigns students to classes based on the students' choices and availability of classes. This same process repeats each time exploratories rotate.

Through this process of teachers scheduling their own students, the responsibility for developing appropriate learning activities and situations is left for teachers and teams to determine. We appreciate the opportunity of making these decisions and now perform this role automatically.[3]

Selecting and Distributing Text and Other Materials. Some middle schools follow a multitext approach to instruction which permits teams to select the texts which best suit their students, and the interests and teaching preferences of instructors. Almost all schools encourage team participation in decisions about texts or materials that the whole school must use. Some administrators turn over a portion of the operating budget of the school to each team. Teams at Fort Clarke Middle School, Gainesville, Florida, for example, are given a budget of $10.00 per student at the beginning of the year, which amounts to about $1500 per team. The teams then apportion these funds as they determine their needs, but team budgets must include basic items such as ditto and construction paper, chalk, film rentals and other items such as field trips, materials for exploratory courses and so on. This type of team budgeting enhances the teams' feelings of autonomy, and frees the principal from the tiresome and sometimes demeaning role of keeper of the purse, doling out sometimes large, other times miniscule, amounts of money, but each time requiring a form or a response to a request.

Team Teaching. When conditions are right (adequate planning time, planning skills and communication skills) teams occasionally engage in actual teamed instruction. A few schools are able to offer thematic units on a regular basis, with a rare school or two actually offering such units on a schoolwide basis in which regular classes are suspended for a week or more in favor of a unit such as ''Spanish Americans'' where everyone teaches every subject area, but the subjects are not fused together as in the thematic units. Even more frequently, two or more members of a team will plan their instruction in a way that permits subject areas to be closely correlated in terms of skills and related concepts. Most teams, however, find fewer opportunities to actually team teach than the members of the team would like.

Other Student Matters. Teams often need to spend time meeting with a counselor for the purpose of placing students into a program for exceptional children. They also find themselves frequently occupied with students leaving school or with new students transferring in from another school; or, rarely, from another team in the same school. Teams also report a significant amount of time spent in conferences with parents of students on the team. The economy of time provided to parents by being able to speak with all their child's teachers at once makes this type of parent-team conference a very popular item with teams that encourage it. As this section should indicate, team consideration of the problems of an individual student is one of the major advantages of team organization.

Relating To Other Staff Members. Teams often need to act as a unit in collaboration with other school staff. There are, of course, many times throughout the year when the principal or the assistant principal would meet with a particular team for a special purpose. In addition to these administrators, there are likely to be dozens of instances when teams confer with other staff members. Many exemplary middle schools have a person who acts as the curriculum coordinator. This person frequently works closely with the teams, often serving as a type of overall team leader and ombudsman dealing separately with each team on issues, inservice opportunities, curriculum development and so on. Just as often, teams meet with counselors, deans or special education teachers regarding individual pupils or small groups of students from the team.

Experience in some middle schools indicates that the energy of the team members is often consumed largely by matters related to the management of team affairs. While such a situation might seem, at first, to be less than ideal, it is important to point out that all working groups function this way. Such day-to-day interaction helps solidify the bonds that unite the team. Since agendas for team meetings reflect these concerns, an examination of what is discussed there should be instructive. One team had the following agenda for some of its meetings from the period October 11, 1978 through May 1, 1979:

October 11, 1978

Field trip plans
Media Center policies
Parent welcome letters
Team discipline issues

November 14, 1978

Bilingual childrens' needs
Speech problems
Summer school
Grading practices & particulars

November 28, 1978

Retention policies & particulars
Christmas plans

December 5, 1978

Duty stations
Team honor roll
Assemblies
Progress reports
Locker check for books
Coffee sharing

December 12, 1978

Use of machines
Budget allocation
Team population enrollment
Eighth-grade test scores

January 4, 1979

Schedules for new students
Parent conference plans
Involvement in Folk Arts Program

Library books due
Teacher inservice workshop
Time out room

February 20, 1979

Plans for desegregation workshop
Promotion and retention decisions
Hospitality
Reality Therapy Pilot Program

February 22, 1979

Discussion of our goals; professionalism
Schoolwide policies for new kids
Postschool planning
Intramural playoff plans

February 27, 1979

MAT testing
Year end field trips
Possible early dismissal
Title I problems

March 15, 1979

Sex education plans
Fifth-grade orientation
Withdrawal forms

April 3, 1979

Schedule for last 3 school days
Social Committee

April 19, 1979

Field trips plans

April 26, 1979

Counselor input
Special media center unit
Honor roll kids

May 1, 1979

Special assembly plans
Money collection
Teachers appreciation week
Eighth-grade testing

At Nock Middle School, Newburyport, Massachusetts, teams are provided with a set of guidelines for their meetings:

The time set aside for team planning each day should be used for that purpose. The meeting itself should take precedence over individual pursuits during that time.

1. *Team members will assume the responsibility of designating a team leader. This could be done on a rotating basis.*
2. *Team leaders will organize and conduct the team meetings.*
3. *Teachers might use planning time to explain and show what work they have planned for their classes for the purpose of planning interdisciplinary activities.*
4. *Suggested topics for discussions:*
   a. *schedules and procedures*
   b. *youngsters with particular problems; what can be done to solve them*
   c. *re-grouping of students for teaching particular skills and concepts*
   d. *evaluation of learning*
   e. *making curriculum more appropriate*
   f. *efforts to individualize teaching and learning*

g. planning interdisciplinary ventures
h. parent conferences
5. The House Coordinator will take part in team meetings on a regular basis.

No middle school has been more specific in its detailing of the duties of team members than Olle Middle School, Alief, Texas. The agenda of team activities (Table 5.1) for the entire school year is introduced as follows:

Horizontal Team Calendar

The suggested list of activities pertinent to team teaching are provided to give structure, continuity, and meaningfulness to our team meetings. While the list may seem formidable, it is in no way exhaustive.

This calendar, under the leadership and direction of the team captain is to be used as a guide and as a checklist. Actually circle each activity which you have accomplished according to the given suggestions during each of the report periods.

It is also recommended that some flexibility be maintained regarding your involvement with each activity during the marking periods. Do not hesitate to alter the sequence or extension of these activities or to suggest additions or deletions to this list.

The Team Leader

In some middle schools team leaders are formally identified, and in others no formal leader is designated. The authors estimate that formally designated team leaders are present in about twice as many cases. No school is known to offer both alternatives. Schools featuring team leaders seem to depend strongly upon them; those without formal team leaders are often equally adamant about the reasons why that way is best.

Valley Middle School, Rosemount, Minnesota; Twin Peaks Middle School, Poway, California; Stoughton Middle School, Stoughton, Wisconsin; and Louisville Middle School, Louisville, Colorado are four exemplary middle schools that use a formal approach to team leadership. Each has a clearly written definition of the duties of team leader. Combining and editing the four lists yields a definition of a team leader's duties that reads like this:

1. Function as the liaison between the administration and the team; individual teachers are encouraged, however, to keep open communication lines with the principal, avoiding any unnecessary hierarchical elevation of the team leader to something in-between teacher and administrator.
2. Program coordination within the team: this is, of course, a task of consuming proportions, including a role in every activity of the team as described above. Together, items one and two here comprise a majority of the responsibilities of the typical team leader.

Other more specific activities of the team leader spelled out in school materials, some of which fall within the scope of the first two above, include:

3. Coordinating between his or her team and other teams and teachers
4. Serving on and appointing team members to various committees

Table 5.1 / Horizontal Team Activities*

1	2	3	QUARTERS
X			1. Select team captain, recorder, secretary and contact person.
X			2. Schedule students for English, social studies, math and science.
X			3. Team members review student orientation manual or handbook for new teachers on team prior to their use of the sequential material.
X			4. Obtain a schedule card for each section taught, and retain them in your classroom for your convenience in locating students.
X			5. Exchange copies of text books with other team members for teacher and student use in classroom discussions and correlating units of instruction.
X	X	X	6. Prior to conferences check file for "Team Conference Cards" for information obtained from student and parental interviews in the past.
X			7. Develop a technique for phoning parents, greeting them when they arrive, opening and closing the conference. Refer to teachers' manual on hints for conducting a conference. Get to the point early and remember that information is held in strict confidence.
X			8. In addition to formal orientation program for sixth graders and new students, develop a thorough explanation of academic policies and procedures in each classroom.
X			9. Distribute and explain the student handbook.
X			10. Check to find whether cumulative record folders are up-to-date and available for each pupil.
X	X	X	11. Disseminate information about children with special problems to teachers who are not familiar with these problems and who now teach these children.
X	X	X	12. Review the statistical data provided for each child in your team. Make full use of anecdotal records in folders.
X	X	X	13. Acquaint yourself with all sixth grade pupils to see whether they are adjusting to middle school. Help other teachers to understand pupils' backgrounds, abilities and achievement. Let the students know that you are going to be interested in them, in the results of their tests, in their work habits, and in their overall academic and social progress.
X			14. Homeroom teachers should schedule individual conference with each student.
X	X	X	15. Initiate a card file for all conferences (parent and student) giving sufficient information on results.
X			16. Prepare for PTO open house meeting.
X	X	X	17. Meet with the librarian and become familiar with her services as a curriculum resource person. Brief her on your courses of study, needs and expectations as the year progresses.
X	X	X	18. Review the district M.B.O.'s and make preparations to meet the guidelines as stated.
X	X	X	19. When necessary, throughout the year discuss the merits of each student for resectioning purposes.
X	X	X	20. Throughout the year refer students who need individual counseling to guidance. Make referrals after the team has briefed the counselor on the need for such counsel.

(continued)

Table 5.1 / Horizontal Team Activities* (continued)

1	2	3	QUARTERS
X	X	X	21. Complete report cards.
X			22. Explain the reporting system to pupils.
X	X	X	23. Throughout the year acquaint nonteam teachers of areas covered by your team in classroom work.
X	X	X	24. Throughout the year check on transcripts of all new children for grades and other information. Designate one member to do this.
X	X	X	25. Coordinate the testing schedule so that pupils are not burdened with too many tests at one time.
X	X	X	26. Discuss the academic standards that will constitute achievement grades for each ability level. Try to arrive at some commonality within the team so that a particular grade has the same value of standards with each teacher.
X			27. Review guidance and discipline procedures in teachers' manual.
X	X	X	28. Review each pupil's disciplinary record and plan positive approaches to rectify this condition.
X	X	X	29. Compile lists of students not achieving at a reasonable level. Begin to confer with these students.
X	X	X	30. Prepare a list of those students who are having difficulties because of physical, social and emotional immaturity. Enlist the help of their teachers, and plan a program of counseling these students in conjunction with the guidance department. That these factors are passively understood is not sufficient. A planned program should be initiated.
X	X	X	31. Contact parents of children having academic, social or emotional difficulties for conferences with the team. Certify that the number of conferences required by M.B.O. has been met each quarter.
X	X	X	32. Confer with the art, music, industrial art and home economics teachers on correlating instruction in certain areas.
X	X	X	33. Exchange courses of study within the team to enable teachers to become familiar with the content of other subject areas. Give explanations to other team members.
X	X	X	34. Interview new students when they arrive.
X	X	X	35. Plan carefully for any large group-small group teaching and team or grade level assembly programs.
X	X	X	36. Distribute homework evenly.
X	X	X	37. Read and discuss current professional publications available in the media center.
X	X	X	38. Review grade distribution.
X	X	X	39. Prepare student progress reports.
X	X	X	40. Check with attendance office on reasons for excessive absenteeism. Enlist the aid of the office as patterns develop.
X	X	X	41. Confer with the Administration as trends in disciplinary incidents develop. Identify offenders and counsel them, or make referrals to the Guidance Department and Administration.
	X		42. Check your inventory and bulletins on future enrollment, and begin planning for preliminary budget considerations.
X	X	X	43. Continue to arrange parent conferences. Begin to conduct follow-up conferences when desirable. (Telephone, letter, note, personal, meeting, and so on.)

Table 5.1 / Horizontal Team Activities* (continued)

1	2	3	QUARTERS
X	X	X	44. Explore the opportunities for joint team participation in testing, group teaching, audio-visual work, and so on.
X	X	X	45. Maintain close contact with children who have been resectioned. Aid them in their adjustments to the new group.
X	X	X	46. Team check on progress of students in Physical Education, Practical Arts, Art and Music.
	X		47. Counsel those students who are failing through the first quarter. Inform them of the dangers of nonpromotion and plan a course of action for successful achievement.
X	X	X	48. Check the condition of all textbooks. Notify students that they are responsible for materials issued and must pay for all damaged and lost books.
	X	X	49. Continue to conduct parent conferences. Encourage parents of well-adjusted, talented students to come in for a conference.
		X	50. Make final check to see that all transcripts on new students have been received.
		X	51. Submit a list of failures to the Principal. A notification of each student's status will be given to the parent.
		X	52. Organize team minutes in final form for the Principal.
		X	53. Complete report cards, cumulative folders, and other closing-of-school tasks.
		X	54. Begin final work on cumulative folders early in marking period.
		X	55. Review student orientation for next year.
		X	56. Check for lost and damaged books.
		X	57. Adhere carefully to the schedule of responsibility in the closing-of-school bulletin.
		X	58. Review with team personnel procedures for determining condition of textbooks and assessments for lost, damaged or misused books.

* From Olle Middle School, Alief, Texas. Columns 1, 2, 3 refer to marking periods.

5. Scheduling and directing the utilization of team-wide criterion-referenced testing
6. Preparing the team budget and requisitions, supplies, textbooks, workbooks, films and equipment
7. Familiarizing new teachers and substitute teachers with school programs and other pertinent information
8. Responsibility for the development of new approaches from within the team by coordinating new schoolwide programs, soliciting creative ideas from other members and actively contributing suggestions for new team programs
9. Scheduling and conducting team meetings
10. Assisting in the selection of new team personnel
11. Directing aides assigned to the team
12. Identifying and encouraging the use, for the team, of other school and district personnel
13. Assisting in organizing volunteer and community resource activities
14. Coordinating reporting procedures and parent-teacher conferences

15. Promoting good home-school relationships
16. Assisting (in some schools) in a positive program of supervision of team personnel
17. Attempting to develop and maintain a high level of morale among team members
18. Facilitating communication between team members
19. Assuming responsibility for equipment, for instructional materials and for their care and distribution
20. Assuming responsibility for the supervision of the work of student teachers
21. Recognizing and encouraging professional growth and initiative on the part of team members
22. Serving as a first recourse for team members who encounter classroom problems
23. Keeping abreast of trends and innovations in curriculum and instruction, and making recommendations to team members and principal and other staff

Chapter 9 gives further consideration to leadership roles in the middle school, including that of team leader.

Purposes and Possibilities of the Interdisciplinary Team Organization

Advantages: Instructional

Now that the interdisciplinary team organization has been defined, an acceptable range of alternatives elaborated, roles and responsibilities delineated, and a number of examples shared, it should be more meaningful to discuss what might be called the rationale for this method of organizing faculty for instruction. The advantages of the interdisciplinary team organization, cited by teachers and administrators of exemplary middle schools, fall into several categories.

Many advantages of interdisciplinary team organization are claimed for the area of instruction, all of which emanate primarily from the combined knowledge, talents and abilities of the team members. One such advantage lies in the team's comprehensive knowledge of student needs, and the power this knowledge provides for educational planning of all kinds. Another is the increased intellectual stimulation for teachers which results from the interaction of people with different academic perspectives and professional points of view. Certainly teachers who develop trust in each other will learn new methods from one another, and this is particularly so in regard to the use of the team in the introduction and orientation of faculty new to the school or to the profession. Particularly in open space schools, but not exclusively so, teacher-teacher interaction often leads to a knowledge of each other's teaching styles that produces improvement among less able or less enthusiastic teachers, or permits the more able teachers on the team to plan team operations in a way that minimizes the damage that might be done by the less skillful teacher. It is also true that teachers learn from working so closely together that even the most skillful and highly motivated teachers undergo periods of greater and lesser crises and stress, and the team organization permits colleagues to support each other with extra efforts during these periods.

Other instructional advantages of the interdisciplinary team organization deal with the group's ability to plan and evaluate the instructional program. The superiority of group problem-solving efforts and greater integration of the curriculum, even in the absence of actual team teaching, seem to be sufficient reason in themselves for the commitment to the interdisciplinary team organization. A more extensive evaluation of course content may also emerge from the interdisciplinary situation, encouraging, as it does, a variety of perspectives. The territoriality sometimes associated with the departmental structure finds little sustenance in the interdisciplinary team organization, and this lack of territoriality, in turn, is more likely to develop better coordination of the curriculum within and across grade levels. Teachers and administrators from exemplary middle schools remark about how dramatically the topics of discussion change, from the defense of a single subject and its place in the curriculum to a consideration of the students on the team and their varied curriculum needs, when teachers are organized in an interdisciplinary way rather than in departments. As might be expected, teachers talk about what they have in common, and when the teachers share the same students rather than the same academic discipline, the students are at the center of discussion and program planning.

Quite naturally, such a situation leads to a more balanced but comprehensive evaluation of individual student progress as well. Deficiencies a student may have in one area can become known to the total group almost immediately. Students experiencing difficulties in more than one academic area can be identified, diagnosed and prescribed for much more accurately and efficiently when, in an interdisciplinary team setting, teachers in all the academic areas are present for discussions.

The interdisciplinary team organization also fits well and works synergistically with other elements of the middle school program, helping each component function more smoothly than it would alone. Advisor-advisee programs function much more effectively when the advisees of a particular teacher have an opportunity to interact with that teacher in a class situation another time in the day. When an advisor works with the other teachers of each of his advisees his knowledge of those students grows in a different way, and the teacher can share with his colleagues pertinent information about a particular child that only he, as advisor, may initially know.

Multiage grouping and the interdisciplinary team organization fit together, since it is virtually impossible to consider the organization of teachers for instruction without being concerned with the process of organizing students for the same purpose. When combined, the two strategies produce a tightly knit learning community that has identity across several years as well as encompassing the various subjects, intensifying and compounding all of the other strengths of the interdisciplinary team organization.

Advantages: Affective and Behavioral

Teachers and administrators in exemplary middle schools refer much more frequently to the affective and behavioral potential of the interdisciplinary team organization, and identify at least as large a number of benefits in this area as in instruction. The majority of the references focus on some aspect of group processes.

Primary among the potentially positive group-oriented aspects of the interdisciplinary team organization is the contribution it seems to make to the development of what might be called a sense of community, with some models of the process going so far as to refer to teams as ''learning communities.'' With dozens of scholars and quasi-scholars decrying the loss of this phenomenon in the larger society, the middle school, through the interdisciplinary team organization, does indeed attempt to move in the opposite direction.

Desmond Morris, author of *The Naked Ape,* has written of the agony produced in humans, essentially still tribal beings, by a modern society in which we are confronted by thousands of strangers masquerading as members of our tribe.[4] Anonymity, amorphousness and anomie seem to characterize contemporary society, and because the schools are in many ways a mirror of the society, these maladies infect the school as well.

The interdisciplinary team organization exercises an ameliorating effect on the degree to which these forces affect the middle school. Such organization has this effect first by limiting the number of people each student must learn with or from. Instead of an amphorphous group of 1500 students and as many as a dozen teachers to get to know, the exemplary middle school is designed in a way that permits students to be members of a team of 150 or less, often with a maximum of six teachers. The dimensions of the group that students must deal with are reduced dramatically, ninefold in this example. The team of students moves together, in various combinations, throughout most of the day. Further, the group spends most of the time in the same part of the building. As a consequence, both numbers and movements of students are reduced to appropriate levels, comfortably between the exclusivity of the self-contained classroom and departmentalized anonymity.

When advisor-advisee programs and multiage grouping are combined with the interdisciplinary team organization, the result is repeated face-to-face interactions between and among the same teachers and students during the day, in several contexts, and over a period of several years. Identity of person, place and time becomes possible. A student knows that he is a member of a specific team, even a specific advisory group; and these structures have dimensions that early adolescents can manage.

In a similar way the interdisciplinary team organization helps the middle school achieve a precarious but precious balance among the demands for a specialized, enriched curriculum and the need for in-depth, enriched interpersonal knowledge among the teachers and students involved in the process of schooling. School size has been a perennial problem of American education. The burden of large schools has, in recent years, been a terrifying anonymity. This has been contrasted with the blessing of size: an economy of scale permitting a stimulating and exciting range of course offerings sufficient to involve the most able students and support the least able. The challenge to the middle school is to develop an exciting array of curriculum plans within a context of schooling where students are known as persons and a sense of community exists.

The junior high school emerged, originally, as at attempt to satisfy those two goals: a richer curriculum than the elementary school was able to offer, and a more personal atmosphere than the high school was able to develop, although it might be argued that the junior high school has failed to achieve the second. Educators in the middle school seem aware of the need to accomplish both. The interdisciplinary team organization can be the answer.

This sense of community can extend beyond the school, involving parents in new and different ways. The interdisciplinary team organization permits the middle school staff to assemble and present knowledge about students to parents in a comprehensive and efficient manner. Parent-teacher conferences take on a wholly different character when they become parent-team conferences, a situation in which a lack of information, leading to misunderstanding, is rare. As time passes, parents begin to realize that students rather than subjects come first with teachers and, often, a new spirit of cooperation and understanding develops.

Cooperation and understanding are not restricted to relationships with parents. It seems clear that the interdisciplinary team organization develops an "esprit de corps" among teachers and the team as well. Teachers on teams evidence a higher morale, report greater job satisfaction, and go on to seek higher levels of professional responsibility than do teachers who work alone.[5] In the last decade, few teachers involved in interdisciplinary team organization have chosen to return to the self-contained classroom or the departmental structure; and an amazingly few schools, having experienced teaming, depart from it.

At the very time this portion of this chapter was being written, one of the authors sat in on a team meeting at a nearby middle school where he was on temporary assignment. The meeting was begun by the team leader, proudly, reading a letter that she had just received from a parent. It capsulizes the above discussion well:

Dear "M" Team,

Just wanted to let you all know how much I appreciate your efforts with Barry. His attitude towards learning is changing and I really believe it is due to your attitude toward teaching. Barry said "This is the best team I have ever been on; they don't just care about me, but they are friends with each other." I think this statement sums up what team teaching should be.

Lucky will be the students that get on "M" Team next year.

Sincerely,
Delores Evans

Educators frequently report that the interdisciplinary team organization generally leads to an improved standard of student behavior. Certainly, the reduction in sense of individual anonymity and group amorphousness, with the consequent development of an increased sense of identity for students is a significant factor in improved student behavior.

Other educators point out that the interdisciplinary team organization, as opposed to the department, cuts back drastically on the amount of movement of students back and forth from one area of the building to the other. Since students remain in the same general area during their study of all four of the basic academic subjects, time and distance involved in movement are reduced by about half. Students have less time to encounter problems in the halls and they do not often find themselves in parts of the building where they are unfamiliar to teachers.

The cohesiveness of the teachers on the team also encourages the development of a degree of consensus about student behavior which leads to a more rational, well-planned and consistent set of rules for students on the team. This consistency itself, of course, makes even further behavior improvement likely. Too, team cohesiveness permits the development of a clearer and more complete picture of actual student behavior in response to rules than the solitary observations possible by teachers working alone.

The rule making and enforcement process so essential to good classroom and school discipline is firmly reinforced by the interdisciplinary team organization. Students are more likely to know that they are cared about and that they have an opportunity to succeed. They can, therefore, accept rules more readily. The teachers on the team can determine whether a particular rule is reasonable by their collective awareness of whether most students follow the rule, whether the best students follow it and whether the rule requires heavy enforcement to make it work.

The team teachers may also be able to model effective group behavior, encouraging imitation among the students. Early adolescents need to see adults working together cooperatively. If there is not interdisciplinary team organization in the school, young people may not witness collaborative relationships among adults at all. The team is also able, functioning as a learning community, to involve students in directly experiencing the group life, sharing in the decision-making process with teachers and their peers.

Such experience is, of course, only possible when the interdisciplinary team organization is functioning fully as a real learning community, and requires that the teachers have a measure of autonomy found only infrequently outside the interdisciplinary team organization. When school principals share power with teams, teams are free to share power among themselves and with the students on the team. A measure of professional autonomy is necessary to the success of the interdisciplinary team organization; and, interestingly, successful teams tend to produce even more autonomous behavior on the part of the teachers on the team. Teachers need to be given the opportunity to make some of the decisions about their team life, regarding the use of time, scheduling of students, distribution and use of funds and a number of other issues. Working together, they can and will make these decisions and carry out such tasks effectively.

Precautions

It would be a less than total exploration of the interdisciplinary team organization if there was no reference to the difficulties encountered by the staff of even exemplary middle schools as they attempt to establish workable interdisciplinary team organizations. That the same difficulties appear in almost every situation should make caution considerably more important. There are several conditions that are crucial to the success of the interdisciplinary team organization, regardless of the particular model followed. One team leader in an exemplary middle school identified the factors she believed to be basic to the existence of authentic interdisciplinary teams.[6] Balanced teacher and student populations, so that each team is a microcosm of the school, are crucial: teachers balanced according to complementing strengths, personal styles, instructional expertise and experience, as well as race, sex and age; students balanced according to sex, achievement, race, exceptionalities and age. Schools that have severely imbalanced teams in terms of the student membership will be likely to find the situation difficult to manage.

Other basics include the need for physical identity, having the members of the team housed in adjacent or nearly adjacent classroom areas. In this way each team has a separate and distinct territory. Without this closeness teams may function only minimally. Another aspect of the physical space needs has to do with the team planning room. Most advocates of the interdisciplinary team organization see the planning room as essential to effective planning, to the storing of materials and for the maintenance of personal relationships.

In addition to place, time together is essential. Some time each week must be designated as team time, allowing regular team meetings and planning sessions to occur. Interdisciplinary team organization does take more teacher time, since teachers require the same amount of time for their individual efforts and additional time for whatever team activities require. Little wonder that early attempts at teaming were frequently disappointing, since team members were expected to teach together as well as work on teams together; the two were seen as synonymous, when, in fact, they are not. Teams that are asked to produce exciting thematic units or integrated lessons all day, every day, require at least 50 percent more planning time than teams which do not focus on actual team teaching. Fortunately, many of the benefits of team organization can be had without team teaching.

In addition to time, as mentioned earlier, teams need autonomy to function well. Given the opportunity, teams can and will assist the school principal with scheduling, budgeting, curriculum, evaluation, long-range planning and dozens of other concerns vital to school progress. Administrators of exemplary middle schools find it essential to involve teams in participatory decision making.

Given balance, time, place and autonomy most teams move forward. Without the proper skills and attitudes, however, forward movement will be minimal. The interdisciplinary team organization requires skills that are slightly different and considerably more sophisticated than those required by nonteaming teachers: planning skills and communication skills. Teachers who do not know how to plan as a group will not do so. Teachers whose interpersonal communication skills are minimal will find their team functioning at a minimal level. Any group that is together regularly and intensely, as in an interdisciplinary team organization, soon discovers that it must devote almost as much time and effort to the interpersonal side of the process as it does to the more work-oriented tasks. This effort requires extra amounts of cooperative spirit and creativity. In attempting to answer the question ''What really makes a team work?'' Doda added four central ingredients: (1) total team spirit, fostered by regular spirit-building activities like projects, field trips, honor rolls and special gatherings; (2) constant and effective team communication and conferences between and among teachers, students, parents and administrators; (3) a team approach to discipline; and (4) when possible, a measure of totally teamed instruction.[7]

The teacher handbook of West Middle School, Aurora, Colorado, deals with team functions and describes the keys to success as:

1. *These are our students—not my students.*
2. *There are many ways and not just my way.*
3. *There are goals to achieve and plans to implement the goals, including long range as well as short range plans and goals.*
4. *The team must evaluate what happened last week before planning for next week.*
5. *The team must be willing to change a plan if it appears to be going wrong.*
6. *Team members should remember that disagreements are normal, but can and should be resolved.*

At Olle Middle School, Alief, Texas, the teachers' handbook includes the following keys to successful interdisciplinary team teaching:

1. *A tactful honesty and a willingness to work and plan together on an idea*
2. *A utilization of the differences, as well as the similarities, among team members*
3. *The ability to accept and recognize failure and a desire to try again*
4. *The realization on each teacher's part that his or her subject is of no more or less importance than the other subjects*
5. *A recognition of new and better avenues to a definite goal (Don't think ''subject matter,'' just . . . THINK!)*
6. *An awareness of how student interest can be employed in teaching the required curriculum*
7. *A knowledge that students recognize ''busy work'' and respect work pertinent to the topic*
8. *The realization that ability grouping may not be compatible with interdisciplinary team teaching*

9. *A flexibility among team members in individual scheduling to meet a particular student's needs*
10. *A knowledge that interdisciplinary thinking compliments individual instruction*
11. *An interest in (not necessarily an understanding of) the other academic subjects*
12. *A sensitivity to the feelings of the other team members; an elimination of petty and/or personal "gripes" that may interfere with the primary objective . . . interdisciplinary team-teaching!*
13. *The awareness that interdisciplinary topics may not include all four disciplines and may, in fact, encompass some electives*

Planning for an Interdisciplinary Team Organization in the New Middle School

Educators involved in or contemplating the move to an interdisciplinary team organization should look forward confidently to the outcome, given attention to several factors. Decisions need to be made regarding the size of teams, and teaching assignments of each member, and the place in the school where each team will be located. Teachers new to this process should be helped to see that they will not be required to make major changes in the type of teaching they have always done. Unless there is a considerable amount of staff development money and time available, and an excess of planning time, teachers ought not be expected to produce any significant amount of actual team teaching. The effort required to make the team organization work will be considerable, and the results of effective teams reward enough. When provided with some tutoring in conducting team meetings and in the process of scheduling their own students, most teams will function quite smoothly, provided the interpersonal mix is right and the communication skills are what they should be. Combine this with a proper location and a comfortable division of teaching responsibilities and things should operate without major problems.

ADDITIONAL SUGGESTIONS FOR FURTHER STUDY

A. Books
McCarthy, Robert J., *How to Organize and Operate an Ungraded Middle School.* Englewood Cliffs, New Jersey: Prentice-Hall, Inc., 1967.
Pumerantz, Philip, and Galano, Ralph. *Establishing Interdisciplinary Programs in Middle Schools.* West Nyack, New York: Parker Publishing Company, 1972.

B. Periodicals
Baker, John A., "Interdisciplinary, Grade-Level Teams: from Jargon to Reality," *Middle School Journal,* 7, 10–1 (March 1976).
DiVirgilio, James, "Guidelines for Effective Interdisciplinary Teams," *Clearing House,* 47, 209–11 (December 1972).

Garner, Arthur E., "Interdisciplinary Team Teaching—Is Your Middle School Ready?" *NASSP Bulletin,* 60, 93–102 (November 1976).

Gerthy, Earl and Others, "An Exploratory Team Approach to Fine and Practical Arts," *Middle School Journal,* 8, 14–5 (August 1977).

Herman, Stanley J., "Middle School Interdisciplinary Teaming and Reinforcement Systems," *Middle School Journal,* 5, 33–6 (Fall 1974).

Levy, Richard D., "Of Mice and Men: An Interdisciplinary Unit," *Middle School Journal,* 5, 43–4, 48 (Fall 1974).

Swick, Kevin J. and Others, "Considerations and Techniques for Team Planning," *Middle School Journal,* 7, 10–1 (June 1976).

Tyrrell, Ronald W., "The Open Middle School: A Model For Change," *NASSP Bulletin,* 58, 62–6 (April 1974).

Waltz, Thomas T., "Exploratory Teaming: An Interdisciplinary Approach to the Fine and Practical Arts," *Middle School Journal,* 7, 18–9 (June 1976).

C. Dissertations and Dissertation Abstracts

Chaemehaeng, Chantavit, "A Comparative Study of the School Climate as Perceived by Team Members and Non-Team Members in Selected Middle Schools in Michigan," *Dissertation Abstracts,* 39 (July 1978) 38–A.

Fuller, Helen Simmons, "Success Indicators of Interdisciplinary Teaming at the Middle School Level," *Dissertation Abstracts,* 39 (July 1978) 170–A.

Kerfut, Andrew Charles, "An Analysis of a Middle School Interdisciplinary Team Teaching Program," *Dissertation Abstracts,* 38 (April 1978) 5825–A.

Marsh, Martha Elizabeth, "Academic Achievement and School-Wide Grouping of Students in Two Middle Schools," Unpublished doctoral dissertation, the University of Florida, 1980.

Stein, Paula Judith, "A Participant Observer Study of Team Teaching Planning Behavior in a Middle School Setting," *Dissertation Abstracts,* 39 (April 1979) 5920–A.

FOOTNOTES

1. Judson T. Shaplin and Henry Olds, Jr. (eds), *Team Teaching* (New York: Harper & Row, 1964) p. 15.

2. For information on IGE, write to the Institute for the Development of Educational Activities, Suite 300, 5335 Far Hills Avenue, Dayton, Ohio 45429.

3. From correspondence between the authors and Virginia Childs, Lincoln Middle School, Gainesville, Florida, March 4, 1980.

4. Desmond Morris, *The Naked Ape* (New York: Dell Publishing Co., Inc., 1969).

5. Paul S. George, *Ten Years of Open Space Schools: A Review of The Research* (Gainesville, Florida: The Florida Educational Research and Development Council, Spring, 1975), pp. 10–20.

6. Nancy Doda, "Teacher to Teacher," *Middle School Journal,* 8, 8–9 (August 1977).

7. Doda, p. 9

Chapter 6

Alternative Methods of Student Grouping

Perhaps more than any other aspect of the exemplary middle school, strategies for grouping students are or should be strongly influenced by the characteristics of the learner. Variability and dissimilarity among students in the middle school, the central developmental features of this group of learners, require schools attempting to implement a unique but transitional educational program to consider a variety of alternative methods of student grouping. The special nature of the transescent is recognized most clearly by educators attempting to design ways of grouping students which accommodate this age group.

Organizing Students for Instruction

Developmentally, students in the primary grades are strikingly similar. Most students in the first three or four grades will be at or below the stage of concrete mental operations in Piagetian terms. Most, if not all, will be sexually immature, not having experienced puberty. Few will have had to deal with the consequences of the early adolescent growth spurt. These elementary school pupils are children, in that they respond to peers, and to parents and other adults, in ways which do not yet reflect the changes they will experience as early adolescents. Mentally, sexually, physically, emotionally, socially, they are developmentally similar.

When chronological age is a reliable guide to the characteristics of the learners, as is the case in the primary grades, it is reasonable to have students grouped for instruction in a manner which reflects this. If six-year-olds are almost all alike, developmentally, it makes good sense to group them in a way that capitalizes on this similarity. Chronological age-graded grouping in the elementary school years appears to have considerable validity, particularly in the earliest years. Of course, flexibility is important even here.

It is also true that, during the primary school years, similarity in academic achievement is at the highest level it will ever be. That is, during the first few years of school, students are more homogeneous in what they have achieved scholastically, than during any later period of school. Academically, as well as developmentally, relative similarity is the rule, so grouping students chronologically, by grades according to age, seems acceptable. Acceptable or not, this is the common practice.

At the high school, the developmental and academic characteristics of the learners also suggest strategies for grouping for instruction. High school students are returning to a position of developmental similarity, one to another, that parallels the situation in the elementary school. Many high school students have matured mentally, one hopes, to the stage of formal operations described by Piaget. Puberty has been negotiated. Physical size and strength reflect the experience of the growth spurt during early adolescence. Much of the stereotypical turmoil of the social and emotional changes is past. Developmentally, high school students are reentering a position of considerable similarity.

Academically, however, the situation is quite different. By the high school years, the students have reached a point where differences in academic achievement levels and areas of interest are at a maximum. As each year has passed, the differences have become more marked. Consequently, strategies for grouping students for instruction in high school reflect this developmental and academic situation.

Since variability among students is quite low developmentally, and quite high academically, the typical high school has responded by grouping students according to their interests in and their achievement of academic goals. Students, historically, select one of three subject matter pathways: general, academic college preparatory or vocational. Students choose courses (for example world history) with little regard to grade level, and it is common to find students from several ages and grade levels in a particular class. Grouping is accomplished primarily by the student's choice of or ability in a particular subject or group of subjects.

The exemplary middle school, too, attempts to group students for instruction in a way that accommodates the special characteristics of the students it serves, but the situation is different in several ways. First, middle school students are dramatically different from both elementary school and high school students when development is considered. Similarity has been replaced by great variability. Middle school students seem to have little in common with each other developmentally, except that they have so little in common. Rapid, pervasive, powerful, unpredictable, personal change is the rule, so much so that it is almost impossible, for example, to describe typical thirteen-year-olds. They may be mature mentally; they may not be. They may have passed through puberty; they may have not yet begun. They may be six feet tall, or four. They may still act like children, they may often seem like adults, or they may range unpredictably from one end of the continuum to the other. Developmentally, students in the middle grades are often described as more dissimilar than they have been or will be at any other period of their lives. Chronological age is frequently not a reliable guide to identify the characteristics of such students, and, hence, not the only guide to grouping such students for instruction.

Academically, middle school students seem far more variable than their elementary school counterparts but less than they will be as high school students. Major changes in achievement and interests may yet reveal themselves, so that grouping these students according to subject matter choices, as will be the case when they reach high school, is likely to be somewhat arbitrary, capricious and against the best interests of the students involved.

If chronological age grouping and subject matter choices are not always totally effective means of grouping middle school students for instruction, are there methods which do more closely consider the characteristics of the students? Do exemplary middle schools often choose an alternative route? If, in fact, the middle school is unique in its attempt to focus on the special characteristics of the learners within, are there some methods which are more likely to be congruent with those characteristics? As the middle school aims at a program that is different from that of the elementary school and the high school but leads smoothly in transition from one to the other, there must be a "middle way" with grouping, too.

A Grouping Continuum

Organizing students for instruction can be thought of in terms of a continuum moving from the most complete age-grade arrangement at one end, to a situation permitting almost total disregard for age or grade of the student at the opposite end. Figure 6.1 illustrates such a continuum.

On one end all students are bound together by the criteria of age, grade and group. At this end of the continuum no student may move more flexibly than these three constraints permit. Students learn with other students of the same age. They study the curriculum designed for the grade level they are placed on, and they move as a unit of students to the next grade level. Teachers in this situation are almost always specialists in one subject at a particular grade level. They do not move with the students, so that while the students may be perceived as a group, the teachers are only temporarily identified with those students. Such an arrangement, while inveighed against by one reformer and innovator after another, remains the norm. The age-

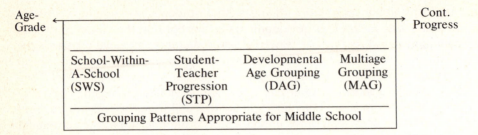

Figure 6.1 / A Grouping Continuum.

graded group arrangement prevails, perhaps, not because it is traditional (only a century old) but because it is thought to be efficient and economical.[1]

At the other end of the grouping continuum is the situation best identified as the continuous progress plan. Having been popularized under other (more confusing) labels such as "nongraded" or "ungraded" programs, continuous progress is the antithesis of age-graded grouping. Here the student is not bound by any of the three criteria: they may learn with other students of widely varying ages, study a curriculum uniquely prescribed for them, and move forward at a completely individual rate. Such a plan would radically rearrange the grouping of students, compared to its opposite, resulting in the most tentative, flexible and temporary groupings possible. It is essentially a nongroup strategy. While extremely popular in theory, it is essentially nonexistent in operational middle schools known to the authors, exemplary or otherwise.

Perhaps three quarters of the middle schools in America can be described as utilizing a standard chronological age-graded student grouping system, and in many cases such grouping is not totally rigid or completely contrary to the best interests of the students. Further, it is possible, in the authors' opinion, to have a healthy, productive middle school with such a grouping strategy. It is, however, the position of the authors that the most fully functioning, exemplary, middle schools choose from several strategies for grouping students, strategies which comfortably avoid either of the two extremes of the grouping continuum. The remainder of this chapter deals primarily with these alternatives; how they appear in schools, and why they are preferable to either age-graded or nongroup continuous progress plans.

Definitions

Many concepts employed in middle school education, and terms used to describe them, lack clarity and explicitness. Terms and phrases are used in so many different ways that communication becomes difficult, and the area of student grouping seems particularly vulnerable. During the next portion of this chapter the discussion will *not* focus on ability grouping or tracking, nor will dealing with special education students be the primary concern. Main-streaming, as an outgrowth of Public Law 94–142, is treated fully in a later section of this chapter. At this point, the problem of general school-wide student grouping is central. The following terms and definitions are important to understanding the discussion:

Chronological age-grade grouping. Organizing students for instruction on the basis of their age and the number of years they have been in school. Most thirteen-year-old students will, for example, be in the seventh grade and the curriculum will be designed for students who have, ostensibly, mastered the curricular requirements of the first six grades. Movement from one grade to another is almost always annual.

Nongraded and ungraded. Two confusing terms which sometimes seem to imply the opportunity for continuous progress learning by individual students unfettered by chronological age-grade levels. At other times the terms are used to apply to the marking and reporting of student academic progress, as in situations where instead of letter grades (A, B, C and so forth), students and parents receive anecdotal reports or learn about student progress through parent and student conferences. The confusion surrounding both of these terms is such that they are best forgotten. Hence, we try to avoid their use in this volume.

School-Within-A-School. An organization which creates a microcosm of the total school in each relatively separate area of the school. A school having grades 5 through 8, for example, might have four "houses" each containing four teams: one fifth-, one sixth-, one seventh- and one eighth-grade team. Students remain in the same house for four years, or as long as they are in the school. Teachers are frequently responsible for teaching one subject at one grade level, although they may occasionally be found teaching more than one grade level.

Student-Teacher-Progress Plan. A school where teams of teachers and students remain together for the entire period the students are in the school. In a middle school containing grades 6 through 8, for example, the teachers and students become a unit in the sixth grade, then stay together through the seventh and eighth grades. Such a program is rare.

Developmental Age Grouping. Students are grouped according to the developmental characteristics they exhibit rather than their age. Three groups are usually designed: older children, pubescents and adolescents. Students may move from one group to another individually during the year, and all students will be reevaluated for grouping at the beginning of each academic year.

Multiage Grouping. Developmental and age characteristics are set aside, as each team of students is designed as a microcosm of the school. Teams represent the total school population in so far as age, sex, race, achievement and other factors are concerned. Each year approximately one third or one fourth of the students move on and are replaced by new students. In a school with grades 5 through 8, for example, the eighth graders would leave the team, and the school, for the high school, and the team would receive a new group of fifth graders.

Continuous Progress. Students learn with small temporary groups not based on age or grade level. They study, at their own paces, a curriculum program designed to fit them. Progress is individual, with movement from one objective to another, or from one grade level to another determined by individual success. Essentially a nongroup strategy.

Alternative Methods of Grouping Middle School Students

Chronological Age Grouping

Of the 5000 or so middle schools in the United States, an overwhelming majority utilize chronological age-grade grouping. Often the administration and faculty of a school will state a preference for an alternative to the traditional process but assert that the conservative nature of their community makes adoption of the alternative impossible. Whether or not there are other more important reasons for the persistence of chronological age-grade grouping, persist it does. Most living Americans have experienced it as students, and most educators have worked with it as the predominant mode of grouping in schools where they are employed.

There is little need to detail the advantages and disadvantages of chronological age-grade grouping. They are well known. Nor is there any compelling reason to illustrate the practice with examples of real schools, since in almost every instance, there is a multitude of examples near at hand. Chronological age-grade grouping, while declining in popularity, is likely to remain a standard method for the foreseeable future, for several reasons. Traditional practice appears even more economical or efficient by comparison, primarily, because the alternatives are so new that they are still accompanied by difficulties which take time to work out. A second reason for the prolonged popularity of the traditional approach is that it is what we all experienced as students and, thus, are comfortable with it. The remainder of this chapter will, therefore, focus on alternatives to traditional practices of grouping students according to their age and the number of years they have spent in school.

In their use of alternative methods of grouping middle school students, exemplary middle schools attempt to find an effective balance between flexibility in responding to individual student needs and benefits of structured group learning situations. In the continuum in Figure 6.1, movement toward the right indicates an emphasis on more flexible approaches emphasizing individual student progress, ultimately arriving at the continuous progress design. Movement from the right toward the center attempts to maintain some elements of the flexible response to students, while emphasizing increasing increments of structured group learning. Our analysis of exemplary middle school grouping programs will begin toward the left of the continuum, with the school-within-a-school program.

School-Within-A-School Grouping

The School-Within-A-School (SWS) approaching to grouping students, as defined here, usually retains the basic format of chronological age-grade grouping, but adds a significant organizational modification. In the SWS approach each school is divided into "houses" or subschools which are representative of the larger school. A number of exemplary middle schools utilize this method of grouping students for instruction, and several objectives are cited by the staffs of schools using a SWS approach.

This grouping strategy, says the staff of Brookhaven Middle School, Decatur, Alabama, in one of their school publications, responds to the concern for the students' sense of identity by designing the school in a way that allows the student to relate to a relatively small component of the total school. Security is fostered, and a spirit of loyalty and pride is developed in a situation small enough for middle students. As one eighth grader at Brookhaven said, "I feel more loyal to Winter House than I am to the school."

The SWS approach, according to the staff at Farnsworth Middle School, Guilderland, New York, is "an attempt at harmonizing the best of both worlds—one of which is small enough to foster a feeling of concern for the individual student, and one which is large enough to offer the varied resources necessary to meet the needs and interests of pre-adolescent and early adolescent youngsters."

The administrative staff at Nock Middle School, Newburyport, Massachusetts, expressed this important concept of balance well. This explanation must have been communicated clearly to the students at Nock. In "Middle Unmuddle," the student handbook, student writers explained the school-within-a-school concept at length; concluding that it was designed "so that we students don't get 'lost' in such a large school."

HOUSE, SWEET HOUSE

The Middle School is divided into thirds. These divisions are referred to as the Red, White and Blue Houses.

Each house is to some degree a "school-within-a-school" and every effort has been made to give each house an identity so that we students don't get "lost" in such a large school.

The head of each house is the House Coordinator who is, in affect, the "principal" of a school-within-a-school.

In each house there are four teams of teachers. Each team of teachers works together to teach us all of our subjects. Sometimes we may have only one teacher in a class; at other times there may be several.

Each of us is assigned to a certain house and within that house we are assigned to a certain team of teachers. Our basic subjects (language arts, social studies, science and math) will be taught in a block of mods and then there will be other mods set aside for special subjects. This includes art, music, industrial arts, home economics, physical education, foreign languages, typing, guidance, skill centers, and the SPARK block. The team to which we are assigned will decide what our schedule will be for each day during the basic subject block.

Actually, the attempt by exemplary middle schools to balance size and program reflects one of the central dilemmas of American education for the last century. The American people have expressed a need for an enriched curriculum, for a comprehensive school program. This need has often come in conflict with the equally important need to design humane, personal institutions which provide satisfying interpersonal relationships and small group experiences. In the middle school the SWS approach is an attempt at a balanced answer to both of those needs.

The SWS approach also attempts to assist in the process of articulation on a K-12 basis. The SWS permits students to enter the middle school from an elementary school and, if necessary, experience an almost totally self-contained classroom atmosphere. In the ensuing years, within the same house, the student moves smoothly and steadily to a more advanced interdisciplinary milieu which will prepare students for the first years in high school. Having students spend their entire middle school experience in the same house permits the house faculty to design each student's learning experience personally. Several examples of excellent operational programs should help illustrate the SWS approach to grouping students.

At Stroudsburg Middle School, Stroudsburg, Pennsylvania, 1200 students are divided into two smaller houses, 600 students in each. Both Mountain and Lake Houses contain students in grades 5 through 8, and while attempts are made to develop the separate identities of each house, grade level associations are clearly maintained. This is done not only through locating each grade separately within each house, but by arranging the schedule so that, for example, eighth graders from both houses have the same basic schedule. Eighth graders appear on adjoining pages in the school memory book, arranged separately by house. Stroudsburg Middle School demonstrates an excellent balance between house identity and grade level unity.

At Nock Middle School, the house identity receives slightly more emphasis. Again, 1200 students in grades 5 through 8 are divided into smaller units; this time there are three houses (Red, White and Blue) of approximately 400 students each.

Each house has its own educational leader, team coordinator or house director who, while a master teacher, also assists in the guidance function. Each house is encouraged to develop a feeling of uniqueness, and the design of the school (with specially colored carpeting for each house, for example) invites this feeling. Oaklea Middle School, Junction City, Oregon, operates in much the same ways, identifying its houses by naming them each after a prominent river in Oregon.

Oak Park and Brookhaven Middle Schools, both in Decatur, Alabama, are strongly committed to the SWS approach in grouping. Here too, each of the three houses of both schools is appropriately named and color coded to assist in the sense of a house or subschool identity. Brookhaven Middle School chose the names Fall, Winter and Spring for its houses. Each house has its own student council, and since each house has its own counselor, students may develop a strong three-year long relationship with that person. Brookhaven Middle School faculty members are particularly pleased with the cross-age groupings which are facilitated by the SWS design. Such cross-age grouping will be discussed in detail when we consider developmental age grouping and multiage grouping.

At Jamesville-Dewitt Middle School, Jamesville, New York, approximately 1000 students are arranged into three houses (including grades 6, 7 and 8) of 330 students, 110 students in each grade level. There are three grade level teams per house. Each house has twelve classrooms, a guidance suite and a team conference room. The students are randomly assigned to each house and heterogeneously grouped on each grade level team. Each house has five teachers per team, with two foreign language teachers, a counselor and a secretary also serving the students of the house. At Jamesville-Dewitt Middle School the counselor also serves as the house educational leader; not so much as an administrator but, reflecting the school's child-centered philosophy, as counselor to the students, consultant to the house teachers, and coordinator and liaison between the house and other adults in and out of the school.

Farnsworth Middle School names its three houses Hiawatha, Mohawk and Tawasentha (Indian tribes that once inhabited the general area), achieving a measure of identity, vicarious distinction and pride for its students. In this large school (1650 students in grades 6, 7 and 8) each of the three houses contains approximately 550 students in four or five interdisciplinary team organizations of 110 to 115 students per team. While separate house identities are encouraged, every team and house is connected both physically and programmatically to the rest of the school. Houses are formed by random assignment of students, but within each house both homogeneous and heterogeneous ability grouping are found. At Farnsworth, each house is directed by its own principal/teacher, and in addition to the regular team teachers, each house has its own secretary, counselor, reading teacher, foreign language teachers and ''learning workshop teacher.''

As an illustration of the way in which the SWS assists in articulation, the fifth grades in each house at Farnsworth Middle School are relatively self-contained. The house principal and the fifth-grade teachers provide the close attention and counseling that they believe the fifth graders require. The house counselors, then, focus their efforts on the students in the sixth, seventh and eighth grades, and assist the teachers who are working in the fifth grade.

Because the students remain in the same minischool setting for the four years, the interpersonal knowledge required for truly child-centered articulation is possible.

Developmental Age Grouping

Donald H. Eichhorn has long advocated a strategy of grouping students for instruction based on the developmental characteristics of the learner.[2] Implemented in 1969 in Boyce and Ft. Couch Middle Schools, in Upper St. Clair, Pennsylvania, following a medical and psychological analysis of the development of middle school students, the process has come to be known as developmental or developmental age grouping. Based on an index of social, physical, mental and academic maturity, students were placed in three cross-age groups. The first group was composed largely of prepubescents, the second of pubescent youngsters and the third, adolescents. The results have been significant, yielding continued increases in academic achievement and self-esteem when compared with Upper St. Clair students in previous years and with students from comparable districts in Pennsylvania. The program has continued, with refinements since that time.[3] Perhaps because such a program appears to require a great deal of time and effort on the part of those involved, few school districts have followed Upper St. Clair's lead.

One middle school has, for the last decade, been involved in what is essentially developmental age grouping. Spring Hill Middle School, High Springs, Florida, has pioneered a program which has proven itself by its continued successful existence, in spite of a relatively low level of funding and in a conservative community. Spring Hill, a small school of approximately 360 students in grades 5 through 8, is divided into three instructional units or teams. Each unit or team includes about 120 students and four teachers, varying in response to enrollment fluctuations.

Students on each team are grouped according to a rough index of chronological age and developmental characteristics. Unit One has the youngest students in the school on this index, about 90 fifth graders and 30 of the youngest sixth graders, a group of 120 students, aged nine to eleven. Unit Two has the 60 older sixth graders and 60 of the youngest seventh graders, a group of 120 students, aged eleven to thirteen. Unit Three has 30 older seventh graders and 90 eighth graders, a group of 120 students, aged thirteen to fifteen. Spring Hill has, therefore, three largely developmental age groups for instruction: prepubescent, pubescent and adolescent. Table 6.1 presents the grouping pattern at Spring Hill schematically.

Since students spend four years in the school, from fifth through eighth grades, they must spend two years in one of the units, assuming that most students move annually from one unit to another. The concept of developmental age serves Spring Hill well in helping decide how many years each student will spend in a particular unit. If the student is identified by the administrative staff, the counselor and the teachers as experiencing a delayed development, he or she will most likely spend two years in Unit One, first as

Table 6.1 / Grouping at Spring Hill Middle School High Springs, Florida

UNIT	ONE	TWO	THREE
GRADE LEVEL	5–6	6–7	7–8
STUDENT AGE	9, 10, 11	11, 12, 13	13, 14, 15
LEVEL OF DEVELOPMENT	Prepubescent	Pubescent	Adolescent

a fifth grader and then as a sixth grader the second year. If the student is older and maturing quickly and early, he or she will be likely to spend the fifth year in Unit One, the sixth year in Unit Two and the seventh and eighth years in Unit Three. A student who is closer to the mode in age and development will probably spend two years in Unit Two.

Spring Hill Middle School has found a way to make developmental age grouping work well. Use of the Kettering Foundation's Individually Guided Education (IGE) curriculum planning model, from the beginning of the school in 1970, has allowed the faculty to design a curriculum that makes effective use of the flexibility offered by developmental age grouping.[4] In a recent self-study, the faculty identified as one of the school's major strengths, the "continuous learning cycle established for each student, unrestricted by chronological age or the number of years in school regardless of the Unit to which he is assigned."[5]

The unit planning process developed by IGE permits the faculty teams to fashion plans for curriculum and instruction that eliminate problems associated with having approximately 30 students on the team who were there the previous year. In reading, language arts and mathematics, a great deal of pretesting and posttesting, and grouping and regrouping, accounts for the personalized curriculum. In social studies and science, a four-year curriculum plan is combined with a great deal of interteam coordination of what is taught each year, to whom, and to what extent or depth.

Spring Hill Middle School is not alone in grouping students in this way, although there are only a comparatively few schools which have opted for this design. Another school which has chosen this process is Glen Ridge Middle School, Glen Ridge, New Jersey. Glen Ridge Middle School demonstrates that such a design can be implemented in a way that fits diverse school sizes. With a population of about 575 students, Glen Ridge is well over 50 percent larger than Spring Hill, but uses the same grouping strategy. The school is arranged into five teams (compared with three in Spring Hill) of approximately 115 students, five teachers and an aide. Each team at Glen Ridge includes two grade levels: two teams cover grades 5 and 6; one team contains grades 6 and 7; and two teams are composed of grades 7 and 8.

Glen Ridge also utilizes an IGE approach to a curriculum focusing on objectives and skills. Students move through the instructional program, within the team, as they master complete components of the curriculum in the various subjects. The flexibility of this program allows the school staff to offer equally flexible promotion and retention opportunities.

Multiage Grouping

The distinguishing feature of multiage grouping (MAG) is the fact that students remain not only in the same house, but with the same team for their entire tenure in the school. In the SWS, students remain in the same house, but move to a different team of teachers each year. In developmental-age grouped situations, students are often placed in a learning milieu which features students whose ages vary over a two- to three-year range, and any particular student may spend up to two years on a team, eventually moving from one team, and group of teachers, to another. In MAG, however, the students almost always begin and end with the same team. Once quite rare, MAG is becoming more popular with schools attempting to implement a complete, fully functioning middle school.

Two Alachua County, Florida, middle schools have set the pace for MAG. Lincoln Middle School, in Gainesville, Florida, and Mebane Middle School, in Alachua, Florida, represent fine examples of successful attempts to develop a school-wide student grouping strategy firmly rooted in an understanding of the nature and needs of the learners involved. The two grouping designs are fundamentally similar, but differ in one or two interesting ways.

Lincoln Middle School has achieved a considerable measure of national attention, due in large measure to the extensive and successful implementation of MAG. Lincoln has something less than 1000 sixth-, seventh- and eighth-grade students, usually fluctuating between 900 and 1000, all of whom are placed on six multiage grouped interdisciplinary teams. Teams consist of from 160 to 170 students, balanced by age, race, sex, academic achievement and other variables such as the section of the city in which they live. Each team reflects the composition of the total school; each team is a Lincoln microcosm.

Students and teachers stay together for three years, with the student population of each team changing by one third each year. In the spring the eighth graders leave the team for the high school, and in the autumn, new sixth graders take their place in the team.

Grouping at Lincoln is essentially grade free. Students on a team may be ability grouped for instruction in only two areas, which usually means either math and reading, or language arts and reading, depending on the team's decision. Within the classes, both academic and exploratory, students are grouped without restriction of chronological age or grade level. Though it often happens that in particular learning situations more sixth graders may be present than eighth graders, for example, many (if not most) classes have students present from all three years.

Visitors to Lincoln expect that the practice of MAG significantly increases the range of achievement levels in each class. But, while the range is extended somewhat, of course, what is more often the case, say the teachers, is that there are simply more students at each point of the achievement curve. Instead of the bell-shaped normal curve, then, the range in Lincoln classes is likely to be more equally distributed, having more students at both ends of the continuum than otherwise might be the case.

Some curriculum adaptations are necessary for MAG to function smoothly, but MAG does not require that each teacher teach three different grade level lessons in each class each day. Some teachers recoil at the thought of being responsible for teaching world history, American history and geography in the same class to three different groups. This is not what happens.

The basic academic program at Lincoln, and at most other schools which have implemented a similar grouping pattern, is modified in two ways. Mathematics, language arts and reading are individualized so that students work independently or in small ad hoc learning groups on specific objectives or tasks which are appropriate for them. Students move from objective to objective or from skill to skill as they demonstrate mastery or complete a particular set of activities. So students may join a team in sixth grade, or at any other point, and move along as quickly as possible from one year to the next.

In social studies and science, the curriculum is arranged on a three-year cycle. Based on the credible assumption that there is very little inherent sequence in learning either of these two subjects, entire teams of students study a particular aspect of the curriculum during the same year, regardless of the age or grade of the students. In social studies, students on two teams may, for example, study American history during year A, world history during year B and geography during the year C of the cycle. Two other teams would study world history during year A, and the final two teams would study geography during year A. In science, the rotation of the cycle would be similar. Table 6.2 illustrates how the cycle revolves in these two areas.

It is important to note that, for new students, placement on a team involves very little difficulty. Since everything major in the curriculum is always being taught on some team in the school, students are placed on the team which most nearly matches the program they had been following in their previous school. This situation also prevents excessive strain on library and other resources for any particular subject.

Mebane Middle School, in Alachua, Florida, may be the most flexibly grouped middle school in America. In operation since 1970, Mebane has approximately 460 students in grades 5 through 8. The school has three multiage-grouped teams, each containing approximately 40 students from every grade level, 5 through 8. Students remain on the team for four years. As at

Table 6.2 / Lincoln Middle School*—Three Year Curriculum Cycle

TEAMS	B & C	D & M	T & W
Years			
A	American History Earth Science	World History Life Science	Geography Physical Science
B	Geography Physical Science	American History Earth Science	World History Life Science
C	World History Life Science	Geography Physical Science	American History Earth Science

* Gainesville, Florida

Lincoln, each team is a microcosm of the total school in terms of grade level, sex, race and achievement.

At Mebane the student population on each team changes by one quarter each year. The eighth graders move on to the high school, and new fifth graders move up from the elementary school. The team or "learning community," as the faculty calls it, remains about 75 percent whole each year. Within each team at Mebane, special grouping for instruction further accommodates the characteristics of the students on the team.

In reading and mathematics, students on the team are divided by ability into two large groups. One group is composed of middle to high ability students, the second contains middle to low ability students. Half of the students study the basic skills in the morning, half in the afternoon. Since the grouping disregards grade levels, it is common for students from at least three grade levels to be together in class. Such a program permits regrouping for mathematics in much the same way grouping is done for reading.

In science and social studies, and in physical education and prevocational classes, the students are grouped without rigid ability or achievement level critieria, but with an attempt to reduce the instructional range. Within each team, students are grouped as follows: fifth and sixth graders together, sixth and seventh, seventh and eighth graders, and occasionally at least three grade levels are in class together if the student characteristics or needs suggest it. Curriculum units are repeated every other year, avoiding duplication for students. Mebane seems to be able to combine both MAG and developmental age grouping into a very efficient and effective overall grouping strategy.

Two exemplary Midwestern middle schools use MAG in large schools and where only two grades are present. At Trotwood-Madison Junior High School, Trotwood, Ohio, 850 students are divided into four teams each containing an equal number of seventh and eighth grades. Each team has five teachers and an aide. At Brentwood Middle School, Greeley, Colorado, the school is divided into six teams of between 100 and 140 sixth- and seventh-grade students, with three to four teachers on each team. At Brentwood, the instructional groupings in the subject areas are based on diagnosed instructional need without regard to student age or ability. Thus, the sixth and seventh graders are mixed in all classes.

As the practice of MAG spreads, a number of schools have found that offering this form of grouping in addition to the continued use of some chronological age grouping makes an effective transitional strategy. Choices may then be offered to parents, students and teachers as to which style of grouping they prefer. Under such circumstances all groups feel considered and well served, and a seemingly controversial grouping strategy is implemented with little or no turmoil.

Several varieties and styles of such combinations are in operation around the country. At Louisville Middle School, Louisville, Colorado, fifth and sixth graders are combined for instruction in mathematics, language arts, reading and exploratory options, but are taught by grade levels in science and physical education. Seventh and eighth graders work together only in elective areas, except during the extensive activity period when students from grades 5 through 8 will frequently be grouped together. This method of interweaving MAG and chronological age grouping is likely to receive support from everyone concerned.

At Nipher Middle School, Kirkwood, Missouri, parents and students are offered a variety of choices in a school containing grades 6 through 8. A self-contained sixth-grade option is available, as well as two- and four-teacher teams; eighth graders all work in interdisciplinary teams. In between, there is an option of a two-year sixth to seventh grade multiage-grouped situation. Materials distributed to parents by the principal explain that the sixth- to seventh-grade team is a two-year curriculum incorporating materials from both years and students would be expected to be on the team for two years.

At Noe Middle School, Louisville, Kentucky, the practice of MAG was introduced to the school gradually, one team at a time. Everyone involved, and particularly teachers, had a chance to become familiar with the concept of having sixth, seventh and eighth graders on the same team. Initially, the students in the school were grouped entirely according to age and grade level. Then a team of volunteer teachers and a selected group of students became a multiage-grouped unit. After a year's successful operation, a second team switched to the multiage format, and the next year a third team changed over. By the 1979–80 year, there were three multiage and three graded teams at Noe.

Fairview Middle School, Tallahassee, Florida, is another example of offering a choice between age level teams and MAG. In a school of 735 sixth, seventh and eighth graders, three teams operate traditionally and three offer the multiage option. At Fairview, a cyclical curriculum operates on the multiage teams in much the same way as it does at Lincoln Middle School.

At Stoughton Middle School, Stoughton, Wisconsin, a "multi-level block program" operates successfully. Here 880 sixth-, seventh- and eighth-grade students are assigned to teams in which all teachers on each team teach all the basic subjects. The sixth and seventh graders on the team are in classes together for mathematics and language arts, with eighth graders grouped separately. In science and social studies, MAG is extensive.

It is important to point out that in several of the examples just discussed the distinguishing feature of MAG was absent. The students and teachers did not develop a unit or community which lasted for the entire time the student was in the school. In this sense, some of the combination options appear to have more in common with developmental age grouping than with MAG as it is defined here.

Student-Teacher Progression

When grouping students is conceived of as being on the continuum described earlier in this chapter, there is at least one other option. It is possible for a middle school to group students chronologically and still have teachers and students remain together for two, three or four years. It is possible for students and teachers to become a team in the sixth grade, for example, and then when the students become seventh graders, for those same teachers to move along to become seventh-grade teachers with their students. Under such circumstances, students and teachers would be intact as a group. After the final year the students move on to the high school and the teacher rotates back to receive a new group of entering students to begin the process anew.

It seems to the authors that such a practice, common in some elementary school districts, and approached in part in the SWS program, might achieve many of the goals of all of the grouping options examined here, without encountering many of the difficulties. No middle school practicing such a grouping strategy is known to the authors.

Advantages and Disadvantages of Alternatives to Age-grade Grouping

Advantages

The thrust of this chapter might be described as the case for more flexible, learner-oriented methods of school-wide grouping, rather than as the case against chronological age-grade level grouping. It is not so much that the traditional process is bad, but that the alternatives seem so much better.

Most important, of course, is that these alternatives more nearly satisfy the twin criteria of offering a unique program to middle school learners and at the same time moving toward continuous progress from the elementary school through the middle grades on to the high school. But there are many more advantages than these.

Continuous Progress. These alternatives, from SWS through MAG, all offer increasing opportunities for continuous progress. Yet each preserves the structure and accompanying economy, efficiency and popularity of group (even grade level group) learning.

In the SWS situation, for example, teachers are familiar with their colleagues in the contiguous grade levels, and may consult with them frequently about the progress or problems of past, present or future students. Records may often be kept in a common planning area. Counselors serve the same students year after year. The scope and sequence of the curriculum and its development in each subject area can be carefully designed and scrutinized by "vertical committees" composed of teachers within the house who teach the same subject. The SWS retains all of the advantages of grade level grouping while providing significant opportunities for continuous progress for the students involved.

Conversely, MAG provides a maximum opportunity for continuous progress learning while permitting grade leveling to occur whenever necessary. Students may begin their studies at whatever point they are when they enter a MAG situation and continue uninterruptedly for two, three or four years or until they move on to a high school situation. For as long as they are in the school there are few if any important grade level barriers to learning.

The student-teacher progress plan proposed earlier in this chapter would, of course, also provide a maximum opportunity for continuous progress while tendering all the advantages of grade level grouping. It would seem to offer the advantages of both so well that it is rather astonishing that the practice is not widespread.

Community. These alternatives offer the promise of continuous progress and also deliver what continuous progress, as a single goal, would prevent—a strong sense of community. This sense of community, the feeling of membership, of ownership, may be the most important advantage of all. Middle school students, because of their nature and because of the character of contemporary society, need a place to belong, a place away from home that feels safe and supportive.

The presence of a sense of community can be observed most dramatically in middle schools practicing extensive MAG. Where teachers and students work together for up to four years, one teacher writes, important parts of the lives of each are invested in the others. "Powerful human bonds are formed and sealed."[6]

In a society that has become, in Vance Packard's words, "a nation of strangers," stability and continuity in human relationships become more and more important in every endeavor.[7] Schools are not exceptions. Loneliness and a feeling of disconnectedness drain the psychic energy from many of the society's efforts and the school suffers in direct proportion. As a poster on the wall of one middle school proclaimed, "True friendship is a plant of slow growth." Relationships that are growth producing do not develop overnight, and the results of such relationships cannot be produced in their absence. There is no substitute for the human factor.

It has long been common knowledge that schools learn a great deal from the military, and that much that occurs in schools has been borrowed from the armed services. It is also the case in learning about the power of interpersonal relationships in human motivation. Long ago the military learned that interpersonal bonds were a more important source of motivation than coercion. Men could be motivated to kill and die for their friends, because of the incredibly powerful bonds that their common experiences had forged. The sense of community that this produced was more effective than the fear of death. If the armed forces have changed from force to relationships to accomplish their most difficult tasks, surely the schools can do no less. If interpersonal bonds can motivate grown men to risk their lives, the same kind of interpersonal power can motivate students to learn.

Discipline. The strength that derives from the sense of community produced by a group of teachers and students spending several years together is evidenced in a number of different spheres, but school discipline and classroom management appear to have significant benefits. In comparison to "single grade centers," which are the opposite end of the continuum from MAG, statistics on factors such as vandalism, expulsions, suspensions and office discipline referrals appear to be significantly lower. In the single grade center, there are often as many as 1500 new students arriving in the fall, knowing no one, possessing no feelings of loyalty or school spirit. In the spring these same students are all transferred to a new school, leaving the wreckage they have created behind, and 1500 new students are delivered to finish the job the first group began.

It is a truism that effective discipline and classroom management depend in large measure upon a positive relationship between the teacher and the students. These relationships take time. In a middle school with MAG, the time is readily available. At Mebane Middle School, for example, at the beginning of each new school year, 75 percent of the students return from the previous year, and only a quarter of the students are new. The entire first grading period of the year, so often wasted in other schools with rule setting, rule testing and a host of other time-wasting activities, can be devoted to real academic effort. The teachers and students at Mebane have, by contrast, been together for as long as three years prior to the beginning of the year.

At the end of the year, the teachers and students in schools with MAG find themselves, again, in a totally different situation. Rather than being desperately in need of release from one another, the eighth graders and their teachers discover that they have come to know and care about each other deeply over the preceding four years. Instead of yells of joy, an observer is often confounded by observing tears produced by the sorrow of separation in the eyes of both students and teachers. Other students in earlier grades, realizing that they will be returning to the same situation next year are much less likely to give up on the academics, and more frequently are found challenging themselves with their efforts to stay on task in spite of the heat. Teachers, also realizing that the large majority of their students from this year will be their students again next year, often find themselves possessed of considerably more creativity than might be typical at the end of the year in other school situations.

The authors, based on their observations of MAG in action over a period of years, believe that school discipline and classroom management problems are considerably reduced by MAG. Teachers and administrators from schools practicing MAG confirm this belief.

Diagnosis and Prescription. MAG, and the other alternatives, considerably simplify the processes of diagnosis and prescription in the program of personalizing instruction. Students who return to the same academic circumstances of the previous year(s) can begin where they left off. New students, because they are a small fraction of the total team, can have their learning needs analyzed much more extensively and carefully than would otherwise be possible. The efficiency benefits the students in more than one way. Because teachers can devote their attention and their energies to directing instruction, rather than to the seemingly endless routines of beginning and ending the year with new groups of students, much more time is likely to be spent in academically direct efforts.

Parental Relationships. Not only do the years together strengthen the bonds between teachers and students, but between teachers and parents, and among the students as well. Teachers and parents have time to discover that both have the best interests of the students in mind. They have time to discover trust, empathy and friendship. Barriers fall.

Peer Relationships. Students also learn that their peers are "okay"; that older students need not be feared so terribly, and that younger students can be valued friends. Peer modeling and peer teaching are much more likely to occur in grouping situations where several ages and grade levels are combined in some way. Cross-age friendships, made possible by the grade-free grouping strategy, allow students to seek support from other students who are similar to them in development, regardless of age or grade level. In fact, teachers who have had experience with MAG report that often the older students seem less hurried in their attempts to act like high school students, and younger students are more likely to imitate the admirable traits of their older classmates than they are the less desirable ones. For some unknown reason, parents and other adults unfamiliar with alternatives to chronological age grouping often assume that putting older and younger students together will result in something socially undesirable. Experiences with these alternatives do not confirm these fears; the opposite is actually much more likely.

Synergism. One of the most important advantages of the alternative grouping strategies is that they act in a synergistic fashion, strengthening the other programs with which they interact. The advisor-advisee programs and the interdisciplinary team are both much more effective, for example, in combination with a grouping plan that extends the life of the team or the advisory group. When teacher and students remain in the same advisory group for two, three or four years, all of the goals of the process become much more realizeable. The interdisciplinary team, and all of the advantages connected with it, are significantly enhanced. Without MAG or another alternative, these programs achieve significantly less than they might with the multiplier effect of the grouping strategy utilized.

Innovation. The grouping alternatives discussed here have a similar effect on innovation in curriculum and instruction. When teachers and students stay together for several years, repetition of the same units and instructional strategies becomes counterproductive, if not embarrassing. Teachers are, therefore, more frequently found in an innovative mode, searching for the most effective and most motivating instructional strategies and curriculum units. This innovative trend is most strikingly noticed during the spring;

weeks before the end of school, when teachers, recognizing that many of the same students will be returning in the fall, implement plans that they hope will not only motivate the students for the remaining weeks, but bring them back with pleasant memories and eager anticipation in the new school year.

Academic Achievement. It is the belief of the authors that, when all the above advantages pertain, increased academic achievement results. Furthermore, for individual students, failure and retention do not carry the social stigma that they might. Because, with MAG, students are frequently unaware of the grade other students are in, and since they were together last year, students often presume that it is normal that they should be together again.

Moral Reasoning. The authors believe that there is some logical support for the likelihood that the development of moral reasoning, as described by Lawrence Kohlberg (see chapter 4), may be enhanced in situations where MAG or related practices are implemented. When students of varying maturity rates are together frequently enough to learn to value each other, exposure to more mature moral reasoning should enhance growth in these areas among less mature students. It also seems likely that the attachment to small groups like the advisory group and the team, strengthened over time by MAG, should encourage students in the first two stages of moral development to move continuously closer to stage three where they differentiate between right and wrong on the basis of the norms of the face-to-face groups to which they belong.

Disadvantages

In the opinion of the authors, the advantages of alternatives to chronological age grouping far outweigh the disadvantages, but no program is without trade-offs. Implementing developmental age grouping or multiage grouping requires a significant departure from previous structure and some program disruption will occur, usually fading after the first year. Most frequently, some stress is experienced as a result of the curricular adjustments required when continuous progress or cyclical curriculum designs replace the graded program. Student turnover and teacher attrition can cause an erosion of the benefits of the program, to the extent that such turnover and attrition occur. Finally, in schools where teachers are already burdened by excessive demands coupled with insufficient funds, the flexibility and innovation required by multiage grouping and developmental age grouping may demand more than teachers have to give.

Requirements for Success

With any new, alternative program, it is important for educators (in schools using an alternative program) to be able to explain it clearly to parents and other community members. In the area of middle school student grouping this need appears to be doubly so, for while parents seem able to accept such practices in the elementary school or high school, they do not, strangely, appear to accept them with equal ease in the middle grades. Perhaps parents are anxious because they are witnessing their children changing into adolescents, and these changes indicate changes in their own lives they find difficult to accept. Perhaps it is only because they have enjoyed their children as children that they are reluctant to have them grouped with students who seem older and more mature. For whatever reason, patience and a willingness to take the necessary time to explain, and explain again, in simple and concrete language, are absolute requirements. School leaders should be especially well prepared to articulate clearly and with conviction the rationale behind the benefits to be received by such a plan. Parents will listen and be supportive if they believe that educators are competent and concerned. After planning carefully and providing ready explanations to new parents, most schools using grouping alternatives find the large majority of parents at ease and in full support of such practices.

Educators involved in grouping students differently must be convinced of the validity of their own efforts when dealing with students, in the same way as with parents. Initially, during the first year or two at the most, older students involved in a transition from chronological grades to developmental grouping or multiage grouping may feel demoted. Students who had been seventh graders in a junior high school, when they become eighth graders in a new middle school and find themselves grouped with younger students, may initially resent what has happened. After one year, however, when these students have moved on to the high school, there will be left only students who have known no other way and most of the complaints will have disappeared. Almost every school using an alternative form of grouping has experienced this pressure from older students but, having resisted it for at least a year, find the problem disappearing with their first group of graduates.

Staff development is, of course, as important here as in other aspects of the middle school program. But with grouping (in contrast to advisory, exploratory or teaming components), the emphasis in staff development should be aimed primarily at curriculum development. As the school moves into its second, third or fourth years, the benefits of the grouping plan will become increasingly obvious, as the need for curriculum adjustments becomes proportionately less.

Mainstreaming: Grouping Exceptional Students in the Middle School

Schoolwide Arrangements

The identification of exceptional students and the provision of special programs for those students has been an important theme in American education for decades. During the first half of the twentieth century, educators became increasingly aware of the inappropriateness of the continued exclusion of exceptional children from the schools. By the early 1960's, these children had been welcomed into the schools, and special classes had become the nearly universal method for educating exceptional students. Concurrently with the development of special classes, research was begun to assess its effectiveness, and by the middle of the seventies, the profession had concluded that this research did not conclusively support the special class process as being superior to other methods. Until November 1976, however, most middle school educators had only an academic interest in the question of the most appropriate method for educating exceptional children. When President Ford signed Public Law 94-142, at that time, professional interest became widespread and practical strategies became considerably more important.

Mainstreaming is the term most often used to describe the attempt to meet the mandates of PL 94-142. The term has been subject to widely varying interpretations and definitions. For purposes of considering its utility in the middle school, in this discussion it is intended to mean the educational placement closest to the normal classroom in which the child can succeed; the least restrictive educational environment. In the past, the placement options for the education of exceptional students were limited to the special classroom. Children were often diagnosed, placed in a special classroom out of the sight of, and out of the mind of, all but special education personnel. Today, PL 94-142 urges schools to use the regular school facilities and program, adapting them to the needs of exceptional students whenever this is possible.

Mainstreaming has several objectives, which research will attempt to assess in the next decade. Special educators hope that moving the exceptional child into the regular program, when possible, will remove the stigma associated with special class placement, and that it will enhance the social status of the handicapped with their more normal peers. Educators expect that mainstreaming will provide a more stimulating environment for cognitive growth, and that contact with the regular classroom will facilitate the modeling of appropriate behavior by their peers within it. Such an environment is intended to provide just manageable difficulty in areas and activities that must eventually be faced in out-of-school environments, such as competition and self-evaluation. Mainstreaming is touted as being more cost-effective, more flexible in terms of the delivery of services to students in need and more acceptable to the parents of exceptional children. It is obvious from an examination of these objectives, that mainstreaming is an ambitious and potentially far-reaching innovation in American education, and the exemplary middle school cannot afford to dismiss it.[9]

The Council for Exceptional Children (CEC), a professional organization for special educators, has identified four major components of mainstreaming:

1. *Providing the most appropriate education for each child in the least restrictive setting;*

2. *Looking at the educational needs of children instead of clinical or diagnostic labels such as mentally handicapped, hearing impaired, or gifted;*
3. *Looking for and creating alternatives that will help general educators serve children with learning or adjustment problems in the regular setting. Some approaches being used to help achieve this are consulting teachers, methods and materials specialists, itinerant teachers and resource room teachers;*
4. *Uniting the skills of general education and special education so that all children may have equal educational opportunity.*

CEC has also identified more common misinterpretations of mainstreaming. Mainstreaming is not:

1. *Wholesale return of all exceptional children in special classes to regular classes;*
2. *Permitting children with special needs to remain in regular classrooms without the support services that they need;*
3. *Ignoring the need of some children for a more specialized program that can be provided in the general education program;*
4. *Less costly than serving children in special self-contained classrooms.* [10]

Middle school educators must deal effectively with the critical question of the students to be placed in these least restrictive environments. PL 94-142 defines the handicapped considered in the law (deaf, deaf-blind, hard of hearing, mentally retarded, multihandicapped, orthopedically impaired, other health impaired, seriously emotionally disturbed, specific learning disability, speech impaired and visually handicapped), but special educators maintain that, all things equal, these students have far more in common with so-called normal students than they have differences. It is a matter of degree, since none of us is perfect. While there are some handicapped who need attention from, predominantly, specially trained teachers within exceptional environments, these are few in comparison to the numbers that can be served effectively in the general education system. [11]

A second question, for middle school educators, follows from the first. If much of mainstreaming is a matter of the degree of the handicap, what are the various degrees of least restrictive environments which are appropriate? Figure 6.2 represents a continuum of placement options that are now available in many school systems, and it has direct application in the middle school program. This chart, originally published in 1962, has been adapted and discussed in countless inquiries on the nature of effective placement of exceptional children since that time. [12] On the chart, the broken lines represent the importance of fluidity (versus rigidity) in classification and treatment of children in and between various levels of the continuum. In essence, children should only be moved as far down the continuum as necessary, and should be returned to a more normal environment whenever the child is prepared to function there.

Figure 6.2 illustrates that at one end of the continuum the regular classroom teacher is almost totally responsible for the education of all the children in the classroom, no matter what may be the degree of variation in exceptionality. From that point on, the amount of assistance to the classroom teacher increases until, at level seven, the students identified have little or

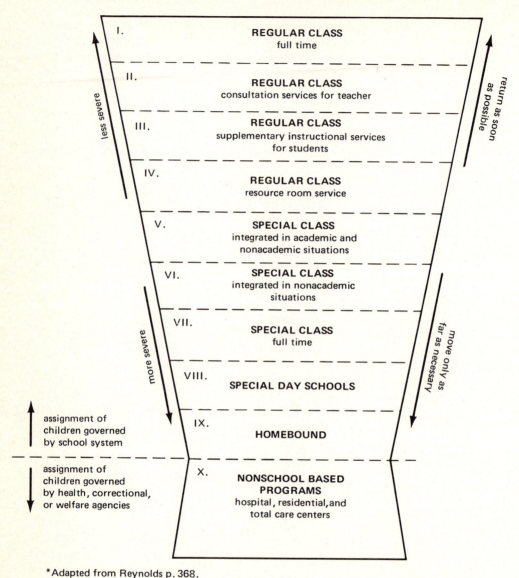

I. **REGULAR CLASS**
full time

II. **REGULAR CLASS**
consultation services for teacher

III. **REGULAR CLASS**
supplementary instructional services
for students

IV. **REGULAR CLASS**
resource room service

V. **SPECIAL CLASS**
integrated in academic and
nonacademic situations

VI. **SPECIAL CLASS**
integrated in nonacademic
situations

VII. **SPECIAL CLASS**
full time

VIII. **SPECIAL DAY SCHOOLS**

IX. **HOMEBOUND**

X. **NONSCHOOL BASED
PROGRAMS**
hospital, residential, and
total care centers

less severe / more severe

return as soon as possible

move only as far as necessary

assignment of children governed by school system

assignment of children governed by health, correctional, or welfare agencies

*Adapted from Reynolds p. 368.

Figure 6.2 / A Continuum of Instructional Settings.

no contact with regular classes. For most middle schools, when help is available to classroom teachers, functioning at levels one through six on the chart, it comes in increasing increments from special teachers, consultants, school counselors and school psychologists, nurses, social workers and the principal.[13]

For many middle schools, however, when mainstreaming is discussed, the major vehicle for implementation is the combination of resource room and regular classroom, students scheduled to attend the special education resource room on the basis of those skills, subjects or situations which can be best handled there. Time spent in the resource room varies with the degree of exceptionality of the student and with the progress being made by the child; with some students spending as little as one hour per week in the resource room, while others spend as much as three quarters of each day there. The use of the resource room exemplifies the commitment of many middle schools that the needs of the individual student will take precedence over the convenience of the delivery system, as in the now outmoded special education classroom to which exceptional students were formerly exiled.

At Farnsworth Middle School, Guilderland, New York, the resource room becomes the Learning Workshop. Clearly committed to the integration of all children into the total school program, the school insures that each student, regardless of the handicap, is a member of a regular team with an assigned homeroom and is entitled to all services offered within the building. The Learning Workshop was developed to aid teachers in responding to as many individual differences among students as possible, drawing upon the services of four professional educators and seven teacher aides.

The majority of the students who are served by the Learning Workshop are divided into two general categories: those who are two to three years below their grade level, and those who are more than three years below their grade level. The Learning Workshop staff at Farnsworth has created two special programs for dealing with these youth. The Curriculum Adaptation Program provides students in the first category with the supplementary instruction, support and materials that permit them to participate in almost all regular classroom tasks; adaptation, modification and enrichment through alternative teaching methods designed for learning-handicapped children. Children who fall into the second category are generally guided to the Basic Skills Instruction program created by the staff of the resource room to provide intensive small group prescriptive instruction in language arts, mathematics, basic sight vocabulary and occupational education.

The Learning Workshop staff at Farnsworth places special emphasis on occupational education in realistic settings. The program is aimed at developing positive work habits, personal responsibility, positive peer interactions and exposure to as many areas of the world of work as possible. Many such opportunities exist within the school setting, involve community volunteers and stress vocational skills in demand in the economy.

Each Learning Workshop teacher must work closely with the teaching teams. Weekly meetings occur with each team to discuss the progress of Learning Workshop students in each academic area, and joint plans are developed to encourage additional learning. Learning Workshop teachers are not assigned to homeroom tasks or other morning duties, so that they will be free for consultation with individual teachers. To further assist this cooperation with teams and within houses, resource room staff operate from small rooms located in each house, and utilize one other regular size classroom for centralized functions. Table 6.3 illustrates a typical day for a Learning Workshop teacher at Farnsworth Middle School.

At Oaklea Middle School, Junction City, Oregon, the resource room functions in a similar way to meet the needs of handicapped learners. The stated goal of the Resource Center at Oaklea Middle is to continue and increase the student's enrollment in the regular program as much as possible, through instruction provided directly to the child, or indirectly through consultation with the teacher. The center also offers services such as program preparation and diagnostic testing. The center, at Oaklea, provides services to middle school students who are functioning at least 1.5 years below grade level, and who need special services to learn most effectively. The Resource Center, staffed by one full-time resource teacher for the retarded, one math

Table 6.3 / Model Learning Workshop Teacher Schedule*

	MOD TIME	CLASS	
1.	9:05– 9:30	Vince-Leon 8th grader's	
2.	9:30– 9:45	Stan-et al. curriculum assistance	
3.	9:45–10:00	Basic Skills Math Class	
4.	10:00–10:15	4 students	
5	10:15–10:30	Peter curriculum 6th	
6.	10:30–10:45	& assistance grader's / Todd	
7.	10:45–11:00	Barry Red /Brian white	Silas-math
8.	11:00–11:15	Mark Day/ Vince day	reinforcement
9.	11:15–11:30	/ Ed	
		John curriculum assistance	
10.	11:30–11:45	LUNCH — teacher consultation	
11.	11:45–12:00		
12.	12:00–12:15	Basic Skills Math Class	
13.	12:15–12:30	4 students	
14.	12:30–12:45	Teacher (Team) Consultation Time	
15.	12:45– 1:00	(Guidance, Parents, etc.)	
16.	1:00– 1:15		
17.	1:15– 1:30	Todd Harvey	Harry-math
18.	1:30– 1:45	Gary	assistance
19.	1:45– 2:00	Peter Curriculum assistance	
20.	2:00– 2:15	Basic Skills Math Class	
21.	2:15– 2:30	5 students	
22.	2:30– 2:45	Team Consultation-8th grade	
			Don Math assistance
23.	2:45– 3:00	Harry	Peter
24.	3:00– 3:15	Kevin } curriculum assistance	math
25.	3:15– 3:30	Linda	assistance

* From Farnsworth Middle School, Guiderland, N.Y.

teacher, two Title One reading teachers and three full-time aides, provides intensive instruction to students after referral by regular classroom teachers.

At Oaklea, a special section of the Resource Center handles both remedial and gifted math students. As in many middle schools, programs for the gifted and talented students have languished until relatively recently, and the staff at Oaklea are developing special programs for these students as well as those with deficiencies. Many middle schools do offer programs for the gifted, often structured in much the same way as the resource center for problem learners, except that the activities and the curriculum are geared for acceleration, independence and in-depth work.

The referral procedure for the Resource Center at Oaklea Middle School seems fairly representative. The following nine steps are followed:

1. Teacher becomes aware of specific problem.
2. Teacher fills out top of referral form in as much detail as possible and notifies parents that child is being referred to Resource Center for individual testing.
3. Teacher places referral in the appropriate Resource teacher's box. Resource Center will get parent permission for individual testing.
4. Resource Center will do individual testing in specific skill areas and notify referring teacher of test results.
5. Resource Center teacher will set up time for staffing if test results indicate a skill deficiency.
6. Staffing will be held including resource teachers, referring teacher, counselor and parent. Resource teachers will present program plan based on test results.
7. Recommendations will be made on the basis of the staffing.
8. If approved for entry in Resource Center, student will begin individual program.
9. If not approved, conference will be held with the referring teacher to determine alternative programs to be utilized in regular classroom.

Once the referral process is complete, for either a handicapped or gifted student, an individualized education plan, required by PL 94-142, is developed and implemented. Such plans are then subject to periodic review. Table 6.4 is an example of the form used at Oaklea Middle School to record the analysis of the plan.

At Steuben Middle School, Milwaukee, Wisconsin, a carefully planned program emerges in a way that demonstrates the centrality of the resource room strategy in mainstreaming at the exemplary middle school. At Steuben, two programs operate simultaneously, providing from one to four hours per day to students, depending upon their individual needs. One program (learning disabilities) is designed to work exclusively within a single team, making it possible for the exceptional education teacher to work closely with the four teachers on the team, an hour each day. This communication enables the faculty to assess a student's functioning in given classes on a daily basis. This organization permits better communication with teachers,

Table 6.4 / Individualized Education Plan Review—Special Services*

				PERFORMANCE		Explain If Unmet					Action	
						Lack Pre-requisite Skill	Objective Too Difficult	Activity Inappropriate	Materials Unavailable	Other	Carry Over Objective	Drop Objective

STUDENT NAME: **SCHOOL:**

Annual Goal Code Number	Objective Number:	COMMENTS:	Met As Stated	Not Met As Stated	Lack Pre-requisite Skill	Objective Too Difficult	Activity Inappropriate	Materials Unavailable	Other	Carry Over Objective	Drop Objective

RECOMMENDATIONS FOR FOLLOWING YEAR:

Teacher: _____   Parent: _____

_____   _____

_____   _____

_____   _____

TEACHER SIGNATURE   DATE   PARENT SIGNATURE   DATE

White: Permanent File   Yellow: Teacher   Pink: Parent

also helps keep parents informed, and strengthens the role of the special education teacher as the fifth teacher on the team. As such, the special education teacher finds herself on an equal footing, no longer on the outside looking in at her students. This permits the planning of activities that will benefit not only the special students in the unit, but the more normal students as well. Since, therefore, more students view the special teacher as a member of the team, the resource room loses the stigma and mystery it once had. Within this model, exceptional students are mainstreamed for at least one regular academic class as well as for most speciality classes. Special education students are also included in regular teams for homeroom, lunch, field trips and other special events.

Mainstreaming and the Regular Teacher

Special educators stress that the methods which regular classroom teachers should use with the exceptional students who are mainstreamed into their classrooms for portions of the school day are actually the methods used by all efficient, well-trained teachers. There appears to be very little that separates the effective special education teacher and the effective regular classroom teacher. Again, it becomes a matter of degree. There are, nonetheless, several suggestions often cited as particularly important when considering students with special needs. Here is one such list:

- Accept the child as he comes to you. Guard against the formation of negative expectations based on appearance, smell or verbal behavior.
- Realize that every child can do better than he is now doing.
- Learn as much as you can about the specific characteristics of the students who will be in your class.
- Survey your resources carefully, within and beyond the school.
- Respect the opinions of other professionals.
- Carefully determine the role and preparation of classroom assistants when available.
- Involve parents realistically.
- Offer a workable, practical curriculum broken down into subunits.
- Do not be overly rigid in your plans for grouping students for instruction.
- Make use of behavior modification and contingency management techniques. Be especially careful to function consistently with special students. Plan to reduce the child's dependence on you.[14]

Grouping: A Comment

It is possible that when first turning to this chapter the reader expected a considerably more lengthy discussion of topics such as ability grouping or the grouping of students with special needs (in other words, mainstreaming). Such topics are of tremendous concern and will continue to be for many years; they are of sufficient importance as to require detailed treatment beyond the scope of the present volume. New research on teacher effectiveness, suggesting the value of more direct large group instruction when teaching basic skills to problem learners may cause a reevaluation of prevalent antiability grouping attitudes. And, certainly, the education of exceptional students is as important to the middle school as any other component. Because of the recency of PL 94-142, however, good programs in exceptional education in the middle school have only now begun to crystalize, and the interested reader will wish to turn to other textbooks that deal adequately with the complexity of such programs.[15]

ADDITIONAL SUGGESTIONS FOR FURTHER STUDY

The discussion of alternative forms of schoolwide grouping of students for instruction in middle schools has been neglected in the professional literature. Theorists, practitioners and researchers concerned with transescents will discover a considerable opportunity for pioneering work in this area. Such a fundamental question as the nature of organizing students for instruction appears, in the authors' opinions, much in need of experimentation, description and study. The suggestions offered here will at least start the reader in the right direction.

A. Books

Brown, B. Frank, *The Appropriate Placement School: A Sophisticated Nongraded Curriculum.* West Nyack, N.Y.: Parker Publishing Company, 1965.

Hillson, Maurie, and Bonge, Joseph, *Continuous Progress Education: A Practical Approach.* Palo Alto, California: Science Research Associates, 1971.

Hillson, Maurie and Hyman, Ronald T., *Change and Innovation in Elementary and Secondary Education,* 2nd Edition. New York: Holt, Rinehart and Winston, Inc., 1971.

Howard, Eugene R., and Bardwell, Roger W. *How To Organize a Non-graded School.* Englewood Cliffs, N.J.: Prentice Hall, 1966.

McCarthy, Robert G., *The Ungraded Middle School.* West Nyack, N.Y.: Parker Publishing Co., 1972.

York, Lilla Jean, *Evaluation of Team Teaching and Children's Continuous Progress.* Dallas: Leslie Press, 1971.

York, Lilla Jean, *Grouping Children for Instruction in Team Teaching.* Dallas: Leslie Press, 1971.

B. Periodicals

Christ, Henry A. "Developing the 'School-Within-A-School' " *Dissemination Services on the Middle Grades,* Springfield, Massachusetts: Educational Leadership Institute, 1–6 (January 1975).

Dixon, Annabella, "Vertical Grouping: A Practice or a Principle?" Forum for the Discussion of New Trends in Education, 21, 19–21 (Fall 1978).

George, Paul S. "Discipline, Moral Development, and Levels of Schooling," *The Educational Forum,* 45, 57–68 (November 1980).

Way, Joyce, "Verbal Interaction in Multi-age Classrooms," *Elementary School Journal,* 79, 178–86 (January 1979).

Yarborough, Betty H., Johnson, Robert A. "The Relationship Between Intelligence Levels and Benefits from Innovative, Nongraded Elementary Schooling and Traditional Graded Schooling," *Educational Research Quarterly,* 3, 28–38 (Summer 1978).

FOOTNOTES

1. John H. Lounsbury and Gordon E. Vars, *A Curriculum For the Middle School Years* (New York: Harper and Row, 1978), 71–81.
2. Donald H. Eichhorn, *The Middle School* (New York: Center for Applied Research in Education, Inc., 1966.)
3. Donald H. Eichhorn, "Grouping for Effective Instruction," Paper presented at the Rider College Institute, July 9, 1974.
4. For information on Individually Guided Education, write to the Institute for the Development of Educational Activities, Suite 300, 5335 Far Hills Avenue, Dayton, Ohio 45429.
5. Spring Hill Middle School Triannual Review, Alachua County Schools, Gainesville, Florida. January 1978, p. 106. Mimeographed.
6. Nancy M. Doda, "Teacher to Teacher," *Middle School Journal,* 9, 8–9 (August, 1978).
7. Vance Packard, *A Nation of Strangers* (Palo Alto, Calif.: Pacific Books, 1974).
8. Doda, p. 9.
9. Terry L. West, Percy Bates, and Rudolph B. Schmeil, *Mainstreaming: Problems, Potentials, and Perspectives* (Minneapolis, MN: National Support Systems Project, 1979), pp. 8–9.
10. West, Bates, and Schmeil, p. 10.
11. Department of Special Education, "Instructional Settings for Exceptional Children, A Continuum of Services" (Gainesville, Florida, The University of Florida, Mimeographed, 1975), p. 4.
12. Maynard C. Reynolds, "A Framework for Considering Some Issues in Special Education," *Exceptional Children,* 28, 368 (March, 1962).
13. Department of Special Education, 10.
14. Department of Special Education, "Fundamental Instructional Practices for Mainstreaming" (Gainesville, Florida: The University of Florida, Mimeographed, 1975), pp. 1–20.
15. See, for example, M. C. Reynolds (ed.), *Mainstreaming: Origins and Implications* (Reston, VA: The Council for Exceptional Children, 1976). Also see J. B. Jordan (ed.) *Teacher, Please Don't Close the Door: The Exceptional Child in the Mainstream* (Reston, VA: The Council for Exceptional Children, 1976).

Chapter 7

Organizing Time and Space in the Middle School

School administrators and others charged with the responsibility for organizing and operating middle schools frequently discover that the successful implementation of an advisory program, exploratory curriculum or interdisciplinary team organization largely depends on the effectiveness of the schedule and the creative use of the facility. Factors which, in the past, were often thought of as separate enterprises, are now recognized as intimately and systematically related. Few schools can overcome the barriers of ineffective schedules or restrictive environments, so this chapter focuses on the proper understanding of this interrelationship between program and the support of the program via schedule and space, and upon the effective organization and use of school time and space.

Organizing Time in the Middle School

The Middle School Schedule

Organizing time in the middle school follows the same mandate to provide a unique and transitional approach as does every other component of the exemplary middle school. Since the program of the elementary school and the high school differ from each other, and from the program in between, it should be no surprise that the methods of organizing the day differ as well. The middle school schedule attempts to lead from that of the elementary school to that of the high school, while reflecting the special program provided for the students in the middle grades. Figure 7.1 illustrates the character of the three time frames.

In the elementary schools known to many of us, the self-contained classroom unit remains the predominant mode of teacher organization, with students allocated accordingly. The elementary classroom teacher often makes almost completely unilateral decisions as to what will be studied, when, by whom, and under what circumstances, and with what processes. One teacher working alone makes the decisions which shape the day. As a consequence, time in the elementary school is organized to facilitate that model. Each teacher works with a large block of time, stretching from the beginning until the end of each day. With just a few interruptions from special teachers and a mandatory lunchtime, most elementary teachers are free to determine the day's schedule entirely on their own. Indeed, it is difficult to imagine a school organized around the model of the self-contained classroom that was not organized this way.

At the other end of the K–12 continuum, the high school has a very different program to schedule, with a completely different set of restraints. The high school program, organized around the departmentalized arrangement of teachers, emphasizing specialization, is usually so large and so complex that efficiency and economy are prime objectives. With as many as several thousand students and teachers to account for, and an amazing array of specialized courses and electives to offer, the most efficient process for organizing time usually turns out to be one which requires centralized control. Individual teachers usually have very little to say about the schedule, since most of these decisions must come from the office. The result is that the school day is most often divided into equal or nearly equal segments called periods, controlled by the office, with student and teacher movement determined by the automatic ringing of bells. While some schools have experimented with modular schedules, featuring a widely varying schedule based on smaller

ELEMENTARY SCHOOL	MIDDLE SCHOOL	HIGH SCHOOL

Figure 7.1 / Organizing Time in Elementary, Middle and High Schools.

units of time and different cycles, most high schools seem to have kept quite closely to the six-, seven- or eight-period day.

The middle school, attempting to accommodate a program which meets the needs of its students, offers a schedule that may be thought of as a compromise between the large single block of time in the elementary school and the smaller periods of the high school. In the exemplary middle school, the organization of time attempts to facilitate the basic organizational framework of the school. And, since in the middle school this is the interdisciplinary team organization, it is the character of this component of the program that determines the nature of the scheduling process.

While there are several varieties of scheduling that are appropriate for the middle school, in order for the schedule to be congruent with the program it serves, it must accommodate the team organization. Not one teacher working alone and making all the decisions about scheduling his or her students; not a massive schedule determined by the office and operated by the bell without any teacher input. The middle school schedule is designed to be controlled by groups of teachers organized into teams in collaboration with the office, a unique and transitional type of schedule for a special type of program. Teachers from several different subject areas, working together to create and operate a comprehensive academic program for the students they serve, need a schedule with flexibility and structure. Any schedule which removes the team's ability to manipulate the daily time frame to suit the objectives of their planning is clearly inappropriate for the middle school.

Objectives of Effective Middle School Scheduling

A schedule is like a budget, used to maximize the opportunities for the balanced satisfaction of basic needs and luxury items. Just as few human beings are able to satisfy all their wants and needs in terms of the financial budget, it is often impossible to acquire enough time and to apportion it wisely enough to accomplish all of the possibilities a school program can muster. Choices must be made and priorities must be set.

First among the priorities is a schedule which molds itself to the other priorities set by the school staff, rather than forcing those items into a schedule designed for the high school. The school schedule is a means to an end, although for those given the responsibility for designing the master schedule, it may often seem like an end in itself. Unfortunately, because many of the administrators who become middle school principals have done their apprenticeships as assistant principals at high schools or have served as principals of traditional junior high schools prior to their designation as middle schools, these administrators frequently have little acquaintance with scheduling options other than the seven-period day as it is worked out in those junior and senior high schools. Consequently, the middle school sometimes is forced into a schedule that is quite like the proverbial Procrustean bed.

The primary objective of the middle school schedule is to facilitate the operation of those school programs determined to be advantageous in the education of middle school students. Interdisciplinary team organization, exploratory curriculum plans, advisor-advisee programs, alternative forms of grouping students on a school-wide basis—all these programs must be organized into an effective schedule. Sometimes priorities which are imposed from outside the school or the district make even the incorporation of these items seem like a luxury.

In addition to accommodating the essentials of an effective middle school program, newer attempts at scheduling usually offer several other reasons for their use. Chief among these appeals is that the more flexible types of scheduling, those which allow teachers in teams to influence the process, avoid the necessity of giving "equal time to unequal subjects."[1] Within the acceptable options for middle school scheduling, all give teachers on the team the opportunity to make judgments about how much time should be given to each of the subjects under their jurisdiction, considering the characteristics of the students in their charge. The proper middle school schedule also allows school boards and other district policy setting groups to mandate greater time and attention to be given to subjects like reading and mathematics with the resulting lower priority to the others.

Effective middle school schedules permit teachers to vary the time given to different subjects on separate days. A team may decide, for example, to devote the first half of every day for an entire week to a review of basic math skills prior to the administering of standardized achievement tests. Another team might decide to teach a thematic unit that required a totally different schedule for as long as four to six weeks. Or one teacher may simply request a few additional minutes to complete a lesson on a particular day. Good schedules, tuned to team decision-making, permit these and many other modifications of the time assigned to each subject in the curriculum.[2]

The school schedule, when designed effectively, permits the use of variable instructional strategies as well. Teams can manage their time to accommodate large group functions, laboratory experiments, individualized and independent study, regular and small group classes. When a particular subject or skill requires a special method or grouping, the schedule permits it. The properly designed schedule can be thought of as an educational blueprint similar in many ways to the architect's work in preparation for the construction of a new building; it arranges for a variety of instructional opportunities but mandates none.

Schedules that offer a greater selection of academic opportunities to students, offer unstructured time when desired, increase teacher influence on school programs and simply break the monotony of the traditional daily period schedule are now much more easily implemented. Since the middle school removes many of the objections raised by those who were threatened by a real or imagined challenge from the Carnegie Unit, college preparation and the standardization required for such accounting simply no longer govern the design of the middle school day. Having gone beyond the grip of the computerized schedule, administrators are discovering that effective time designing can happen with lower cost, fewer irrevocable errors, increased options and greater flexibility.[3]

Options for Organizing Time

There is no right way to organize the middle school day, except insofar as the schedule facilitates or interferes with the program of the school. The authors believe that a seven-period day can, if designed correctly, accommodate the programs of a middle school equally as well as a block or a modular schedule, and it is unnecessary for the staff of a school to feel either self-satisfied with one type of schedule or ashamed with another. The question is not "What kind of schedule is best?" The right question is "How can we schedule our day to facilitate the priorities we have established?"

All schedules, no matter what variety, are arbitrary divisions of the total school day into smaller units. The only major differences are in the size of the smaller units and in who influences or controls the manipulation of those units. In the middle school, the size of the unit is more varied than it often is in either the elementary school or the high school. Thinking of the division of time units on a continuum may help. Figure 7.2 illustrates this division of time into progressively smaller pieces. The essence of scheduling wisdom is to manipulate some chosen series of units into a schedule that allows groups of teachers to operate in the most effective manner. As will be seen, blocks, periods and modules are interchangeable. That is, modules can be used to construct blocks and periods of time, periods of time can be combined into blocks, and can be as small as a module, and so on. The idea that one of these varieties of schedules is, in and of itself, superior to the others is simply false.

Each of the three examples that follow permits a very similar program to function smoothly in each school. All three have the basic components of team organization, teacher guidance, special school-wide student grouping and an exploratory emphasis in the curriculum plan.

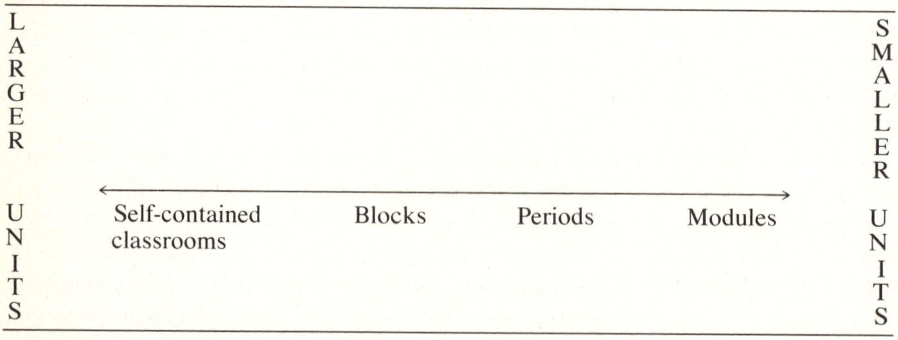

LARGER				SMALLER
UNITS	Self-contained classrooms	Blocks	Periods	Modules	UNITS

Figure 7.2 / A Scheduling Continuum.

Table 7.1 / Spring Hill Middle School* Schedule, 1976–1977

TIME	UNIT I	UNIT II	UNIT III
8:00– 8:55	Teacher Planning Time		
8:55– 9:25	ADVISOR-ADVISEE		
9:30–11:00	Reading/ Language Arts	P.E./ Expressive Arts	Reading/Math
11:00–11:30	P.E./ Expressive Arts	Social Science	Social Science
11:30–12:00			
12:00–12:30		Lunch	
12:30– 1:00	Lunch	Math	Spelling-Lang. Arts
1:00– 1:30	Social Science		Lunch
1:30– 3:05	Math	Reading/ Language Arts	P.E/ Expressive Arts
3:05– 3:30	Teacher Planning		

* High Springs, Florida

Table 7.1 presents the master schedule for Spring Hill Middle School, High Springs, Florida, an excellent example of the block schedule. In this school, time appears to be broken into unequal units, with little continuity from one team to another. It should be pointed out, immediately, that the school is organized into multiage teams (called units at Spring Hill), and readers may want to refer to other chapters for a more complete review of this school's organization. This schedule makes teaming attractive, offering team planning time before (fifty-five minutes) and after (twenty-five minutes) school as well as for ninety minutes during the school day.

In this schedule, as in many others, team planning time during the student day must be inferred from the position of the time during which a team of students is sent to physical education and to the unified arts. Team (Unit) One at Spring Hill, for example, has team and individual teacher planning time from 11:00 a.m. until 12:30 p.m., while their students are in other curricular areas. Team Two has their planning time from 9:25 a.m. until 11:00 a.m. and Team Three from 1:30 p.m. until 3:30 p.m. The students and teachers, all teachers, are involved in the Advisor-Advisee time for thirty minutes, from the moment students enter school for the day at 8:55 a.m. until 9:25 a.m., when classes begin. Students on all three teams spend forty-five minutes per day in physical education and the unified arts. Teachers from these areas must extract their planning time from the times during the day when all students are engaged in the basic academic program with their team of teachers in each Unit. In this case the planning period is from 12:30

p.m. until 1:30 p.m. These specialists also manage to gain some additional planning time during other parts of the day, and to exchange some duties with the academic teachers to equalize their teaching loads.

The schedule at Spring Hill shows that while the same basic program is offered to each student on each of the three teams, individual teams have had something to say about the placement of the various subjects in the space of the day and about the amounts of time devoted to each. Lunch, physical education and unified arts times are fixed, but beyond that there is a great deal of opportunity for teacher input. Team One combines reading and language arts and devotes ninety minutes each day to that topic, while social studies and science are combined and given about an hour daily. Math receives about an hour at the end of each day. Team Two operates in an almost identical fashion, while Team Three combines the time periods for reading and math into a total of ninety minutes, provides an equal ninety-minute block for the social studies-science time, and devotes a special thirty minutes to spelling. Teams of teachers are obviously collaborating with the administration to insure a smoothly running, well-integrated master schedule.

On a lighter side, readers can test their own knowledge of the characteristics of middle school students by looking closely at the Spring Hill schedule. Remembering that students are grouped into older children (Unit One), pubescents (Unit Two) and adolescents (Unit Three) at Spring Hill, can you determine why the schedule for Unit Three was specifically designed so that these students would have their physical education at the last time of the day? One hint—built originally as an elementary school, Spring Hill has no gymnasium, no locker facilities and no showers. Now, readers who guessed that the schedule is designed to give the older students (whose glands are working overtime,) physical education, then put them on the bus and send them home, are correct. The staff reports that, in a school without windows, this practice is absolutely essential! A school schedule can be used, as this anecdote illustrates, to serve a multitude of purposes.

The schedule for North Marion Middle School (Table 7.2) demonstrates the considerable flexibility of the traditional seven-period schedule. Once again, the school is organized into interdisciplinary teams, but in this case the students are organized primarily in a chronological age-grade level pattern, with three teams each of sixth, seventh and eighth graders. The numbers to the right of each team designation (for example, 6A[4]) indicate the number of teachers, and hence the approximate number of students on each team. Variability in the size of the team is an excellent device for compensating for the unequal distribution of numbers of students across and within grade levels.

Taking team 6A as an example, it can be seen that out of the seven periods in each school day, teachers are involved in instruction during five, and that these periods of instruction can be handled in a variety of ways. Here, too, lunch, physical education and the unified arts are fixed at specified times of the day, and teachers are relatively free to use the remainder of the day as they see fit. At North Marion, teams most frequently follow a tradi-

Table 7.2 / Schedule at North Marion Middle School, 1977–1978

TEAM	1	2	3	4	5	6	7
6A (4)			ACADEMIC BLOCK			Plan	SGG
6B (4)			ACADEMIC BLOCK			Plan	SGG
6C (2)						Plan	SGG
7A (4)	BLOCK	SGG	Plan		ACADEMIC BLOCK		
7B (4)	BLOCK	Plan	SGG		ACADEMIC BLOCK		
7C (2)	BLOCK	SGG	Plan				
8A (4)		ACADEMIC BLOCK		Plan	SGG	ACADEMIC BLOCK	
8B (4)		ACADEMIC BLOCK		SGG	Plan	ACADEMIC BLOCK	
8C (2)				SGG	Plan		
Phys Educ (5)	Plan	7	7	8	8	6	6
Exploratory (7)	Plan	7	7	8	8	6	6
Reading (3)	6–7–8	6–Plan–8	6–Plan–8	6–7–Plan	6–7–Plan	Plan–7–8	Plan–7–8
Art and Music (4)	6–7–8–6	6–8–6–Plan	6/Plan/8/6	6/7/6/7	6/7/6/7	Plan/7/Plan/8	7/Plan/7/8
Special Educ (6)		Planning Varies Depending Upon Exploratory and P.E.					

School day for students 7:30 a.m.–1:55 p.m.
Periods approximately 45 minutes long
Student body = 1100

William Caton, Principal
904-622-3111

tional path, permitting each teacher to teach only one or two subjects. However, the schedule allows each team to vary teaching assignments so that each teacher could teach all four of the basics if they wished, or the team could suspend the regular schedule for a period, of, perhaps, a week or more and engage the whole team of teachers and students in a thematic unit that exemplifies the best in teamed instruction. The important point is that the schedule, a traditional seven-period day, permits a variety of teaming modes, from the simplest to the most difficult and complex.

Following the first five periods, the students on team 6A move to physical education and exploratory (in other words, unified arts), as can be seen by examining the arrangements for the physical education and exploratory teachers near the bottom of the schedule. Teachers of team 6A have a planning period during the sixth period and small group guidance during the last period of the day. This schedule, as traditional as it is, also permits the entire sixth-grade group of teachers to plan at the same time, making grade level curriculum planning a reality at North Marion. Finally, a glance at the lower left-hand area of the schedule reveals the presence of several groups of teacher specialists, in addition to a complement of physical education teachers. These teachers receive their planning time during those times of the day (for example, first period) when all students are in an academic team mode.

The schedule at Stroudsburg Middle School (Table 7.3) exemplifies the virtues of the modular schedule. A glance at the schedule will reveal that here, too, the teachers are organized into interdisciplinary teams, and the students into chronologically graded groups in a school-within-a-school format as described in the chapter on student grouping. This type of grouping permits the use of varying sized teams while maintaining a balance in the size of the two houses. The size of the fifth-grade teams could, for example, be three teachers each, while the size of the sixth-grade teams could, if the number of students required it, be four teachers on each team. The schedule also shows that, at Stroudsburg, the program contains both a formal and an informal advisory time, an exploratory period for all students every day and a free activity period during the lunchtime. The division of the day into smaller modules of time provides for both larger blocks of time and for standard periods, too.

The basic modular unit of time at Stroudsburg is fifteen minutes, but it could be just about any desired specific portion of an hour. The day is divided into twenty-seven modules, allowing the school staff to divide the day as they see fit, so long as it is made up of combinations of modules. School begins with two modules of advisory home base time, the second of which becomes the first formal module of the day. The remainder of the morning, modules 2–13 are devoted to a combination of academic time and physical education-unified arts. During the day, each team has thirteen modules of academic time, about fifty minutes for each of the four basic subjects. So while it may look quite different to the uninitiated, in actuality it is almost exactly the same as the standard six- or seven-period day, in the total amounts of time that are devoted to each area. Students receive physical education instruction twice weekly with other opportunities during lunch and the period of time offered by modules 21–23. The Stroudsburg schedule illustrates the practice of using time in a different way to accomplish the same ends as those of schools using a more standard scheduling practice.

Three different methods of dividing time into units are, therefore, appropriate for consideration when designing the middle school schedule. The criterion for evaluating their relative effectiveness is how well a particular method serves the specific purposes of the middle school, especially the sup-

Table 7.3 / Master Schedule, Stroudsburg Middle School

TIME	MOUNTAIN HOUSE 5	6	7	8	LAKE HOUSE 5	6	7	8	MOD
8:30									
8:45	INFORMAL HOME BASE ADVISOR ACTIVITY								
9:00	FORMAL HOME BASE ADVISOR ACTIVITY								1
9:15	PE–M, W		ACADEMICS	ACAD	UA–M, W PE–T, TH ACAD–F	ACAD	ACADEMICS	ACAD	2
9:30	UA–T,	ACADEMICS							
9:45	TH, F								3 / 4
10:00				ACAD–M, T, W, TH UA–F		ACAD–M, W, TH, F UA–T		ACAD–T, W, TH, F UA–M	5
10:15									6
10:30	ACADEMICS				ACADEMICS		UA–TH		7
10:45			PE–M, W UA–T, TH, F	ACADEMICS		ACAD	UA–M, W PE–T, F ACAD–TH	ACADEMICS	8
11:00									9
11:15									10
11:30		UA–M, T, TH PE–W, F	ACAD	ACADEMICS		PE–M, TH UA–W, F ACAD–T	ACAD	ACADEMICS	11
11:45									
12:00									12
									13
12:15	LUNCH	LUNCH	FREE ACTIVITY	FREE ACTIVITY	LUNCH	LUNCH	FREE ACTIVITY	FREE ACTIVITY	14 / 15
12:30	FREE ACTIVITY	FREE ACTIVITY	LUNCH	LUNCH	FREE ACTIVITY	FREE ACTIVITY	LUNCH	LUNCH	
12:45									16
1:00									17
1:15	ACAD	ACAD	ACAD	UA–M, W PE–T, TH ACAD–F	ACAD–M, T, W, TH UA–F	ACAD	ACAD	ACAD–M UA–T, TH PE–W, F	18
1:30									19
1:45									20
2:00	ACAD PE ENR 1 MON 3 MON	ACAD PE ENR 1 TUES 3 TUES	ACAD PE ENR 1 WED 3 WED	ACAD PE ENR 1 TH 3 TH	ACAD PE ENR 2 MON 4 MON	ACAD PE ENR 2 TUES 4 TUES	ACAD PE ENR 2 WED 4 WED	ACAD PE ENR 2 TH 4 TH	21
2:15									22
2:30									23
2:45									24
3:00	EXPLORATORY PROGRAM								25
3:15									26
3:30	FORMAL HOME BASE ADVISOR ACTIVITY								27

port it may provide for the interdisciplinary team organization and other basic program components. In a very real sense, schedules reflect the program knowledge possessed by those who arrange the structure of the school day.

Building the Master Schedule

Prerequisite Decisions. There are no two school schedules that are exactly alike. The processes of developing those schedules are, therefore, unique to each school, although there are similar operations which appear in each effort. The most important steps in the scheduling process, it seems, may be those steps which precede the actual construction of the schedule. There are a number of important factors that influence the scheduling process and about which decisions must be made prior to the beginning of the schedule building itself.[4]

The most important decision concerns the organization of the faculty and students for instruction. In many ways the organization of the school and the school schedule are the same thing; the process of designing one places inevitable restrictions on the other. Scheduling cannot begin, the present authors believe, without a firm commitment to one of the several types of teacher instructional organization. The interdisciplinary team organization of teachers will, for example, mold the remaining steps in the scheduling process in quite a different way than will a decision to have a departmentalized structure. A decision to have multiage grouping, the student-teacher progression plan or some other alternative to or modification of the graded group will have tremendous implications for the schedule which will ultimately emerge. These decisions regarding the organization of teachers and students for instruction must be made before effective scheduling can begin.

Almost as important, in the impact on the schedule, are the decisions that are made about curriculum. Since the master schedule is really like a budget, a budget of time, each schedule depends for its final shape on the curriculum priorities established. And, because no school day can adequately contain all of the demands of the parents, school board, state department of education and national curriculum movements, decisions establishing priorities must be made before scheduling of the day can proceed. No schedule can contain everything; something must always be left out. A considerable amount of frustration with the scheduling process actually can be seen to be a matter of establishing curriculum priorities which, when clearly set, can lead to a smoother scheduling process. Knowing how many curriculum components will comprise the basic day for each student is a crucial prerequisite to the beginning of scheduling. Will reading and language arts be offered together or separately? Will there be daily physical education, or some other arrangement? Will there be an advisor-advisee program? What kind of exploratory emphasis will the curriculum offer? Will there be a full year each for social studies and language arts? Will students from different grades study completely different subjects? All these questions, and many others, need to be answered before scheduling can begin.

Ideally, the school scheduling team will be able to make many of these decisions themselves, in collaboration with the rest of the staff. In practice, however, these decisions and many others come to the staff as givens, decided for them by others beyond the school. It may even be that the unit of time into which the school day is divided (module, block or period) will have been previously determined along with the number of units in a daily schedule. Regardless of where these decisions are made, those who schedule must incorporate these data into the process. Additional decisions will have to be made: How much passing time will be permitted between classes? What length of time will be required for each of the parts of the curriculum each day or week? Are there restrictions which arise from the nature of the school building? From the student-teacher ratio or other funding concerns? Answers to these questions, and others unique to each school, must be clearly known before scheduling can begin, otherwise barrier after barrier will arise during and after the construction of the schedule.

Steps in Scheduling. Veteran schedule builders begin with equal amounts of humility and determination. Accepting that all of one's priorities cannot be achieved is as important as the dogged determination to achieve them in spite of the impossible nature of the task. The objective of the scheduling process becomes the struggle to achieve as much as possible from the list of priorities with which one begins. With this in mind, one expert schedule builder known to the authors recommends the following steps in the construction of a workable schedule for a fairly conventional, but exemplary, middle school:[5]

The first step in designing a schedule follows the establishing of curriculum priorities: determination of the number of teachers needed to offer all of the required daily subjects that have been selected. In the form of a question to be answered, it would be "How many teachers must I have for each subject?" One way to answer that question is to divide the number of students to be served by the number of students per class. This calculation gives the number of sections needed for each class to be taught daily. Next, divide the number of sections needed by the number of periods per day that each teacher will teach. The resulting figure is the number of teachers needed to serve the students in each subject.

The second step is the formation of teams of teachers and students. If the school has committed itself to a version of grouping which permits groups of students to be brought together without regard to grade level, the process is simplified considerably, and involves developing as many teams as you wish, based on the type of team you desire. If the school is committed to a version of chronological age grouping, it will be necessary to determine whether the numbers of students in each grade are evenly divided. When the numbers are even, balanced teams may be designed, but when there are more students in one grade than another, the teams may not be exactly the same size. In large schools, the number of students will even require, at times, that there be teams of different sizes at the same grade level. Under these circumstances, teams of two, three, four, or five teachers will be found in the same school.

The third step is to determine the manner in which the students' day will be divided; the number of units of time in the day during which students will receive instruction. Generally, the pattern most common in middle schools we have observed is to arrange units of time for each of the four or five basics, a period for physical education, and a period for unified arts. This basic pattern is then modified in many schools to accommodate the separation of reading from language arts, the addition of other exploratory options, and so on. These units of time can, of course, be periods, blocks, or modules.

The fourth step is to determine what special features will be added to this basic schedule. Compensatory mathematics or language arts education, advisor-advisee periods, special interest periods when the whole school is involved, uninterrupted sustained silent reading efforts that require everyone's participation, and other special programs can be added in at this point.

The fifth step never ends; master schedules are almost never finished. More often than not, the scheduling team simply reaches a point where they believe that the best possible schedule has been produced. It may be that the final product fails to accomplish a number of priorities that were established at the beginning of the process. Unfortunately, in the real world of conflicting priorities, this often happens. It is impossible to have twice as much of everything. After you have done all that you can do, and asked for assistance from others you respect, the schedule is probably as good as it can be. Remember, however, that if you designed it to accommodate the interdisciplinary team organization, each team will be able to adjust to the schedule in individual ways that will make the ultimate fit of the schedule to the program seem a bit more acceptable.

North Marion Middle School provides an excellent illustration of the application of the scheduling process just outlined. North Marion is a large rural school serving just over 1,000 students in grades 6, 7 and 8. The school funding situation in this part of the state is, perhaps, slightly below average for the nation. The students come from a wide geographic area, some riding the bus for as many as fifty miles each way. The master schedule at North Marion is prepared in accordance with the steps discussed above.

While the preparation of an actual schedule for a school of 1,000 students involves many smaller substeps that are impossible to include here, following the process of the major steps in the construction of the North Marion schedule should be helpful. As we discuss the steps, it will be helpful if you will turn to Table 7.4, a more detailed version of the school's master schedule.

In step one, the number of students to be served at North Marion (1049, minus 32 educably mentally retarded students who are scheduled separately, yielding a total of 1017) is divided by the number of students per class (1017 divided by 30 students per class equals approximately 34 sections of each class to be taught daily). Then the number of necessary sections (34) is divided by the number of periods per day each teacher is to teach (5). This yields the number of teachers required to serve the students in each subject

Table 7.4 / Schedule at North Marion Middle School 1978–1979

NORTH MARION MIDDLE SCHOOL			HR	1	2	3	4	5	6	7	LUNCH	1978-79 SCHEDULE
Scott	6A	LA	6	ACADEMIC					PLAN	SGG	10:18	
O'Connell		M	6						PLAN	SGG	10:25	
Rosier		Sc	6						PLAN	SGG	10:18	
Tyler		SS	6						PLAN	SGG	10:25	
Clifton	6B	LA	6	ACADEMIC					SGG	PLAN	10:32	
Dixon		M	6						SGG	PLAN	10:25	
Beckerman		Sc	6						SGG	PLAN	10:25	
Bredahl		SS	6						SGG	PLAN	10:32	
Caswell	7A	LA	7	ACAD.	PLAN	SGG	ACADEMIC				11:14	
Hicks		M	7		PLAN	SGG					11:21	
Brown,G.		Sc	7		PLAN	SGG					11:21	
Parra		SS	7		PLAN	SGG					11:14	
Cahill,J.	7B	LA	7	ACAD.	SGG	PLAN	ACADEMIC				11:07	
Thomas		M	7		SGG	PLAN					11:14	
Johnson,E.		Sc	7		SGG	PLAN					11:14	
Estes		SS	7		SGG	PLAN					11:07	
Hovater	8B	LA	8	ACADEMIC			PLAN	SGG	ACAD.		12:10	
Priscott		M	8				PLAN	SGG			12:03	
Johnson,R.		Sc	8				PLAN	SGG			12:10	
Cahill,R.		SS	8				PLAN	SGG			12:03	
Creveling	8A	LA	8	ACADEMIC			SGG	PLAN	ACAD.		12:24	
Nichols		M	8				SGG	PLAN			12:17	
McLean		Sc	8				SGG	PLAN			12:17	
Clegorne,A.		SS	8				SGG	PLAN			12:24	
			6,7,8	6,8	6,8	6,7	6,7	7,8	7,8		
Clegorne,C.N.	Skills-Basic		7		PLAN						11:00	
Snyder	L.Arts-Basic		6				PLAN				11:00	
Brown,A.	Math - Basic		8		PLAN						12:03	
Johnson,L.	Reading-Basic								PLAN		11:00	
Billings, Marian	PE			PLAN	7	7	8	8	6	6	11:49	
Lavan, William	PE			PLAN	7	7	8	8	6	6	11:49	
McKelvy, Barry	PE			PLAN	7	7	8	8	6	6	11:49	
Miller, Gary	PE			PLAN	7	7	8	8	6	6	11:49	
Poole, Patricia	PE			PLAN	7	7	8	8	6	6	11:49	
McEwen, Barry	Agriculture			PLAN	7	7	8	8	6	6	11:49	
Reynolds, David	Construction			PLAN	7	7	8*	8**	6	6	11:49	
Smith, Lester	Graphics			PLAN	7	7	8	8	6*	6**	11:49	
Wyman, James	Manufacturing			PLAN	7**	7*	8	8	6	6	11:49	
Mack, Carol	Business Ed.			PLAN	7	7	8	8	6	6	11:49	
Thomas, Vernita	Food & Textiles			PLAN	7	7	8	8	6	6	11:49	
Jackson, Mary	Food & Textiles			PLAN	7	7	8	8	6	6	11:49	
Rubly, Annell	Dev. Reading			6A	6A,B	6A,B	6A	6A	PLAN	PLAN	10:11	
				6B	6A,B	6A,B	6B	6B	8AB,7	PLAN	10:11	
				7B	PLAN	PLAN	7A,B	7A,B	7B	7B	11:49	
Watson, Martha	Dev. Reading			8A	8A	8A	7A,B	7A,B	PLAN	8A	11:49	
				7A	PLAN	8A	Band 7A,B	Band 7A,B	8AB,7	7A	11:49	
				8B	8B	8B	PLAN	PLAN	7A	8B	11:49	
Smith, Billie K.	Art			7A	EMR	BASIC	BASIC	PLAN	7B	7B	11:00	
				8B	8B	8B	6A	6A	Basic	PLAN	10:11	
				6B	BASIC	6A,B	6B	6B	PLAN	7A	10:11	
Hergert, Linda	Art			7B	BASIC	PLAN	6B	6B	Basic	7A	10:11	
				8A	8A	PLAN	BASIC	7A,B	7A	7B	11:49	
				6A	6A,B	BASIC	6A	6A	EMR	PLAN	10:11	
Cotton, Johnnie	Vocal Music			6B	8B	8B	EMR	PLAN	7A	8B	11:00	
				7B	BASIC	BASIC	7A,B	PLAN	7B	8A,B		
				7A	8A	3A	BASIC	PLAN	BASIC	8A		
Henry, John	Instr. Music			8B	6A,B	6A,B	7A,B	7A,B	8AB,7	PLAN	11:49	
				6A	6A,B	6A,B	7A,B	7A,B	8AB,7	PLAN	11:49	
				8A	6A,B	6A,B	7A,B	7A,B	8AB,7	PLAN	11:49	
Hilker, Larry	EMR										TBA	
Noll, Beverly	EMR										TBA	
Rosenvinge, Arlene	EMR										10:11	
Kirkwood, Karla	SLD								PLAN & TEST		TBA	
Campbell, Kenneth	EH										TBA	
Parker, Tommy	Gifted			7	8	6						

Hackmyer, Scott	Guidance Counselor	Caton, William	Principal
Rowe, Kathie	Guidance Counselor	Livingston, John	Assistant Principal
Mills, Nancy	Media Specialist	Lane, Elaine	Asst.Prin./Curr.Coord.

* = P & T Semester 1
** = P & T Semester 2

(7). North Marion will need seven teachers in each of the basic subjects: math, science, social studies and language arts; a total of 28 teachers for the academic group of subjects.

At the second step, North Marion has elected to offer an interdisciplinary team model which includes four teachers, one representing each of the basic subjects. This results in the construction of seven teams. Opting for the standard version of chronological age grouping, this means two teams at each grade level, and one additional team. This additional team, or individual teachers, could have been assigned to the grade level where the largest number of students were that particular year. Assuming, for example that projections for the following year indicate 50 more students in the sixth grade than in the other two grades, plans would be made to utilize these additional teachers at that level.

Step three requires the North Marion staff to consider the enormous geographic area (800 square miles) served by the school, and the largely rural and economically disadvantaged character of the population there. Consequently, in an attempt to offer as many enriching experiences as possible, with an emphasis on programs which will be beneficial to later needs of the students as they become adults, North Marion divides the day into seven periods, approximately forty-five minutes per period. Notice, however, that the seven periods are conveniently grouped into two blocks, a five-period academic block and a two-period enrichment block.

Each team at North Marion is assigned approximately 150 students. While the students are divided into four homeroom groups, for instructional purposes they are reassigned to five groups. During any one instructional period, four of the groups are with the academic team and the fifth is in art, music or reading. A glance at the bottom of the schedule will show that, during period one, the fifth group of students from team 6A went to reading the first twelve weeks, music the second twelve weeks and to art during the last twelve weeks. In essence, this is a five-teacher team, but with four homerooms. Schools which have five teachers on a team, by adding reading as a yearlong subject, function in much the same way.

The enrichment period for team 6A appears where it says "Plan," in the sixth-period spot. At that time all students from the team are sent to the seven prevocational areas, providing a common planning time for the academic teachers on the team. During the seventh period, team 6A is involved in small group guidance and physical education. Each academic teacher works with 10 advisees in a small group while the other 30 go to physical education. By the end of the week, each student has had four periods of physical education and one period in a small group with his advisor.

The small group program is an example of the implementation of the fourth step in planning the master schedule at North Marion. Having survived for more than ten years in this school district, this program demonstrates the importance of proper scheduling to the life of an idea such as small group guidance. The existence of the Basic Skills Team is another example of this step in the planning process. Because many of the students at

North Marion are considerably deficient in skill development when they arrive at the school, the staff has designed a special team for the slow learner who while not specially classified by the state, seems unable to keep up in the regular classroom. To serve these students, many of whom are functioning at the second- or third-grade level in skills, the school designed a special multiage grouped team which would focus on the rapid development of basic skills. Using the same type of scheduling process for this team, the teacher-student ratio was reduced to approximately 12 to 15 students per teacher. The exceptional students who have been staffed into special programs are also able to participate fully in the two-period block of small group guidance, physical education and enrichment. These students also move in and out of the team's academic time on the basis of individual needs, with eighth graders successfully mainstreamed.

Recognizing step five (the unfinished step) at North Marion means that while living with one schedule, the staff has already begun to consider changes for the following year. Because of the nature of the sixth-grade students, and the larger number of them, the staff is considering a return to teams of two teachers each, with each teacher reponsible for two subject areas and a smaller group of students. And, in response to continuing pressures to shore up the basic skills area, building on the success of the present basic skills team, the school plans to exchange several teacher units so that two additional math lab teachers can be added. This will allow all students to spend twelve weeks each year in developmental reading, and almost all students to spend twelve weeks in the math lab. The result is that students will receive the normal instruction in math and language arts daily for the entire year, but in addition, each student will receive social studies for twenty-four weeks, with math lab the final twelve.

Those who schedule at North Marion emphasize the importance of flexibility and persistence. The schedule which we have analyzed here is the last in a series of five attempts, all of which permitted the retention of the team concept, the common planning periods and the small group guidance program. Scheduling is, obviously, never finished at North Marion, nor will it be in any exemplary middle school.

It is important to remember that in any effort in scheduling the basic process is the assignment of units of time to elements of the program. The names of those units, whether module, period or block, are arbitrary and beside the point. Arranging the day to fit the program, and giving teams of teachers some role in the use of that time is the objective. There are many different ways to achieve that objective.

Fort Clarke Middle School, Gainesville, Florida, is an example of an exemplary effort in schedule development and modification. Faced with a number of priorities derived from school board guidelines, teacher contracts, an open-space school where movement is a problem, a commitment to team organization and several other complicating factors, the staff responded creatively and practically to scheduling concerns. While space limitations herein prevent a complete discussion of the scheduling process as it

Table 7.5 / Former Five-Period Schedule*

60	60	60	L U N C H	60	60

* Fort Clarke Middle School, Gainesville, Florida

evolved over a six-year period at Fort Clarke, some description of the basic design should be enlightening.

Fort Clarke is a school of approximately 1,000 students in grades 6 through 8. Teachers are organized into three unusually large grade level teams, each with three language arts-reading teachers, three social studies-science teachers and two math teachers. The students on each team are grouped according to achievement and ability levels in math and reading. Fort Clarke has a 300-minute instructional day.

Students have a daily schedule of five periods, but not the 45- or 50-minute periods that one might expect. When the school board mandated that the students at Fort Clarke should have extra amounts of reading and math (approximately twice that of science and social studies) the staff was able to respond creatively, as a result of a flexible schedule that was based on a team organization.

Table 7.5 illustrates a typically basic five-period student day for the sixth grade prior to the school board mandate. Table 7.6, however, represents a simple but profound modification of the basic student schedule that permits the school to respond effectively to the board mandates. Each grade level team was divided into two groups, roughly by ability and achievement, and given schedules that provided for 75 minutes of daily instruction in language arts-reading, and 75 minutes in a combined science-social studies program.

Table 7.6 / Revised Sixth-Grade Schedule*

G R O U P A	75	75	L U N C H	50	50	50
G R O U P B	50	50	50	L U N C H	75	75

* Fort Clarke Middle School

Table 7.7 / Sample Sixth-Grade Student Schedule*

Language Arts Reading	Social Studies Science	L U N C H	Math	P.E.	Exploratory

* Fort Clarke Middle School

With this schedule, each student also receives 50 minutes of physical education, 50 minutes of mathematics and 50 minutes of an exploratory course. Table 7.7 illustrates a typical day for the sixth-grade students at Fort Clarke: five periods of five subjects with the lengths of the periods modified according to the significance attached to a subject by school board members and parents. Half of the students begin the day with a 75-minute period of language arts and reading, the balance between the two topics to be determined by the teachers based on the needs of the students. Next comes a 75-minute period of either science or social studies, a half year of each. After lunch this half of the sixth graders has three successive 50-minute periods of mathematics, physical education and exploratory. The other half of the sixth-grade team has a schedule that is basically the reverse. These other sixth graders have their math, physical education and exploratory courses in the morning, followed by the two larger time blocks for language arts-reading and science-social studies in the afternoon. And it appears that the two groups could exchange schedules at midyear with little difficulty. Similar schedules exist for seventh- and eighth-grade teams.

The teachers at Fort Clarke like this design. For the mathematics, physical education and exploratory teachers the program is still very much as it was—six 50-minute periods with planning time before and after school. For the language arts-reading teachers and the science-social studies teachers, this design is very comfortable. None of them have more than four classes a day, with class sizes equal to the other teachers, since compensatory program students and other special and exceptional students are sent from the team for their special classes during these times. This design also provides for a great deal of teamed planning and instruction within these smaller mini-departments on each team.

Actually, this schedule seems to work well for almost everyone at this particular school. The school board is satisfied and the teachers' union is content. The parents approve of the extra emphasis on reading and mathematics. The students are doing well on tests of academic achievement. The administration likes the situation where only a fraction of the students are changing classes at any one time, hand scheduling is simple, changes are uncomplicated and the entire process (when one has all the information) seems relatively traditional and rather easily understood.

It is crucially important, however, to point out that this schedule has evolved to its present form over a six-year period in response to the special characteristics of a particular school in a particular place at a particular time. The caution against the folly of attempting to impose a schedule from one school directly upon another cannot be repeated too often.

Special Schedules. Experienced schedulers know that a master schedule cannot be built to respond to every changing need of a school population. There are often special alternative schedules that are used, infrequently, whenever the special need requiring it arises. Some schools use floating period schedules to add an additional elective to an already full day. Others use a rotating schedule in which subjects appear at different times each day of the week. Many schools use a minimum day schedule which allows all classes to meet for something less than their regular allotment of time, permitting an early dismissal of students while the faculty remains for special activities such as inservice education or parent conferences. Many schools use "A and B day" schedules which allow students to attend two different subjects (for example, physical education and unified arts) on an every other day basis. Even more schools follow a pattern similar to that at C.L. Jones Middle School, Minden, Nebraska, of designating one of the periods (usually the last) of the day as a special exploratory period. At Beck Middle School, Cherry Hill, New Jersey, the activity period is filled with difficult-to-schedule programs such as minicourses, intramurals, independent study, group guidance, study hall and so on. This type of schedule can also be used to offer special assemblies, to permit school field trips and so on.

At the middle school level, however, stability and continuity are as important to the arrangement of the school day as are variety and change. Older high school students may be able to function effectively in a situation which manifests constant schedule changes controlled from the office. The authors believe, as do many educators from outstanding middle schools, that most needs for change and variety can be met within the structure of the interdisciplinary team organization, and met more effectively there than through some other mechanism. Once a school has found a team organization that works and a schedule that fits this process, fewer complicated special scheduling maneuvers are necessary or popular.

Scheduling Within the Schedule. Beyond the construction of the master schedule lies an entire world of time management. Effective master schedules permit teachers on teams to adapt time to the goals of the program of the team, and to accommodate the activities of the team to those of the larger school with a minimum of inconvenience. Moving students on the team to the unified arts program, scheduling students for academic learning within the team and arranging special whole team learning programs are all important scheduling efforts that must be designed for individual teams.

At Beverlye Road Middle School, Dothan, Alabama, the design of an effectively simple master schedule in block form, permits the movement of students in and out of a fine unified arts program. Table 7.8 illustrates the master schedule at Beverlye. Based on the discussion earlier in the chapter,

Table 7.8 / Beverlye Middle School, Winter Quarter

SIXTH GRADE	SEVENTH GRADE	EIGHTH GRADE
8:00–8:20	Advisor/Advisee Period	
P.E./Exploratory Team Planning 8:30–9:55	8:30–11:30 A.M. Basics Content Area	8:30–10:05 Content Area
A.M. Basics Content Area 10:05–12:30		P.E./Exploratory 10:05–11:40 Team Planning
	11:30–11:55 Lunch	
Lunch 12:30–12:55	11:55–1:00 P.M. Basics	Lunch 11:40–12:05
		P.M. Basics Content Area 12:05–2:35
P.M. Basics Content Area 1:00–2:35	1:00–2:35 Team Planning	
2:35–2:45	HOME BASE	

2:45 Escort students to loading zone exit
Exploratory and physical education teachers will have their planning time and lunch
 period from 11:40 until 1:00
Team planning scheduled from 2:45 until 3:15

the reader should be able to identify a number of middle school program components within the schedule at Beverlye: interdisciplinary team organization (there are two teams at each grade level); an advisor-advisee period during the first period of the day (8:00–8:30 a.m.), and an extended time (ninety-five minutes) for exploratory experiences.

The Dothan, Alabama, middle schools are committed to a strong exploratory emphasis in the unified arts and physical education. The schedule is, consequently, designed to facilitate that program commitment; and it does so very well. Table 7.9 illustrates the scheduling for these curriculum areas that is built into the master schedule, but not obvious by looking at it. The sixth grade is used here for explanatory purposes; seventh and eighth grades follow similar schedules. While the academic teachers in the sixth grades have their planning periods, their students are involved in the exploratory program. During the first half of the ninety-five minute exploratory time, half of the sixth-grade students are involved in an outstanding exploratory curriculum. One group each is in art, home economics, industrial arts and music. At the same time, the other half of the sixth grade is divided into three equal sections and sent to physical education. During the second half of the long period, the two halves of the sixth grade exchange places. This basic rotation program can be modified to fit just about any local condition or demands, just about any division of the year into grading periods, and practically any type of curriculum offerings.

Analyzing the program of one of the teams at Noe Middle School, Louis-

Table 7.9 / Beverlye Road Middle School, Sixth-Grade Exploratory Schedule

* F I R S T	¼ 6A Art	¼ 6A H Ec	⅓ 6B-PE
			⅓ 6B-PE
4 7 ½	¼ 6A Ind. Arts	¼ 6A Music	⅓ 6B-PE
S E C O N D	¼ 6B Art	¼ 6B H Ec	⅓ 6A-PE
			⅓ 6A-PE
4 7 ½	¼ 6B Ind. Arts	¼ 6B Music	⅓ 6A-PE

ville, Kentucky, illustrates just how flexible the master schedule permits creative teachers to become. Table 7.10 illustrates the schedule at Noe Middle School. Notice that there are six teams, one sixth; two seventh; one eighth; one unified art and one designated MA, which stands for the multiage group team at Noe. (Attempting to change from chronological age

Table 7.10 / Noe Middle School Master Schedule, 1977–78

TEAM	TEAM DATA	TEAM SCHEDULE (ALL TEAMS WILL HAVE HOMEROOM FROM 7:30–7:40.)					
6:1		7:45–9:40 TEAM		9:45–10:40 UA	10:45–2:00 TEAM		
7:1		7:45– 8:40 TEAM	8:45– 9:40 UA	9:45–2:00 TEAM			
7:2		7:45– 8:40 TEAM	8:45– 9:40 UA	9:45–2:00 TEAM			
8:1		7:45– 8:40 UA	8:45–2:00 TEAM				
MA		7:45–1:00 TEAM				1:05–2:00 UA	
Unified Arts		7:45– 8:40 8:1	8:45– 9:40 7:1–2	9:45– 10:40 6:1	10:45– 12:00 Cafe	12:05– 1:00 Plan	1:05– 2:00 MA

grouping to multiage grouping smoothly and slowly, the school began to change, in 1977–78, one team each year.) The multiage (MA) team at Noe, as does each of the teams there, has the responsibility for scheduling the advisory time within the extended periods of time allocated to them for their interdisciplinary instruction. Each team tends, therefore, to structure the advisory time in a way which suits them best. The MA team reports that, because the teachers get along so well together in other aspects of team life, they often arrange the advisory time in a team fashion, using it to teach aspects of social and emotional education. Table 7.11 illustrates the team's plans for the advisory time over a period of three months. The column at the left indicated when the various topics will be covered; column two, the topics themselves; column three lists the teachers on the team who will be responsible for the major planning of each separate unit. Scheduling the advisory time this way permits the team to deal with a wide range of important topics while it keeps individual teacher planning to a minimum.

This same team of teachers utilizes the maximum amount of flexibility when designing the academic time for its students. During a week that included an interdisciplinary thematic unit on the West, the team utilized a scheduling procedure that reaches the zenith of both flexibility and individual student choice within a teacher-designated structure that provides stability and continuity.

The following illustrations and explanations clarify the set of steps through which the team and its students moved during the last week of the unit on the West, and some additional science and language arts activities. The process begins with a series of team meetings during which teachers plan the activities and develop a schedule for each week to come. Table 7.12 illustrates the activities for social studies, science and language arts for the week. (Because mathematics was not involved in this particular unit, and was taught by the team at another time of the day, it does not appear in these plans.) The list tells us what topics will be dealt with, and the learning activi-

Table 7.11 / Advisor-Advisee Topics At Noe Middle School

March	24–30	Values Clarification	Davis
	31–April 6	Decision Making	
April	7–13	Friendship Week	Sindalar
	14–20		
April	21–27	Development of Self-Confidence	McLaughlin
	28–May 4	and Identification of Strengths	
May	5–11	Development of Self-Awareness	Brakmeier
	12–18		
May	19–23	Interpersonal Relationships	Warner
May	24	Drug Day	All
May	25	Follow-up	All
May	26–June 2	Dating and Sex	All

Table 7.12 / Topics and Activities—Unit on the West*

SOCIAL STUDIES		
Monday	Movie: "The Red West", narrated by Gary Cooper	2 Mods
Tuesday	Discussion of Life on an Indian Reservation	2 Mods
Wed.–Fri.	Stations on the "Old West"	6 Mods
Thursday	Guest Speaker, William Owl	2 Mods
LANGUAGE ARTS		
Monday and Thursday	Skills and Application (Groups A,B,C)	4 Mods
Tuesday	Skills and Application (Groups D,E,F)	2 Mods
SCIENCE		
Monday	Discussion on the Use of the Microscope	2 Mods
Tuesday	Lab Using the Microscope to View Prepared Slides	2 Mods
Wednesday	Lab Using the Microscope to Prepare and View Self-Made Slides	3 Mods
Thursday	Review of the Use of the Microscope	2 Mods
Friday	Test on the Microscope	2 Mods

* From Noe Middle School, Louisville, Kentucky.

ties which will be used for each subject. Science, for example, deals with the use of the microscope, and involves discussions, laboratory activity, a review and an exam. Social studies focuses directly on the topic of the West and involves a series of learning stations, a movie, a guest speaker and some group discussions. Language arts focuses on skills and the application of these skills using the social studies topic of the West. Table 7.12 lists the topics in each of the three areas, the days they will be offered and the number of periods (or mods) that each student is required to take, even to the extent of assigning students to different language arts groups.

Once the teachers have laid out their plans for the coming week, the entire team of teachers and students meets during the last two mods of the week, from 12:15 until 12:55 on Friday. Table 7.13 is the program that the teachers distribute to the students during these two planning periods. Students can see quickly which activities are required and which are not, how many mods of each activity will be needed and which teacher will be in charge of each activity. The next step is to divide up into advisory groups for the actual choosing of activities for the next week.

Table 7.14 illustrates the second planning form given to the students, on which they record the plan for their learning. The upper square section lays out the different mods during which these activities will be offered for the week. Each mod contains the numbers of the activities that will be available at that time of that day. Tuesday, at 11:05 a.m., for example, students can choose from among the microscope lab, learning stations on "the West," discussion of life on an Indian reservation, a language arts group and inde-

Table 7.13* /

NUMBER	MODS	TOPICS FOR THE WEEK	GROUP	TEACHERS
1	2	Discussion-Use of the microscope		Brakmeier/ McLaughlin
2	2	Lab-Microscope techniques of viewing slides		''
3	3	Lab-Microscope-preparing and viewing self-made slides		''
4	2	Review-Microscope		''
5	2	Test-Microscope		''
6	2	Movie-"The Red West"		Sindelar
7	6	Stations-The West		Warner and/or Sindelar
8	2	Guest Speaker-William Owl, Cherokee Indian from North Carolina		Warner
9	2	Discussion-Life on an Indian Reservation		Sindelar
10†	4	Literature skills & application	A	Davis
11†	4	'' '' '' ''	B	''
12†	4	'' '' '' ''	C	''
13†	2	'' '' '' ''	D	''
14†	2	'' '' '' ''	E	''
15†	2	'' '' '' ''	F	''
16	—	Independent Study		
17	2	Team Meeting-Plans for camping trip	A,B,C, D,E,F	

D,E,F-Critical Analysis Notebooks due in to Ms. Davis on Friday
All "Old West" Projects due in to Mrs. Warner or Mr. Sindelar Thursday
Special Arts Project students are to report to Mr. DeGiovanni at 12 noon Tuesday

* From Noe Middle School.
† Language Arts Group attendance required.

pendent study. The bottom half of the form is initially left blank, so that students can record their choices. Referring to the list of choices (Table 7.13), students work out their own schedule for the week, within the limits and the structure which the teachers have built. Table 7.15 illustrates the choices of one student on the team. Notice that many activities are really offered at very limited times (for example, the planning time for the following week, activity 17, is for everyone and must be scheduled for 12:15 until 12:55 on Friday). Nevertheless, it seems that most students will experience this opportunity for choice as a very positive experience, and that students will gain in self-discipline and responsibility as a result of it.

The team planning and scheduling by this team exemplify the effective use of the freedom and autonomy which well-designed master schedules offer. It is hard to imagine teams of teachers and students functioning in a

Table 7.14 / Student Decision-Making Form — Schedule of Topics*

	MONDAY	TUESDAY	WEDNESDAY	THURSDAY	FRIDAY
10:45–11:05	1,6,7,10,16	2,7,9,13,16	3,7,16	4,7,8,12,16	5,7,16
11:05–11:25	1,6,7,10,16	2,7,9,13,16	3,7,16	4,7,8,12,16	5,7,16
11:30–11:50	1,6,7,11,16	2,7,9,14,16	3,7,16	4,7,8,10,16	5,7,16
11:50–12:10	1,6,7,11,16	2,7,9,14,16	3,7,16	4,7,8,10,16	5,7,16
12:15–12:35	1,6,7,12,16	2,7,9,15,16	3,7,16	4,7,8,11,16	17
12:35–12:55	1,6,7,12,16	2,7,9,15,16	3,7,16	4,7,8,11,16	17

	MONDAY	TUESDAY	WEDNESDAY	THURSDAY	FRIDAY

* From Noe Middle School.

manner nearly as effective without the benefits of a schedule designed especially for the middle school situation. The high school departmentalized schedule could never achieve these ends. Perhaps, only the most effective middle school teachers could make this flexibility and student autonomy work smoothly.

Table 7.15 / Student Decision-Making Form — Illustrative Choices*

	MONDAY	TUESDAY	WEDNESDAY	THURSDAY	FRIDAY
10:45–11:05	1,6,7,10,16	2,7,9,13,16	3,7,16	4,7,8,12,16	5,7,16
11:05–11:25	1,6,7,10,16	2,7,9,13,16	3,7,16	4,7,8,12,16	5,7,16
11:30–11:50	1,6,7,11,16	2,7,9,14,16	3,7,16	4,7,8,10,16	5,7,16
11:50–12:10	1,6,7,11,16	2,7,9,14,16	3,7,16	4,7,8,10,16	5,7,16
12:15–12:35	1,6,7,12,16	2,7,9,15,16	3,7,16	4,7,8,11,16	17
12:35–12:55	1,6,7,12,16	2,7,9,15,16	3,7,16	4,7,8,11,16	17

	MONDAY	TUESDAY	WEDNESDAY	THURSDAY	FRIDAY
10:45–11:05	1	2	7	4	16
11:05–11:25	1	2	7	4	16
11:30–11:50	6	14	7	8	5
11:50–12:10	6	14	3	8	5
12:15–12:35	7	9	3	7	17
12:35–12:55	7	9	3	16	17

* From Noe Middle School.

Scheduling in Perspective

Few aspects of the exemplary middle school are both as fraught with difficulties and as crucial to the success of the program as the process of scheduling. Most middle school administrators recognize that an effective schedule is the fulcrum upon which the remainder of the program is moved. Yet the scheduling process has probably received less attention from research and development than any other item. Training in the skills necessary for effective schedule construction is still almost nonexistent. Much remains to be done.

Organizing Space in the Middle School

The Middle School Building

The famous aphorism "We shape our buildings; thereafter they shape us," attributed to Winston Churchill, applies directly to the discussion of school buildings. Often placed in the position of inheriting old high school or junior high school buildings, middle school educators find themselves in possession of a building designed for purposes and programs that are foreign to those the middle school advocates. With declining enrollments apparently likely to continue for some time, it seems possible that middle school educators who pin their hopes for a fully functioning school on the opportunity to design a new building to fit their program will often be disappointed. As this section of the chapter will demonstrate, however, exemplary middle schools can function beautifully in all kinds of physical plants.

Since, in architecture, form should follow function, comments on the most appropriate organization of space in middle schools must be accompanied by the familiar requirement to provide a unique and transitional approach. What the middle school building looks like and how it is organized will depend upon the type of program intended. The building should be designed to serve the program. Consequently, building construction should follow program design; organization of space in existing facilities which become the site of newly organized middle school programs should follow the acceptance of program changes. All too often, however, this does not happen.

Middle school buildings should be different from elementary and high school buildings. In the elementary school, where the emphasis is upon close relationships built in self-contained classrooms or those that are nearly so, where the curriculum focuses on skill development of the most basic kinds, and where teachers frequently work alone, the building is designed to accommodate this style. In spite of some recent changes in the construction of elementary schools, the building which focuses on single classrooms remains the model structure. Many elementary schools seem to be a series of single classrooms strung together for reasons that are difficult to determine. Because of the nature of the children they serve and the programs they offer, elementary schools tend to be smaller and less expensive than middle schools.

The high school building also reflects the program within it. Committed to the departmentalized organization of teachers, high schools are almost inevitably organized to reflect this design. The science department is housed in one wing, the mathematics department in another, the English department in a third and the social studies in a fourth area. Specialization is the key to high school programs, and the building reflects it with a myriad of special rooms, equipment and areas. High schools, because of this focus of specialization, and the increased costs that accompany it, tend to be much larger and much more expensive than middle schools.

Middle schools serve a kind of students and offer a kind of program which fits somewhere between the elementary and secondary positions. Middle schools attempt to provide a middle way, balancing the twin goals of personalized climate and enriched curriculum. Most middle school students would be lost in buildings housing between 3,000 and 5,000 students, like some high schools. These same students would often be challenged less than optimally by the programs which very small schools can afford. The middle school building must be large enough to hold the number of students necessary to justify the inclusion of expensive special programs so essential for effective early adolescent education. The cost of industrial arts, agriculture, music, art, home economics and other expensive programs place them beyond the reach of the elementary school, which because of the young children involved, must remain small and connected with the neighborhoods it serves. The number of students required to offer high school programs, however, produces a school building and student body large enough to drown the average middle schooler in a sea of anonymity and amorphousness.

The challenge of the middle school building, thus, is to be large enough to hold a number of students which will justify the expenditure of funds necessary for the exploratory programs which educators believe these students require. At the same time, however, the middle school building must be organized in a manner which insures a sense of community and a personalized educational experience for each student. This is no simple task.

It is not an impossible task, however, even though it is made more difficult by the frequent need to implement middle school programs in buildings designed initially as elementary or high school facilities. Middle schools can be designed originally or modified later to accommodate: advisory programs; the interdisciplinary organization of teachers; just about any type of school-wide student grouping pattern desired; enlarged library and media facilities; new programs in the unified arts; more complex and sophisticated opportunities for physical education and, if preferred, sports. These same schools can be organized in a way which permits the development of close personal relationships with teachers and a sense of community which leads students safely away from the protective atmosphere of the elementary school. Middle schools are the most effective way to educate older children and early adolescents, in part because they allow us to offer stimulating programs and enriched educational experiences without sacrificing the atmosphere most conducive to growth-producing interpersonal relationships. Neither program nor school climate needs to be subjugated to the other.

Flexibility

There is no single type of physical facility which is required for the implementation of the middle school program. Programs are influenced by the buildings they inhabit, but they are not completely determined by those buildings. It is possible to reach the status of an exemplary program in an old motel-style high school building, a converted elementary school, a new open space school or a structure built around pods of one kind or another. What one asks of a building matters most.

Earlier in the life of the middle school movement, near the end of the decade of the sixties, some educators seem to have been convinced that middle school and open space facilities were synonymous, that open space buildings were required for effective middle school programs. As a result, a great deal of public dissatisfaction with the way open-space schools were used in some school districts transferred to the middle school concept. Luckily, just as we seem to have realized that the middle school concept is not totally dependent on a particular instructional strategy (for example, individualized instruction), so, too, it seems that educators understand that many kinds of school buildings can be made to serve the middle school concept, and almost no building can totally prevent the concept from developing. Buildings without permanent walls offer the maximum amount of flexibility, but old high school buildings often present teachers and students with a great deal more space than might have been available if a new middle school building had been constructed. Almost every type of building has its strengths and weaknesses. The key to the use of the facility resides in being able to use the strengths of a particular building to enhance the program offered within.

No more effective demonstration of the truth of these comments could be found than the simple fact that of the many exemplary school programs described in this volume, no two are alike. Outstanding programs are found in old buildings and new, large and small, open and conventional. Some of the schools had the buildings designed especially for the programs, others took old high school, junior high school or elementary school buildings and modified them for new programs in highly effective ways. Equally true, in the opinion of the authors, is the observation that sterile, unimaginative and ineffective programs can be found in buildings which were designed to accommodate much, much more than they do. A reasonably flexible school plant is necessary for a good program, but is far from being sufficient to guarantee that program.

With this latitude in the kind of building in mind, however, it is interesting to note that the schools described in this volume represent three different kinds of building style. Similar programs have evolved in three different sets of physical surroundings: older structures often inherited from previous occupants; new buildings focusing on flexible use of space and individualized programs and even newer facilities designed with the idea of smaller schools within the larger building.

Middle school buildings can be classified in one other way that is significant. Some buildings were designed with a sophisticated middle school program clearly in mind. Others inherited the building, or grew within it after it was built to highlight another purpose. In the experience of the authors, the number of middle school buildings seems to be divided unevenly; far fewer buildings have been designed specifically to incorporate all the components of the middle school. Those for whom the middle school was an afterthought, if it was a factor at all in the design of the building, are far more numerous. The future, dominated as it may be by declining enrollments, will almost certainly include large numbers of middle schools that inhabit quarters designed to serve another student population. Both types of schools will, however, continue to offer exemplary programs for the remainder of this century.

Adapting Older Buildings

Perhaps because it may be easier to establish an exemplary middle school program in a new building designed specifically for that purpose, fewer schools which might be labeled exemplary are found, in our experience, in older buildings that have been adapted. This is certainly influenced by the likelihood of being able to assemble a new faculty, specially selected for the middle school program, whenever one opens a new middle school building. While it is, of course, possible for new faculties to be assigned to older buildings, it is almost mandatory in a new facility, since the staff has never been there before the building opened. Unless, that is, the faculty moved to the new building, en masse, from earlier quarters. Most middle school administrators in our acquaintance assert that it is many times more difficult to change from an existing junior high school to a middle school program than it is to begin a middle school program where no prior school existed. While the faculty makeup can be the most important factor, the building itself is quite important in determining the ease with which the new program is established. The simple fact that older buildings were almost always designed for other purposes and, therefore, require adaptations, establishes a measure of additional difficulty.

Sometimes middle schools inherited their space from elementary schools, but more frequently the program moved into a plant that housed a high school or junior high school. In the relatively infrequent instances where the middle school took over space from an elementary school the major problem stemmed from inadequate space and from facilities which did not contain areas or equipment to house the unified arts and other new programs which may have been in the planning. Since these enrichment areas were central to the middle school concept, their absence was serious. Accommodations for these programs usually came in the form of portable buildings or additions to the existing facilities, or they did not come at all. Schools fortunate enough to convince district planners to add the space had a new chance to excel; those who were refused were forced to accept severe limitations in the program they offered to their students.

Middle school programs that inherited their space from older secondary programs were more fortunate, or at least their problems were of a different nature. Moving into an older secondary school building usually meant that the enlarged library and media space was there, if the books and the equipment were not. The areas where the unified arts had been offered were still there, even if the spaces looked like vacant airplane hangers. Inheriting a high school building has usually also meant that there would be more space of all kinds; offices, cafeteria, study areas, auditorium, laboratories and larger classrooms. High schools, simply, were bigger. So, the problems were not connected with having enough space to put all the program components.

The major problem with inheriting the high school or junior high school building seems to be related to the differing practices of organizing teachers for instruction. Most secondary schools have operated on the departmentalized model of curriculum and teacher organization. In addition, in the headlong rush to erect buildings large enough to offer expanded, comprehensive programs, consolidating (read eliminating) the smaller schools in the process, few architects or school planners seem to have given any thought at all to the need to design the new structures in a way that preserved the sense of community that existed in the smaller schools. New middle school programs in older secondary buildings, thus, found themselves with space that was often difficult to adapt to new needs.

Most older secondary school buildings were constructed so that classrooms were not grouped together in any type of recognizable pattern, except in the case of the science program. The department concept required the science laboratories to be grouped in the same area, and this simple construction decision has caused an endless round of difficulties for middle school planners as they have attempted to adapt the buildings to the pattern of interdisciplinary teacher organization. Finding convenient groups of classrooms, and surmounting the science department problem so that teams could be close together in the middle school, presents a major stumbling block to new programs in old school buildings. Once these problems are solved, the rest seems to be relatively easy.

Middle schools choose one of two or three ways to deal with the need to make the science area more flexible. Some planners organize the day and the teams so that teams are able to schedule the time in the available science laboratory areas, avoiding major conflicts. With some notable exceptions, many middle school science programs seem to be relatively independent of the need for constant access to a science laboratory, and being able to schedule special lab time when necessary seems to be enough. Other schools have found that portable minilabs or demonstration tables often suffice. Still others are able to arrange their teams in the space so that while the science teachers have their rooms in what was the science department, interdisciplinary groups are still quite close together. Some other schools have found themselves so stymied by the placement of the science rooms that they have had to resort to interdisciplinary teams composed of mathematics, social studies and language arts teachers, leaving the science teachers together in a department. The authors believe that this is the least acceptable option, but that it is still considerably better than having the entire faculty remain in a departmentalized structure.

The authors also believe that, in almost every case, these science area problems can be resolved without sacrificing the interdisciplinary team concept. Faculties which find it difficult to do so may be philosophically resistant rather than spatially troubled. Since the authors believe so strongly that the interdisciplinary team concept is central, and must come first in the development of an exemplary middle school, it is important to take the time to help the staff to see the need to make both the philosophical and the territorial changes.

One school that has done an outstanding job of adapting an older secondary school building to the middle school program is Lincoln Middle School, Gainesville, Florida. Lincoln inherited a building that had a history as a segregated high school for several decades, followed by a period of vacant idleness after schools in the district were integrated in 1970. Opened several years later as a vocational school, it was changed to a middle school in 1974. Figure 7.3 is a floor plan of Lincoln drawn in 1973, prior to the opening of the middle school program there.

Lincoln houses approximately 1,000 students in a building intended to hold considerably more, when it was designed several decades earlier. A glance at the floor plan will show that the school was not intended as a middle school when built, but that the Lincoln staff did make the necessary adaptations to convert it to serve the team concept well. Believing that teams work better when located in contiguous classrooms, and having inherited enough space to give each team a planning area, the school was organized along these lines. Each of the six teams at Lincoln were assigned to team areas: C Team was given rooms 25 to 28 as classrooms, and room 15 as a team planning space; B Team was given rooms 31 to 34 as classrooms, and room 13 as their planning area; D Team was given rooms 44 to 47 as classrooms and room 40 as a team room; W Team was housed in rooms 48 to 51, with 42 as a planning room; G Team had rooms 52 to 55 as teaching areas, with 56 as the planning room; M Team was located in rooms 87 to 89, 90 and 91, with their planning space in room 88, which had been an automotive mechanics shop during the years the high school had been there. Six teams, six areas.

Other rooms and areas in the school are used quite conventionally:

- Gymnasium—76
- Cafeteria—19 to 24
- Auditorium—62
- Industrial Arts—93
- Media Center—67 to 68

- Special Education—12 to 17
- Typing—18
- Home Economics—39, 41
- Offices—1 to 8

Since the opening of school that first year, many changes have occurred at Lincoln. New programs which affected the entire district, in areas like bilingual education, deaf education and so on, have been located there. Enroll-

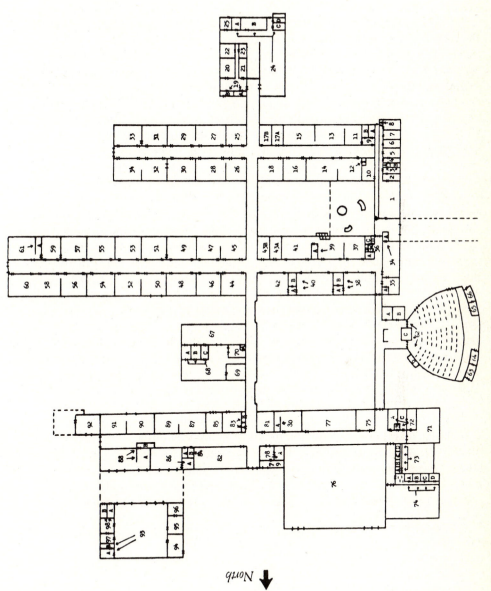

Figure 7.3 / Floor Plan, Lincoln Middle School, Gainesville, Florida.

ment fluctuations and other factors have required space to be adjusted, but the concept of team areas and planning spaces has been guarded jealously and never sacrificed. Very much the result of this, Lincoln is still an exemplary middle school nearly a decade after it was opened. Room 38, at one time the science laboratory for the high school, has always served as the science laboratory for the middle school, with teams scheduling their time in the lab on a first come, first served basis.

Many other middle schools have made creative adjustments of their inherited space in ways which have allowed them to develop and maintain outstanding programs. Schools mentioned elsewhere in this volume that have done so include: Tipton Middle School, Tipton, Iowa; West Middle School, Aurora, Colorado; and Stoughton Middle School, Stoughton, Wisconsin. But some school districts, more than most others, seem to exemplify the ability to make creative programs develop and prosper in school settings of widely varying types. The district of Dothan, Alabama, is such a place.

In early 1974, the school district of Dothan, Alabama, began to implement a well-planned project, with funding assistance from several sources, to close three junior high schools in the city and open four middle schools in the fall of 1977. Two of the four junior high school buildings were to be used as middle schools, and two new middle school buildings were to be built. The plan included a commitment to almost identical programs in each of the four middle schools, but the buildings that were intended to house these programs were radically different. Two were to be brand new flexibly spaced pod-type structures, one was a relatively modern junior high school of conventional classroom design, built about twenty years previous to the middle school plan and the fourth was a building that needed monumental renovation to make it acceptable to members of that community. Since the middle school plan also included a total reassignment of teachers throughout the district's middle level, the teachers had a vested interest in the building construction and renovation.

As it turned out, the programs for the four schools are, in fact, virtually indistinguishable from each other, with talented faculties operating within nearly identical team designs. Advisory programs function in each school, along with exploratory curriculum plans that should be the envy of neighboring districts. The most interesting thing about the program, in this respect, is that all four middle schools function with roughly identical schedules as well. The schedule for Beverlye Road Middle School, illustrated earlier in this chapter (Tables 7.8 and 7.9), is almost exactly like the schedules of sister middle schools Honeysuckle, Girard and Carver.

Pod-Style Middle School Facilities

The pod-style middle school building is the midpoint between the self-contained classroom school, which must adapt as described above, and the more completely open-space school designed to foster individualized instruction. The pod-type construction seems particularly suited to the middle school program, accommodating the interdisciplinary team organization in a special way. An analysis of the floor plan (Figure 7.4) of the Beverlye Road Middle School, Dothan, Alabama, illustrates the features of the pod design. The Beverlye plant also illustrates the flexibility that permits a number of program modifications to be installed without major plant renovation.

Beverlye Road Middle School houses approximately 750 students in grades 6 through 8. The program is almost identical to the program in the other three middle schools in the Dothan school district, in spite of the radically different physical facilities of the separate schools. Beverlye obviously offers an opportunity for an extensive exploratory program, described in the scheduling section of this chapter, including physical education, vocal and instrumental music, drama, business education, interior management (home economics), arts and crafts and industrial arts. The building, constructed in 1977, accommodates these programs beautifully. All parts of the building look out on to a central courtyard, and the outstanding media center is particularly fortunate in this regard.

Most important, however, is that the school was designed with a middle school program in mind, and with the realization that the interdisciplinary team organization was the heart of the program. The school building, therefore, is especially facilitative of the team and its community. At Beverlye, each grade level is housed in a separate pod. There are two teams for each pod, with up to four teachers on each team. Between each grade level team in the pod is a commons area for the grade level. The commons area radically expands the instructional space available to teachers and, therefore, contributes a flexibility to the academic program that is far beyond the capacity of schools without this design. The commons area also serves as a quasi-cafeteria, a place for all students and teachers on the team to eat the hot lunch which, cooked in the kitchen, is served in the pod. Students, therefore, leave the pod area only for physical education, exploratory subjects or for occasional trips to the media center.

The Beverlye plant, and other pod-style plants in schools elsewhere (for example, Jamesville-DeWitt Middle School, Jamesville, New York; Nock Middle School, Newburyport, Mass.), offer the maximum flexibility to middle school programs. The pod area at Beverlye, for example, permits educators to organize teachers and students for instruction in a variety of ways. While the staff in Dothan has decided to remain with the standard chronological grade level pattern, should there be a decision to move to a school-within-a-school program it could easily be accomplished with this building. Even a move to complete multiage grouping could be accommodated without plant modifications, simply establishing six such teams. Placements for flexible partitions and the opportunity to expand the building outward add to the amazing flexibility of this kind of building, and consequently to its desirability as a middle school facility.

A number of schools described in this volume can, quite reasonably, be described as pod-type schools, even though their actual physical plant may or may not have been designed with this purpose initially in mind. Pro-

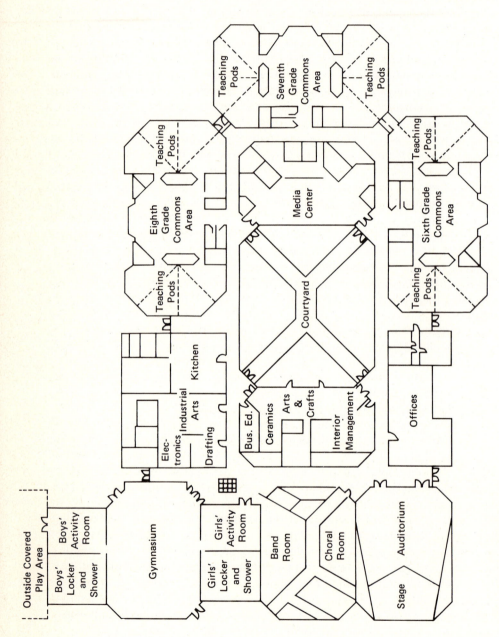

Figure 7.4 / Floor Plan, Beverlye Road Middle School, Dothan, Alabama.

grams at schools such as Farnsworth Middle School, Guiderland, New York, are assisted by spaces that match the programs beautifully. Figures 7.5, 7.6, 7.7 and 7.8 illustrate the floor plans of exemplary middle schools with outstanding accompanying facilities. Figures 7.5 and 7.6 illustrate both the first and second floors at Farnsworth, where each house extends over both levels. Designed to accommodate 1650 students, each house consists of four or five interdisciplinary teams, from grades 6 through 8. The staff at Farnsworth express their commitment to "harmonizing the best of two-worlds—one which is small enough to foster a feeling of concern for the individual student and one which is large enough to offer the varied resources necessary to meet the needs and interests of pre-adolescent and early adolescent youngsters." Examining the floor plan at Farnsworth creates an excited expectation that this type of program is really possible there.

Figure 7.7 illustrates the floor plan of Brookhaven Middle School, Decatur, Alabama, recognized since the late 1960's as an outstanding combination of program and plant. Notice the similar program potential in comparison to other schools described in this volume, and the flexibility to make changes in program without major building renovations. The strength of this type of building plan is a major factor in the ability of the school program to maintain a standard of excellence during more than a decade of challenges of all kinds. Figure 7.8 shows the features of the building that houses another outstanding program, that of Olle Middle School, Alief, Texas. Olle illustrates a kind of facility that reaches out to bridge the gap between the pod-style school and the more sweeping open-space schools. Houses at Olle are clearly in evidence, but the program could also be easily modified to focus on an open-space individualized grade-level program.

Open Space Buildings

Many exemplary middle schools are housed in what have been known as open space facilities, originally designed to accommodate programs also described as open, featuring the centrality of individualized instruction and actual team teaching. Following a decade of sometimes painful illumination about the relationship between form and function, many open-space schools have been modified in major ways and have, therefore, come to be known more legitimately as flexibly spaced facilities. The use of moveable walls has transformed rigidly open schools into schools where the faculties can shape the facility to fit the program they wish to offer there.[6]

North Marion Middle School, Citra, Florida, offers an example of the ultimate in flexible space. Figure 7.9 highlights the floor plan at North Marion. Simply stated, almost every wall in the school is moveable or removeable. Classrooms in the sixth-, seventh- and eighth-grade team areas can be opened to feature one large space, closed to accommodate conventional classrooms or arranged for varied sizes to fit almost any purpose. Notice the program reflected by the floor plan, and its emphasis on team areas, and exploratory curriculum opportunities. Teams of any size, reflecting the vicissitudes of

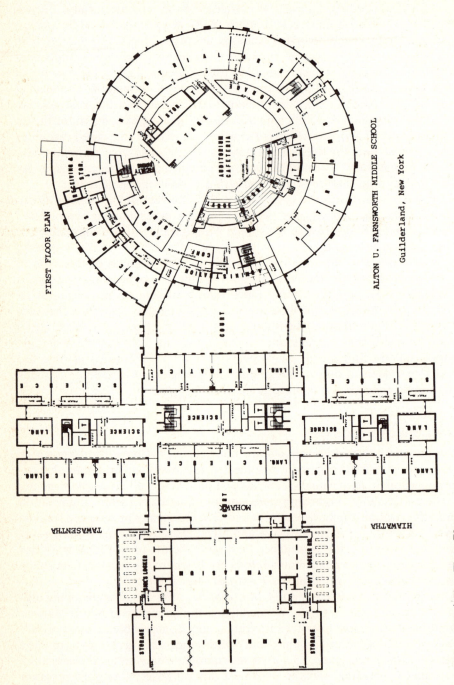

**Figure 7.5 / First-Floor Plan,
Farnsworth Middle School, Guiderland, New York.**

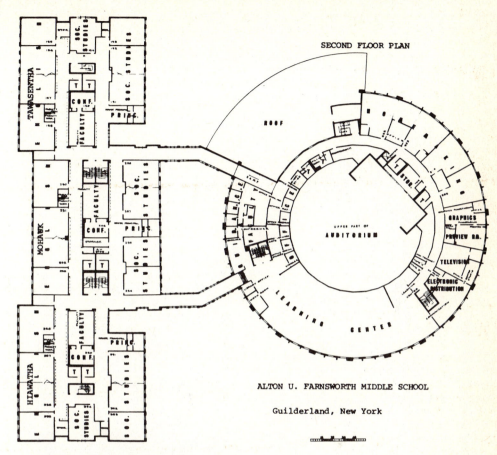

ALTON U. FARNSWORTH MIDDLE SCHOOL

Guilderland, New York

Figure 7.6 / Second-Floor Plan,
Farnsworth Middle School, Guiderland, New York.

shifting enrollment patterns in central Florida, can be fitted into each area.

Shelburne Middle School, Shelburne, Vermont, exemplifies the effective use of the flexible open space facility to strengthen the middle school program. Figure 7.10 shows the entire plant, housing 750 students in grades 5 through 8, with an opportunity for a multiage team as well. Team areas and exploratory spaces are clearly in evidence. Figure 7.11 details a classroom area, listing as advantages of this style: maximum flexibility in accommodating changes in teaching methods and curricula; efficient use of classroom space to provide for teaching groups of various sizes; corridors utilized as part of the educational spaces; carpeting for acoustical treatment and a homelike atmosphere; completely accessible resource materials, stimulating their use by students; development of appropriate social attitudes based upon the increased awareness of other students; and the use of moveable teaching aids, storage units, chalkboards and tackboards for greater flexibility and increased use.

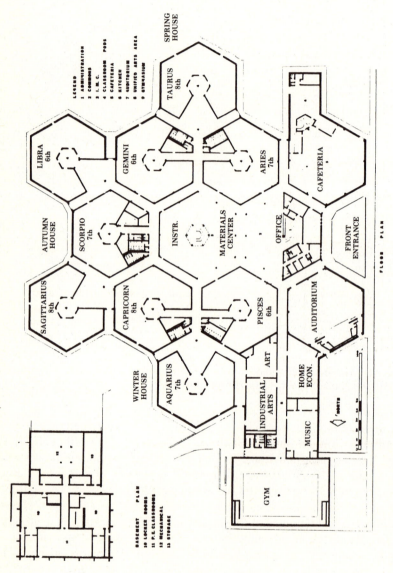

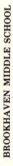

Figure 7.7 / Floor Plan, Brookhaven Middle School, Decatur, Alabama.

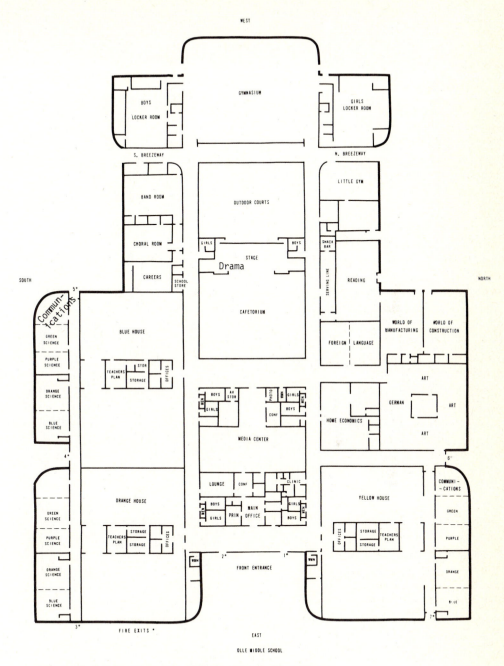

Figure 7.8 / Floor Plan, Olle Middle School, Alief, Texas.

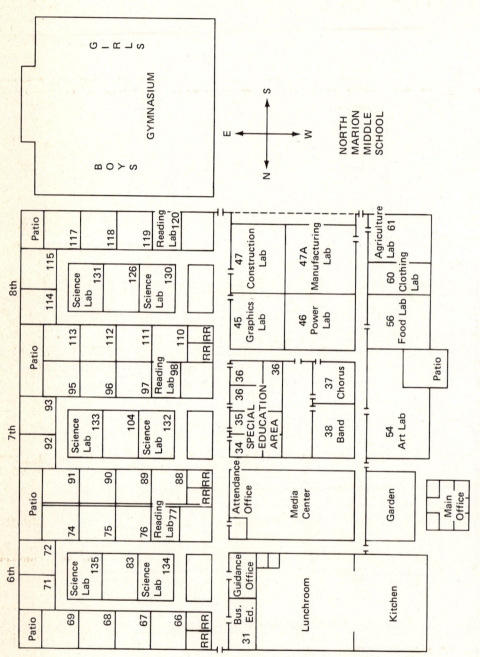

Figure 7.9 / Floor Plan, North Marion Middle School, Citra, Florida.

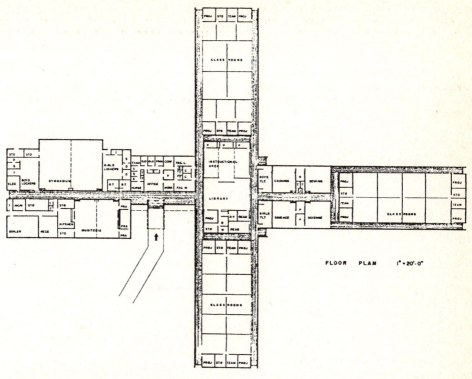

**Figure 7.10 / First-Floor Plan,
Shelburne Middle School, Shelburne, Vermont.**

Many other middle schools have capitalized on the flexibility of the open-space school to offer a challenging and stimulating middle school program. One of the oldest, and most successful, is MacDonald Middle School, East Lansing, Michigan. Designed to accommodate 850 students in grades 6 through 8, MacDonald has been operating in this facility since 1968. The school has been recognized as a special facility and received a great deal of recognition for its design.[7] A number of journals (for example, *The American School Board Journal, Nation's Schools*) offer numerous and detailed descriptions of new and different designs for use by school programs. Readers interested in an in-depth treatment of individual schools are encouraged to seek out examples in this part of the professional literature.

Time and Space in the Middle School: A Staff Development Comment

The effective use of time and space in the middle school is absolutely critical to the successful implementation of the other portions of the middle school program. If a component of the middle school program cannot be

CLASSROOM AND CORE PLAN

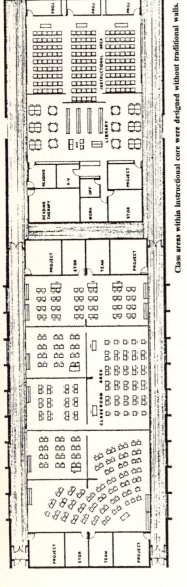

Class areas within instructional core were designed without traditional walls.

CONSTRUCTION STATISTICS

Grades...5–8
Designed Capacity 750
Site 30
Building Area ....85,500 sq. ft.
Cost of Construction (excluding
  land, landscaping, fees and
  furniture)...................$1,515,819.00
Construction Cost per sq. ft..$ 17.73
Construction Cost per pupil..$ 2,021.00

OPEN PLAN ADVANTAGES

Provides maximum flexibility for accommodating changes in teaching methods and curricula.

Efficient use of classroom space to provide for teaching groups of various sizes.

Corridors are utilized as part of the educational spaces.

Carpeting is used for acoustical treatment and homelike atmosphere.

Resource materials are completely accessible to stimulate their use by all the students.

Social attitudes are developed based upon the increased awareness of other students.

Teaching aids, storage units, chalkboards and tackboards can be movable for greater flexibility and increased use.

Figure 7.11 / Classroom and Core Plan, Shelburne Middle School, Shelburne, Vermont.

scheduled, it cannot be offered to the students. If there is no space which can be adapted to the use of a program part, that part will be unlikely to become a regular component of the program. In a sense, the organization of time and space stands as the ultimate restriction on the type of program possible in any particular middle school. But in the opposite sense, properly designed, these two factors represent a liberating opportunity for the expansion and enrichment of complex yet community-building school programs.

School planners interested in helping the staff of a middle school program get the most from the schedule and the building they use, must foster the development of several important skills. For administrators, a clear understanding of program priorities and the knowledge of the steps involved in the construction of a master schedule to accommodate team organization are crucial. The ability to place teams together within the building seems almost as important. For teachers, directors of inservice programs will assist most effectively when they help teachers learn how to use the schedule to their own advantage, to schedule their own students and special activities within the schedule and to turn the design of the plant, however constructed, to the enhancement of the life of the interdisciplinary team.

ADDITIONAL SUGGESTIONS FOR FURTHER STUDY

A. Periodicals

Barber, Ralph W., "Organizing Clusters in a Traditional Building," *Clearing House*, 50, 314–5 (March 1977).

English, John J. and Canady, Robert Lynn, "Building the Middle School Schedule," *Middle School Journal*, 6, 59–62 (Winter 1975).

Fliegner, Laura R., "Moving Toward the Ideal Middle School," *NASSP Bulletin*, 62, 74–7 (May 1978).

Huie, David L., "Organizational, Technical and Physical School Features," *NASSP Bulletin*, 58, 30–5 (April 1974).

Tyrrell, Ronald, Johns, Frank, and McNally, Margaret, "Are Open Middle Schools Really Open?" *Elementary School Journal*, 76, 2–8 (October 1975).

Wilson, Laval S., "Can An Open Space Middle School Meet the Needs of Minority Youngsters?" *Journal of Negro Education*, 44, 368–76 (Summer 1975).

B. ERIC

Bick, Lowell W., *New Concepts in Design of Middle Schools*, July 1975. (ERIC ED 109 798)

The Changing Middle School, ERIC Clearinghouse on Educational Management, Oregon University, Eugene, National Institute of Education (DHEW), Washington, D.C., 1977. (ERIC No. ED 136 345)

Johnson, Donald W., *Developing and Implementing an Effective Student and Teacher Assignment Schedule*, Practicum Report submitted in partial fulfillment of requirements for Doctor of Education Degree, Nova University, July 1976. (ERIC No. ED 131 532)

C.   Dissertations and Dissertation Abstracts

Fleener, Duane Shafer, "A Study of the Scheduling Practices of Middle Schools, Junior High Schools, and High Schools in Indiana," *Dissertation Abstracts*, 37 (February 1977) 5020–A.

Kennedy, James Arthur, "A Comparison of Physical Plant Facilities of New Junior High and Middle Schools Built During and Since 1965," *Dissertation Abstracts*, 35 (December 1975) 3345–A.

Phillips, Byron Clayton, Jr., "A Categorical Analysis of the Organizational Climate and Self-Concepts of Children in Selected Open and Closed Construction Middle Schools," *Dissertation Abstracts*, 39 (September 1978) 1398–A.

Taylor, James Hubert Jr., "A Study of Design Features in Fifteen Selected Virginia Middle Schools and Three Nationally Recognized Middle Schools," *Dissertation Abstracts*, 37 (December 1976) 3329–A.

FOOTNOTES

1.   Donald C. Manlove and David W. Beggs, *Flexible Scheduling* (Bloomington, Indiana: Indiana University Press, 1965), p. 29.
2.   Alexander M. Swaab, *School Administrator's Guide to Flexible Modular Scheduling* (West Nyack, N.J.: Parker Publishing Co., 1974), p. 20.
3.   Swaab, p. 46.
4.   For more detailed discussions of these and other factors, see Anthony Saville, *Instructional Programming: Issues and Innovations* (Columbus, Ohio: Charles E. Merrill Publishing Company, 1974).
5.   The authors gratefully acknowledge the assistance of Mrs. Elaine Lane, Assistant Principal, North Marion Middle School, Citra, Florida, for the preparation of this material.
6.   Paul S. George, *Ten Years of Open Space Schools, A Review of Research* (Gainesville, Florida: The Florida Educational Research and Development Council, Spring 1975).
7.   See the extensive description of the school facility and program in the *American School Board Journal*, 156, 22–26 (May 1969).

Chapter 8 Instruction

In exemplary middle schools effective instruction is the primary goal. The design of the building, and the shape of the master schedule, even the organization of teachers and the school-wide decisions about the grouping of students; all are prerequisites for the delivery of effective instruction. Even instruction's pedagogical partner, curriculum, is, in a sense, dependent upon instruction for its effective implementation. All of this heightens the significance that should be attached to the design and conduct of instruction in middle schools. The behavior of teachers, as they plan and implement their instruction, is at once both the most obvious and the most difficult aspect of middle school education.

Characteristics of Effective Instruction in the Middle School

Teaching, at any level, can be thought of as a chain of decision making. A host of decisions are involved: decisions about who will be taught, about the curriculum to be implemented, about the instructional style to be employed. At the middle school level, educators have felt a commitment to several principles guiding the decisions about teaching. Instruction in the middle school, most educators agree, focuses on helping pupils understand themselves as unique individuals with special needs and important responsibilities. Instruction attempts to guarantee every pupil some degree of success in understanding the underlying principles and the ways of knowing in the academic disciplines. Certainly, instruction aims to promote maximum individual growth in the basic learning skills, while at the same time it permits the widest possible exploration of the world of knowledge and of the personal interests of each student. Finally, effective instruction fosters the ability to work and learn independently on the part of every pupil. Decisions about instruction in the exemplary middle school are strongly influenced by these commitments.[1]

In addition to the principles that form the basis for our decision making about instruction in the middle, there are a number of other factors that affect teaching. Research on teacher behavior and student learning styles should affect instruction. Many states have special learning objectives that elicit particular emphases in teaching, and the federal government has a steadily increasing number of guidelines and restrictions that require certain practices. The state of the art in educational technology both extends and limits what teachers may attempt. The structure of knowledge imposes its own demands, as does teachers' understanding of the process of learning and their preferences for one or another of the current explanations of the process. Long before teachers begin to instruct their pupils, many influences have been felt in the design of that instruction.

No influence is likely to be more significant than the middle school teachers themselves. The literature of middle school education is replete with references to the special characteristics desirable in persons electing to teach middle school youngsters. List after list of special talents has been drawn up. Yet the authors believe that the qualities that distinguish a good middle school teacher from a good elementary teacher or high school teacher are probably quite limited, albeit critically important. We believe that effective middle school instruction is implemented by teachers who have the flexibility of the generalist, the expertise of the specialist and the enthusiasm of one who understands and enjoys the special nature of the middle school student.

Until quite recently universities and colleges seemed unable or uninterested in developing teacher education programs that had as their goal the preparation of teachers specially trained to teach at the middle level.[2] Where such programs did begin, efforts were often frustrated by the lack of supportive certification regulations. University educators discovered that prospective teachers would not enroll in large numbers for teacher education programs that offered either sharply restricted or nonexistent certification, and therefore severely limited employment opportunities. In addition, realizing that the large majority of teachers who will be practicing in the middle schools of the year 2000 are already working makes the hope for a trained cadre of committed teachers emerging from our universities to infuse schools with new vigor and expertise a dim one indeed. The training necessary to produce effective middle school teachers will, in the years ahead, occur as a process of inservice education and staff development. Declining enrollments in public schools seem likely to make this prediction even more certain, since fewer and fewer districts will have unfilled vacancies in which to place the teachers from the universities which do manage to install middle school teacher education programs. Public school people seem destined to be left with the task of identifying and training the staff of their programs, in addition to designing and implementing those programs. For additional comments on the area of staff development for middle school, readers should refer to chapter 9.

Perhaps the most important characteristic of effective instruction at the middle school level is that it, too, carries the obligation to be both different from instruction at the elementary and high school levels, but also to bridge the gap between the two. In the elementary school, effective instructional practices are often much more likely to be teacher-directed, whereas the high school has the burden of assisting students to become self-directed and responsible for their own learning to a far greater extent than students are capable of in the elementary school. Not that student-directed instruction is impossible or unadvisable in the elementary school, but it is accurate to describe most young children as in need of a tremendous amount of teacher direction in their learning in school. It would also be foolish to claim that the average high school student is capable of sustained and satisfactory patterns of totally independent learning for prolonged periods of time. Certainly older students need guidance and direction of varying amounts throughout their latter school years, but the amount of student responsibility for their own learning should increase as each year in the public school passes.

If the emphasis of instruction in the elementary school is on a teacher-directed introduction to the world of the school and to the process of learning, and the stress at the high school level focuses on developing increasing increments of student responsibility, the middle school's obligation is to weave together these two divergent paths so that students may move from following one to pursuing the other without loss of educational momentum. Middle school teachers strive to accept students who are comfortable with almost total dependence upon the teacher for every learning experience. They act to help these students move to the place where they can survive in an academic environment much less tolerant of the personal idiosyncracies of each learner. At the same time, the pattern of instruction in the middle school aspires to be sufficient to help students reach success in mastering the learning tasks that the curriculum of the middle grades imposes upon the learner.

The instructional strategies of the middle school are, therefore, a combination of structure, balance and flexibility: structure, to provide the teacher-directed efforts without which the basic skills of the middle school student would remain largely unextended; balance, to offer the opportunities which will teach students the skills necessary for learning on their own and the attitudes that support such learning; flexibility, to permit teachers to know when a particular instructional strategy is appropriate and when it is not, and the disposition to make the changes in style when it is necessary for the students' benefit to do so. Instruction in the middle school emanates from the purposes of the school. Teaching methods mirror the functions of the total institution, with care needed to relate to knowledge of the characteristics of the students served. Teachers are prepared to teach a variety of different kinds of students with a wide range of learning skills and styles. The faculty must accept the challenge to become proficient with an array of methods and techniques, choosing one or another in relation to the purposes that motivate their actions.

The middle school has never been committed to any one particular instructional strategy to the exclusion of any other. Although the literature of middle school education would sometimes seem to argue in the affirmative, the authors are convinced that the elevation of one particular strategy over all others is a dangerous and unproductive step to take. Because middle school educators believe strongly in the special nature of the students they serve, it seems that the enthusiasm resulting from this commitment may have caused an overemphasis on the use of individualized instruction in middle schools. While individualized instruction is certainly one of the most important instructional strategies to be employed in middle schools, it is just as certainly not the only such strategy to be used. Middle school and individualized instruction are not synonymous.

The question is not, ''What is the best way to teach middle school students?'' It is now quite clear, from the evidence of both research and practice, that there is no one right way to teach all middle school students all the time. The method chosen depends upon the objectives of instruction, the nature of the particular group of students being taught, even the grade level involved. The right question to ask about instruction in the middle school is likely to be, ''What is the right method to use for these objectives in this area with this particular group of students?''

Whatever the method may be, there are a number of perennially important factors to be considered in the selection of an instructional approach. Most important is the assurance that the method chosen does not conflict with knowledge of the characteristics and needs of the students in the middle school. Equally significant, however, is the requirement that the blend of instructional strategies finally designed be consistent with the obligation of the middle school to strike a balance, pedagogically, between the elementary school and the high school. In addition, the selection of teaching methods involves criteria such as: clarity of the learning task in the eyes of the learner when using a particular method; motivational power of the method; provision of immediate feedback of a method; opportunities for continuous progress provided; avoidance of excessive frustration and failure; likelihood of transfer of learning to other situations outside the classroom; and, the ability to develop and preserve positive attitudes toward self, teacher, subject matter and school in general.[3]

A consideration of teaching methodology appropriate for middle schools might also include several other factors. First, the particular teaching method must match the instructional skill of the teacher intending to use it. Some methods are considerably more difficult to conduct effectively than others, and the expectation that all teachers will be able to use a method with equal effectiveness is bound to meet with disappointment. Second, the method chosen must not demand more of a teacher's energy than is reasonable. The phenomenon of teacher stress and burnout are too well known to ignore. Teachers in the middle school often seem, by the very nature of their tasks, to be frequently subject to considerably more stress and exhaustion than are teachers at other levels. Methods which demand even more energy and time are likely to be successfully implemented in a very few situations and for very brief periods of time. Third, methods that require a great deal of staff development time to learn will have a low priority, simply because there is so much competition for inservice education funds. Finally, methods which, while they may be effective in producing achievement gains, conflict with the basic values and philosophy of the school and community must be examined closely prior to extensive implementation.

Selecting instructional strategies for use in middle schools is not a simple or easy process. Many factors must be considered. But there are, nevertheless, a number of methods which research and experience recommend for use with the students served by the middle school. The remainder of this chapter is a consideration of these methods, the uses they serve and the situations where they are and are not appropriate. For simplicity, the methods to be discussed are categorized in terms of the number of students usually served and the number of teachers involved in the planning of instruction. The chapter will conclude with some comments about learning style, the influence of school organization on instruction and ability grouping.

Total Class Instruction

Research on Teacher Behavior

In the past five to ten years, research on teacher behavior has contributed mightily to our understanding of the relationship between how teachers act and the academic achievement of their students. Where for years it was not, now it is very clear that teachers do make a difference in the academic achievement of their students. What students do in the classroom makes a difference in their learning, and what teachers do makes a difference in what learners do. Research has helped us to see that it is not only the characteristics of the students in a school that determines the achievement within the building. In any given school, academic achievement will vary from one class to another, based, in part, on the teaching behavior exhibited in those classes.[4]

While much of the research has been conducted with young children in the early grades of the elementary school, it is the belief of the present authors and of many of the researchers that there are good reasons to analyze the research for implications for middle school learners. Not everything in the research can be applied to middle school classes, of course, but for teachers and administrators interested in raising the standardized test scores in basic skills, it seems fairly certain that teacher-directed total class instruction of a fairly traditional nature is often superior to either the discovery approach or individualized instruction as it is currently practiced.[5]

Teacher behavior does make a difference; but not single, discrete, separate teaching acts. What does seem to make a difference in student achievement are the teacher behaviors that tend to group together into patterns or clusters. These clusters of teacher behavior appear to be responsible for differences in academic achievement among students exposed to different patterns. Several clusters seem consistently related to increased achievement on standardized tests: patterns of teacher expectations and role definitions; classroom management; and what might be called the direct instruction process. This research on teaching behavior and academic achievement suggests some changes in instructional strategies currently in vogue in the middle grades.

There are some limitations in the application of the results of the research to the middle school. Most importantly, the research can be most confidently cited when dealing with basic skills instruction, and when working in these skill areas with students who might be described as less successful, less motivated or of lower ability. Beyond these considerations, the age of the students also seems to be significant. It is also important to recall that much of the research focused on teacher behaviors that were readily measurable by low inference measures, and that perhaps much of teaching that is subtle and artistic, and therefore, difficult to observe and record, is not included in the results. Teaching is a terribly complex act, and when the object of the instruction happens to be middle school students, the difficulties and complexities seem even more important. With all of these limitations in mind, however, there do seem to be some important recommendations that can be made to teachers who have the task of teaching the basic skills, reading, writing, spelling and mathematics, to middle schoolers.

Jere Brophy summarizes the effective process of basic skills instruction:

> The instruction that seems most efficient involves the teacher working with the whole class (or small groups in the early grades), presenting information in lectures/demonstrations and then following up with recitations or practice exercises in which the students get opportunities to make responses and get corrective feedback. The teacher maintains an academic focus, keeping the students involved in a lesson or engaged in seatwork, monitoring their performance, and providing individualized feedback. The pace is rapid in the sense that the class moves efficiently through the curriculum as a whole (and through the successive objectives of any given lesson), but progress from one objective to the next involves very small, easy steps. Success rates in answering teacher questions during lessons are high (about 75 percent), and success rates on assignments designed to be done independently are very high (approaching 100 percent).[6]

Classroom Management and Achievement in Basic Skills

Teachers who are able to produce increased amounts of on-task behavior without increasing the amount of time devoted to discipline or the level of negative teacher affect are teachers who help students score higher on tests of basic skills than the students would be likely to do with some other type of teacher behavior. Apparently this objective is easier to achieve with large group instruction than with either discovery or individualized instruction. Task oriented but relaxed classrooms (and both aspects are equally important) are places where increased achievement is found. Large group instruction is more likely to display this binary characteristic.

Time spent on task is of the essence in increasing academic achievement while classroom discipline efforts detract from this time. Teachers who find themselves taking significant amounts of time dealing with deviant and disruptive behavior are likely to have less time to devote to the skills to be tested. Classrooms where a great deal of pupil freedom of movement exists are classrooms where learning of basic skills is less. Socialization of pupils with each other, and of the teacher with the pupils, is also negatively correlated with pupil growth in the basic skills. Actually, within reasonable limits, the less physical movement and off-task talk the better.[7]

Tight control of the classroom and negative affect are not the same thing. In fact, positive affect and negative affect are not opposite ends of the same continuum of affect. That is, the elimination of negative teacher affect from the classroom does not always, or even often, mean that the more positive a teacher is, the more learning that will occur. There are, actually, many occasions when positive affect on the part of the teacher is either unrelated to increased achievement or negatively correlated such that the presence of positive affect actually produces less achievement. The use of praise is not uniformly helpful, so that when it is used it must be used very specifically and with individuals. It seems, according to the research, that classrooms with a neutral atmosphere, where neither positive or negative affect abound, are likely to be classrooms where students spend more uninterrupted time at the tasks of learning set before them.[8]

Establishing a classroom where tasks are taken seriously by both the teacher and the students, and where students are performing their task as much as is appropriate and possible, is important to achievement in the basic skills. How the teacher manages the time of pupils over which he or she has control is as important as establishing a classroom where negative affect is at a minimum. Since learning is a process that takes place in time, and what a student does is essential to his learning, influencing how pupils use their time becomes a critical variable. Research has indicated a number of factors associated with uses of time in the classroom and the connection with achievement in the basic skills.

Teachers concerned with managing their classrooms to maximize the effective use of time need to know several things. Recent studies, for example, indicate that what a student learns is directly related to the uses to which he puts his time. That is, simply, the more time devoted to the study of a subject, the better the subject is learned. If basic skills have a priority, then more time in the school day needs to be devoted to those topics. Apparently, research does not seem to indicate that there is a point of diminishing returns; there is no apparent limit to increasing the time devoted to learning tasks. When breaks and wasted time are decreased, learning goes up. Increasing breaks will not raise productive behavior or achievement.[9]

Although balance with other activities is important, there does seem to be quite strong research support for spending as much of the student time as possible in large groups in face-to-face contact with the teacher. In a typical classroom hour, for example, it might be effective to devote about two thirds of the hour to large group teacher-directed instruction. The remaining one third of the time could then be spent in closely supervised and monitored seatwork that is directly related to the preceding large group instruction. Seatwork that is not closely monitored by the teacher actively moving around the room is negatively correlated to achievement. It is very clear that students spend more time on task when working directly with the teacher (84 percent) than when working alone in seatwork (70 percent).[10]

Basic Skills Instruction

Assuming that large group teacher-directed instruction does generate greater degrees of student on-task behavior with less need for negative teacher affect, the question still remains as to what specific form this large group instruction should take. Here again, recent research has some important statements to make. When it comes to teaching the basic skills, there are some very definite steps to take. Rosenshine, referring to the recommended process, calls it "direct instruction."[11]

The Basic Skills Instruction Process (BSIP), or direct instruction, whatever one calls it, may be thought of as containing a series of specific steps, beginning with the assumption of personal responsibility for student learning by the teacher.[12] That is, teachers who feel personally responsible for whether or not their students achieve the objectives set for them, are, not surprisingly, more effective in producing higher levels of student achievement. Teachers who believe that it is up to the students to learn and that the teacher has no rule or duty to motivate, inspire or promote students' learning are less likely to act in ways that produce it. The power of teacher expectations is manifested very clearly in teaching the basic skills.

The second step in the BSIP, following the assumption of personal responsibility by the teacher, involves a series of decisions, all made primarily by the teacher. In the BSIP, it is the teacher who decides what curriculum goals and objectives should be pursued, not the students. It is also the teacher who decides the materials to be used, the settings in which instruction occurs and the time to be devoted to the process. It is the teacher who assumes the primary role in planning instruction, and students do little or no such planning.

The teacher makes a considerable effort to focus the time of both teacher and students on academic goals. Distractions, pleasant or otherwise, which draw the class away from the academic objectives at hand are discouraged. Socializing is diminished. All persons involved realize that their job is to pursue the academic objectives which have been set for them. There is no other choice.

With this mindset, the teacher then sets about to promote, through an actively directive teacher presentation, extensive coverage of the objectives that have been selected. When the teacher has arranged the class effectively, students will be sitting with their backs to the rest of the class, while the teacher is facing the class. Having done so, the teacher begins with an overview of the lesson that ties it to previous work and which provides advance organizers to prepare the students for the skills work to come. In doing so, the teacher concentrates on the whole class, rather than a small group. Brophy goes so far as to specify that this review and orientation should last about eight minutes. Following the introduction, the teacher should collect and check the homework, if there has been some assigned.[13]

After the review and the checking of homework, in large groups, the teacher continues the total class instruction with about a twenty-minute presentation that develops the new concepts or skills. Again, this process is highly teacher directed, with a minimum of opportunities for student input or questions. As a part of this lesson, however, the teacher should eventually begin to ask questions and solicit student responses on the concepts or skills that have been introduced. Such questions should be of a low cognitive level, simple enough to result in a very high success rate.

The question and answer session toward the end of the lesson is very important, and the research speaks very clearly about it. Most of the questioning should be done by the teacher, and most of the answering should be done by the students. Avoiding extensive student questions and extended answers and amplifications of student questions by the teacher seem well supported by the research data. There are other surprises, though, for teachers who have been told that teacher-directed instruction is evil, including support for using a predictable pattern when calling on students during the recitation portion of the lesson. Random and unpredictable questioning seems counterproductive, while the structure and stability of the pattern process appears to support the anxious student. It seems important, too, when questioning, to wait at least three seconds for the student to answer (the average teacher waits one second), before interrupting with a new question or calling on a new student. It is also important to see that other students wait to be called upon, and when they do not, to remind them that everyone will get a turn and that they must wait for theirs. Focus on one student at a time, but set up the questioning session so that everyone in the class has had a chance to answer a question. Praise correct answers only, but accept questions in the form that they are asked.

The lesson, and question and answer session included, should be followed by a shorter period (for example, fifteen minutes) of closely monitored seatwork. Such seatwork should be highly correlated to the lesson and should, ideally, lead to uninterrupted successful practice.

BSIP requires that the teacher set the pace at which students work, both during the lesson and while at work at their seats. Students should be held accountable for their seatwork by a teacher who spends the time during seatwork walking from student to student, checking work, delivering brief praise quietly to specific individuals. Under appropriate circumstances, and with great care, homework should be assigned, homework which should take little more than fifteen minutes, but which will be collected and checked regularly. The final step in the BSIP is to conduct weekly and monthly reviews of the concepts and skills which are being taught.

Important Modifications

It is terribly important to stress that the same type of instruction, no matter what type or for what purposes, cannot be applied equally to all types of students. The BSIP must be modified and adapted to take into consideration the types of students with whom one is working. The particular strategy we have been discussing, using a directive instructional process to teach the basic skills, seems especially appropriate when teaching students who might be described as less successful, with lower academic motivation, more dependent and anxious. Some researchers point out that these characteristics often appear with greater frequency in populations of schoolchildren from lower socioeconomic groups. Students with what has been called an external locus of control also seem to profit from the direct instruction of the BSIP.[14]

When using the BSIP with these students, the general recommendation seems to be to follow the direct instruction model to the letter, but with some important emphases. Students who are less successful need a slower pace, with more drill and repetition, and more overlearning in small pieces. More individual monitoring is important, as is more teacher warmth, encouragement and personalized teaching in general. Students who are anxious and dependent need less challenge, but not less than they are able to handle. They do require lower levels of criticism and of demands, and they need to know that help is always available.

Less successful students need to be gently prodded into making actual responses each time they are asked a question, but with less rigorous probing, and a greater stress on facts and on thinking operations at the lower end of the taxonomy. The oft-repeated statement that factual questions are bad and higher level questions are good is not borne out by the research on academic achievement, as far as these students are concerned. More success with lower level questions, more repetition and more structured help of all kinds are called for.[15]

It is also important, when working with less successful students, to be aware of teacher expectations which subtly lead to teacher behaviors associated with lower achievement in students. Teachers who expect lower ability students to learn give adequate amounts of feedback, provide equal amounts of individual attention and are as patient with the slower students as with the higher ability pupils. It is comforting to know that such expectations are not consciously formed and that teachers, when notified of such behaviors, change immediately.[16]

When working with students at the other end of the continuum, those with high ability and a high record of achievement, with an internal locus of control and so forth, a different emphasis is required. Such students should be asked more difficult questions, with more rigorous probing and redirection. Incorrect answers from these pupils should be corrected. More homework should be assigned to these students, or homework of a more detailed and demanding nature. It is also possible to admit more student initiation of teacher-student interaction, and to be more flexible in response to student input generally. Less structure imposed by the teacher, and more student-designed activity is desirable with higher ability, less dependent, children.[17]

Teachers using the BSIP model must also be prepared to further modify the process, depending upon the age or grade level of the students they teach. Generally, middle school teachers can rely on the use of more large group and whole class instruction, and less small group work, than teachers in the primary grades. Older middle school students should be able to handle more extended discussion, with slightly less drill and repetition. More cognitive challenge and higher level cognitive level activity should be encouraged, along with more sustained concentration on academic activities. A more rapid pace than would be comfortable for younger students, and less individual feedback are both possible at the middle school level. Less positive affect and praise are necessary, but not to the point of having a higher level of negative affect and criticism.

Figure 8.1 illustrates the application of the BSIP with different grade levels, student characteristics and academic objectives in mind. In the primary grades, and in most of the middle school grades, where basic skills are the focus, and especially where the students are less successful or less academically motivated, the BSIP model works well. As students mature, become more successful and the curriculum includes more and more objectives that are beyond the basic skills, the emphasis on the use of BSIP should lessen and the search for alternatives that permit more flexibility and more student direction of the learning process should be increased.

Brophy points out that the findings concerning the process of direct instruction do generalize to students at the middle school level, but that the most important qualification is that basic skills must be the primary goal. The instructional objective pursued seems to be the guiding factor when deciding what instructional strategy to pursue. When the focus is on basic skills in reading and math, in particular, teachers should consider the BSIP model. When creativity, problem solving, complex thinking, appreciation or social and emotional education are the goals, the BSIP may not be the best instructional method. It may even be that the direct instruction process

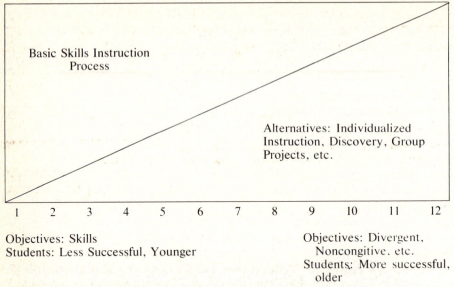

Basic Skills Instruction
    Process

Alternatives: Individualized
Instruction, Discovery, Group
Projects, etc.

1   2   3   4   5   6   7   8   9   10   11   12

Objectives: Skills   Objectives: Divergent,
Students: Less Successful, Younger   Noncongitive, etc.
                                                Students: More successful,
                                                   older

Figure 8.1 / An Instructional Continuum

is inimical to student growth in some areas other than basic skills, especially
if students are older or more academically successful. BSIP may be inconsistent with the goals of social studies, humanities, the arts and other essentially less cognitive and less factual areas.[18]

Why does the BSIP work better than individualized instruction or discovery modes, when teaching basic skills, especially to less successful students? Because using this method, under these circumstances, makes it possible to encourage higher levels of student on-task behavior with lower levels
of negative teacher affect. The traditional whole class method seems easier
to plan and easier to manage, leaving more time and energy for the teacher to
focus on the tasks and objectives at hand. The structure provided by BSIP
apparently helps the anxious, dependent, distractable students to stay on
task, and it is easier to establish standards and hold students accountable for
the accomplishment of those standards. The BSIP provides large helpings of
teacher contact, and middle school students, who often measure the significance of tasks they are asked to complete by the amount of attention the
teacher pays to them as they work on it, place greater significance on
teacher-directed learning tasks than on those that primarily involve materials without teacher intervention. The BSIP takes less time in changing activities, requires the training and use of fewer additional adults in the classroom, and, consequently, provides more time for instruction and less time
for directions and transitions. There is more modeling and less of the elitism
and labeling that sometimes occurs in rigid ability grouping within a class.

The BSIP permits teachers to take an active role, one which allows them
to, as one teacher said to the authors, "really teach." The goals of instruction seem reachable with this process, as it does not require magical talents
or hidden energy reserves to implement and continue. It is realistic and prac-

tical, and it inspires confidence in teachers which they pass on to their students. It develops a sense of community. It works.

But, as we have pointed out in the discussion above, it does not work for all objectives with all students at all grade levels. When the objectives go beyond the basic skills, or when teachers are dealing with students who possess a great deal of self-discipline and personal responsibility, there are other instructional strategies that may be preferable. Some of these strategies are effective because they build upon the characteristics of the students with whom middle school teachers work, and these same methods may be preferred because they provide a setting in which social and emotional education may occur along with the academic objectives. Under these circumstances, methods that forsake the large group teacher-directed process become more desirable.

Small Group Instruction

Small group instruction, in the discussion which follows, refers to situations in which the teacher arranges the class in groups significantly smaller than the entire class, excluding individualized instruction. The teacher, in these situations, often acts more as organizer and facilitator than direct instructor. The distinguishing characteristic of small group instruction, in the authors' opinion, is that in this mode students often work together, rather than attending solely to the teacher or working entirely alone. In both peer teaching and group or team learning, the emphasis is on cooperative experience.

Peer Teaching

Middle school teachers are frequently aware of the need for their students to improve the skills and attitudes that they possess in working cooperatively with their peers. As in so many other ways, often the best process for attacking these attitudes and skills, with middle school students, is to do so indirectly. Peer and cross-age tutoring is one quite good method to teach both academic content and social attitudes and skills.

Several respected educators have articulated the need for using more peer teaching. In 1962, Hilda Taba wrote that the greatest untapped source of learning is in the efficient use of group relations in the classroom, and ten years later Urie Bronfenbrenner urged teachers to design two-pupil teams composed of students of differing abilities so that the students could become involved in responsible tasks on behalf of others within the classroom.[19]

Wagner, surveying the literature of peer teaching, identified a number of additional advantages to this instructional method, in addition to the improved human relations skills and attitudes:

1. *He who teaches others, teaches himself.*
2. *Self-concepts of students are improved when they teach others.*
3. *Students who are taught by other students have an opportunity to develop a*

sense of warmth and recognition as a result of the attention and identification with the other student.

4. *A more efficient use of human resources results when students are used to help each other.*
5. *Individualized instruction is more nearly possible when students are involved in teaching one another.*
6. *Students are more highly motivated to achieve when involved with each other in tutoring relationships.*
7. *Pupils like working together.*
8. *Because it depends on a new kind of interaction, peer tutoring can be a focal point for eliminating some forms of discrimination.*
9. *Students become more active participants in their own learning.*
10. *Academic achievement is higher than in some other forms of instruction.*[20]

While there are many types of peer and cross-age teaching, the type that most middle school teachers are likely to be able to use involves one middle school student teaching another. Cross-age tutoring, involving the teaching of elementary school students in another school setting, is frequently impractical. That does not mean, however, that cross-age teaching is not possible within the confines of the middle school. Several methods of school-wide grouping of students provide good settings for cross-age teaching.

Multiage grouping of some sort, and the school-within-a-school format, seem particularly facilitative of cross-age tutoring. In schools with two, three or four grade levels represented on one team, designing a cross-age tutoring program should be quite simple. Where teams are arranged in a school-within-a-school format, students from the higher grade level(s) can teach or tutor those from the lower grade levels. Because teams of different grade levels are located near each other in the school-within-a-school framework, moving from one team area to another is relatively easy. In schools with a conventional grade level team design, cross-age teaching is certainly not impossible, since all that is required, in most cases, is for the teachers on the teams to have the desire to do so. Under these more traditional circumstances, designing a teaching or tutoring situation in which students from the same grade level work in peer teams is just as simple as the teachers on the team wish it to be. Individual teachers who wish to arrange peer teaching situations in their own classrooms often find it relatively easy to do so. The existence of mainstreaming, following PL 94–142, provides particularly exciting opportunities for the use of peer teaching, even with single grade level classrooms.

While there are many possible models to follow when designing a peer tutoring process, it seems likely that this method, like any other, will profit from careful planning. One model known to the authors offers a well-structured process labeled the "Four T's of Tutoring."[21] Beginning with a recognition that the tutor is as much a focus of the project as the tutee, the model has, as its first step, a testing process that is used to determine the match between tutor and tutee. Tutors may, optimally, be selected so that their instructional level is just slightly higher than those that they tutor, especially in reading skills, but it is absolutely necessary that the tutor's academic level be at least equal to that of the tutee.

The second phase of the peer teaching process, as described here, is the training period. Once the tutors are selected, Smith recommends that some discussion of the characteristics of the learner and the learning situation be conducted. For example, assuming that the tutors are eighth graders and tutees are sixth graders, the discussion could develop from the following questions:

1. How have you changed since you were in the sixth grade?
2. What types of things did you do then that you think are silly now?
3. When you were in the sixth grade, how did you feel about eighth graders?
4. What types of things do you see sixth graders doing that you think are silly? Why do you suppose they do those things? Do you suppose that sixth graders think those things are silly?
5. In what ways do you act differently from sixth graders? Tenth graders?

If the tutors have a better understanding of how younger students behave, the tutoring situation should move more easily.[22]

The preparation of the tutor should also include some discussion of effective learning and teaching, since peer teaching works best when the tutor does not exceed the tutee's learning rate, gives positive reinforcement and helps the tutee to be aware of his progress. Smith points out that such discussions do not have to be uninteresting, and that most students would welcome the opportunity to discuss questions related to learning:

1. *What happens when the teacher gives you too much work?*
2. *How do you feel when you are asked to do something that you are almost certain that you can do, but is neither too easy or too difficult?*
3. *How do you feel when the teacher is uncomplimentary about your work?*[23]

It is also important that the tutor be helped to master a simple series of steps in a teaching process. Tutors might, for example, be taught to: give an overview of the lesson, with an appropriate review; present the purpose of the lesson; present new words or terms; work through the lesson, whatever it is; and follow the lesson with a question and answer period. In essence, the tutor is presenting a teacher-directed style, but to a class of one. Instructing the tutor in the steps of a directed teaching activity should not only help the tutor do a beter job with his student, but it should also help both students gain a better understanding of the process the teacher follows during those times the class is involved in whole group instruction.

According to Smith's model, just prior to the tutoring session, the teacher should teach the lesson to the tutors in very much the same way that she expects the tutors to present the lesson to their students. The worksheets and other materials that the tutors use during this lesson become the answer sheets for the lesson that will be presented to tutees.

The third step in the process is the actual tutoring, which should follow the training session as closely as possible. Smith recommends that the tutoring session last about thirty minutes, and be divided into three parts, approximating the parts of a teacher-directed lesson: presentation, drill or recitation and practice. In a reading lesson, tutor and tutee might takes turns reading, followed by a worksheet or series of questions about the lesson, ending with an enjoyable application of some kind, such as a game or puzzle.

Smith uses the term "translating" to describe the fourth and final step of the peer teaching process. It is a step that involves the tutor, but it could certainly also involve the tutee. During this phase, essentially an evaluation, the tutor is asked to write answers to questions like these:

1. *What skill did you teach today?*
2. *Describe at least one successful task accomplished by your student.*
3. *Did your student enjoy the tasks? Please explain.*
4. *How did you feel about helping your student with his or her work today?*
5. *Did you find any part of the lesson difficult to teach? Please explain.*[24]

A number of benefits to the tutor accrue as a result of this experience. Students who need the skills that they were expected to learn in an earlier grade can usually be found to be more receptive to confronting their deficiencies when it is a part of a tutoring process in which they have status and responsibility. In addition, the peer teaching process provides a number of instances of meaningful repetition of skills that the tutor may need to review. Tutors also receive practice using processes of listening, speaking, reading, writing and spelling as a part of their labors. The tutor is, of course, not the only one who is expected to improve as a result of this process.

Group Inquiry and Team Learning

The attempt to develop small group instructional strategies that combine both academic inquiry and the democratic process has led to the use of a number of related but somewhat different methods for use in the middle school classroom. Individual teachers have, for the last two centuries, used group projects and other team learning situations, to achieve a variety of objectives. More recently, several clearly defined and researched models of group and team learning have made their appearance in the classroom.

These models of teaching have been most clearly cataloged and described by Bruce Joyce and Marsha Weil, of Teachers College, Columbia University.[25] These authors categorize several types of teaching methods into a family of models which emphasizes the social dimension of learning and teaching. Middle school and junior high school teachers have been using these methods, or portions of the methods, for many years without labeling or describing their uses for others. It is even possible to trace the origins of these methods to the theories of John Dewey who, as long ago as 1916, advocated the use of teaching methods that would combine both academic inquiry and democratic learning.[26]

Organizing the students in a class into small groups whose task is to react to, inquire into the nature of and attempt to solve social problems that the teacher helps them to select is a method that teachers of older children and early adolescents have used effectively for many years. Ascribing the most authoritative elaboration of the model to Herbert Thelen,[27] Joyce and Weil list six steps in the application in the classroom of the group investigation process:

1. The students in the group are confronted with a stimulating problem that arises naturally or is supplied by the teacher.
2. The students react to the problem and the teacher draws their attention to the diversity of their responses and reactions to the problem.
3. As the students become interested in the differences in their responses to the problem, the teacher helps them formulate a problem statement.
4. Following the formulation of a problem statement, the students organize themselves to attack and resolve the problem.
5. The students pursue the study of the problem and, at the conclusion of their study, report their results to the teacher and the rest of the class.
6. With the assistance of the teacher and the rest of the class, the investigating group evaluates the solution to the problem.

In this and other varieties of the group and team learning process, the teacher plays a much more indirect role than in the large group teacher-directed basic skills process. In the group learning mode, the teacher is very careful to ensure that the students examine what they are doing, that they are conscious of the methods of learning they are using, that they are learning skills of group management and that they are involved in the examination of personal meaning in the group context.

Joyce and Weil identify and describe a number of other small group models, all of which feature interaction-oriented learning. There is the jurisprudential model of Donald Oliver and James Shaver, which teaches students to analyze and take positions on public issues in American society. Byron Massialas and Benjamin Cox have developed what has been described as social inquiry learning, similar in many ways to the group investigation model of Herbert Thelen, except that it strenuously emphasizes the solution of societal problems, advocating that the school assume a position of involvement in the creative reconstruction of the culture. Teachers everywhere will recognize these methods as descriptions of time-honored processes that remain highly effective in classrooms where instruction attempts to go beyond the standard cognitive objectives of the basic skills. Readers interested in the detailed descriptions of these models are referred to the sources noted earlier in this section.

One of the freshest twists in the old method of group and team learning has been added by work done at the Johns Hopkins University Center for Social Organization of Schools. Student Team Learning (STL) is the result of the effort at the Center to produce and use scientific knowledge of how school and classroom organization affects the students within. Student Team Learning is a new method of using small groups, based on years of research on student learning in cooperative teams at the Center for Social Organization of Schools.[28]

The basic idea of STL is that "when students learn in small, carefully structured learning teams and are rewarded for working toward a common goal, they help one another learn, gain in self-esteem and feelings of individual responsibility for their learning and increase in respect and liking for their classmates, including their classmates of other races.''[29] STL draws upon the group spirit that emerges from common effort, harkening back to the experiences of each of us as we grew up and participated in team sports, music groups and other such efforts. The exciting experience of working toward a cooperative goal, either in competition with other groups, or in comparison to some ideal goal, provides a strong motivational force that, the originators of the STL process argue, can be used by teachers to infuse classroom learning with the same urgency. Students in an STL classroom are involved in a learning process that provides the same kind of peer support, excitement and camaraderie that are characteristic of team efforts elsewhere.

Following eight years of research, the Team Learning Project staff at the Center developed two team techniques and adapted a third that had been designed elsewhere. According to the literature of the Center, all three of these team techniques have positive effects on achievement, on students' mutual concern and self-esteem and on race relations in integrated schools. The Center staff asserts that these team efforts are easy for teachers to use and that the materials are inexpensive to obtain.[30]

The best researched of the three is the Teams-Games-Tournaments (TGT) process. In TGT, students are assigned to learning teams of four or five members. After the teacher presents the lesson, the teams study together, trying to make sure that every team member understands the lesson, since the success of the team depends upon each member functioning effectively in the slot he is assigned. At the end of a period of time (for example, a week) the teams engage in a tournament with other teams in the class. Each team member competes with students from other teams on a more or less ability-grouped basis. At the end of the tournament, winners from each competition level move up to the next highest position, competing there with those whose scores on the last set of games classifies them as on the same level. It is the spirit of competition that changes rote memorization from a dead and deadly affair into one of challenge and enthusiasm. Under these circumstances, it is also competition that begets, ironically, higher levels of cooperation.

According to one teacher known to the authors, the equal competition makes it possible for every student to have a good chance of contributing equally to the success of the team. A weekly class newsletter prepared by the teacher recognizes successful teams and students who have contributed effectively to their teams' success. The dynamics of the process combine to produce a classroom where the objectives of small group instructional processes are quite effectively realized. For example, Geoffrey Pyne, mathematics teacher at Mebane Middle School, Alachua Florida, said, ''. . . the students love to play the tournaments, and I believe I can honestly say that this was true for all my students. When presented as an alternative to the customary classroom methodologies in mathematics, it is accepted in a very positive manner by the students.'' The TGT process also allows the teacher in a school where racial issues are unusually sensitive to promote regular interaction without resorting to an unpopular seating chart, since all teams must be balanced, racially, sexually and academically. As Pyne points out, the TGT process does not affect the teacher's own individual style of teaching, since it structures the way in which students work together on any objectives or content presented to the class through any chosen style or method of presentation.[31]

The two other versions of team learning produced by the Johns Hopkins group are similar in many ways to the TGT process. The Student Teams-Achievement Division (STAD) uses quizzes instead of games, and as a result, is easier to use and takes less time in the classroom. Jigsaw, the third version, involves the student teams in the study of content units, with each member assuming responsibility for learning a specific topic or section of material. Then the student must return to his or her group, after having become an expert on that topic, and teaches what they have learned to their teammates. This process, then, resolves itself with the standard tournament.[32]

All of these small group instructional strategies are important for middle school educators interested in providing a balanced instructional program for the students they teach. Peer teaching, group investigations, team learning—all work toward several important objectives for the middle school. Each of these methods is built, intentionally or not, on a solid grounding in the characteristics of the transescent student. Each accomplishes the objectives for which middle schools are accountable, academically. And, each serves effectively in the attempt to pass on to students the social and human relations skills and attitudes that students require for effective citizenship. Middle school teachers who attempt to fashion their instructional styles without any effort to include some small group instruction will, in the opinion of the authors, serve their students less effectively than they might.

Individualized Instruction

The evidence from research cited above, testifying to the superiority of large group instruction in the teaching of the basic skills, might tempt some educators to cast aside any other instructional methodologies. This would be a mistake. While the research evidence is indeed convincing, it does not necessarily invalidate the use of recently developed methodologies that attempt to individualize instruction. Whether or not a teacher selects a method that falls within the category of individualized instruction depends upon the particular style and strengths of the teacher and, more importantly, upon the objectives that must be pursued and the students who are pursuing them.

Teachers whose classroom goals include the development of greater degrees of individual responsibility and self-discipline in learners, persistence and personal creativity (and many other objectives that can be pursued best, if at all, with some method of individualization), should be urged to do so. Teachers who find their preferences for and strengths in teaching expressed best through a method of individualized instruction should be encouraged to include these methods in their repertoire. All teachers, in the attempt to provide a balanced instructional program that fits every learner, must seek to develop the competencies required for individualized instruction.

The research on instruction does not tell us to do away with individualization. It suggests that on the whole, one kind of instruction is better under one set of circumstances. With the proper objectives and the correct group of students, teachers who have the skills to implement individualized instruction effectively should feel confident in doing so.

Such teachers, present in every middle school, seem to prefer several methods of individualized instruction. When resources permit, there are several quasi-commercial systems for individualizing instruction that ought to be investigated by educators searching for effective methods. The Individually Prescribed Instruction System (IPI) is one of the most widespread and best known of the quasi-commercial systems for individualized instruction. Westinghouse has produced the Program for Learning in Accordance with Need (PLAN) as a computer-managed system offering both academic and guidance programs on a wide spectrum. The Individually Guided Education System (IGE), developed by the Kettering Foundation's Institute for the Development of Educational Innovations (IDEA), has branched into two varieties and has been adopted in both forms by dozens of middle schools throughout the nation.[33]

Many teachers, however, find themselves without the resources to avail themselves of the rich opportunities that commercial systems may provide. Too, schools and classrooms that strive to offer the balance, instructionally, that the authors believe to be so essential, may find it difficult to adopt a commercial system and provide the necessary time and resources to include other methods as well. For these teachers and schools, several methods of individualizing have become common responses to the need to achieve academic objectives without sacrificing the goals of increasing student self-direction and independence.

Many of the methods of individualized instruction currently popular, whether commercially produced or teacher designed, appear to follow a quasi-systematic approach to the elaboration of the learning experience. Perhaps it could not be otherwise, and some would argue that all effective instruction proceeds from the same framework, but it does seem that in the effort to individualize instruction, the systems aspects appear much more conspicuously. Each method seems to begin with an attempt to set or derive goals and objectives, followed by an assessment of some sort. This assessment leads, if done correctly, to a set of learning activities. The entire process is capped by a summative evaluation of student progress, and movement on to the next set of objectives, or back to a previous position for remediation. The various methods of individualization differ in the emphasis they give to the different parts of the system and to the packaging of the learning activities, but, for the most part, the methodology is quite similar and one method can often be used side-by-side with another.

It also seems fair to say that, with very few exceptions, most methods of individualization focus primarily on the differentiation of the pace of learning that each learner keeps, rather than on the opportunities for the learner to choose from a variety of objectives those which he or she particularly prefers to do. Variety and choice in learning objectives are certainly not absent in the middle school, however, since the exploratory element of the middle school curriculum is one of the strongest and most popular aspects of the program in almost every middle school in the nation. But when it comes to standard academic classrooms and the objectives which remain dominant there, even though there are exceptions, individualization most frequently refers to the pace of learning rather than to the direction it takes.

Learning Centers

Learning centers constitute one of the methods that seem to provide a popular balance between academic effort and the goals of increasing student self-direction, independence and responsibility. Learning centers, or stations, as sometimes called, usually refer to "an area for study and activity, in or near the classroom, that has been provided for the structured exploration of a particular subject, topic, skill, or interest. It is a place for using and storing materials that relate to a special interest or curriculum area. It may be on a wall, in a corner, next to a bookcase, or on a table; but it exists somewhere in the physical space of the classroom or school."[34] It is not the library or media center of the school. Learning centers frequently exhibit the following characteristics:

1. *Learning centers are auto-instructional. When properly designed they do not require the constant and continuous intervention of the teacher. Students, after consulting with the teacher, may go directly to a learning center and begin work. Consequently, a well-designed learning center will contain clear, easily-discovered objectives and plainly written directions for beginning, continuing and completing work at the center.*
3. *A learning center invites each student to achieve specific objectives that are clearly communicated. The directions must specify the nature of the task and the exit behavior that is required.*
4. *Each learning center includes a method of recording the student's participation. The teacher may provide individual folders for each student, stored with others in an area removed from the centers but convenient to both students and teacher. Students make additions to their folders whenever necessary.*
5. *Similarly, a learning center includes opportunities for assessment of pupil learning. Ideally, a center contains both pre-assessment and post-assessment, which students can administer to themselves or to each other without the constant supervision of the teacher.*

6. *Each learning center involves the opportunity for student decision-making and steps towards the assumption of increased degrees of independent learning. Students should be making decisions about the management of time, use of resources, goals, evaluation of products, and other concerns.*[35]

Learning centers have a variety of uses in middle school classrooms. They can be used on a part-time basis to accomplish a wide variety of purposes. Enrichment centers, where students may go for additional work, in greater depth, on a particular topic, are effective ways to use this method, since every classroom inevitably has a small group of students who are brighter and more motivated than the remainder of the class. For the students on the opposite end of the ability and motivation continuum, centers can be useful as remediation or reinforcement opportunities. The use of centers for motivational purposes is another way to make part-time use of this method, offering an early preview of a unit that may be as much as six weeks away. And, of course, learning centers can be used to bring closure to a unit that had other methods as the primary instructional strategies.

At Spring Hill Middle School, High Springs, Florida, one team of teachers used learning centers as a regular part of the day. The daily schedule of the team provided the teachers with a thirty-minute unit of time following lunch that seemed too short to do anything difficult or complex, so the team searched for a constructive way to use the time. It was decided that this would be an excellent time of the day to encourage independent study. Student interests were assessed and a dozen or so brightly colored, well-designed learning centers appeared on the walls of the team area. Following a conference with their advisor, each student contracted for an amount of learning center activity, small group discussions with the counselor or other independent learning that could be supervised by the teachers on the team. Students who had difficulties, initially, in taking hold and making the most of the opportunity met with one of the teachers and worked on the skills and attitudes necessary for effective independent study. The program, with learning centers at the heart, lasted for three years and became one of the favorite times of the day for both students and teachers.

Another effective way to introduce learning centers into the classroom is in the form of a short course within another, larger, unit. In the average six-week unit, for example, there are usually many different activities planned, one or more of which can be learning centers involving a self-contained short course. A unit on ''Comparative Government'' might include a short course on ''Dictatorship'' offered as a learning center, with its own objectives, directions, assessments and learning activities, all relating to the subtheme of dictatorial government. Another appropriate short course for the same unit might focus on the process of ''Comparing.'' Such centers can be a part of the unit, but separately so.

Once students have been introduced to using learning centers, know what is expected of them when using a center and have used them on a part-time basis, additional learning centers can be introduced. They can easily become the major instructional strategy for a short unit or for a particular subject.

Centers can be used, in this way, one day a week, one week during a unit or on any other schedule that a teacher finds effective. A unit on the Civil War, in American history class, could be taught using learning centers as the primary instructional strategy. Such a unit might have centers on some or all of these topics: The South Before the War; The North Before the War; The Causes of the Civil War; Significant Battles of the Civil War; Music and Art of the Civil War Period; Civilians and the War; The End of the War; The Results of the War; Why the North Won the War. Individual teachers could manage such a unit in their own special ways, using the centers as the focus. Learning centers, thus, can be a supplementary strategy or the major pedagogical tool, depending upon the goals and preferences of teachers.[36]

The process of developing good learning centers follows the same steps involved in designing any good instruction, with a few modifications. Teachers must first decide what the role of the learning center will be in their instructional program: enrichment, remediation, motivation, short course or major method. Will they be used during the whole period, the entire week or on some other schedule? Will they be required or optional? Will they be used in one classroom, or for an interdisciplinary team unit? Many teachers recommend that the teacher new to the use of learning centers begin with using this approach for one subject or for a few hours out of the day or week. Teachers and students can, in this way, learn how to use centers effectively, with the least amount of disruption or confusion in their classes.

Once the teacher has determined the extent to which centers will be used, other steps toward implementation may be taken. Teachers and students may plan the identity of the centers. Learning activities can be designed. Assessment and evaluation plans can be drawn. One of the authors of this book lists these six steps as those necessary in constructing and implementing a center:

1. *Decide, perhaps with the students, the theme of the center.*
2. *Identify from two to five objectives that will comprise the learning goals of the center. The objectives should be precise, behavioral if possible. Resist the temptation to write the objectives after designing the learning activities.*
3. *Create at least two learning activities through which each learning objective may be accomplished.*
4. *Pretests and postassessments should be developed when the objectives and learning activities have been designed. At this point it is appropriate to write the introduction, with its crystal clear directions. The clearer the directions, the more time the teacher will have to devote to uninterrupted helping.*
5. *When the essence of the center has been completed, design an attractive backdrop to appeal visually to the students. The purpose of the backdrop is to attract student attention and interest, and to have signs and signals that lead the students through the center.*
6. *Before students begin to work at the center, the teacher should take them on a tour of the center, answering as many questions about the center as possible. Then let them begin.*[37]

One teacher used learning centers in a unit on library reference skills, with the following results:

I have discovered that students responded, in time, with increased self-direction when using learning centers. For this particular unit, I designed 14 learning centers, each covering one or two pre-determined objectives. The glaring pre-test results indicated that all but a small, select group needed instruction in all the centers. Consequently, I divided each class into half-groups of about 16 students and set up seven centers in both the classroom and our media center for almost all the students to complete. Students could work through these centers with little or no teacher help. As they completed a given center, their mastery of that center's skill was tested. Mastering a skill became a pass to another center. The children paced themselves, learning to listen to their own rhythm as learners. Those students who finished earlier than others were given a unipac, an additional individualizing tool, on the Card Catalogue and the Dewey Decimal System. Meanwhile, the other students would continue with the original centers until they finished. All students found success![138]

Learning Activity Packages

Learning Activity Packages (LAPs) are similar in many ways to the larger more complex learning center. The basic components of each are quite alike: introduction, objectives, preassessment, learning activities, postassessment and sometimes an optional extra credit or quest activity. Each is an acceptable method of individualizing instruction for teachers in classrooms that are not involved in the exclusive use of a commercial system. Each is inexpensive, relatively simple, adaptable to many uses, interesting to students if not abused. Each is used by teachers attempting to encourage student self-direction while tackling academic tasks. But the LAP is also different in some important respects.

The LAP is also commonly known as a unipac, referring to the characteristic feature, a design intended to cover the content encompassed in a single objective. If it is well written, the LAP is like a sentence in that it should cover one complete thought, concept or skill. Judging when one covers too much comes from experience, but one rule of thumb is that an effective LAP should involve approximately two to five hours work for the average student. Because a LAP is almost always a paper and pencil learning activity, anything longer than five hours tends to become tedious for the student; anything shorter requires too much management and design work for the teacher. One way to conceptualize the length and complexity of a typical LAP would be that if this were the only teaching method used by a teacher (which the authors do not, of course, recommend), thirty to thirty-five LAPS or unipacs would cover the entire school year. LAPS can be used as an effective learning activity in a class unit or as a part of a larger learning center. Suggestions for the successful use of LAPs (unipacs) include the following:

 1. *Include, in the introduction, a brief motivational rationale telling the student why this objective needs to be completed and why it is important to him. Follow this with an overview of the purpose and activities of the LAP. Wind up this very brief*

introduction with some clear, step-by-step directions for completion of the LAP, making the directions as simple as the teacher can possibly make them.

2. *List the objective separately, spelling out exactly what the student will be able to do upon successful completion of the activities that will follow.*
3. *The pre-assessment should be brief, and if successfully completed, should lead directly to the more comprehensive post-test.*
4. *There should be at least five major activities for each objective. The activities should present some opportunity for success and challenge for each student. Such activities should relate directly and clearly to the objective of the LAP, and most of the activities should be able to be completed by the student at his seat, with little or no help from the teacher.*
5. *The post-test should relate directly to the objectives, and may be contained in the LAP, or it may be the teacher who administers a final post-test of his or her own, following the successful completion of the post-assessment in the LAP. It should be easily scored.*
6. *There should be a section that pemits the student to evaluate the LAP.*
7. *Try using a different color paper for different sections of the LAP, or for different LAPs.*
8. *Keep consumable materials separate, or have students use their own paper for completion of the activities.*
9. *When designing the LAP for use in a heterogeneous class, develop the vocabulary at a level that aims at the low average students in the class. Since the LAP is designed to be a roadmap to learning, it should be clear to as large a number of students as possible.*
10. *As with learning centers or any other method where students are expected to learn on their own, they should be given an appropriate orientation to the tasks.*[39]

As with learning centers, the role of the teacher using unipacs is significantly different than that of the teacher involved in the use of large group instruction. The teacher sheds the roles of presenter, demonstrator, driller, questioner, and adopts the mantle of decision maker, planner, evaluator, facilitator, initiator, monitor, coordinator. The manner in which the teacher relates to the students in these styles of individualized instruction is much like the way in which the teacher must respond to the small group learning situation.

Excessive use of either of these strategies carries with it the same dangers that accompany a too heavy reliance on any other major instructional act. When correctly understood and used, both methods can be powerful instructional alternatives. In classrooms where more student involvement and greater personalization of the learning activity are major objectives, these modes offer attractive opportunities to teachers and students alike. Little wonder that in the past decade these methods have continued to attract interest and use rather than dust.

Mastery Learning

Mastery learning is an attempt to individualize instruction within a systematic framework that preserves the advantages of personalizing the instruction while attempting to avoid the excesses of exclusively individualized instruction. If successful, it may be an acceptable compromise between large group teaching, small group work and individualization.

Advocates of the mastery learning approach make a number of very bold assumptions about teaching and learning. They claim, for example, that when using mastery learning, from seventy-five to ninety-five percent of the students in school can achieve the same level of excellence that the best students attain under traditional circumstances. These advocates also assert that mastery learning is more efficient, takes less time and produces higher levels of motivation and better attitudes in students.[40]

The startling contention of mastery learning is that, if each pupil is permitted to spend the time needed to learn to the level of mastery, then progress will be almost inevitable. When students are not allowed the time they need, failure is almost automatic. Mastery learning, thus, stresses the direct relationship between time spent on task and the level of achievement, something very similar to the focus of recent research on teacher behavior discussed earlier in this chapter.

Mastery learning denies the inevitability of the normal curve in academic achievement. The normal curve appears when time and the quality of instruction are held constant, leaving aptitude to determine the levels of achievement reached by different students. Block, a prominent proponent of the mastery learning approach, maintains that when each pupil is provided with the most appropriate type of teaching and given the required amount of time to learn, that the close relationship between aptitude and achievement (and therefore the normal curve) will disappear.[41]

There are four primary variables that influence achievement and that are attacked by the mastery learning approach. First, the idea of aptitude for learning must be thought of in new terms, as the amount of time required for a person to learn a task, and not the innate ability of the student to learn at all, as in the intelligence quotient. Some students need more time and help, and may need to expend more effort, but almost all are capable of learning what the school demands. Second, the quality of instruction must be adjusted so that students are provided with learning activities that adapt to their individual learning styles. A variety of learning activities from which students can choose becomes crucial. Third, individual perseverance (and motivation) in the learning task is significant. If a student needs twenty-five hours to learn a particular skill, but is only willing to spend ten, learning will not occur. Fourth, and most important, is the time allowed for learning. An effective mastery learning strategy must find ways of altering the time framework so that individual students are able to spend the time they need. Block[42] expresses these four factors in the following way:

$$\text{Degree of learning} = f \frac{\text{1. Time allowed} \quad \text{2. Perseverance}}{\text{3. Aptitude} \quad \text{4. Quality of instruction}}$$

In addition to these four primary factors, there are several other items of concern that give shape to mastery learning. One is an insistence that learners complete the necessary prerequisites before attempting to learn something new. Moving on to a new task before learning well what has been left behind is seen as a primary cause for failure in school. Mastery learning also places great significance on the role of formative and summative evaluation in facilitating learning. Formative learning helps to decide whether the learner should move on to a new task or return to a review of a previous or current task. Summative evaluation helps to determine, in a final way, whether the learning has been effective, and forms the basis for grading. If mastery learning is implemented, say proponents, there will be far more "A's" and far fewer grades in the "D" and "F" levels.

The process of implementing mastery learning, while considerably more complex than the present space permits, generally follows a series of five steps:

1. *Deriving the program standards. For individual classroom teachers, this may involve an analysis of the present curriculum, followed by the development of smaller units which lead to objectives that can be taught in one or two weeks (for the average student).*
2. *Selecting the pattern of instruction. This involves the designing of learning activities that present a variety of approaches to mastering the subject. A rule of thumb, followed by one of the authors when using this approach, is to have at least five activities for each objective.*
3. *Developing formative evaluations for each objective, specifying the level of attainment that constitutes mastery.*
4. *Prescribing learning correctives for students who fail to attain mastery after working through learning activities. Learning correctives are either additional learning activities that the student did not choose the first time through, or special remedial techniques reserved for recycling.*
5. *Administration of summative evaluations to students who have arrived at the appropriate point.*[43]

There appear to be two major varieties of mastery learning, each of which follows this basic pattern. One approach, designed by Bloom, begins the instruction regarding each objective with large group teacher-directed sessions, followed by a formative evaluation that lets students know about their progress and the need or lack of need for further work on that objective. Students who need extra work on a particular objective then turn to the learning correctives, while also participating in the next large group presentation. At the end of a particular period of time (for example, a school grading period) a summative evaluation constricted as far as the major variable (time) is concerned, still manages to combine into one package several attractive instructional processes. The second approach, called the Keller model, does not use the large group instruction process and relies on the accumulation of satisfactorily completed objectives for the grade for each student.[44]

After a period of more than a decade of experimentation with mastery learning, its advocates report a number of positive results. One review of the research reported that for ninety-seven comparisons of average achievement scores between mastery learning and other techniques, fifty-nine comparisons indicated statistically significant results in favor of the mastery learning approach, while only three favored the alternatives. In the remaining studies, while none was statistically significant, most (twenty-eight of the thirty-four) favored the mastery learning style. Other reviews appear to support mastery learning in a similar fashion. Recent uses of even more sophisticated statistical devices, such as meta-analysis, also indicate moderate to strong effects in favor of mastery strategies. One researcher concluded that mastery learning not only works, but that it works very well.[45]

As with any instructional approach, however, there are some unanswered questions. Researchers would like to know whether mastery learning works equally well with different types of educational goals and objectives. They would also like to learn whether this approach is equally effective with different types of students. Others question the relationship between the presence of mastery learning and appearance of grade inflation. Still others, impressed with the promise of mastery learning, point to the need for highly specific, and widely agreed upon educational goals, a not too widespread condition in American school systems. The lack of sophisticated assessment and diagnostic tools, inadequate corrective treatment, exhausted teachers, the problems with time and content variables and the stigma of a behavioristic-based model of teaching have been identified as challenges to the smooth operation of mastery learning strategies.[46]

Horton summarized the case for mastery learning this way:

> There are many unanswered questions arising from mastery learning, but it does provide some exciting and provocative assertions that should cause us to question the way we presently view teaching and learning. We will probably find that it will never be ''the'' answer for everyone or even for most but we may very well find it useful for ''some'' teachers to use in ''some'' situations to teach ''some'' children ''some'' things.

Individual Learning Styles and Instruction

One of the most promising developments in the area of personalizing instruction is the attempt to identify the individual learning styles of learners and to adapt instruction they receive to those styles. Since middle schools are dedicated to the recognition and nurture of individual differences in learners, these relatively recent attempts to do so should continue to grow in popularity and practicality in the years ahead. Three approaches have been singled out by the authors for brief mention here.

Rita and Kenneth Dunn have, through their writing and speaking, become identified with the attempt to identify and utilize the individual learning styles of students in the educational process.[47] Citing what they perceive to be a great need for individual student diagnosis and related prescriptions for learning, the Dunns have developed a process of analyzing each of eighteen separate elements of learning style as they conceive it to be. The general elements that comprise learning style, as described by the Dunns, include environmental, emotional, sociological and physical components.

Once the individual learning styles of the students in the classroom have been detailed, the Dunns recommend that the teacher move to redesign the classroom to accommodate the differences. Classrooms, argue the Dunns, must be transformed from nondescript boxes into multifaceted learning environments capable of responding to and supporting the diversity of learning styles. In their text, the Dunns offer detailed and practical strategies for bringing about this classroom transformation. These suggestions are followed by a wealth of ideas for designing instruction to match the learning styles of the students: small group techniques, contracts, programmed instruction, multisensory instructional packages, "tactual" (sic) and kinesthetic resources; and case studies illustrate the ideas.

Another area of interest, in connection with the topic of learning style, is the approach known as cognitive style mapping. Based on the assumption that each individual has an idiosyncratic approach to the process of learning, the advocates of Educational Cognitive Style attempt to identify the modes of behavior that make up an individual's cognitive style and to design a display of that style in the form of a graphic printout that is called a map. Once an educator has the information on learning style yielded by the mapping process, he or she can attempt to design instructional settings that are based on an individual's strengths. Preferences for large group, small group and independent learning modes can be determined. Options for written, visual or programmed materials can be exercised on the basis of an individual's cognitive style. The possibilities are as numerous as the diversity of learning styles present in the classroom.[48]

Mullally points out, however, that this approach to capitalizing on individual learning style (and, the present authors believe, with all such attempts) has several limitations imposed upon it by the very nature of the quest. Specialized training, skills and materials are required of teachers who attempt to design, implement and manage instructional activities planned for the various cognitive styles uncovered in the class group. There is also the danger that an individual child's cognitive style, once determined by the teacher, will be assumed to remain unchanged and students may be mislabeled or permanently classified on the basis of a cognitive style that no longer exists. It is possible, however, that the seriousness of these limitations only mirrors the importance of the attempt to determine and utilize data about individual learning styles.[49]

A third approach to the recognition and use of information concerning learning style comes from the study of psychological type. Based on the theory of the great Swiss psychologist, Carl Jung, this approach postulates that there are four basic mental processes (sensing, intuition, thinking and feeling) used by everyone, but that each person differs to the extent that these processes are preferred and developed. Our preferences for certain processes appear at very early ages, almost as if the preferences were a part of our nature. As we grow, we are likely to rely more and more on those mental processes we prefer. Skills and interests, as well as characteristic ways of behaving toward others, develop into patterns which can be grouped into psychological types. Research in the theory of psychological type has determined that there are sixteen separate types, and that each type has a characteristic style when it comes to learning. What's more, every teacher has a preferred pattern, or type, that determines the ways in which each prefers to teach.[50]

Students' psychological types differ in several important ways in regard to learning style. Some students prefer to be active and extraverted in their learning, often learning as they speak. Others prefer to be reflective and introverted, learning by inner analysis. Some students prefer learning directly through the senses, maintaining direct contact with the real world, while others learn quickly by leaps of intuition, by putting two ideas together to get a third. Some students make decisions about themselves and their world by rational, logical analysis; others weigh the values involved, the people concerned and how they will be affected, and additional affective elements of decision making. Some students prefer a very planned, structured, controlled experience, while many of their classmates may respond more flexibly and spontaneously, perhaps procrastinating instead of planning. All of these preferences influence the effectiveness of various instructional settings.

Many educators, when faced with the seemingly infinite variety of factors that determine an individual student's learning style, may grow weary at the mere thought of attempting to arrange a classroom to fit such conditions perfectly. The three approaches which are noted here seem to require almost Herculean efforts of middle school teachers already overburdened. Lawrence succinctly summarized the dilemma posed by the knowledge of the existence of individual learning styles:

> Matching instruction to each learner's uniqueness is, in most situations, an unrealizable objective. Yet, to ignore individual differences in learners is foolish. Without straining to attend to uniqueness, it is possible to identify patterns in students that can serve as shortcuts to matching instruction to individuals.[51]

What we are faced with, then, in the area of learning style, is not an insurmountable problem arising from the uniqueness of each learner, but the task of identifying patterns of style and motivation that allow us to think about smaller groups of students with relatively similar patterns. This task, in the minds of the present authors, seems much more likely to be accomplished than efforts based on the assumption that each individual student has an irreconcilably different learning style from every other.

Other Approaches to Individualization: A Comment

Some writers in education believe that the processes involved in the individualization of instruction will soon be drastically modified by the utilization in

schools of advances in the design of what have come to be called minicomputers. Such devices may well have a considerable impact on the management of individualized instruction, vastly improving our capacity to store
and recall information about pupil progress. Minicomputers, assuming
equally dramatic advances in the design and availability of appropriate soft-
ware, may also significantly improve the ability of the school to provide instruction itself. The present authors, however, believe that those who predict revolutionary growth in individualized instruction via the minicomputer
are likely to fall short of their hoped-for quantum leap toward a completely
technologically based instructional program for the middle school.

The special significance of the research on teacher behavior and student
learning discussed earlier in this chapter is in the ability of the results of this
research to call into question those who make sweeping claims for the superiority of any single instructional strategy for all students or for all educational objectives. So long as the learning tasks we ask of our students are of
radically different types, and as long as the students we serve are dramatically different in the ways in which they function in schools, no one instructional strategy will or should serve all the needs of the middle school and its
students.

The authors discussed the organization of teachers into interdisciplinary
groups in chapter 5 and the significance of interdisciplinary teaching units
of instruction in chapter 3. The following treatment of teamed instruction
relies heavily on the concepts elaborated in these other sections of the text.

Teamed Instruction

The complexity and diversity of the attempt to properly instruct middle
school students has led teachers in virtually every middle school in the nation to attempt, in one way or another, to combine their talents and their
efforts to bring about a more effective educational program for the students
they serve. The interdisciplinary teacher organization, as the foundation of
the entire middle school program, recognizes, by its existence, the mandate
to form team efforts to meet the needs of the students. While the authors
have steadfastly maintained that interdisciplinary team organization and team
teaching were not synonymous, and that the presence of the first does not
always require or imply the presence of the second, it is hard to imagine an
interdisciplinary unit that did not evolve from a team organization of at least
rudimentary dimensions. It is also difficult to conceive of an interdisciplinary group of teachers who, having dealt effectively with the myriad problems that confront them regularly, did not at least discuss the possibility of
coordinating their instructional efforts more closely. From this point to actual teamed instruction is a very small step, indeed.

Teams must, of course, deal with all of the team management issues that
confront them, but teamed instruction is usually a much more voluntary
practice, dependent upon several very important conditions. A sufficient

amount of common planning time, supplementing the planning time that individual teachers need, is probably the most important of the prerequisites to teamed instruction. Many exemplary middle schools are able to provide teachers with two planning periods per day, one for the team efforts and another for the individual teacher. Teamed instruction simply requires additional planning time, and without it few teams will be able to maintain the effort for long.

A second, and perhaps no less critical, requirement for the success of teamed instruction emerges from the nature of interpersonal communication. Teaming resembles married life in several ways: when it is working well it is beautiful, and when it is not it can be horrible. Much of the work of the team on a regular basis will require interpersonal skills and attitudes of the highest caliber. An especially large supply of patience and tolerance always is in demand. Much of the success of the team will depend on how well members communicate with each other: knowing how to listen so that others will talk to you; knowing how to talk so that others will listen to you; and knowing how to solve problems in an essentially democratic fashion. Teachers who enjoy being with each other will seek opportunities to plan and teach together.

The third major component in successful teamed instruction deals with the level of proficiency among the team members in the area of planning thematic units. Since team planning is quite different from the lesson planning that individual teachers must do, it will consume large portions of teacher time if the level of skill in planning as a team is not what it should be. Team members must know how to plan for instruction as a group.

The extent to which these three factors are satisfactorily resolved will determine the amount of actual teamed instruction that will occur. Where time, predisposition and skills are at a minimum, there will be few effective interdisciplinary thematic units offered to the students. Minimally functioning teams will find themselves consumed by the mechanics of team management and unable to find the necessary time or energy to engage in actual team teaching of the type most educators admire.

Many schools begin to investigate teamed instruction as the effort to reorganize from a departmentalized to an interdisciplinary teacher grouping occurs. For example, one new team in a junior high school that had begun the reorganization process (Walker Junior High School, Orlando, Florida) recognized the deficiencies of departmentalization: little or no correlation between and among the disciplines; territoriality; focus on the discipline rather than the student; and lack of flexibility. In an effort to establish a program that would remedy these deficiencies, a pilot team was formed at the seventh-grade level.

The pilot team at Walker Junior High School has worked to interrelate the four academic disciplines represented on the team, in a successful effort to accommodate students coming from self-contained elementary school classrooms into a school requiring six changes of classrooms, six different teachers and six different subjects. Their effort was described this way:

As much as possible, the four teachers select a subject that all can emphasize, each in his own area. Unlike the traditional intermediate school where, for example, the metric system is taught exclusively by the math teacher, at Walker each teacher on the team teaches aspects of the metric system. In math, the students learn the various comparisons and conversions of the metric system. The English teacher emphasizes the spelling and proper use of the metric system terms within sentence structure. In science, students use the metric system in their lab and classwork. And, in social studies, the teacher emphasizes the historical background of metrics and its use in other parts of the world. In each academic area, the teachers function consistently in requiring the students to use correct grammar, spelling and usage while learning about the metric system.

Another example of our efforts to correlate and interrelate the academic subjects comes from the period between Thanksgiving and Christmas. By taking advantage of a season that almost all students love, the team was able to capture the interest and motivation of the pupils by relating the curriculum to the season. The geography teacher emphasized the cross-cultural celebration of this season. The students decorated each of the classrooms in ways that emphasized the traditions of four continents. Students researched and presented oral reports of their research on how the season is celebrated elsewhere. Food that emphasized the customs and traditions of the various areas was prepared. In English classes, the students read from Dickens, from literature from other parts of Europe, and other continents. Vocabulary from the stories was inserted in the curriculum of other subject areas. In science, some interest was focused on plant and animal life and how these things fit into the season. Math was difficult to correlate, but was worked in wherever it was possible to do so.[52]

Such a change has been exceedingly important for the group of teachers and students at Walker Junior High. It is also significant in that it represents a dramatic departure from the previous patterns of instruction at that school, and it signals important reorganization efforts that have begun to appear in many formerly traditional junior high school systems. It is not done easily and should not be taken lightly.

Many exemplary middle schools have been able to move from this position to one which permits the frequent offering of interdisciplinary units throughout the school. Time, interpersonal skills and planning skills are such that teams work together effectively and efficiently, offering an exciting thematic program to the students fortunate enough to be involved. The terms used to describe the typical effort at teamed instruction are many and varied: core, multidisciplinary, interdisciplinary, thematic and so on. Most frequently, however, the process and the end product are quite similar, regardless of the name applied. Here, the term teamed instruction will be used to stand for all efforts of teachers from interdisciplinary groups who plan and teach together.

Given adequate time, and the interpersonal resources to carry on, the planning process becomes extremely important. One writer with considerable experience in the design and implementation of teamed instruction described a model to assist teachers in offering the type of teamed unit that most would prefer. Fox suggests that a team try only two to four such units in the first year, using a planning cycle of six weeks followed by implementation of the unit on the seventh week. Stressing the need to interpret the model flexibly, Fox identifies the following seven-step process:

1. *Week One: Brainstorming of possible themes drawn from one or more of the yearly goals as identified previously. End with a tentative selection of a theme for the unit.*
2. *Week Two: Development of subject area objectives by specialists from different academic disciplines. Exchange all of these materials among the members of the team. A meeting toward the end of the week should serve the purpose of combining objectives and skill areas, producing a package of not more than four to eight objectives or skill areas.*
3. *Week Three: Team members work independently, gathering resources and developing learning activities.*
4. *Week Four: Team meets to examine the activities and materials developed by each teacher, and to decide about the length of time to be set aside for the unit. A tentative schedule of events is produced at this meeting, tasks are divided, and the remainder of the week is spent in preparations related to these tasks.*
5. *Week Five: The final schedule for the unit is produced, with available resources, speakers, room schedules, student regrouping and other details worked out.*
6. *Week Six: A meeting toward the end of the week will help teachers check on last minute details and make emergency assignments and last minute changes.*
7. *Week Seven: Implementation of the unit.*[53]

Considering the painstaking efforts required to develop and implement plans for teamed instruction that involve as many as five or more teachers and up to 200 students, it is little wonder that there are only two to four such units produced throughout a typical school year. The authors are aware, however, that many teachers in many schools seem to defy the laws of human effort in their determination to provide the best possible program for their students. Some schools (for example, Indiantown Middle School, Indiantown, Florida) have even produced thematic units that were planned and taught involving the entire school. More often, what emerges is the joint effort of the academic teachers on the team, supported and supplemented by specialists from other areas. One example of the hundreds of fine interdisciplinary units that take place in middle schools everywhere occurred in the autumn of 1979 on ''W Team'' at Lincoln Middle School, Gainesville, Florida:

Following a discussion on the team of the need for greater team unity, the teachers decided to ''build some bridges,'' which led eventually to the theme for an interdisciplinary unit titled ''Bridges.'' The teachers identified three general goals for the unit, in addition to the need for greater unity: to offer students a different, yet meaningful experience in learning; to move team teaching from theory to practice on the team; to strengthen parental involvement. Since it was the first attempt of this team to produce such a unit, it was decided to limit it to one week's duration. Subsequent team meetings produced a series of learning objectives, and learning activities to match the objectives. Several of the teachers decided to venture into teaching areas other than their regular speciality. On the Saturday before the unit began, the team met at school to put up the props of the unit, and on Monday, following six weeks of intermittent planning, the unit was ready to go. To arouse student interest, the team posted riddles that hinted at the coming special unit. An advertisement in the school newspaper brought students to school on the first day of the unit at a peak of interest.

A variety of objectives and learning activities were offered in several different subject areas: language arts, social studies, science, industrial arts and the advisor-advisee program. The language arts teacher worked on the understanding of the literal and symbolic meanings of the word, bridge, upon exposure to "bridges" in different genres of literature, and in offering the opportunity for creative writing. The social studies students were involved in locating famous bridges, reading about them, reviewing the historical development of bridge design, and in an investigation of local bridges. In science, the teacher emphasized the physics of three types of bridge structures. In an exploratory model building class, the students worked in groups applying their knowledge and understanding of the physics of bridges to the construction of a model bridge. In the team's advisor-advisee groups during the week, an emphasis was placed on building interpersonal bridges, using activities such as one called "The Friendship Bridge." One of the most exciting activities involved parents and students in the construction of a mural for each advisory group based on experiences that had "bridged the generation gap."

As the reader might imagine, both teachers and students felt excited and revitalized by the unit described above. A follow-up survey revealed that 82 percent of the students had enjoyed the unit, and a similar number wanted another such unit sometime during the remainder of the year. Parent feedback was generous and plentiful. As the teachers said, "For one week teachers, students, and parents worked cooperatively towards a goal, but more importantly, we have laid a strong foundation for the bridges we have yet to build and cross."[54]

Teams able to produce units like the one described above are often found in schools where the leadership has strongly encouraged teamed instruction and provided the training necessary for the fulfillment of the mandate to do so. Few systems, in the opinion of the authors, provide a more comprehensive approach to the systematic planning of middle school instruction, on both a team and schoolwide basis than does Individually Guided Education (IGE), the instructional program of the Institute for the Development of Educational Activities (IDEA), an offshoot of the Kettering Foundation's educational efforts.[55] The IGE program organizes the entire instructional program around the principles of democratic decision making, individual responsibility and the worth of each person involved in the school. IGE offers a structure that includes: thorough interdisciplinary team teaching, balanced instruction, an advisory program for teachers and students, flexible student grouping, independent study, models for team and school-wide decision making, strategies for self-improvement for teachers and teams and much more. Many of the exemplary middle schools cited in this volume have, as their organizational foundation, the IGE program.

The IGE program for middle schools is consistent with the basic premises of middle school education. It is more difficult to implement and maintain than some supporters of the IGE program would admit, but for educators looking for a comprehensive and systematic approach to planning instruction in the middle school, IGE is something that can be strongly recommended for study. In connection with teamed instruction, IGE provides a model for team planning and teaching that is unmatched in its comprehensiveness, solid structure and ease of understanding for teachers.

Instruction: Concluding Comments

There is much more that can be written about effective instruction in the middle school than can be included in a single chapter. There has been little reference here to the characteristics of effective middle school teachers, to middle school teacher education or certification. Nor has there been any provision for a look at ability grouping, teacher burnout or the effects of the school organization as an instructional phenomenon. Further, we have assumed that readers will not look to this volume for beginning instruction in the basics of lesson planning and the other characteristics of effective instruction at any level of schooling. This chapter has, instead, focused on major instructional strategies that have significance for all middle school teachers.

Like the curriculum of the middle school, the topic of effective instruction for the middle school is complex, as yet poorly researched and inadequately understood. It is likely that there will be more growth in our understanding of this topic than, perhaps, in any other aspect of the exemplary middle school. The more clearly we perceive the characteristics of our students, agree upon our purposes and research the effects of our behavior, the more we will experience progress in the area of instructional strategies.

ADDITIONAL SUGGESTIONS FOR FURTHER STUDY

A. Books

Bloom, Benjamin, *Human Characteristics and School Learning* (New York: McGraw Hill Book Company, 1976).

Gagne, Robert M. and Brigg, Leslie J., *Principles of Instructional Design,* 2nd ed. (New York: Holt, Rinehart & Winston, Inc., 1979).

Klingele, William C., *Teaching in Middle Schools* (Boston: Allyn and Bacon, Inc., 1979).

Peterson, Penelope L. and Walberg, Herbert J., eds., *Research on Teaching: Concepts, Findings and Implications* (Berkeley, Calif.: McCutchan Publishing Corp., 1979).

Travers, Robert M.W., ed., *Second Handbook of Research on Teaching* (Chicago: Rand McNally and Company, 1973).

B. Periodicals

Allington, Richard L., "Improving Content Area Instruction in the Middle Schools," *Journal of Reading,* 18, 455–61 (March 1975).

Barmore, Judith M. and Morse, Philip S., "Developing Lifelong Readers in the Middle Schools: Teaching Ideas," *English Journal,* 66, 57–61 (April 1977).

Brown, James, "The Middle School Learner: Instructional Planning for a Transitional Stage," *History and Social Science Teacher,* 13, 157–62 (Spring 1978).

Bushman, John H., "Achieving Student Interaction in Creative Junior High/Middle School Programs: Teaching Ideas," *English Journal,* 66, 67–72 (April 1977).

Castallo, Richard, "Listening Guide—A First Step Toward Notetaking and Listening Skills," *Journal of Reading,* 19, 289–90 (January 1976).

Deller, Don K. and Wright, Jack E., "An Associate Faculty Program Incorporates Community Resources," *Middle School Journal,* 8, 11 (August 1977).

Fazekas, Steve and Mauch, Irene, "Organizing a Responsive Curriculum for the Middle Grades: the RISE Program," *Middle School Journal,* 6, 41–3 (Fall 1975).

Hepburn, Mary A., "Are Middle School Teachers Prepared to Teach Civics?" *Clearing House,* 50, 151–6 (December 1976).

Hofman, Helenmarie, "Middle School/Junior High Survey Report," *Science and Children,* 14, 33–5 (January 1977).

Manning, Gary, Manning, Maryann, and Bumpus, Robert, "Ten Do's and Why's of Reading to the Middle School," *Middle School Journal,* 7, 12 (June 1976).

Merritt, Daniel L., "Middle School: Organization for Learning (LAGs, LAPs, and CAPs)," *Middle School Journal,* 5, 55–9 (Winter 1975).

Morse, Sandy, "Middle Schoolers Are Special," *Language Arts,* 52, 1155–6 (November/December 1975).

Stewart, W.J., "What Causes a Middle School to be Ineffective," *Clearing House,* 49, 23–5 (September 1975).

Rathbun, Dorothy, "How to Get Middle Schoolers to Read When They're not too Thrilled About the Idea," *Learning,* 6, 122–36 (August/September 1977).

Vacca, Jo Anne L. and Vacca, Richard T., "Learning Stations: How to in the Middle Grades," *Journal of Reading,* 19, 563–7 (April 1976).

Vacca, Richard T., "Reading Comprehension in the Middle School: Instructional Alternatives," *Middle School Journal,* 8, 12–3 (August 1977).

Vacca, Richard T., "Teaching English: A View from the Middle," *English Journal,* 66, 42–6 (April 1977).

Whitmore, Sue, "Books and Kids Belong Together," *Middle School Journal,* 8, 14–5 (May 1977).

C.   ERIC

Allington, Richard, *Differentiating Instruction to Improve Comprehension in Middle School Content Areas,* A Paper Presented at the Annual Meeting of the International Reading Association, New Orleans, Louisiana, May 1974. (ERIC No. ED 092 882)

Golub, Lester S., *Reading in the Middle School Using an IGE/Teacher Corps Instructional Model,* Paper presented at the Annual Meeting of the International Reading Association, Houston, Texas, May, 1978. (ERIC No. ED 158 229)

D.   Dissertations and Dissertation Abstracts

Fenlon, John L., "An Examination and Development of Recommendations for Implementing Selected Components of a Middle School Instructional System Based on the Cognitive Characteristics of the Pre- and Early Adolescent," *Dissertation Abstracts,* 36 (January 1976) 218–A.

Glenn, Devurn H., "The Effects of a Series of Human Relations Training Sessions on the Attitude of Middle School Students Toward Study," *Dissertation Abstracts,* 35 (January 1975) 4075–A.

Green, Gerald Weakley, ''The Effects of Three Different Teaching Strategies on the Reading Comprehension of Middle School Language Arts Students,'' Unpublished doctoral dissertation, The University of Florida, 1976.

Keilocker, Sister Francette, ''An Experiment in Modification of Middle School Teachers' Behavior Through Using a Training Module on Personal Knowledge of Students,'' *Dissertation Abstracts,* 34 (May 1974) 6973–A.

Morrison, Jona Bradshaw, ''A Study of Self-Directed Learning Instructional Practices in Selected Middle and Junior High Schools,'' *Dissertation Abstracts,* 38 (September 1977) 1341–A.

Ruth, Eugene Dorsey, Jr., ''A Description of the Elements Comprising a Learner-Centered Teaching/Learning Approach with Illustrations from the Calhoun Middle School: 1971–72,'' *Dissertation Abstracts,* 36 (July 1975) 243–4–A.

Smith, James Arthur, ''A Comparison of Middle School Instruction and Conventional Instruction with Respect to the Academic Achievement and Self Concept of Pre- and Early Adolescence,'' *Dissertation Abstracts,* 36 (September 1975) 1420–1–A.

Welsch, Vicki LaFreniere, ''A Comparison of Two Organizational Approaches to Reading Instruction in the Middle School,'' Unpublished doctoral dissertation, The University of Florida, 1977.

Whitley, Theodore Walker, ''Some Effects of a Locally Developed Program of Individualized Instruction on the Attitudes of Middle School Pupils Toward Various Aspects of the School Environment,'' *Dissertation Abstracts,* 37 (June 1977) 7656–A.

Young, Jerry Lynn, ''The Identification of Mathematical Concepts for a Middle School Mathematics Program,'' *Dissertation Abstracts,* 36 (September 1975) 1354–5–A.

FOOTNOTES

1. William M. Alexander and Others. *The Emergent Middle School* (New York: Holt, Rinehart and Winston, 1968), pp. 84–86.
2. Paul S. George and C. Kenneth McEwin, ''Middle School Teacher Education: A Progress Report,'' *Journal of Teacher Education,* 29, 13–16 (September/October 1978).
3. James L. Kuethe, *The Teaching-Learning Process, Keystones of Education Series* (Glenview, Ill.: Scott, Foresman and Company, 1968), 126; cited in Joseph C. DeVita, Philip Pomerantz, and Leighton B. Wilklow, *The Effective Middle School* (West Nyack, N.Y.: Parker Publishing Company, 1970) p. 173.
4. N.L. Gage, ''The Yield of Research on Teaching,'' *Phi Delta Kappan,* 60, 229–35 (November, 1978). See also N.L. Gage, *The Scientific Basis of the Art of Teaching* (New York: Teachers College Press, 1978).
5. Jere E. Brophy, ''Teacher Behavior and Student Learning,'' *Educational Leadership,* 37, 33–38 (October 1979).
6. Brophy, p. 34.
7. Frederick J. McDonald, ''Report on Phase II of the Beginning Teacher Evaluation Study,'' *Journal of Teacher Education,* 27, 39–42 (Spring 1976).
8. Conversations with Robert Soar and Donald Medley, held at the Seminar on Research on Teacher Effectiveness, University of Florida, Gainesville, Fla., May 9–10, 1979.
9. Walter R. Borg, ''Time and School Learning,'' *BTES Newsletter,* (Sacramento,

Calif.: The Commission on Teacher Preparation and Licensing, March 1979), pp. 2–7.

10. Barak V. Rosenshine, "How Time Is Spent in Elementary Classrooms," *BTES Newsletter* (Sacramento, Calif.: The Commission on Teacher Preparation and Licensing, March, 1979), pp. 7–10.

11. Barak V. Rosenshine, "Recent Research on Teaching Behaviors and Student Achievement," *Journal of Teacher Education,* 27, 61–64 (Spring 1976).

12. The Basic Skills Instruction Process (BSIP) is the authors' label for a series of instructional steps which form a pattern that has been called different things in different places and times. The research that supports the process is scattered throughout the literature of teacher education. Readers interested in the research support, data and documentation in greater detail are referred to the October, 1979 issue (Volume 37, Number 1) of *Educational Leadership,* specifically pages 29–60. This issue deals intensively and sensibly with the impact and implications of research on teacher effectiveness, and articles published therein offer bibliographic citations that will permit readers to trace the research reports to their original sources.

13. Brophy, p. 37.

14. Penelope L. Peterson, "Direct Instruction: Effective for What and for Whom?" *Educational Leadership,* 37, 46–48 (October 1979).

15. Barak V. Rosenshine, p. 61.

16. N.L. Gage, Address to the Seminar on Research on Teacher Effectiveness, University of Florida, Gainesville, Fla., May 9–10, 1979.

17. Gary D. Borich, "Implications for Developing Teacher Competencies From Process-Product Research," *Journal of Teacher Education,* 30, 77–86 (January/February 1979).

18. Brophy, p. 35.

19. Hilda Taba, *Curriculum Development: Theory and Practice* (New York: Harcourt, Brace and World, Inc., 1962); and, Urie Bronfenbrenner, *Two Worlds of Childhood: U.S. and U.S.S.R.* (New York: Pocket Books, Inc., 1973); cited in John Henry Wagner, "Peer Teaching in Spelling: An Experimental Study in Selected Seventh-Day Adventist High Schools" (unpublished doctoral dissertation, University of Florida, 1978) p. 11.

20. Wagner, pp. 12–16.

21. Lawrence L. Smith, "A Model for Cross-Age Tutoring," *Middle School Journal,* 9, 3, 26–27 (February 1980).

22. Smith, p. 26.

23. Smith, p. 6.

24. Smith, p. 10.

25. Bruce Joyce and Marsha Weil, *Models of Teaching* (Englewood Cliffs, New Jersey: Prentice-Hall, Inc., 1972); see also several more recent additions to this literature by the same authors, *Personal Models of Teaching; Social Models of Teaching;* and *Information Processing Models of Teaching,* all published in 1978, by Prentice-Hall, Inc., of Englewood Cliffs, N.J.

26. John Dewey, *Democracy and Education* (New York: Macmillan, 1916); cited in Joyce and Weil, *Models of Teaching,* 1972.

27. Herbert Thelen, *Education and The Human Quest* (New York: Harper and Row, 1960), in Joyce and Weil, *Models of Teaching,* 1971, p. 45.

28. "Student Team Learning" (Baltimore, Maryland: Johns Hopkins University Center for Social Organization of Schools), n.d. Additional materials describing

the process for implementing Student Team Learning in the classroom are available from the Center, 3505 N. Charles Street, Baltimore, Maryland, 21218.

29. "Student Team Learning," p. 1.

30. Silvain, Robert E., *Using Student Team Learning: The Johns Hopkins Team—Learning Project* (Baltimore, Maryland: Center for the Social Organization of Schools, Johns Hopkins University), 1978.

31. Conversations with Geoffrey Pyne, mathematics teacher, Mebane Middle School, Alachua, Florida, Summer 1979.

32. The Center for Social Organization of Schools will provide interested educators with further information, filmstrips and tape materials, curriculum units already prepared and a host of other materials. The Center also conducts workshops throughout the United States, and has established a network of trained facilitators to help teachers and districts interested in adopting Student Team Learning.

33. Leslie W. Kindred, et. al., *The Middle School Curriculum: A Practitioner's Handbook* (Boston: Allyn and Bacon, Inc., 1976), pp. 120–21.

34. Paul S. George, and Others, *The Learning Centers Approach to Instruction* (Gainesville, Fla.: The Florida Educational Research and Development Council, Fall, 1973), p. 4.

35. Paul S. George, "Individualized Instruction in Secondary Social Studies: The Learning Centers Approach," *American Secondary Education*, 4, 4 (September 1974).

36. George, "Individualized Instruction . . . ," p. 8.

37. George, "Individualized Instruction . . . ," pp. 9–10.

38. Nancy Doda, "Teacher to Teacher," *Middle School Journal*, 7,9 (December 1976).

39. For more information on unipacs, see John H. Hansen and Arthur C. Hearn, *The Middle School Program* (New York: Rand McNally, Inc., 1971). See also William C. Kingele, *Teaching in Middle Schools* (Boston: Allyn and Bacon, Inc., 1979).

40. See Ron Brandt, "A Conversation With Benjamin Bloom," *Educational Leadership*, 37, 157–161 (November 1979) for a report of an interview with an outstanding authority on mastery learning.

41. James H. Block, Ed., *Mastery Learning: Theory and Practice* (New York: Holt, Rinehart and Winston, Inc., 1971).

42. James H. Block, *Schools, Society and Mastery Learning* (New York: Holt, Rinehart, and Winston, 1974), pp. 5–8.

43. Jerry W. Klein, "Designing a Mastery Learning Program," *Educational Leadership*, 37, 144–49 (November 1979). The entire issue of this journal is devoted to the exploration of mastery learning.

44. James H. Block, "A Description and Comparison of Bloom's Learning for Mastery Strategy and Keller's Personalized System of Instruction," in J. Block, Ed., *Schools, Society and Mastery Learning* (New York: Holt, Rinehart and Winston, Inc., 1974), pp. 15–27.

45. Robert B. Burns, "Mastery Learning: Does It Work?" *Educational Leadership*, 37, 110–11, (November 1979).

46. Lowell Horton, "Mastery Learning: Sound in Theory, But . . . ," *Educational Leadership*, 37, 154–46, (November 1979).

47. Rita Dunn and Kenneth Dunn, *Teaching Students Through Their Individual Learning Styles: A Practical Approach* (Reston, VA: Reston Publishing Company, 1978.)

48. Lee Mullally, "Educational Cognitive Style: Implications for Instruction," *Theory Into Practice,* 16, 231–242 (October 1977).
49. Mullally, p. 241.
50. Gordon Lawrence, *People Types and Tiger Stripes: A Practical Guide to Learning Styles* (Gainesville, Florida: The Center for Application of Psychological Type, Inc., 1979).
51. Lawrence, p. vii.
52. From personal correspondence between Mr. Ed Hamil, Assistant Principal, Walker Junior High School, Orlando, Florida, and the authors, January 3, 1980.
53. James H. Fox, "Planning Interdisciplinary Units Within A Team Structure," *Middle School Journal,* 5, 49–51 (Winter 1975). For a similar description of the planning process from the teacher's point of view, see Nancy Doda, "Teacher to Teacher," *Middle School Journal,* 9, 8–10 (May 1978).
54. The authors gratefully acknowledge the assistance of Ms. Carla Hoy, team leader, and of the entire W Team, Lincoln Middle School, Gainesville, Florida, in the preparation of this description of the "Bridges" Unit.
55. For additional information on IGE, write to the Institute, Suite 300, 5335 Far Hills Avenue, Dayton, Ohio, 45429.

Chapter 9 Leadership Roles and Staff Development in the Exemplary Middle School

Middle schools are affected by many factors as they seek to become exemplary, but none more significant than the quality of their leadership. Theory, observation and research all attest to the great importance of the leadership of the school principal and also of the various other individuals who may at one time or another have roles as leaders. Some person or persons must bring together the people and ideas that start a good school, especially a new school organization and program like the middle school, and some person or persons must keep operating all the processes necessary for continued program effectiveness. More specifically, we see these major functions of the responsible leadership of a school:

1. Maintaining a good school that satisfies generally accepted criteria of such a school and fulfills its stated goals;
2. Motivating the performance required by students, faculty and others directly concerned, to maintain continuing high quality of the school;
3. Providing opportunity and utilization of shared decision making;
4. Facilitating processes of educational improvement within the school community; and
5. Working cooperatively and effectively with other school personnel in the school and district for optimum educational continuity.

The school principal is certainly the key individual in the discharge of these functions, but there are roles for associates in leadership and special service positions, as well as roles of a nonstatus, informal nature for all personnel associated with the school—faculty, staff, students, parents and citizens. Major approaches to these functions are made through staff development programs. This chapter is devoted to descriptions and illustrations of all these roles, with a major section on staff development.

Leadership Roles of Principals and Other Status Leaders

The five major functions of a school's leadership prescribe the roles of the principal and any other persons designated by official title and job definition to have leadership roles. The positions are variously entitled associate principal, assistant principal (both without a qualifying phrase such as "for instruction," and with such qualification), coordinator (usually of something, such as curriculum) and administrative assistant. All of these positions are leadership roles affecting an entire school. Although our concern is primarily with leaders in individual schools, we do recognize in this section the relationship of leaders in the school to others in the district and state. We also note in a subsequent section the existence of various special leadership roles, such as house director, that affect a part of the individual school.

Maintaining a *Good* School

The most generally recognized role of the principal and any administrative associates is that of maintaining a *good* school; indeed it is to this goal that all other functions must relate, for having a good school is the common expectation of the taxpayers, parents and community in general. What is "good" is not necessarily agreed upon or even defined, but what is "bad" gets identified readily, frequently and fully if not uniformly.

We have devoted most of the preceding pages of this text to describing the essential elements of a good middle school. As we see it, the first and most important and indeed most pervasive role of the principal and associates is to implement as rapidly and as fully and well as possible the organization, program, instruction and services we have described. To do so, faculty must be chosen, organized, supervised and helped. Students must be organized for instruction in a program that must first be carefully planned and thereafter continuously improved. Students must be served through counseling and various special services. Schedules and facilities must be provided to match curriculum and instructional needs. Any funds under school control must be allocated and accounted for. And along with all this there must be continuing communication with parents and the community, and continuing planning and evaluation to ensure the maintenance of quality. The school administration has great responsibility and arduous tasks, but what a challenge and opportunity!

This historic development of the principal from the role of teacher and then "principal teacher" should be regarded in the training and selection of principals. We like the emphasis of an early author in middle school education, Theodore Moss, on the concept of the principal as teacher: "Briefly stated, this concept of the role of administration is that building principals ought to be teachers, first, last and always."[1] Moss argued that the principal need not neglect other responsibilities in order to maintain instructional leadership:

There are numerous ways that the principal teacher can keep in touch with teaching children and at the same time not neglect important administrative responsibilities. Through his teaching, he is in direct contact with middle school students and their needs and also maintains his perspective as a professional educator. He is thus not the cool, impersonal, papershuffler, button-pusher, intercom announcer and decision maker which too many building principals have become. The principal teacher remains a teacher, working with children and colleagues to improve instruction.[2]

The present authors would in no way deprecate the various tasks of the principal already alluded to that are apart from direct instruction, but we do see curriculum and instruction as the central function of the middle school. The principal needs to know firsthand curriculum and instruction in order to provide school leadership, and his or her knowledge needs to be kept current by continuing association with students and classrooms. Unless he or she is well grounded in curriculum and instruction the principal simply cannot discharge well such critical duties as these four (of eight) stipulated for the principal of the Rupert A. Nock Middle School, Newburyport, Massachusetts, in the school's personnel handbook:

1. *Guide and encourage the school's professional personnel in their professional work and their professional growth, so as to secure continuous improvement of instruction and to promote healthy growth and adjustment of the pupils.*
2. *Create an environment wherein teachers and pupils may achieve mutual understanding, a high sense of morals and the best possible working conditions.*
3. *Take all necessary precautions to safeguard the safety, health and well being of pupils and staff members, including formulation of plans to meet emergencies.*
4. *Be responsible for maintaining close and cooperative relations with parents and community, and interpreting to them the educational program of the school.*

To provide the needed leadership in curriculum and instruction and the other related tasks required to have a good school, the principal and associates must stimulate and involve as much help as possible. We turn now to these roles.

Motivating Optimum Performance

We agree with a 1978 issue of the NASSP's *The Practitioner* that *"the most prominent—and common—component of successful schools is a motivated teaching staff,"* and further that *"the principal is the key to a motivated and* dedicated staff."[3] We would also assign to the principal the role of leadership in setting a school climate in which students too become better motivated for performance as learners. The *Practitioner* charge is heavy:

Who then must assume the responsibility for teacher motivation? It is the responsibility of only one person—the principal. He must become the motivational catalyst, for no one else will. His school will never be great and neither teachers nor students will ever perform or grow to their full potential unless the principal assumes this responsibility. This is critical to the success of every student and teacher within the building. *A monumental task, yes, but critical to success.*[4]

The importance of the principal's human relationships and his or her administrative behavior is so well recognized that these matters are studied and written about very widely and often.[5]

Our own knowledge of theory, research and practice concerning the middle school principalship leads us to suggest that such behaviors as the following characterize middle school principals and their associates who have seemingly better motivated and better performing faculties and student bodies. These exemplary principals:

1. Use a maximum number of opportunities for person-to-person communication with faculty and students and parents
2. Are enthusiastic about the school, the students, the faculty
3. Emphasize the values and uses of goal setting and goals in all elements of the school program
4. Seek opportunities to secure and use feedback about their own performance as well as each aspect of school operation
5. Praise faculty, staff and students whenever praise is due
6. Avoid embarrassing students and faculty and staff members before other persons but provide constructive criticism when needed
7. Reward performance of students and faculty and staff members by the most appropriate means available, including salary increases for employees when possible
8. Eliminate conditions, including disruptive students and faculty members, which are inimical to the effective performance of others
9. Conduct meetings skillfully to achieve their purposes
10. Participate in faculty work assignments such as monitorial duties

Sharing Decision Making

We have assumed throughout this book that much decision making in the middle school must be shared by the administration with the groups concerned; thus in both chapters 2 and 3 in appropriate sections on planning, we used various examples of planning councils of parents and teachers and others. Here it is the importance of the administrator's sharing the decision making we wish to emphasize. A section on "Shared Decision Making As It Relates to the Middle School Program" in Milwaukee's plan for middle schools cites this practice as "one of the key components of the middle school program," and describes eight levels of shared decision making: (1) student and student, (2) student and teacher, (3) teacher and teacher, (4) teacher and administrator, (5) administrator and administrator, (6) school and parents, (7) school and community and (8) parents and community.[6] The plan itself was the result of extensive shared decision making, according to the Superintendent's letter of transmittal:

> The Middle School Steering Committee, central office personnel, teachers, administrators, and parents developed *A Working Draft for the Plan for the Transition to the Middle School* during the first semester of the 1978–79 school year. The purpose of the *Working Draft*, dated November 9, 1978, was to stimulate input by parents, students, community residents, School Board Directors, teachers, field administrators, and central office personnel in the planning and development of a quality educational program, for pre- and early adolescent students enrolled in the Milwaukee Public Schools.
>
> The Working Draft was reviewed by the Instruction Committee at its November 20, 1978 meeting. Members of the Steering Committee met with school parent groups, the Committee of 100, middle/junior high teachers and administrators, elementary and high school administrators, and central office personnel to involve them in the development of a middle school plan. Additionally, elementary, middle/junior high and senior high school administrators held meetings at local schools to involve parents and staff. As a result of this extensive input, *The Plan for the Transition to the Middle School,* was completed in December, 1978.[7]

Suggestions for the implementation of the Plan caused the Board to adopt it as a two-year transition. Such careful involvement and consideration of the move to middle schools seems essential to the success of the movement.

Within the individual school once established and in operation the need is especially great for some group representing the faculty to participate actively in the decision-making process, and as appropriate in the implementation of decision. In Milwaukee the responsible group is the School Coordinating Committee:

> The basis for school planning and decision-making procedures is the School Coordinating Committee (SCC). This group, with the leadership of the principal, consists of the learning coordinator, a teacher representative from each of the basic teams and vocational/arts teams, exceptional education, an aide representative, and an MTEA representative and meets weekly to determine school policies, to coordinate activities, and to review the total school operation. Staff involvement in the decision-making process is the key to the successful operation of the total program.[8]

At Oaklea Middle School in Junction City, Oregon, decision making is aided by the Administrator's Council, an advisory group meeting weekly to advise and serve as a communication group for the entire staff. According to the school's Certified Handbook, the main mission of this Council "is to provide more immediate communication where total staff participation is not required" and the group determines the need for faculty or staff meetings of a nonemergency nature and the agenda for faculty meetings. It includes representatives from each team (called "River," and the Council is referred to as

"River Rep"), and from two special teacher groups and the classified employees group.

The Graveraet Middle School of Marquette, Michigan, uses the model of the staff decision-making process shown in the accompanying figure (Figure 9.1); note the continuing opportunities it provides for staff participation. Decision making in the Marshall, Michigan, Middle School, is shared with the Faculty Council described as follows in a 1979 bulletin from the school:

> Marshall Middle School's faculty has an effective means of assuming a leadership role in our school through its Faculty Council. Each team and special area elects and is represented on the Council by one of its members. The officers are nominated from the Council and elected by the total staff. . . .
>
> Our Council is a vital part of Marshall Middle School. For example, in the past year we have completed or are currently working on a revision of our skills inventory (reporting system), the promotion of our Faculty Follies, the content and schedule of assemblies, a committee to reevaluate the goals and philosophies of Marshall Middle School, the training and placement of Tutors and Aides in the middle school, a new student orientation program, to name some. Our Faculty Council continues to show growth in Marshall Middle Schools' decision-making policies.

Some middle schools have adopted the Program Improvement Council (PIC) plan included in the Individually Guided Education (IGE) program of the Kettering Foundation's IDEA organization. Defined in this program as "a decision-making body especially concerned with school-wide policies and operational procedures" PIC is further described as follows in an IGE publication:

> With the principal as its chairman, it establishes school-wide policy and oversees the many wide-ranging aspects of the total program. LC leaders who make up the balance of the PIC's membership have teaching and advising as well as administrative duties in their Learning Communities. They combine a thorough understanding of LC operations and problems with an overall appreciation of the task of implementing IGE successfully throughout the school.[9]

Facilitating Educational Improvement

If the foregoing three functions of administration are well handled, facilitating educational improvement will be corollary and almost inevitable. In a good school with a well-motivated faculty already sharing in decision making, the principal simply needs to keep the way clear for improvement to come, helping the process as the occasion arises. Many specific types of help are needed, and it may well be the principal's role to provide them or see that they are provided. The following list is illustrative:

1. Setting a budget which includes provision for the various items essential to staff development and school improvement such as travel for professional meetings, purchase of professional books and periodicals, employment of substitutes for teachers visiting schools or working on curriculum

The staff of the Graveraet Middle School recognize that decisions affecting our school are best made with the consensus and involvement of as many people as possible. The purpose of this model is to provide for a decision-making process which can be followed when members become interested in bringing about change in our Graveraet programs.

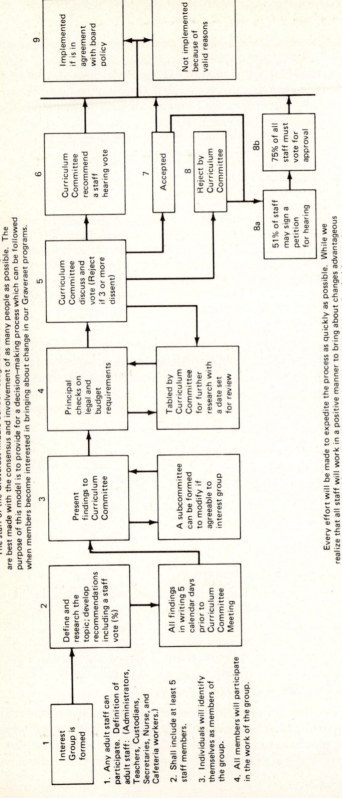

Every effort will be made to expedite the process as quickly as possible. While we realize that all staff will work in a positive manner to bring about changes advantageous to our total school program, the final authority for all administrative decisions rests with the building principal.

It is understood that no administrative policy pertaining to Graveraet would be contrary to rules or policy established by the Marquette Board of Education.

Figure 9.1 / Staff Decision-Making Process, Graveraet Middle School, Marquette, Michigan.

and instructional projects involving absence from regular teaching duties, and provision of consultant help as needed and available. (A later section of this chapter deals fully with staff development guidelines.)

2. Taking or arranging for a class or other assigned duty for a teacher who cannot otherwise readily arrange to complete a meeting or other assignment essential to an improvement aim.

3. Maintaining a school climate in which an experiment does not have to succeed since its goal is viewed as finding out whether or not some change works.

4. Keeping communication open between the various groups and individuals involved in planning, operating and evaluating the school.

5. Providing emotional support to the person or persons attacked for trying something new and different, and helping to bring together the critic and the criticized whenever appropriate.

6. Setting and keeping in operation the links between schools, school and central administration, school and community, that must hold together groups and institutions whose mutual understanding and cooperation are essential to ongoing improvement.

Many more specific types of facilitation could be listed, but the authors suggest that each school situation is the primary base for determining roles in educational improvement. One middle school principal put the emphasis on instructional leadership:

The principal is a key person in implementing the middle school program. As an instructional leader, the principal must be strong and an agent of change. Principals must take advantage of the opportunity to be instructional leaders, and they must not abdicate their roles to obtain time to complete reports, get bogged down in paper work, or spin their wheels doing tasks that could be completed by the assistant principals, department heads, team leaders, secretaries, or other staff members.[10]

Working for Educational Continuity

We noted in chapter 2 the seeming lack of practices for the purpose of developing closer ties and fewer barriers between the levels of precollege education—elementary, middle and secondary. We also listed there various approaches that could be used in relation to the middle school. If the middle school can really achieve one of its original aims involved here, improved educational continuity, it will contribute greatly to educational progress. And certainly as the school in the middle, it is in the logical position to bring about better transition and articulation.

Various approaches to educational continuity within the middle school are succeeding very well, we believe, in the exemplary middle schools of the United States: advisor-advisee plans, interdisciplinary teaming, curriculum planning at the school and team level, balanced instructional systems, flexible time and space arrangements. The problem is to get these plans understood at the other levels, especially in the high schools, with easy links existing between these plans and what precedes and follows. One key to solving this problem, we believe, is in the hands of the middle school principal. If he or she can represent well the middle school to the elementary and high school administrators and faculty, and take leadership in arranging for the communications channels and situations in which faculty can talk and understand each other across levels, and in which parents and teachers get and use well the information available from the earlier level, educational continuity can be advanced. Middle school faculties need to understand what the feeder elementary schools are doing, and vice versa. Intervisitation, meetings, teacher-to-teacher contact, visual aids and other devices can overcome the ignorance and inertia of faculties about each other, *if* some powerful catalyst intervenes. Principals and central office coordinators are the potential catalytic agents. If they are effective, a district's schooling from elementary school entrance to high school exit has optimum educational continuity.

Curriculum planning on a K-12 basis is one important step toward educational continuity. Utilization of elementary school principals in this task is illustrated by a report from the Hendrick Hudson School District, Montrose, New York:

> We have broken with the traditional pattern of the role of the elementary principal by assigning each of the four principals to chair a district curriculum committee in the area of his particular interest and knowledge. Each principal works with two teachers from each of our four elementary schools, a middle school teacher, and a high school teacher in the specific subject area. The charge to each committee is to construct a plan to develop, implement, and evaluate a revised curriculum in the subject area.[11]

In larger districts with multiple middle schools, middle school principals might appropriately chair such curriculum committees, with teacher representatives from the elementary, middle and high school levels. In addition to the development of a curriculum plan for educational continuity, the give and take of representatives of the various levels itself makes for cooperation and understanding.

Special Leadership Positions and Roles

In addition to principals and their associates having general leadership roles, most middle schools have one or more other positions for particular service that is perceived as leadership or as having leadership potential. These positions include those of house director, dean, team leader and various specialists.

House Director

The school-within-a-school organization of the middle school was described and illustrated in chapter 6. As noted there, each of the small units, usually called "houses," in this organizational plan, has an educational leader, the house director (or house principal or coordinator or dean). Illustrative of the responsibilities of this position is the following statement from the Farnsworth Middle School, Guilderland, New York, of the areas in which the effectiveness of the teaching principal (one for each of three houses, with each teaching principal responsible for teaching one academic class daily) is assessed:

1. *Planning and implementing constructive change;*
2. *Supervising and evaluating employees; quality of candidates recommended;*
3. *Implementing budget of assigned department and negotiated employee agreements;*
4. *Protecting the health, safety, and welfare of pupils;*
5. *Engaging in personal professional growth activity;*
6. *Maintaining a positive climate for pupils to learn and teachers to teach in his house and department;*
7. *Keeping parents informed and building good school-community understanding;*
8. *Cooperating in implementing district policies, programs, directions;*
9. *Participating and leadership in professional projects and organizations.*

A comprehensive description of *The Middle School in Philadelphia* lists a dozen duties of the house director of such specific nature as "serves as a resource person for all members of the team" and "serves as a chairperson at all general meetings of the House." This statement also suggests that the duties "may be performed by more than one person depending on staffing structures," perhaps because the title of house director in Philadelphia middle schools "is an unofficial title filled on a voluntary basis."[12]

Since the purpose of the house organization is to provide smaller school units and thereby facilitate interpersonal relationships of faculty, administration, students and parents, the house director is first of all the head facilitator of these relationships. Personal leadership of the faculty, and personal acquaintance as early as possible with students and parents, are critical for this role, as are the knowledge, experience and skill required for program development and maintenance. The house director is also occupied with liaison roles with the school principal, with the other house directors and faculties, with the central services and personnel of the school and the district and with the various community agencies which work directly with the house.

Dean

The position of dean seems to be found less frequently in middle schools as compared with former and present junior highs. In many middle schools assistant principals have taken over administrative functions and discipline, and counselors and teachers the guidance function. Yet many larger middle schools do have deans. We doubt if any position other than principal has such generally understood functions as to argue for its maintenance or elimination without reference to specific situations. Traditionally in secondary education, the dean is a dean of students, with a wide range of duties relating to their behavior, guidance and welfare; in junior high schools and especially in middle schools deans are likely to have a wide variety of functions. For example, at the Twin Peaks Middle School in Poway, California, curriculum and evaluation is listed by the school as the No. 1 item in the duties of each of the two deans, with the various curriculum areas divided between them. Among other duties for one dean are: discipline and attendance, A–L; schedule; books and textbooks; field trips; assemblies; curriculum development and high schools; substitute teachers. The other dean's duties include: discipline and attendance, M–Z; counseling and testing; report cards and progress notices; new student orientation; curriculum development and elementary schools; teacher aides. Such individual building assignment of duties which provides for school needs, and also for leader qualifications and interests, seems far better than some standard definition of duties of a particular position that must be implemented for accreditation or other external requirements.

Team Leader

We dealt with the role of the teaching team leader in our chapter 5 on interdisciplinary team organization, and presented there a composite list of team leader activities constructed from descriptive materials provided by several school districts. Here we would like to emphasize the significant opportunity team leaders have to bring about the desired educational results in middle schools. If a major part of instruction in the middle school is to be done by interdisciplinary teams, and we and many others believe it should, the way these teams are constituted and led are very important. Lipka's research study on the role of team leaders in middle schools noted that team teaching was generally desired and was found in most exemplary programs, but that the role of the team leader was largely undefined both in the literature and in practice.[13] Her study provided a base for further definition and examination of the role of team leaders in individual situations. Her own specific definition of team leader was: "A designated member of the teaching team who serves as instructional leader as well as coordinator for the team's program."[14] On the basis of the literature, and the judgment of practitioners and authors in middle school education, Lipka developed a sixty-one-item checklist of tasks of the team leader in the middle school. The sixty-one items were logically organized into these five categories: team relations, organizational relationships, instructional coordination and development, management activities, public relations. Completion of the checklist by team teachers, team leaders and principals revealed that the team teachers and leaders had similar perceptions of both the ideal and actual roles of team leaders but that the perceptions of team leaders and principals and of team teachers and principals differed significantly. Deliberate consideration needs to be given by the principal and faculty members concerned to the role of the team leader in order to capitalize fully on the potential of this position.

Special Services

A variety of special services are offered by exemplary middle schools. Note, for example, the following statement about student services in the "Middle Schools Parent/Student Handbook" of the Weld County School District, Greeley, Colorado:

The staff and students of each middle school will be able to draw on the resources of the district's student services program. Each school will be served by a school nurse, a school psychologist, and a speech pathologist. Students with educational or physical handicaps will receive expert attention either in the classroom, or in an educational program tailored to meet individual needs. Speech, hearing, or visually handicapped students will receive individualized care in helping them to overcome their handicaps.

In addition to such special services as mentioned in this excerpt, middle schools offer the services of media specialists, guidance counselors, special education personnel not included in the preceding statement, cafeteria and office and plant personnel, the entire range of instructional specialists and perhaps other specialists. We do not have space to discuss further the duties of all these personnel, but we do want to emphasize that each person is a potential leader at some time and place for some other individual or group. Indeed most of these specialists, in fact most all school personnel, are regularly influencing the educational experience of students. The exemplary school provides maximum opportunity for students to make use of these services, and it is an ever-present challenge to the general administrator and associates to employ carefully and utilize efficiently the most capable specialists needed and available.

Other Leadership Roles for Faculty and Staff

Each adult in the middle school has a potential leadership role in relation to students, who are influenced most directly by the teachers and service personnel they contact daily as contrasted with the principals, dean and other status leaders they rarely see. Furthermore, as we have described in detail in an earlier portion ("Shared Decision Making") of this chapter, instructional personnel in exemplary middle schools have much opportunity to help determine and execute school policy. The members of the Program Improvement Council or the School Coordinating Council or other named representative groups have a major opportunity to lead in policy determination, but in effective school organizations the persons represented also have power to elect, even instruct their representatives and in some situations (see the Gravaraet model, Figure 9.1) to approve or reject the actions of the representative group.

But it is in the implementation of policy that all faculty and staff members provide most direct leadership. In middle schools as at other school levels, faculty committees and chairpersons lead or execute many of the special, usually noninstructional functions of the school. A sample listing of faculty committees (the last six are one-person assignments) from the Hobbs Middle School, Milton, Florida, illustrates this common practice:

- Instructional Materials Center
- Student Handbook
- Social Sunshine
- Activities/Calendar
- School Plant/Grounds
- Guidance
- Lunchroom
- School Policies
- Student Discipline
- Budget
- Drug Abuse
- Newspaper
- Memory Book
- Master Plan
- ETV Contract
- Environmental Contact
- Career Education Contact

Regardless of special committee and individual assignments, it is within the power of each teacher to affect student attitudes toward learning, the school and the society, as well as toward self and teacher. It is within the power of school secretaries to affect the attitudes of students, parents and teachers toward the school, the administration and each other. Every school employee, including those working in the media center, the lunchroom, the custodians' areas, the health clinic and elsewhere is a public relations representative, as well as an adult who helps children form their notions of adult behavior. We think there may be no more important task for the total school staff than the development and careful maintenance of a code of human relations shaped with especial attention to the adult-child relationship. As the adult leaders of the school population, the quality of their relationships with students is of primary importance for students in those impressionable and responsive years of development toward adolescence and adulthood.

Leadership Roles for Students

Students, too, have many opportunities for influencing people and programs in the middle school. They may even help draft the materials used to inform other students and parents about a school: *Middle Unmuddle,* the student handbook of Rupert A. Nock Middle School, Newburyport, Massachusetts, according to its Foreword, "was originally written by a group of students from the Belleville, Brown, Currier, Davenport, Kelley, and Jacksman Schools before the Rupert A. Nock School opened."

In addition to leadership services given by students as monitors, office and library assistants, tutors and safety patrol members, many schools provide students an opportunity to provide leadership through membership on some type of student council. The purposes of the Aberdeen, Maryland, Middle School Student Advisory Committee, which includes one representative from each home-base group, illustrates our statement in chapter 4 that the home-base or advisory group constituted a significant unit for transacting school business:

1. *Serve as liaison between students and administration.*
2. *Make recommendations to the principal about student functions, intramural programs, and other student activities.*
3. *Recommend to the principal any curricular changes or problems which should be considered by the school curriculum committee.*
4. *Assist in the evaluation of the Aberdeen Middle School Curricular program.*
5. *Explore the possibility of student involvement in corridor, cafeteria, and bus control, and make recommendations to the principal.*

An extremely comprehensive, indeed revolutionary, leadership role was developed in the Gilman, Vermont, Middle School, as described in a very interesting and detailed 1978 article.[15] According to this article:

. . . the Thaler System has matured over the last two years into a complex economy whose currency is backed by hard cash. It features a student government that shares power with an adult council and a legal system that relies on peer-group judgment for resolving disputes. Annually, the economy generates a volume of goods and services amounting to $5,000 at a conversion rate of one thaler to the cent. None of the work is 'make work.'[16]

Students earned their thalers by a variety of jobs in the school during and after school hours, and they had to spend the thalers earned in amounts of $2 to $8 per week on goods and services provided at the school (with 25 percent of a student's income available for mail-order items bought through the school). The government of the school gave major responsibility to students for the Thaler System, and the legal system relied mostly on peer judgment. Bumstead reported very favorably on the program:

In the final analysis, Grove and his staff are teaching their 72 students to take responsibility for their goals, rather than sit back and have things done for them or to them. And the students practice this active, responsible way of dealing with the world, which the Thaler System imitates, in the safety of their school where the consequences of making a mistake are not really so bad.[17]

The size of the Gilman School, with 72 students, five teachers, seven support people and a principal, is a factor favoring success. But larger middle schools can certainly use to advantage the ideas of giving students some share of responsibility for their behavior and government, of performing real service and work and of handling a real economy.

Leadership Roles for Parents and Other Citizens

In addition to serving as participants in the various councils and task forces involved in planning middle schools (see chapter 2), parents and laymen in general provide many types of leadership service in exemplary middle schools. Some of these are as follows:

1. Speaking at community meetings on accomplishments and problems of the school

2. Representing the school at civic and service club meetings discussing educational issues
3. Campaigning for votes on school fiscal elections
4. Serving on boards of education and other official education-related community boards and commissions
5. Conducting polls of parents and other laymen on school issues and evaluation
6. Rendering expert service as advisors to the Board of Education and/or the school administration on many types of problems requiring expertise not available within the school organization
7. Providing resource help as speakers, interviewees, panel members and consultants in curriculum areas
8. Arranging and/or transporting and supervising students on field trips
9. Preparing press releases, scripts for radio and television and other public relations materials
10. Helping in articulation with other levels by reporting and evaluating their own children's experiences in moving from one school level to another
11. Organizing and participating in work days for school and grounds improvement purposes
12. Providing volunteer services in school offices, libraries, classrooms, playgrounds and other facilities

Many of these services may be provided through the parent or community council operating as an advisory and service organization for many middle schools. For example, the objectives of the Parent Council for the Marshall, Minnesota, Middle School were stated as follows in a communication to parents:

1. *To assist in identifying needs of students and how to work toward fulfilling those needs.*
2. *To bring community information and attitudes directly to school officials.*
3. *To provide a channel of communication for all aspects of education, between parents and the school.*
4. *To provide a vehicle to harmonize differences—educational differences—between home and school.*
5. *To provide a means to discuss problems of child development so coordinated efforts of home and school might work for the benefit of children.*

Each homeroom of the school was represented by a parent or parent couple in the organization.

As indicated in the list of services above, opportunities for volunteer services are varied and many in the middle school. An area in which particular use of community resource persons is essential is career education. For example, the student handbook of the Albert D. Lawton Intermediate School of Essex Junction, Vermont, invites parents to help in remedying "the isolation of many young people from exposure to essential occupations" by sharing information regarding vocation, profession, hobby or interest, and also to have a student spend a day with the volunteer at work. The handbook includes forms for completion and return.

Leadership Resources from Outside the School Community

We described in chapter 2 the many steps to be taken to maintain effective relations between middle schools in the same district and between middle schools and the schools that precede and follow. Although the leadership of the individual school has an important role to play in these relationships, they really cannot be effective without the leadership of the central office or the district, usually that of the school superintendent and any associates involved. The success of the middle school in closing the traditional gap between elementary and secondary education is highly dependent on the vision and wisdom and action of the central administrator. He or she, whether superintendent, assistant superintendent or other administrator having system-wide responsibilities, can exert great leadership in bringing together representatives of the various schools and levels, and facilitating cooperative ventures to share promising practices, to solve common problems and to maintain closely knit ties between school units and levels.

A major function of the central administration is to assist in the identification and utilization of consultant and staff development assistance in planning and establishing and maintaining exemplary middle schools. Although consultants may be employed from outside the school organization for assistance in developing the total program or any phase of it, they are especially useful for the development of understanding and skill needed by all middle school personnel, particularly in the planning and implementation stages. We turn now to the total staff development problem and opportunity in middle school education.

Staff Development Roles and Guidelines

Prerequisites for Effective Staff Development

At its core, the middle school movement is, beyond anything else, a reconceptualization and reorganization of the ways in which people work with each other to facilitate the learning process. As such, it is possible to interpret the failure of other attempts to meet the educational needs of middle school students (in other words, some K-8 and 7-9 schools) as due to their failure to respond to the need to prepare people for this new way of being together professionally. Reorganization efforts that were stimulated solely by reasons essentially external to the operation of a school itself, however salutary (for example, integration, efficient use of plant facilities), often achieved much less than might have been accomplished. The authors believe that effective staff development is the key to comprehensive program implementation. When this is acknowledged and planned for, effective programs emerge; when it is not, little changes except the external elements that demanded the initial efforts. Even the most carefully designed multiyear implementation plan cannot overcome the deficiencies imposed by inadequate staff development.

During the 1960's and 1970's middle school educators have learned a great deal about effective staff development, but nothing more significant than that there are very important prerequisites to the entire inservice process. First, and long before the process of staff development begins, is the need for, the absolute necessity of, straightforward clarification and disclosure of the initiating circumstances for the move toward middle school reorganization. The fact that most middle schools, to this point, have emerged as a concommitant to other fundamental changes such as racial integration and changing enrollments is nothing to hide; it does not demean the middle school to have it born out of a need to meet other commitments. It has been the experience of the authors, however, that whenever staff development projects are undertaken without the real reasons for the move to middle school being fully clarified, elaborated and discussed by all parties, enthusiasm for and willingness to participate fully in such projects is far less than desirable. When there is no choice for the professionals involved, there is all the more reason to surround the staff development process with the opportunity for questioning and discussion.

The school district of Columbia Heights, Minnesota, offers a good example of the openness that permits a more objective investigation of the merits of moving to middle school. Faced with a drastically declining enrollment over the decade of the seventies, the district entered 1980 with the unavoidable need to reorganize the K-12 school plan and to develop a list of teachers who may eventually have to be given unrequested leave for an indeterminate period. Under these circumstances, to have ballyhooed the implementation of the middle school, as a quasi-coverup for the issue of declining enrollments would have been a terrible error. As it is, the district leaders have faced the issue squarely and openly, and have dealt fairly with everyone involved. Consequently, the bad feelings that might have blighted the move to middle school have not developed. In Columbia Heights, the middle school plan is enthusiastically accepted.

Staff development efforts will, we believe, almost always be more successful when, as a second prerequisite, the commitment of the central administration to the middle school is clearly perceived and easily discussed by those who are asked to undergo the training to equip them for the move to the new school organization. Teachers and others at the school level have learned to measure the commitment of others farther up in the district hierarchy by, among other things, the amount of visible time that central office personnel and school administrators devote to participation in the fundamental efforts of retraining. People budget their time to projects they assign importance to, and when central office staff are seldom seen at the staff development activities, or when teachers and others never have an opportunity to listen to these persons articulate their interest in or support for the reorganization effort, enthusiasm and effort wane. Modeling is an important tool for stimulating learning, even at such an advanced professional level.

Again in Columbia Heights, effective long-term planning processes permitted the central office personnel to anticipate the need for the middle school option. As early as two years before the planning process was formally begun, the district superintendent, the director of instruction and building leaders were exploring and expanding their understanding of the middle school program. By the time classroom teachers became involved, the central office staff was committed to and could clearly articulate this commitment to the basic components of the middle school program. They both planned and participated in every staff development effort.

Similarly, staff development efforts are enhanced whenever those involved have the opportunity to hear school board members demonstrate their understanding of and commitment to the reorganization effort. Early efforts to advise and inform the school board almost always, the authors believe, result in increased personal and financial support for professional staff development efforts when they become necessary. The adoption of a wait and see attitude by board members often seems to almost guarantee less than optimal success in retraining the professional staff.

A third prerequisite to effective staff development is the appointment of a coordinator for the retraining effort. One person must be seen as the central figure responsible for the inservice education of those to be a part of the new middle school. This coordinator should, ideally, have training and experience at both the elementary and secondary levels, in addition to an in-depth exposure to the middle school movement. Such a broad perspective is important to the design of appropriate components of the staff development program. Without such a broad background, it is all too likely that the staff development program will take on a character that reflects the narrower perspectives of an educator wearing professional blinders. It is only human to design programs, staff development or otherwise, that reflect one's own experience and training.

In Dothan, Alabama, planning began three years prior to the implementation of middle schools. The position of Supervisor of Middle Schools was created fully eighteen months prior to the opening of the new schools, and even before that time other school personnel had served as the coordinator of exploratory efforts. In Dothan, this position was filled by a person whose teaching and administrative experience had been exclusively at the middle school level in another district that had implemented middle schools some years earlier. As the number of districts with middle schools continues to increase, this opportunity becomes more possible.

The design of a comprehensive staff development program is, however, too complex to be left entirely to one person. Consequently, another prerequisite to effective efforts is the presence of a broadly based staff development committee to assist the coordinator. There should be representatives from both administration, curriculum specialities and the potential faculty, ensuring a balance between organizational and programmatic emphases in the staff development plan that emerges. This committee should find it possible to prepare an acceptable rationale for extensive staff development, and to articulate a sensible long-range plan of such activities, complete with timelines, learning experiences, funding requirements and identification of participants. This committee should be able, further, to assist the district in escaping the trap of expecting too much too soon. Permanent change requires careful and realistic planning.

An additional prerequisite for maximally effective staff development is the early identification of participants. Teachers, we believe, are not inherently opposed to change or even anxious to avoid extra duties. They are, however, likely to perceive the change to middle school as a positive one for them to the extent that they are provided with early opportunities for information and involvement. Kept in the dark about the future of the school, and especially about their own place in that future, teachers will find it difficult to concentrate on the purely professional aspects of the impending changes. Since the great majority of teachers care deeply about children, a great deal can be gained by extending to them the earliest possible opportunity to assimilate the meaning of the changes, and the chance to opt for inclusion or exclusion from any further participation. There seems to be, in the authors' experience, a direct connection between voluntary participation in the change to middle school and the success of the staff development efforts that accompany it.

In Columbia Heights, Minnesota, the faculty of the middle school to come was selected and informed eighteen months before the school was to open. Each faculty member was asked to give his first and second priorities as to preferred level of teaching: elementary, middle or secondary. In all but a very few cases, even in a district with severely declining enrollment, teachers were given the choice they preferred. The faculty will, in addition, be given a central role in the development of the local rationale and the unique components of the program that will emerge there.

Three Phases of Staff Development

The authors' experience with staff development programs leads us to conclude that there is a series of three phases into which the process of staff development flows. The first phase has to do with the encouragement of awareness and commitment among the potential members of the new or reorganized school. Since the success of any staff development effort is always dependent, in large part, upon the commitment, desire and talents of the persons involved, significant portions of time and energy should be focused on the objective of creating excitement about the impending changes and commitment to the success of those changes among the staff to be involved. Teachers and administrators should be clear about the nature and the importance of the changes to come, or much of the staff development efforts that follow will be much less successful than desired. An early understanding of and commitment to the entire reorganization effort is the fulcrum upon which all remaining staff development activities must move. Involvement, as in Columbia Heights, is the key.

The second phase of the staff development program focuses on a comprehensive understanding of the organizational components to be a part of a particular middle school plan and the sharpening of the skills necessary for the successful implementation of those programs. If the first phase of staff development could be called resocialization, the second could be labeled re-education. And if implementation is jeopardized by teachers and administrators who are unwilling to perform the necessary roles, it is crippled by a staff who may be willing but unable to perform the proper duties. Everyone involved in the change effort must understand and be able to exhibit the requisite skills, or implementation will not occur.[18]

The third phase of staff development coincides with the implementation of the middle school program. Much of what will be needed by way of insights and skills will not be clearly perceived until the program is underway. This phase actually extends throughout the existence of the reorganized program, since many exemplary middle schools discover the need for continuing staff development for new faculty, and for revitalizing experienced staff.

Successful Staff Development Strategies: Seven Recommendations

There are, of course, many more suggestions for effective inservice education than the seven to be discussed here. A great deal of research on the characteristics of successful staff development programs is now beginning to surface, and the cautious will review this literature carefully before embarking on any program of this nature.[19] Indeed, the entire field of organizational development is quite relevant to the effort to reorganize the middle grades, under almost any circumstances.[20] The few suggestions made here come primarily from the testing ground of the authors' experiences in middle school staff development efforts. With these disclaimers, here they are:

1. Operate on a 90/10 philosophy. That is, with the limited funds that almost inevitably accompany these activities, spend 90 percent of the funds available on 10 percent of the people. Permanent change comes when the staff is changed permanently, and this means that some of the faculty and administration must undergo a training experience that is sufficient to alter their ways of thinking and acting, professionally, forever. When the staff with the commitment, desire and talent are also provided with the skills necessary to do the tasks required for implementation, we believe that these persons will train those with whom they work on a daily basis. A small cadre of expertly trained personnel can grow; a large group of confused and unskilled faculty members, no matter how professional in their attitude, can only grow smaller.

Spend 10 percent of the staff development money before the school is opened, and 90 percent afterward. Providing answers for questions that the staff does not yet have is a highly inefficient use of time and money, and the same amounts of time and money will bring much higher yields of understanding and skill development when applied as the needs become evident. Only the most alert and farsighted among us are able to suspend present needs in order to attend to issues we do not yet face, and most of this group is so highly professional that the training is almost unnecessary for them in the first place.

Another way of expressing this principle of expending staff development funds is to think in terms of pyramids. That is, when funds for inservice are limited, expend the funds with an inverted pyramid in mind; see that the majority of the opportunities are offered to those who will bear the greatest responsibilities when the reorganization arrives: school administrators, team leaders and counselors, for example. When in rare cases such as a special grant, a significantly greater amount of money is available, the luxury of making enriched staff development opportunities available for the majority of those who will be involved can be possible. In these instances, using the model of the pyramid (with the greatest effort at the base) becomes logical.

2. Be prepared to make difficult choices when it comes to deciding who will be included in the staff development activities. While it may sound somewhat Machiavellian, a person who has been designated as the coordinator of the middle school reorganization plan must develop leadership that will last, with the most efficient and economical expenditure of scarce resources. It may not even be too farfetched to suggest that coordinators take a page from the book of French battlefield medicine, investigating the usefulness of the concept of "triage" as applied to the development effort. Confronted with inadequate time and medical supplies, in the midst of a battle that would not stop, French physicians applied the concept of triage, which meant that the casualties were divided into three groups: those who would die regardless of the amount of help they received; those who would get well without help; and those who would recover only with help from the physician. The physician then spent the time and scarce supplies where they would do the most good, in essence applying the principle of the greatest good for the greatest number. It may behoove the middle school reorganization coordinator to think in similar ways. There are teachers and administrators who need little if any assistance in making the transition successfully, and many of these persons can be used to assist in the training of others less able or ready. There are teachers and administrators who, no matter what opportunities are afforded them, will never be able to make the adjustment but who may make superb professionals at other levels; they should be helped to do so. There will be another, larger, group who will guarantee the success of the reorganization effort if they are able to receive the training opportunities that will allow them to develop the insights and skills that will be required. It is likely that concentrating a greater proportion of available

opportunities for growth on this third group will result in the most effective deployment of meager staff development funds.

3. Develop a multiyear staff development plan. Based on the time-honored principle that spaced practice assists learning more effectively than does massed practice, it will be advantageous to have a long-term staff development plan that initiates different components at different times following the implementation of the middle school reorganization effort. A program component (for example., an advisor-advisee program) could be introduced one year, with a full-blown inservice effort, followed periodically during the next several years by supportive services that take new faculty into account and that solve new problems as they arise. Middle schools do not spring forth fully formed like Athena from the forehead of Zeus, and haste is the enemy of effective staff development.

It is important to recognize that some elements of the middle school program appear to be prerequisites to others. That is, it is the opinion of the authors that the firmly established interdisciplinary organization of teachers must come before other program changes are attempted. It also seems evident that the basic organizational effort, from departmental or self-contained to interdisciplinary, requires much less actual staff development than do other components of the new program. Teachers can be organized in an interdisciplinary fashion without being asked to perform dramatically new or different tasks. The teacher who, for example, has been teaching math for twenty years in a departmentalized junior high school, can continue to do very much the same sort of thing in an interdisciplinary organization. Because it makes all the other programs easier to establish and maintain, and because it can be implemented with the minimum of staff development, interdisciplinary team organization should come first.

Consider arranging the remainder of the programs in terms of the difficulty of implementing them with a minimum of inservice education, so that the most difficult are last to be brought on line. Doing so would probably result in a decision to group students for learning in some way that would go beyond simple chronological age grouping, since only the most extreme forms of multiage grouping require a significant amount of retraining of the staff or redesigning of the curriculum. This might be followed, in a wisely designed staff development plan, by an attempt to structure the curriculum in a way that would permit the infusion of a more exploratory type of program. A more flexible schedule, if it emerges from the effort to regroup teachers and students, will follow naturally. Only when all of the above elements of the program have been effectively planned and implemented will it be wise to implement an advisor-advisee program of teacher-student guidance, since this is a program that requires more staff development than possibly all of the others together. All the components of the middle school program are not equal, in terms of the amount of staff development time and effort required for successful implementation, and it will be wise to plan the sequence in which each is introduced.

Priorities sometimes also intervene in the planning of the staff development program in another way. Because the reorganization effort is, in many ways, a curriculum planning process, it is too frequently seen as a curriculum rewriting effort. That is, the middle school plan is sometimes perceived, narrowly, as an adventure in rewriting the social studies, science, language arts, mathematics and unified arts programs. When this happens, a great deal of activity centers around curriculum revisions, and committees write furiously, producing volumes which are very much like the curriculum of the junior high school. Then the crucial nature of the new organization arrangements is ignored. It is important that curriculum coordinators who become the motivating force for the new middle school remember that the curriculum plan goes far beyond a mere shuffling of the courses of study or a restatement of objectives in terms of observable skills. The middle school is also a new way of working and learning together and attention must be given, equally, to these new relationship patterns.

4. Seek assistance in arranging and conducting the staff development program, but seek it very carefully. The first middle schools established during the decades of the sixties and early seventies were, primarily, on their own. A few guidelines had been suggested, but fewer school systems had actually established successful and long-running programs to which new middle school educators could turn. It was a time of experimentation and innovation in the middle grades, and, fortunately for middle school educators, for the nation in general. A plethora of new programs were attempted, some surviving, others failing. Since the middle school movement shows little sign of slackening, in the number of new middle schools being established, it is fortunate indeed that twenty years of experimentation and innovation will now pay dividends in the coin of knowledge that can be relied upon. Whereas in 1960 there were few, if any, educators who could boast of years of experience in middle schools, this is no longer true. Educators seeking to establish a new program in the middle grades of their school systems can now reach out for assistance from hundreds of experienced educators who, remembering their own eager first efforts, are pleased to help in any way they can.

Consultant help can often be important to the success of a middle level reorganization effort. Chosen carefully, outside consultants can help a school district in the decision making and planning phases of the move to a middle school. But, more often, consultants are needed to assist in the development of local expertise, leadership and skills. Since it is in the area of actual daily operation of middle schools that most districts need help, it is important to choose consultant help on the basis of demonstrated successful experience in the areas in question. Many districts report that the combination of university and public school personnel into a small consultant team leads to both a clear conceptualization of the needed skills and the credibility that makes the tasks acceptable to local teachers and faculty. The best clue to the potential effectiveness of any particular consultant would seem to be whether or not close proximity to and involvement with one or more exemplary middle schools is a prominent part of that person's regular professional experience. When districts are clear about the needs they have, and select a consultant on the basis of demonstrated experience with effective programs related to those needs, a satisfactory relationship is more likely to develop.

5. At all costs, develop and maintain a high degree of local expertise. No consultant, regardless of how expert, can substitute for the existence of local school district employees who have developed a commitment to and the skills necessary for the implementation of an exemplary middle school program. The consultant's effectiveness depends in part upon the availability of an alter ego in the district or school who sets the stage and follows through, before and after the consultant. The authors believe that the performance of many programs depends in large part upon the emergence of strong local leadership. Staff development efforts should begin at this point. If at all possible, these persons (curriculum coordinators, school principals, team leaders) should be given the opportunity to participate in a mini-internship in a middle school away from home, a school that has the characteristics which the local district wishes to build into its program. Hearing about the middle school concept, studying about it, even having participated in intensive workshops on how to do it are simply not enough for the development of exemplary programs that will last a decade or more.

In the authors' experience, the most permanently successful programs are those that were built upon the resources that created an opportunity for direct involvement, of the local leadership, in fully functioning middle schools elsewhere. Implementing a middle school program guarantees that, no matter now well it is done, a great deal of anxiety, doubts and new pressures will result. School leaders who have had an opportunity to experience a successful program directly will be much more likely to bear up under those pressures and see the program through to a successful future. Team leaders who have both seen it and made it happen elsewhere will be confident that it can happen in their own schools and will be able to bring it about. The funds required to provide such opportunities are so well spent that it seems impossible to mount an effective argument to the contrary. So many good middle schools are available for such assistance that it might be foolish to proceed without it.

The school districts of Alachua County, Florida, and Dothan, Alabama, offer convincing examples of the importance of this direct experience in other programs. Prior to the opening of Spring Hill and Mebane Middle Schools, in 1970, the leadership (team leaders and principals) of both schools spent two weeks participating in schools in another state that had been identified as having the type of program that educators in Alachua County wished to implement. Over a decade later, these two schools continue to offer the same experience to educators from across the continent. Before implementing their own program, a close tie was developed between the Dothan and Alachua County systems, resulting in having dozens of teachers and administrators from Dothan spending mini-internships in Alachua County schools. The exemplary nature of the Dothan middle schools is testimony to what was learned through this process. Since the Dothan schools are quite different from the schools in Alachua County, fears that one school system will be tempted to undertake the wholesale adoption of the program designed for another are obviously untenable.

6. Realize that changing an existing junior high school to a middle school plan is much more difficult than implementing a new middle school program where no previous junior high school existed. When a new faculty is being gathered, and perhaps a new school building being opened, innovative programs are much more readily implemented. When a faculty and building with a heritage remain and only the program is to be changed, one might be led to think that the tasks would be even easier, but such is not the case. Such transitions seem infinitely more difficult.

When faced with the task of changing the program with an existing faculty within a facility that will not be changed, the approach must be more deliberate, and will often be more costly. Interpersonal loyalties and differences, subject matter preferences, established ways of doing things and working together and pure inertia interact to make this sort of transition one of the most difficult processes in the educational profession. It is a task that ought not be taken on lightly. For those who find themselves involved in such a project, several factors are important for planning the staff development program:

Plan for the transition to take about twice as long as other reorganization efforts.

Plan for a staff development budget that will be about twice as much for each program component implemented, as in the prior plan.

Plan to include, from the outset, those faculty members who are experienced and who have shown their leadership ability within the faculty over previous years. One real advantage to having a sizable number of experienced (in other words, over twenty years) teachers is that one can be certain that whatever they agree to implement will work and will last.

Plan to involve a great deal more visitations to exemplary schools, and to attend more conferences, and cut back drastically on the number of expert-led after-school workshops.

When staff development funds are miniscule compared to the needs, refuse to yield to the temptation to implement the programs without the inservice! Very little else will contaminate future change efforts more than the taint of badly managed present failures.

Be prepared to insist, however, that the change from departmentalized organization of teachers to an interdisciplinary grouping take place. Without this change nothing else is likely to be successful for long. Teachers who have taught in one subject, and in one grade level for many years may still do so with the interdisciplinary framework. It may be that several years of becoming accommodated to the interdisciplinary organization will be necessary before any additional program components can be easily brought on line. Once comfortable with and acclimated to the interdisciplinary organization the faculty is likely to view other new programs much more favorably.

7. The concept of synergism is important when planning staff develop-

ment activities. The programs of the middle school (for example, interdisciplinary organization, advisor-advisee and so on) are complementary; the presence of one strengthens the others. So it is with staff development. Working on one component of the middle school program will contribute to the improvement of the others.

The Focus of Middle School Staff Development: Skills

While it is very important to allow ample opportunity and time for the development of proper attitudes toward the change effort, behavioral psychologists have long maintained that changes in attitudes often follow changes in behavior. When behavior changes (in other words, when new skills are developed and used) changes in attitudes are close behind. With this in mind, staff development planners may be wise to focus on the new skills that will be required in the new organizational framework, on the assumption that with skills mastered will come confidence and assurance, followed by increasingly positive attitudes toward the coming new programs.

There are, of course, specific skills for both school administrators and for the faculty.

Staff development for school administrators will usually focus on two different areas: knowledge of the new program and organizational development expertise. Principals need to understand the team organization, the advisory program, the curriculum plan, the grouping strategies and other elements of the planned changes so that they can assist teachers in implementing those programs. The principal needs the knowledge so that he or she can effectively communicate the purposes and the structure of the program to parents and community members who will have dozens of questions that will need to be answered. Principals need this knowledge to bolster their own confidence in the efficacy of the proposed changes and to give them the courage to venture into areas that the district has not yet attempted.

Most of all, however, school principals need to know how to use the building and the daily schedule to accomplish the demands of the new program without placing unreasonable stress on the faculty and students. If a place in the building is not available for an activity, that activity will not occur. If there is no time in the schedule for the program, there will be no program. And, since many new middle school principals come from a secondary background, having often served successfully as an assistant principal in a high school, it cannot be assumed that the necessary skills were learned prior to assuming the leadership of the new middle school. It might be more likely that there will have to be some unlearning of certain skills that may actually lie at cross purposes with the new duties at the middle school.

In addition, because the middle school will be an adventure in new relationships of all kinds and in new patterns of teaching and learning, the school principal must be skilled at helping people solve the problems that these new patterns create. He or she must also be able to assist in the process of ongoing change and adjustment that any dynamic organization will encounter. And the principal must, whenever possible, represent an unwavering source of support and enthusiasm for the staff. These are behaviors that can be learned.

Teachers, whether team leaders or not, will need dozens of new skills when the reorganization is complete, and most of these skills are spelled out in detail in other chapters. It is important, however, to underline several needs. First, in order to make the team organization function at its optimum, teachers need to be effective communicators with each other. They also need help in planning and managing a program for a large group of students: ordering supplies, planning activities, conducting parent conferences, arranging student schedules, team budgeting, reporting pupil progress and many other management activities. They need to learn how to schedule an advisor-advisee program so that they are not involved in making new lesson preparations for each new day of the week. They need to be helped to discover activities for advisory programs that can be repeated on a once weekly basis, and activities that require little or no teacher planning but which deliver considerable power to the advisor-advisee relationship. Teachers will require curriculum writing assistance if alternatives to chronological age grouping are implemented on a school-wide basis. Exciting exploratory programs require creativity and high levels of energy from teachers, but assistance in learning how to develop and conduct an exploratory minicourse that students will enjoy can go a long way toward releasing that creativity and energy. Teachers must be helped to develop a repertoire of instructional skills and the knowledge of when each is effective. Above all, many would say, teachers must understand the characteristics and needs of the students they serve, and be able to respond to those needs in ways that are satisfying for both student and teacher.

The selection of effective school leaders and outstanding classroom teachers will go a long way toward ensuring the success of the new middle school program, but it is not sufficient. Staff development, even with the most outstanding recruits, is essential. Just as no corporation would introduce a major new product without assigning and carefully training some of its most talented staff, no school system can afford to introduce a major reorganization without a similar effort. Product knowledge is essential in private enterprise and in education.

ADDITIONAL SUGGESTIONS FOR FURTHER STUDY

A. Books

Bondi, Joseph, *Developing Middle Schools: A Guidebook,* New York: MSS Information Corporation, 1972.

Brandt, Ronald S. ed., *Partners: Parents and Schools.* Alexandria, Va: Association for Supervision and Curriculum Development, 1979.

Lipham, James M. and Froth, Marvin J., *The Principal and Individually Guided Education.* Reading, Mass.: Addison-Wesley Publications Co., 1976.

McCarthy, Robert J., *The Ungraded Middle School.* West Nyack, N.Y.: Parker Publishing Co., 1972.

B. Periodicals

Anderson, Robert H. and Snyder, Karolyn J., "Preparation of Staff for Middle School Implementation," *Middle School Journal,* 10, 5, 27, 30–1 (August 1979).

Applegate, Jane H., "The Rhetoric of Middle Grade Teacher Preparation: A Look at the Last Ten Years," *Middle School Journal,* 8, 5, 22–3 (August 1977).

Cooke, Gary and DeBruin, Jerome E., "Principles for Principals: How to Plan Successful Teacher In-Service Workshops," *Middle School Journal,* 6, 45–8 (Fall 1975).

Costantino, Peter S., "What Kind of Teacher for the Middle School?" *NASSP Bulletin,* 62, 84–90 (November 1978).

George, Paul S. and McEwin, C. Kenneth, "Middle School Teacher Education: A Progress Report," *Journal of Teacher Education,* 29, 13–6 (September/October 1978).

Johnston, J. Howard and Markle, Glenn C., "What Research Says to the Practitioner —About Teacher Behavior," *Middle School Journal,* 10, 14–5 (May 1979).

Jones, Paul and Garner, Arthur E., "A Comparison of Middle School Teachers' Pupil Control Ideology," *Clearing House,* 51, 292–4 (February 1978).

Markle, Glenn C. and Others, "Students' Perception of the Ideal Middle School Teacher," *Middle School Journal,* 8, 6–7 (August 1977).

McCarthy, Robert J., "Student and Staff Advocates in the Middle School," *NASSP Bulletin,* 60, 90–4 (March 1976).

Powell, William W., "Preparing Teachers for the Early Adolescent," *Middle School Journal,* 9, 22–3 (November 1978).

C. ERIC

Range, Dale G., *Staff Development: Still a Major Challenge for Middle School Administrators,* Paper presented at the Annual Meeting of the National Association of Secondary School Principals, New Orleans, Louisiana, January 1979. (ERIC No. ED 136 363)

D. Dissertations and Dissertation Abstracts

Andaloro, Russ Joseph, "Components of a Junior High/Middle School Teacher Preparation Program," *Dissertation Abstracts,* 37 (September 1976) 1479–80A.

Armstrong, Marvin Cara, Jr., "A Model of an Internship for Pre Service Middle School Teachers," *Dissertation Abstracts,* 36 (September 1975) 1445–A.

Coney, Charles Edward, "Perceptions of the Role of the Middle School Principal in Selected School Systems of Southeast Louisiana," *Dissertation Abstracts,* 36 (June 1976) 7765–A.

Hudson, Stanley Eugene, "Immediate Superordinates' Perceptions of the Middle School Principal's Functions," *Dissertation Abstracts,* 36 (March 1976) 5961–A.

Moon, Howard Herbert, Jr., "Middle School Teacher Development: A Continuous Education Model," *Dissertation Abstracts,* 36 (February 1976) 4925–6–A.

Nolan, John Andrew, "Identification of Inservice Education Purposes and Middle School Characteristics by Principals in Selected New Jersey Middle Schools," *Dissertation Abstracts,* 37 (March 1977) 5665–A.

Payne, Cretchen Bradley, "A Teacher Education Curriculum for the Middle School," *Dissertation Abstracts,* 38 (February 1978) 4553–A.

Skinkus, John Richard, "Principals', Counselors', and Teachers' Perceptions of Professional Roles in Middle School Pupil Personnel Services," *Dissertation Abstracts,* 37 (October 1976) 1927–A.

Skoczylas, Robert Francis, "An Analysis of Cooperative Decision Making in Selected Middle Schools," *Dissertation Abstracts,* 39 (August 1978) 653–A.

Walker, Mary Louise Richardson, "Assistant Principals in Junior High or Middle
Schools' Role as Perceived by Educators in Selected States in 1975–78," *Dissertation Abstracts,* 39 (September 1978) 1252–A.

Wiederholt, Richard Joseph, "Ideal and Actual Leadership Styles of Middle School
Principals," *Dissertation Abstracts,* 39 (November 1978) 2681–A.

Williams, Leona Clarice Wellington, "The Middle School Principal and the Curriculum Director: Locus of Decision-Making," *Dissertation Abstracts,* 39 (January
1979) 3974–A.

FOOTNOTES

1. Theodore C. Moss, *Middle School* (Boston: Houghton Mifflin Co., 1969),
   p. 178.
2. Moss, p. 179.
3. National Association of Secondary School Principals, "Providing Leadership
   for Teacher Motivation," *The Practitioner,* 5, 1 (November 1978).
4. National Association of Secondary School Principals, p. 4.
5. For relevant reports and articles in addition to *The Practitioner* issue cited, see
   current and past issues of the *NASSP Bulletin* and the NAEP *National Elementary Principal* and other publications of the respective associations, National
   Association of Secondary School Principals and National Association of Elementary Principals. Also see such standard works in school administration as
   Ralph B. Kimbrough and Michael Y. Nunnery, *Educational Administration: An
   Introduction* (New York: Macmillan, 1976), and Paul B. Jackson, James D.
   Logsdon and Robert R. Weigman, *The Principalship: New Perspectives* (Englewood Cliffs, New Jersey: Prentice-Hall, Inc., 1973).
6. Milwaukee Public Schools, *The Plan for the Two-Year Transition to the Middle
   School* (Milwaukee, Wisconsin: The Schools, March 1979), p. 80.
7. Milwaukee Public Schools, p. i.
8. Milwaukee Public Schools, p. 23.
9. Jean A. Coakley, *The School* (Dayton, Ohio: Institute for Development of Educational Activities, Inc., 1975), p. 45. LC is for Learning Community—a type of
   interdisciplinary team organization.
10. Elliott Y. Merenbloom, "The Role of the Principal in Implementing the Middle
    School Program," *Dissemination Services on the Middle Grades,* 11, 6 (Febru-
    ary 1980).
11. Charles V. Eible and Joseph A. Zavarella, "Curriculum Development: A Model
    for Action," *NASSP Bulletin,* 63, 87 (March 1979).
12. Department of Curriculum and Instruction, The School District of Philadelphia,
    The Middle School in Philadelphia: A Tentative Statement (Philadelphia: the
    District, 1979), p. 45.
13. Lipka, Cheryl Fountain, *Perceptions of the Role of Team Leaders in Florida
    Middle Schools.* Unpublished doctoral dissertation, University of Florida, 1977.
14. Lipka, p. 6.
15. Richard Bumstead, "The Thaler System: A Slice-of-Life Curriculum," *Phi
    Delta Kappan,* 59, 659–664 (June 1978).
16. Bumstead, p. 659.
17. Bumstead, p. 664.

18. See Jerry L. Patterson and Theodore J. Czajkowski, "Implementation: Neglected Phase in Curriculum Change," *Educational Leadership,* 37, 206 (December 1979).

19. See, for example, Gordon D. Lawrence, *Patterns of Effective Inservice Education* (Tallahassee, Florida: Florida State Department of Education, 1974). Available from the Panhandle Area Educational Cooperative, Drawer 190, Chipley, Florida. Also available from P.A.E.C. are about twenty inservice education modules on middle school education that have been used in staff development efforts across the state of Florida and many other places in the country.

20. Readers interested in more about the application of the principles of organizational development applied to public school staff development should consult the February, 1980, issue (Volume 37, Number 5) of *Educational Leadership* for a series of articles dealing with that topic.

| Chapter **10** | Evaluation in and of
a Middle School |
|---|---|

Inevitably schools are accountable for their results. Evaluation is the process whereby results are determined and judged. In a middle school as in other educational institutions, evaluation includes direct measures for evaluating the progress of students, and indirect measures for evaluating the various aspects of the school which are believed to determine the performance of students. This chapter gives attention to both the direct and indirect processes following further discussion of the purposes and scope of evaluation in and of the middle school.

Purposes and Scope of Evaluation

We recognize the following four major purposes of evaluation in the middle school:

1. To provide information regarding the progress of each student in order to assist in the attainment of optimum individual progress
2. To provide data regarding the attainment of school goals to help in the continuing process of goal setting, program planning and modification
3. To provide feedback regarding specific practices and programs in order to modify and improve them
4. To provide a data bank for consultation by the school administration and other concerned groups in decision making regarding such matters as finance, school organization and research projects

To serve these various related purposes the program of evaluation must include many different data-gathering techniques and instruments. They are grouped in this chapter into one section on evaluating student progress (Purpose No. 1) and another on evaluating a school as a whole (other purposes above) with a final section devoted to the problem of evaluation of the middle school movement.

Before turning to these sections we should note three major types of evaluation classified according to the use of data involved.[1] First, diagnostic evaluation includes the processes involved in identifying the status of whatever condition of the individual or school is being treated (instructed) and/or evaluated over time. This evaluation is usually at the beginning of the period of instruction, in the evaluation of student progress or at the beginning of a program of school evaluation and improvement in the case of school evaluation. A diagnostic evaluation is more frequently called a "needs assessment" for the school or district. Second, formative evaluation includes those processes that evaluate the individual's (or the school's) progress in an ongoing program. Generally formative data can serve as feedback to make corrections in faulty plans as instruction (or the program) continues. Formative evaluation is an integral part of the planning process, both for the individual student and the school. Third, summative evaluation includes those processes involved in reaching a somewhat terminal or final decision as to the focus of evaluation, whether of the progress of an individual, a school or a movement. Summative data may include recapitulation of diagnostic and formative data; the difference is in the use of the data. Thus diagnostic data tell teachers the initial status of learners; formative data tell what is happening in the process of instruction, indicating possible changes in plan and procedures; and summative data tell how well the student's progress has met teacher expectations, indicating whether the plan of instruction should be used again, and how. Or, in terms of school evaluation, diagnostic evaluation provides a needs assessment initially of aspects of the school needing improvement; formative evaluation yields data measuring changes in these aspects; and summative evaluation provides a comparison with the original, diagnostic evaluation to determine if the changes made worked well enough to continue them. Value judgments are involved, of course, at each stage and especially at the end in summative evaluation. The evaluative data provide significant input for teachers, in student progress evaluation and for school planners, in school evaluation. Evaluation helps to eliminate guesswork and facilitate valid, systematic educational decisions.

Evaluation Models

During the 1970's new emphases on evaluation and accountability stimulated the development of new models of evaluation and the synthesis of new and old techniques into other systems and models. In their comprehensive chapter on curriculum evaluation, Saylor, Alexander and Lewis described, with extensive citations of related sources, five evaluation models which they recommend for consideration in the development of an evaluation plan for a particular program or institution.[2] These models are briefly identified in the following paragraphs with our suggestions as to the use of each in middle school evaluation processes.

1. Behavioral Objectives Model—This model, widely used following its introduction by Bobbitt and Charters in the scientific management movement and its further development by Tyler and such more recent advocates as Mager and Popham, can be effectively used in evaluating student progress but not as the only model even here.

2. Decision-Making Model—This model, developed by a Phi Delta Kappa Committee chaired by Stufflebeam, emphasizes the use of evaluation data in decision making about a program. To us it is a comprehensive approach that we recommend. We suggest some procedures in this section intended to fit the decision-making processes of middle school planning, evaluation and improvement.

3. Goal-Free Evaluation Model—This model, developed by Scriven to free an evaluator of the bias of the program developer, might be useful for evaluating particular innovations but it is deficient in yielding formative data for purposes of program improvement.

4. Accreditation Model—This model, characteristic of twentieth century regional, state and national (specialized higher education programs) accreditation, includes certain techniques such as use of criteria, self-study and visiting committee reviews that we include in this chapter as possibly desirable phases of middle school evaluation. Our view of the purpose, however, is continuing improvement of the school whether or not accreditation is involved.

5. Responsive Model—Stake's evaluation model organizes evaluation procedures around issues or problems raised by students, teachers, parents and administrators. It can constitute a comprehensive plan from which various interested parties can select data needed for school evaluation.

We see the foregoing models as useful systems of classification for evaluators, but believe that most readers of this book will be more concerned with specific evaluation procedures they can utilize in evaluation of student progress and of their middle schools. Those interested in further information can find full treatments of the models in the sources cited.

Evaluating and Reporting Student Progress

No subject is more certain to secure and hold the interest of both students and teachers in the middle school than grades and report cards. Unfortunately, the predominant interest of parents and, we fear, teachers, and, certainly, students is in the grades (we think the term 'marks' less confusing), the report cards, and the tests forever underlying grades and reports. A discussion of the evaluation and reporting of student progress seems more logically and correctly based on the purposes of evaluation and reporting, which we suggest as the following:

1. To assist each student in maintaining optimum progress toward becoming a fully self-directed learner
2. To help parents and other student advisors in their role of assisting student progress
3. To provide data on student progress that can serve such purposes as consultation by future teachers, use in school evaluation and use in decision making for program planning

A subsequent section describes techniques of evaluating and reporting student progress that relate to each of these purposes.

Data Sources

Before turning to sections on the respective purposes, we wish to emphasize the point that student progress is progress on all goals set for student's education; it is not just the standing on written tests, standardized or otherwise. Important as test standings are in respect to the knowledge objectives they usually test, there are also significant goals in attitudes and behavior that are less readily tested. An adequate program of student progress evaluation and reporting may well include data taken from most or all of the following sources, as these are relevant to educational goals:

1. Conferences—with school personnel, parents and others to secure data regarding student learning and behavior
2. Diaries and logs—kept by students and analyzed by teachers
3. Interviews with students—to get information about their progress
4. Inventories of many types—for information about personality development, interests, activities outside school, use of time, study habits
5. Observation—of individuals and of groups to determine various data about behavior and learning
6. Performance tests—including creative work, oral reports, skills in group work, physical skills and similar items best evaluated through performance
7. Pictures (still and motion)—for later observation of performance, appearance, behavior and so forth
8. Rating scales—used by teachers, peers, parents and others to estimate student behavior on specific traits and also to evaluate any aspect of the school program
9. Recordings—of individual voices and group discussions for later analysis
10. Records of many types—achievement, attendance, disciplinary, health, participation in activities, time studies, cumulative
11. Written papers, notebooks, workbooks and other materials produced by individual students

12. Written tests—standardized, teacher made, group made: to test knowledge, skills, attitudes and performance.

Although the last two items are outnumbered in the list, they remain in practice the predominant sources of information used in evaluating and reporting student progress. Significant improvement in this important phase of middle school education requires the use of other, more relevant data for determining progress on some goals as well as more widespread concern for goals other than those which can be adequately evaluated by pencil-and-paper student products and tests.

Assisting Student Learning

Historically, grades and reports have been powerful pressures to coerce students to study and learn, much as educators may have decried this use. As there has been increasing recognition of the importance of internal motivation and decreasing use of failure and other punitive measures, experimentation with different systems of evaluation and reporting for broader purposes has increased. Especially below the high school and college levels, with their emphasis on grades as determiners of graduation and admission to the next level, attention has been given to assisting student learning through techniques of self-evaluation and individualized instruction. Individualized progress systems, as described in chapter 8, make extensive provision for checking of progress at each step, and this is one of their major advantages. Immediate knowledge by the student of the quality and extent of his progress at every step is probably the most powerful force toward maintaining continuous progress.

Middle school classrooms provide many opportunities for student self-evaluation. Teacher-student conversations in which teachers ask such successive questions as "How are you doing on—?" "What mistake(s) did you make?" "How will you do it now (later)?" can be effective in stimulating and guiding student self-evaluation. Progress checklists and charts are widely provided in commercially prepared instructional materials, and may also be developed by teachers to fit individual situations. Such self-checking plans may include assignment of marks or simply status of completion, and are usually completed first by students and checked by teachers or teacher aides, with teacher-student conferences held as student self-evaluations are considered to need discussion. Forms can also be supplied any day by teachers to aid student self-analysis by such questions as follow:

- How did I do today?
- Did I ask the questions I needed to?
- Did I get the answers I needed?
- Did I find out what to do next? How to do it?
- How do I feel about this class? How can I make it better?

Tests can also be effectively used for self-evaluation purposes. Test exercises to help students check up on their reading comprehension or their skill in using a book or their ability to find materials in reference books and other library resources, may be very useful to students for determining skills needing practice. When test results can be disassociated from the grading system, self-correction of tests can be a valuable experience. Checking of papers by pairs with the teacher available to answer questions and suggest improvement measures, can also be very helpful. Students can also maintain and use effectively in self-evaluation efforts several types of records in addition to those of tests and progress in an instructional system: student diaries and logs; time records; letters to parents reporting school experiences; lists of readings; and papers corrected by teachers. Each of these materials can be useful in the student's efforts to identify progress and make improvements where needed.

Inevitably in our graded school systems the use of marks and evaluation is related to the question of whether students move automatically from one grade to another. From his vantage point of a half century of observation of promotion and curriculum practices, Hollis L. Caswell summed up the problems of evaluation for promotion purposes quite well in the following statement concerning emphasis on the basics of communication and computation:

> One of the first things we tried was to apply grade standards more vigorously, often retaining pupils two or three years in the same grade. In due course we learned that cumulative nonpromotion resulted in a situation bad for all pupils. . . .
>
> Gradually a substantial proportion of schools reduced the use of nonpromotion, and in many cases it was practically eliminated. But we found that this did not solve the problem either. . . . Even in my day it had become clear that neither holding pupils in lower grades nor passing them automatically with their chronological age group would provide a setting in which optimum development of the basic skills of communication and computation could be achieved.
>
> It came to be widely agreed that the problem could be solved only by designing a curriculum that varied as much in opportunities as the individual differences of the pupils to be taught. . . .[3]

We wholly agree that it is curriculum and instruction which must cope with the problems of great differences in the learners of middle school age. Evaluation and reporting systems can merely provide data which teachers, parents and especially the students can use to make appropriate choices as to learning opportunities and instructional modes. These systems can also be used to determine the students failing to achieve minimum competencies or other standards, and thereby, if the promotion system employs such standards, the students who are and are not to be held back. We would hope that the school faculty members responsible would consider fully the data in terms of each student's own status and probable future, determining whether to promote in each case on the basis of what action would most likely assist the student to perform better.

Communicating with Parents for Student Progress

Three major questions about evaluating student progress must be answered as we consider means of communicating with parents about their children's progress: (1) What standard of comparison is used? (2) What symbols are used to denote progress? (3) What means of communication with parents are used? Although the first two of these questions have to be considered in student self-evaluation and in records and reports in general, they usually are dealt with as issues in school reports to parents. Accordingly we deal with them in this section.

Standards of Comparison. The traditional standard of comparison of the individual is with the group, of which the average or midpoint is considered the norm. In this normative evaluation, the student's progress is spoken of as exceptionally high, above average, average, below average and very poor, or some such terms, frequently equated respectively with A,B,C,D and E or F. In comparison of standardized test scores the norm is the midpoint of the population used for norming, and scores may be reported in percentiles, with the 50th percentile representing the norm of the group. This is essentially a competitive system, and its use or nonuse usually involves debate as to whether the school should foster or restrict competition.

In criterion-referenced evaluation, there is some minimum standard set as the criterion. Thus the criterion for achievement on a test for example, may be set as 75 of a possible 100; in writing exercises, not more than 3 errors in spelling; in mathematics, 9 of 10 problems correct; and so forth. In continued learning skills and other curriculum opportunities wherein learnings are specific and sequential, this pattern of evaluation seems logical; it may not operate effectively in curriculum areas in which there are knowledges and behaviors involved that cannot be tested so as to yield adequate quantitative data.

Other standards that are employed are effort, attendance and progress or improvement. For example, the Kirkwood, Missouri, middle schools use a dual marking system in their "Basic Skills" and "Exploratory" grade report forms, as illustrated in the accompanying form (Table 10.1). Note that "effort" requires an "outstanding," "satisfactory" or "unsatisfactory" mark on three factors—behavior, use of class time and completion of assignments. Attendance is frequently included in reports to parents, and it is a very prominent criterion for decisions as to promotion, disciplinary action and other critical matters. Full implementation of a philosophy emphasizing progress as the consistent aim in every goal of the school for its students, really requires that the progress of the student be evaluated; to meet this requirement diagnostic evaluation is needed for every objective with follow-up evaluation yielding an estimate of progress. Then there is still needed some criterion for judging progress—is it adequate? Frequently, marking and reporting systems make some effort to appraise progress in terms of the student's ability; the report form or the teacher's oral statement may include language such as "is working up to ability" or "is not working up to abil-

Table 10.1 / Kirkwood Middle Schools,*
Nipher and North—Basic Skills Grade Report 19__–__

Last Name   First Name

Grade/Team   Subject   Teacher

Student Working _____ Grade Level

GRADES		QUARTER			
		1	2	3	4
Achievement					
Effort	Behavior				
	Use of class time				
	Completion of Assignments				

1st Quarter Comments:

2nd Quarter Comments:

3rd Quarter Comments:

4th Quarter Comments:

EXPLANATION OF GRADES

Achievement	*Effort*
E —Outstanding	1 —Outstanding
S —Above Average	
M—Average	2 —Satisfactory
I —Below Average	
U —Failure	3 —Unsatisfactory

Parent Signature

* From Kirkwood, Missouri, Public Schools.

ity." The illustrative mathematics report form (Table 10.2) from the Albert D. Lawton Intermediate School of Essex Junction, Vermont, permits the teacher to mark in relation to either (or both) the students or the class, and emphasizes classwork and self-motivation.

We believe that the standard of comparison used should be the one most clearly related to the goal involved, and the one that seems most likely to give parents and other advisors information they need to help students

Table 10.2 / Sample Subject Report Form*

NAME _____ GRADE _____ SECTION _____

MATHEMATICS

This is an evaluation of the student's achievement in relation to:
        himself _____
        his class _____
Each student's strengths and weaknesses are taken into consideration.
The grade is derived by averaging homework or tests or both.

PERIOD REPORT

I.   CLASSWORK
        Seeks help when needed.
        Comes prepared to class.
        Work completed on time.
        Prepares for tests.

II.   SELF-MOTIVATION
        Effort
        Respect
        Attentiveness
        Cooperation
        Works independently

III.   OVERALL GRADE

Teacher _____ Teacher _____ Teacher _____

COMMENTS:

---

* From Alfred D. Lawton Intermediate School, Essex Junction, Vermont.

Table 10.3 / Comprehensive Report Form*

STOUGHTON MIDDLE SCHOOL
STUDENT EVALUATION

THIS EVALUATION HAS BEEN PREPARED ESPECIALLY FOR _____
BASED ON HIS/HER INDIVIDUAL ABILITIES.

BLOCK _____ SIXTH GRADE _____ SEVENTH GRADE _____ TEAM LEADER _____ Phone - 873-6624

SUBJECTS

A - Academic   C - Conduct

LEARNING SKILLS AND GENERAL BEHAVIOR
THAT NEED IMPROVEMENT ARE NUMBERED
ACCORDING TO SUBJECT.

	1	2	3	4
Listening carefully				
Following instructions				
Participating in class				
Completing work thoughtfully				
Completing work promptly				
Using time efficiently				
Understanding concepts				
Working well independently				
Working well in a group				
Completing work neatly				
Bringing materials to class				
Relating well to peers				
Being sensitive to others' needs				
Showing respectful behavior				
Obeying school rules				
Respecting self				
Out of class conduct				
Study hall conduct				

SUBJECTS:

1) Art
2) Band
3) Chorus
4) Communication Arts
5) General Music
6) Home Ec.
7) Ind. Arts
8) Language Arts
9) Math/Algebra
10) Orchestra
11) Phy. Ed.
12) Reading
13) Science
14) Social Studies
15) Speech
16) Spelling

EXPLANATION OF GRADES

ACADEMIC

A -- All objectives met with excellence, superior work based on teacher-established criteria including in-depth assignments, creativity, promptness, etc.

B -- All objectives met with good quality.

C -- All objectives met.

D -- All objectives met minimally, work not commensurate with student's ability.

Inc/F -- Objectives not met. Students will be given an opportunity to make up incomplete assignments. If assignments are not completed, the grade of F; signifying failure to complete objectives, will become part of the student's record.

CONDUCT

O -- Outstanding
S -- Satisfactory
U -- Unsatisfactory

COMMENTS

First Quarter _____ Second Quarter _____

Third Quarter _____ Fourth Quarter _____

TIMES ABSENT

	1	2	3	4
Art				
Band				
Chorus				
Communication Arts				
General Music				
Home Ec.				
Ind. Arts				
Language Arts				

Times Absent con't.

	1	2	3	4
Math/Algebra				
Orchestra				
Phy. Ed.				
Reading				
Science				
Social Studies				
Speech				
Spelling				

* From Stoughton, Wisconsin, Middle School.

make optimum progress. For instructional purposes, criterion-referenced tests are very helpful in individualizing student progress within particular areas, especially those having highly sequential material. For parent information, there may be a need for normative comparisons which are easily understood, but this need should be met only if there is also help given for understanding why students are below average and what means if any are available for helping them. As to effort, attendance and other such factors, we see their chief use in teacher and parent understanding of individual students and their student progress.

Symbols for Marking and Reporting. Numerical marks on the 100 percent scale were once popular in the United States and still are given in a few schools, but it is the traditional letter grades (A,B,C,D,E and/or F) that have been used most widely now at all levels, and almost universally in high school and college. The grades are variously interpreted, with some districts equating each letter to a range on the 100 percent scale (for example, A = 90–100), and others using such varied explanation of A, for example, as "Outstanding Progress," "All objectives met with excellence" and "Excellent." A single grade may be assigned to a subject, or there may be marks on each of several objectives or other items used as criteria. The accompanying report form (Table 10.3) from the Stoughton, Wisconsin, Middle School, illustrates several features of middle school report forms, few of which include so many features as Stoughton: checklist of skills and behavior items that can be checked by subject to show improvement needed; record of attendance by subject; one system of letter grades, related by definition to objectives, for academic evaluation and another system for conduct in each subject area.

Means of Communication with Parents. The traditional and dominant means of communication with parents is the report form or card, developed by each district and even by individual schools. Great variety exists in the forms used. Some districts use different forms for different subjects and grades; for example, the Carleton W. Washburne School of Winnetka, Illinois, uses a variety of forms, differing by subjects, covered by a checklist showing reports included for each student, up to the second semester of the eighth grade, when the accompanying form (Table 10.4) much like that of the typical high school, is used. Most of the individual subject report forms from various districts using them, list objectives of the subject with some indication of student strengths and weaknesses. The report forms vary especially in the use of the various symbols and in the standards of comparison as discussed earlier in this section.

Middle school educators also use a variety of plans for communicating with parents about student difficulties, before and between report cards. For example, the accompanying form (Table 10.5) from the A. G. Currie Intermediate School, Tustin, California, can be used by any teacher to report unsatisfactory achievement and/or conduct, although it lacks any positive

Table 10.4 / Sample Subject/Grade
Eighth Grade Report Form,* **Second Semester**

Name _____   Total days absent _____

(Sept.–June)

Advisor _____   Times tardy _____

(Sept.–June)

The progress evaluations herein are based upon reasonable expectations for the individual child in each area.

(5. Outstanding/4. Above Average/3. Average/2. Below Average/1. Unsatisfactory)

ACHIEVE-MENT	EF-FORT		COMMENTS (WHERE NECESSARY)	TEACHER'S INITIALS
		English		
		Social Studies		
		Mathematics		
		Introductory Physical Science		
		Physical Education		
		Art		
		Band/Orchestra		
		Child Study		
		Choral Music		
		Dramatic Arts		
		French		
		Graphic Arts		
		Homemaking		
		Industrial Arts		
		Resource Center		
		TV Productions		
		Typing		

Parent's Signature _____

* From Carleton W. Washburne School, Winnetka, Illinois.

comments. In some schools interim progress reports differ by subjects; see the one reproduced here (Table 10.6) from the Esperanza Middle School, Lexington Park, Maryland, for Industrial Arts.

There seems no categorical, universal answer to the question of what means of communication to use with parents to assist student progress. Three principles are seen as especially valid and important:

1. The communication with parents should be as direct and personal as possible: to this end many districts have relied on parent-teacher conferences for much of their reporting in elementary schools, and some middle

Table 10.5 / A.G. Currie
Intermediate School*—Progress Report to Parents

STUDENT'S NAME _____ GRADE _____ DATE _____
SUBJECT _____ TEACHER _____
Number of Misconducts _____ Grade unsatisfactory for ability _____
Achievement to date _____ Conduct unsatisfactory _____

DAILY ASSIGNMENTS

_____ Incomplete   _____ Suggest parent conference
_____ Inconsistent quality _____ Class participation poor
_____ Not turned in   _____ Poor work habits in class
                               _____ Frequently fails to bring materials
TESTS   _____ Misuses or wastes school ma-
_____ Test not made up   terials/time
_____ Low test scores   _____ Performance does not meet class
_____ Inconsistent quality   standard
                               _____ Excessive talking in class
SPECIAL PROJECTS   _____ Too many tardies
_____ Incomplete   _____ Inattentive in class
_____ Poor quality   _____ Excessive dress cuts in P.E.
_____ Late   _____ Uncooperative
_____ Not turned in   _____ Absent too often
                               _____ Other side for teacher's comments
                               PARENT'S SIGNATURE _____
                               (Comments may be made on reverse side)

* Tustin, California.

schools are using conferences when possible. The case for them is well summed up in this excerpt from the "Parent Teacher Conference Guide" used in the Jamesville-Dewitt, New York, Middle School:

The Middle School regularly sends you progress reports and report cards which summarize your child's scholastic progress. However, it's impossible to reduce to a few sentences, an assortment of check-marks, or any collection of letter or number marks a unique and infinitely complex human—including your child. Telephone conversations are good, but the best base of cooperation is found in the interchange of face-to-face conferences between parents and teachers.

The Teacher Handbook of the Woodlawn Middle School, Mebane, North Carolina, classifies parent conferences as (1) impromptu—chance meeting; (2) telephone conference—quick means of contact; and (3) scheduled school conference which "is especially valuable in that it is planned in advance and the teacher has time to prepare fully for it." To help in the advance planning, the accompanying form (Table 10.7) is used at Woodlawn.

2. The report, whatever its form, should be intelligible to the parents. Since parents do not generally possess a pedagogical vocabulary and may not want to spend as much time studying explanations as the report form makers anticipate, the form must not be overly complex, explanations must

**Table 10.6 / Esperanza Middle
School—Interim Progress Report for Industrial Arts**

| | Student's Name | Homeroom | Date |

Students are expected to perform to the best of their ability in special subject areas. Your child is in need of improvement in some areas at this time. He/She should make a special effort in each area checked below.

	Shows an abililty to function in a group
	Practices safety habits
	Practices self-control
	Respects the rights and property of others
	Follows directions
	Participates in clean-up activities
	Works carefully and accurately
	Utilizes time effectively
	Exhibits ability to conduct research
	Exhibits ability to speak before a peer group
	Exhibits proper communication skills
	Exhibits ability to share scarce resources
	Exhibits ability to exercise self-direction
	Shows respect for tools and machinery

We are providing you with this information so that your child can have the best possible chance to receive a satisfactory evaluation at the end of the marking period. COMMENTS:

	Teacher

be specific and clear and any follow-up conferences or other action well spelled out. The best guarantee of this principle lies in the development of the form; careful pilot use with representative parents to eliminate flaws and ambiguity helps greatly.

3. The ultimate purpose of the report, whether oral or written, is to increase cooperation for the student's progress. Both teacher and parent may need an occasional reminder of the purpose, for progress reports sometimes get used as punitive measures, or as bases for rewards extrinsic to the educational program. Positive reports are also desirable; note the letter form on page 302, used in the Oaklea Middle School of Junction City, Oregon, for commendation:

**Table 10.7 / Parent/Teacher Conference
Planning Form—Woodlawn Middle School***

DEAR _____

     Your parent-teacher conference is scheduled for

     Date _____ from _____ to _____

     This appointment is to exchange information about

     _____. Please indicate below any area(s) that
you are particularly interested in discussing.

_____	Work habits	_____	Social Studies
_____	Growth as an individual	_____	Science
_____	Growth as a group member	_____	Mathematics
_____	Reading	_____	Art
_____	Writing	_____	Music
_____	Listening and Speaking	_____	Physical Education
_____	Spelling	_____	Other _____
_____	Language		

     Please RETURN this prior to the conference.
     If you are unable to attend at the time above, please indicate other
convenient dates and times.

                            _____
                                   (Parent's Signature)

TEACHER _____

_____

                        (Detach here)

REMINDER: Conference to exchange information about _____
_____ on _____ from _____ to _____.

* Mebane, North Carolina

Sample Progress Letter Form

                     Date _____

To the parents of _____ :

    We at Oaklea School believe that outstanding achievement as well as conscientious effort toward improvement should be encouraged and recognized in our students.

    Your child has displayed these commendable qualities during the past four-week period and we are proud to send you this statement of merit for personal effort and achievement.

                          _____
                          Class

                          _____
                          Teacher

                          _____
                          Principal

Much money and effort go into maintaining an evaluation and reporting system. Parents do need to know how Johnnie and Mary are doing at school so that they can be helped at home; they can and do help in such ways as improving study conditions, offering parental encouragement and arranging for extra help at school or otherwise as teachers recommend. Parents can be helpful only as they understand their children's learning status and problems, and communication must first of all convey as accurate data as possible on this score.

Records for Other Purposes

The same basic data used by the student in his or her self-improvement activities and by the teacher and parent in determining how to counsel and help the student serve several purposes as records. For example, the student's own cumulative record, with its compilation of test scores and other quantitative data regarding student progress as well as informative material about the student's family, health, school attendance and other items, is important for consultation by future teacher and counselors.

Compilations of evaluative data about various populations of students become exceedingly important data sources for use in school evaluations and in program planning. Certainly the ultimate criterion of school quality is the progress its students attain, and any adequate program of school evaluation provides for consideration of such measures of student progress as available. And the first source of data for school planning committees is that of data about student achievement, behavior and attitudes. Hence carefully maintained records of the evaluation of each student's progress are prerequisite to the other phases of evaluation which follow in this chapter.

Evaluating a Middle School

Although the ultimate criterion of the value of schooling is that of student progress, educators and school patrons also need to know what the strengths and weaknesses of the school are. Many aspects of student progress are very difficult to appraise, and attention has to be given to the factors believed to influence the quality of schooling and its results. And we are especially interested in a choice of components which will provide adequate data for making decisions about school improvement. This section describes several such components.

Use of Single Criteria

Evaluation of a middle school on the basis of achievement test results in a particular area such as reading or mathematics may occur. In fact, any use of achievement data for school evaluation is an example of the use of a single criterion. If this is the only criterion, it is an example also of the fallacy involved in judging a total program on the basis of only one criterion. Another example of the use of single criteria is the evaluation of school personnel, or, better, of a single group of personnel, as teachers. And the evaluation of teachers may use single criteria also, such as the degrees attained, years of experience, rating of teaches by the principal or achievement of students on a particular objective.

An evaluation always employs a single criterion or a group of single criteria. It is the former practice, use of a single criterion alone, that can be least helpful in identifying strengths and weaknesses and needs for improvement of a school. Hence our suggestion is that data regarding many specific criteria are needed, and may be gathered singly or in combination as is feasible but should be used in concert so that the school is not labeled good or bad on any single testing, opinion poll, visit of an evaluator or other one aspect. Practice differs with this principle primarily in the use of achievement test data, although the state of the school building or the personality of the principal or the band program or any other single item may also unduly weight the general appraisal of the school by students, patrons and visitors. Such weighting has be avoided or at least minimized by a comprehensive evaluation program employing a variety of criteria closely related to the goals of the school—all of them, not just one.

Feedback Opportunities

"Feedback" is used, perhaps loosely, in educational evaluation to denote almost any type of reaction, formal or informal, made by a variety of individuals regarding one, many or all aspects of a school. We ourselves believe it well to maintain a flexibility of definition in order to encourage the securing and use of reactions from appropriate sources. Thus, feedback includes not only formal opinion polls and systematically collected and organized data in a self-study program, but the informal comments of visitors and other persons. It is the latter type of feedback with which we are concerned at this point.

Middle school student feedback is immediate and direct. Student reaction to a person, an event, a class session or a program of instruction is readily available, and indeed may get expressed too quickly without adequate thought on the student's part. But student feedback is highly relevant to almost all aspects of middle school education, and should be reviewed and itself evaluated as new elements in the school program or new groups of students in the school population make feedback timely.

Feedback is frequently all too obvious when parents come to school to discuss their children's problems, but more objective data are too infrequently sought. Every parent conference is an opportunity to secure feedback, as is every meeting of parents in parent-teacher organizations, advisory councils and other groups. In addition to the questionnaires and other polling instruments that may be used, informal, well-guided discussions can yield much information as to the reactions of those participating, to whatever aspects of the school program and issues therein are under discussion.

Perhaps the most insightful feedback can be secured from professional educators visiting an exemplary middle school, or one seeking to become exemplary. Middle schools, especially those in new buildings and those reported upon in professional journals and other publications, get visited by personnel from other middle schools, especially from schools in the process of reorganization or initial planning. These well-motivated visitors, frequently with some background information about desirable practice, form definite opinions about what they see. Some exemplary middle school personnel quite effectively invite the visitors' reactions in a final conversation before the visitors' departure.

Somewhat similarly, visitors from classes at nearby teacher education institutions are frequently informed about middle school programs and practices, and may have worthwhile reactions. Some student teachers may lack experience but not self-confidence, and can and do offer with candor their opinions and reactions; others may need to be urged to express theirs. The middle school principal or other representative conducting an informal feedback session can improve the flow of reactions and suggestions by avoiding argumentative and defensive statements, by indicating that all opinions and reactions are valued and will be considered, and by a generally courteous and grateful attitude, even in the face of undeserved criticisms.

Opinion Polls

An opinion poll is another form of feedback data: opinions of some group of people are sought through a written form or guided interviews or a combination of forms and interviews. In addition to the annual Gallup Poll on Education and the inclusion of questions on education in other national, state and local polls, many school districts and individual schools use polls of their own to get opinions from many students, and also parents, that can be tabulated and interpreted. Teachers are also frequently included as a polling group.

Several issues must be dealt with in developing an opinion poll as an instrument to yield data for evaluation purposes. First, is opinion to be sought on a particular issue or facet of the school program, or on many issues and/or facets? Polls on specific controversial issues may secure more responses but be less useful for broad purposes of evaluation than polls on many questions. But if the issue is whether a new school program—course, activity or service—is believed by the students to be helpful (or interesting or generally good) it may be easiest to use a very simple fill-in form on the program. If parent opinion is desired for reactions to several programs, a more comprehensive poll is indicated.

A second issue in the use of opinion polls is that of whose judgment is desired. Will the most reliable data come from students, teachers, parents or citizens in general? And if comparable data are wanted from two or more groups, can the same instrument be used for both? An especially significant, related question is whether the poll is to be on a sample basis or to include the total population of the group to be polled. If only a sample is needed, is it to be random, representative or of some other type? And what percentage of returns will be considered adequate? Resolution of these issues is beyond the scope of this book and should probably be done at the school or district level with the help of some research specialist.

We would especially urge that the opinionnaire be carefully constructed. Some important precautions are suggested:

1. If the response may be influenced by the possibility that the respondent's identity is known, the poll should be made completely anonymous.
2. The respondents should be supplied with adequate background for expressing opinions.
3. All directions should be as clear and simple as possible.
4. The instrument should be tried out several times, with needed revisions made before its final use; the tryout should be on members of the group to be polled.
5. The questions and the responses should be constructed in such a way as to facilitate tabulation and summarization.

The accompanying parent questionnaire (Table 10.8) from the Nipher Middle School, Kirkwood, Missouri, is illustrative of the many seen by the authors. The reader will note that several of the items on this instrument were definitely localized, as we believe they should be. The letter to a random sample of parents regarding the form asked for their help and stated that the parents need not sign their names.

In view of the great importance of communication of parents and school personnel, the parent opinion poll is believed to have especial significance. It must be planned and constructed as above, and particular care must be given to the handling of it to get an adequate return. One procedure that may get good returns is a phone call requesting the parent to complete a form, followed by mailing the form to those agreeing to complete it. Of course this procedure may be feasible only for a sample, although phone calls by teachers to their advisees' parents might be possible for the total population. Such general questions as these can be somewhat reliably answered when parent polls are used effectively:

1. Are parents satisfied or dissatisfied with the curriculum? To what extent and in what particulars?
2. What are parents' expectation regarding the middle school? Are the school's goals confirmed by parents? If not, what changes in goals need to be made?
3. How well do parents understand what the school is trying to do for their children? What problems in communication are indicated?
4. In what middle school curriculum areas do parents believe their children's experiences are adequate and inadequate?
5. What problems of the total middle school program and its individual aspects are indicated by the poll?
6. What suggestions for solving these problems (#5) are suggested by parents?

Table 10.8 / Parent Questionnaire*

1. Nipher Middle School helped my child to develop effective study habits.
   - A. Strongly Agree
   - B. Agree
   - C. Disagree
   - D. Strongly Disagree
   - E. No Opinion

2. Nipher Middle School encouraged my child to do his best.
   - A. Strongly Agree
   - B. Agree
   - C. Disagree
   - D. Strongly Disagree
   - E. No Opinion

3. Nipher Middle School helped my child to become responsible.
   - A. Strongly Agree
   - B. Agree
   - C. Disagree
   - D. Strongly Disagree
   - E. No Opinion

4. Nipher Middle School helped my child improve his basic skills.
   - A. Strongly Agree
   - B. Agree
   - C. Disagree
   - D. Strongly Disagree
   - E. No Opinion

5. The exploratory courses—living arts, home economics, shop, vocal music, drama, creative writing, health and art were helpful.
   - A. Strongly Agree
   - B. Agree
   - C. Disagree
   - D. Strongly Disagree
   - E. No Opinion

6. The instrumental music program at Nipher was helpful to my child. (Instrumental music parents only)
   - A. Strongly Agree
   - B. Agree
   - C. Disagree
   - D. Strongly Disagree
   - E. No Opinion

7. The physical education program was helpful to my child.
   - A. Strongly Agree
   - B. Agree
   - C. Disagree
   - D. Strongly Disagree
   - E. No Opinion

8. Nipher Middle School has helped my child to find ways to solve problems.
   - A. Strongly Agree
   - B. Agree
   - C. Disagree
   - D. Strongly Disagree
   - E. No Opinion

9. Nipher Middle School's sixth-grade camping program was a good experience for my child.
   - A. Strongly Agree
   - B. Agree
   - C. Disagree
   - D. Strongly Disagree
   - E. No Opinion

10. The Olympics were a good experience for my child.
    - A. Strongly Agree
    - B. Agree
    - C. Disagree
    - D. Strongly Disagree
    - E. No Opinion

11. The twenty-three minute daily reading period was helpful.
    - A. Strongly Agree
    - B. Agree
    - C. Disagree
    - D. Strongly Disagree
    - E. No Opinion

12. The total educational program at Nipher was helpful.
    - A. Strongly Agree
    - B. Agree
    - C. Disagree
    - D. Strongly Disagree
    - E. No Opinion

13. Teachers gave too much homework.
    - A. Strongly Agree
    - B. Agree
    - C. Disagree
    - D. Strongly Disagree
    - E. No Opinion

14. Teachers gave too little homework.
    - A. Strongly Agree
    - B. Agree
    - C. Disagree
    - D. Strongly Disagree
    - E. No Opinion

15. My child enjoyed attending Nipher.
    - A. Strongly Agree
    - B. Agree
    - C. Disagree

(continued)

Table 10.8 / Parent Questionnaire* (continued)

D. Strongly Disagree
E. No Opinion

16. The curriculum at Nipher met the needs of my child.
    A. Strongly Agree
    B. Agree
    C. Disagree
    D. Strongly Disagree
    E. No Opinion

17. Reports from Nipher concerning my child were adequate.
    A. Strongly Agree
    B. Agree
    C. Disagree
    D. Strongly Disagree
    E. No Opinion

18. The co-curricular courses (mini-courses) were helpful for my child.
    A. Strongly Agree
    B. Agree
    C. Disagree
    D. Strongly Disagree
    E. No Opinion

19. Discipline in the school should have been more strict.
    A. Strongly Agree
    B. Agree
    C. Disagree
    D. Strongly Disagree
    E. No Opinion

20. The principals at Nipher were interested in helping the students.
    A. Strongly Agree
    B. Agree
    C. Disagree

D. Strongly Disagree
E. No Opinion

21. The teachers at Nipher were interested in helping the student.
    A. Strongly Agree
    B. Agree
    C. Disagree
    D. Strongly Disagree
    E. No Opinion

22. The counselors at Nipher were interested in helping the student.
    A. Strongly Agree
    B. Agree
    C. Disagree
    D. Strongly Disagree
    E. No Opinion

23. My child liked the cafeteria food.
    A. Strongly Agree
    B. Agree
    C. Disagree
    D. Strongly Disagree
    E. No Opinion

COMMENTS:

_____
_____
_____
_____
_____
_____
_____
_____
_____
_____

* From Nipher Middle School, Kirkwood, Missouri.

We should also note the utility of short opinion polls of appropriate groups on specific issues. The middle school beginning a new program does have early and serious need to determine student and parent reactions to the program. Even before beginning new programs need for them may be assessed in part by polls. Especially when polls can be validated by samplings of interviews, the data from them may be highly significant formative evaluation data, data to help in modifying and improving a program.

Unobtrusive Measures

Lamenting upon the "overdependence upon a single, fallible method," that of questionnaires and interviews, for research in the social sciences, Webb and his associates in 1966 published a very useful book[4] on unobtrusive methods of gathering data. These authors especially objected to the use of any one method alone, but also noted that interviews and questionnaires "intruded" into the social setting and had several other weaknesses:

> Interviews and questionnaires intrude as a foreign element into the social setting they would describe, they create as well as measure attitudes, they elicit atypical roles and responses, they are limited to those who are accessible and will cooperate, and the responses obtained are produced in part by dimensions of individual differences irrelevant to the topic at hand.[5]

Unobtrusive measures, by contrast, do not require the cooperation of the respondent and do not depend on the respondent's attitudes toward the interview or questionnaire. We see tests also as examples of the obtrusive measures; wider use of unobtrusive measures seems increasingly necessary to avoid the use of a single method, testing, and especially of one so influenced by individual differences in interest and ability.

Miller has suggested a long list of unobtrusive measures that can be used for gathering data in schools about the achievement of school goals. Several excerpts we consider illustrative of such measures for evaluating a middle school follow:

> Number of situations in which students are:
> 1. *Voluntarily remaining after school to chat with teachers*
> 8. *Writing, rehearsing, and polishing their efforts*
> 15. *Working independently*
>   Data about students:
> 3. *What percentage of students skip each day?*
> 4. *What percentage of students are tardy each day?*
> 7. *How many students know the principal's name?*
> 13. *How many students attend optional school events?*
>   Number of situations in which teachers are:
> 2. *Complimenting students*
> 7. *Attempting to measure student progress in other than academic areas*
> 15. *Making positive remarks about students in the staff lounge*
> 21. *Voluntarily staying after school to chat with pupils*
>   Data about staff:
> 1. *What is the teacher absenteeism rate?*
> 2. *What is the teacher tardiness rate?*
>   Number of situations where administrators are:
> 2. *Involving staff, parents, students, and community in setting priorities, assessing progress, and reviewing rules*
> 5. *Providing means whereby students can attend school at different hours, take different courses, where class periods are different lengths, etc.*
> 6. *Listening to students*
>   Data about administration:
> 1. *How many principals has the building had in the last three years?*
> 8. *What percentage of the time in staff meetings are staff members talking?*
> 9. *How many new courses or programs have been added this year?*[6]

Readers can undoubtedly add many such items that might be useful in their own schools. Obviously any school faculty using such measures in evaluating the school must be prepared to defend the validity of each item as a measure or indicator of school quality. It is important also to select items which are truly unobtrusive, that is, not requiring the cooperation or other involvement of students or other groups concerned. And note that most of the illustrative items we selected from Miller's list involve some type of quantitative data; this is to facilitate the collection and comparison of such data from time to time to provide a true measure of change.

Self-Study Programs

We turn now to a more frequent, comprehensive effort to evaluate a middle school, a self-study program. There are many types of such studies, ranging from a fairly cursory compilation of faculty responses to a questionnaire or in a group evaluation session, to a complete analysis of each aspect of the school by the faculty followed by the review of a visiting team or committee. The complete review has most possibilities, we believe, for affecting program development and school quality, and we give it primary attention here. It should be noted that less comprehensive self-studies can be done for almost any aspect of the school by the designation of study committees and guides for the aspect(s) concerned, with the use of visiting individuals or committees also possible.

Purposes of the Self-Study Programs. Two overlapping purposes dominate self-study programs: (1) to evaluate the school in order to improve it and (2) to satisfy accreditation requirements of the regional and/or state accrediting agency. These purposes should not conflict since accrediting agencies require self-studies in order that the schools may improve, but it can happen that the immediate goal of accreditation overshadows the long-range goal of improvement.

Accreditation of a middle school by the state department of education or any agency designated by the state is essential for public schools, although the requirements for accreditation vary widely in the fifty states. The requirement of a periodic self-study program is a sensible means for the school to determine its status and maintain improvement, and an effective way for the agency to have data basic to accreditation. Regional accreditation is an option for the school; being accredited by the regional association is recognition for status purposes desired by some school boards, faculties and patrons. Both purposes of the self-study program are stated in the following illustrative excerpts from the Superintendent's foreword to a self-study report of the Noe Middle School of Jefferson County, Kentucky:

Accreditation by the regional accrediting agency is a worthy goal. For many years our high schools have been accredited with obvious advantages to our high school graduates, especially those who pursue higher education. The inclusion of our elementary, and middle schools in the accreditation process, a relatively new endeavor, enables our district to seek high standards at all levels in a systematic and objective way. . . .

Everyone involved in a Southern Association self-study benefits from the experience. The involvement required by self-evaluation can provide insight which will result in a stronger program and improved learning experiences for boys and girls.

A major problem in accreditation standards and processes for middle schools has been the tendency of accrediting agencies to expect the middle schools to use guides developed for secondary and/or elementary schools that may not provide for unique elements of the middle school. In the absence of applicable regional or state guidelines for middle school self-study programs, local districts may effectively develop their own guides for improvement. For example, middle schools in Alachua County, Florida, follow the same pattern of self-study as elementary schools, a pattern that does provide for considerable flexibility of programs and criteria. The purpose of the five-year review is stated as follows in the Alachua County guide:

> The review of a school's program should be viewed as a positive professional process. It provides the school's staff an opportunity to utilize self-study, peers, and other resource persons for a systematic comprehensive look at its programs every five years. The object of the review is to analyze the school's programs to ascertain strengths, weaknesses, and plans for improvement in terms of appropriate state, school board, and local school guidelines/criteria.[7]

The Self-Study Phase. The period in which the school faculty carries on its own study of the school varies in length, although a major part of a year seems essential for a thorough study, carried on as it must be in addition to the regular school operation. The National Study of School Evaluation program followed widely in high schools and junior high schools, and in many middle schools, specifies that the self-study usually requires a minimum of one year and that the steering committee should be appointed a year before the evaluation is to be completed.

The process of the self-study generally encompasses the total school program and its personnel and facilities. The *Evaluative Criteria* of the National Study of School Evaluation includes these sections for junior high and middle schools:

    I. Manual
    II. School and Community
    III. Philosophy and Goals
    IV. Major Educational Priorities
    V. Design of Curriculum
    VI. Learning Areas
    VII. Individual Faculty Data
    VIII. School Staff and Administration
    IX. Student Activities Program
    X. Learning Media Services
    XI. Student Personnel Services
    XII. School Plant and Facilities[8]

Most middle school self-study reports include the foregoing elements, although the terms and combinations may differ.

Table 10.9 / Bases for Evaluating Learning Areas*

I. PRINCIPLES

Introduction

The learning areas include instructional experiences that maintain and extend knowledge, attitudes, values and skills begun in the elementary school and ones that initiate new areas of learning.

Listed below are a number of specific principles regarding "Learning Areas" to which faculty, parents, and students should address themselves. This introductory part is designed to encourage introspection concerning this section of the self-study. It is a starting point for discussion and for interaction among participants preparatory to delving into the nature of this aspect of the school program. Participants should avoid lengthy debate over the adequacy or the inadequacy of each principle. Rather, it is important that the committee assigned this responsibility react to each statement in terms of an overview of how the school community generally accepts and implements each principle.

The committee should indicate by circling the appropriate number in the first column to the right of each principle the extent to which that principle is accepted by the school, and indicate by circling the appropriate number in the second column the extent to which that principle is being implemented in the school. Where necessary, in order to be consistent with the stated philosophy and goals, specific principles may be modified and others added.

The descriptions of the numbers listed immediately below apply to the numbers in the columns to the right of the principles and should be borne in mind when marking the degree of acceptance and the degree of the implementation.

Degree of Acceptance
1. Unacceptable
2. Questionable
3. Accept with reservations
4. Accept in general
5. Endorse completely

Degree of Implementation
1. Not implemented
2. Weakly implemented
3. Average implementation
4. Strongly implemented
5. Fully implemented

Principles	DEGREE OF ACCEPTANCE					DEGREE OF IMPLEMENTATION				
The content and instructional activities in this learning area:										
1. Are based on the philosophy and goals of the middle school/junior high school	1	2	3	4	5	1	2	3	4	5
2. Are based on an analysis of the educational needs of pre and early adolescents	1	2	3	4	5	1	2	3	4	5

3. Contribute to a balanced program of general education for each student	1	2	3	4	5		1	2	3	4	5
4. Articulate the learning experiences of the middle school/junior high school with those of the schools above and below	1	2	3	4	5		1	2	3	4	5
5. Provide an educational opportunity for students in accordance with their own needs	1	2	3	4	5		1	2	3	4	5
6. Provide opportunities for exploration within the learning area	1	2	3	4	5		1	2	3	4	5
7. Provide opportunities for a limited amount of specialization in areas of interest or ability . .	1	2	3	4	5		1	2	3	4	5
8. Are flexible enough to meet the changing needs of students	1	2	3	4	5		1	2	3	4	5
9. Provide for evaluation of student achievement in accordance with each individual's aptitudes and abilities .	1	2	3	4	5		1	2	3	4	5
10. Are analyzed periodically in an effort to determine why students fail	1	2	3	4	5		1	2	3	4	5
11. Are structured in such a way that all students in a given class, regardless of the number, have the maximum opportunities for learning	1	2	3	4	5		1	2	3	4	5
12. Are examined in detail periodically in order to determine what contribution this learning area makes to the total education of the students . .	1	2	3	4	5		1	2	3	4	5
13. Others	1	2	3	4	5		1	2	3	4	5

* From National Study of School Evaluation. *Middle School/Junior High School, Evaluative Criteria*, (Arlington, VA: The Study, 1979, p. 67). With permission of the National Study of School Evaluation, 2201 Wilson Boulevard, Arlington, VA 22201.

The NSSE *Evaluative Criteria* follows for junior high and middle schools the basic pattern of the volume long guiding the accreditation self-studies of high schools throughout the United States. This guide has been regarded by many middle school educators as being more appropriate for secondary than middle schools. However, the 1979 edition of *Middle School/Junior High School Evaluative Criteria* has been made more relevant to middle schools than the prior edition, and we believe this can be helpful in middle school evaluations. Certainly the group concerned should be free to eliminate inappropriate sections and to adapt the guide, which has considerable flexibility, to the local situation.

The *Evaluative Criteria* calls for quite specific data to be supplied in the school report. For example, Section II, School and Community, includes directions and blanks for these data: annual student enrollments by grade and sex for the past five years; number of years students have been in the school and number of schools students have attended; age-grade distribution; ethnic composition; reading and mathematics levels by grade and sex; analysis of withdrawals (reasons); occupational and educational status of parents; population, enrollment and financial data about the school district; and identification of educational and other resources of the community. The study outline for Section VI, Learning Areas, is intended to be used for each subject area the school identifies; it includes the accompanying rating form (Table 10.9) on acceptance and implementation of certain principles, five pages of fill-in blanks listing questions regarding the nature of the program, and other pages for fill-in items having to do with evaluation plans for improvements and rating of current status in the subject area.

Schools using the NSSE *Evaluative Criteria* as the guide for their self-study may follow the form of this completely, having the report written into the fill-in spaces of its sections. Of course schools not using this guide for accreditation purposes, may also elect to use some sections and not others, or to follow another outline. Whatever the elements of the school studied, the general pattern of self-study is one by committees, primarily of the faculty, corresponding to the major sections of the study. Thus if the *Evaluative Criteria* plan is utilized there will be a committee responsible for each of the sections listed earlier, and usually multiple committees on the subject areas, one per broad field. Interdisciplinary organization is recognized in the 1979 edition, but committees may need to develop a more suitable study guide. If the school has a departmental organization the department members may constitute the committee for their subject field. Each committee gathers the data required by the guidelines used, and works out the summarization, analysis and presentation of the data for the report. The work is time-consuming and even tedious at times, but many middle school educators believe that the effort of a self-study is exceedingly well rewarded in the exchange of ideas, arrival at program changes and the improvement of school, faculty involvement and student and faculty morale.

The aspect of the self-study that is most crucial is the setting of recommendations for improvement of the school. The recommendations may be made at several points: (1) preliminary ones based on first discussions of an element of the school that seem feasible for immediate implementation at least on a trial basis; (2) recommendations based on the self-study prepared by the respective committees and frequently reviewed and modified by steering committees and/or the total faculty; (3) recommendations made by the visiting committee; and (4) recommendations made by the school faculty and administration after reviewing the report of the self-study, and the report of the visiting committee. The latter two reports will be considered in later sections, but we should emphasize at this point the very great importance of carefully determined and stated recommendations of the faculty study groups. The following suggestions are offered as to the development and statement of recommendations in the report of the faculty self-study:

1. Each recommendation should clearly flow from the data presented in the self-study section immediately preceding the recommendation(s).
2. Each recommendation should be so clearly and fully stated that it can be understood by whomever is responsible for its approval and implementation.
3. Each recommendation should indicate clearly by what person or group it must be approved and implemented.
4. If the recommendation represents the judgment of persons other than the responsible committee—for example, the judgment of parents, students, community representatives or educational consultants—this fact should be included in the statement of the recommendation.
5. Recommendations involving additional financial cost should include estimates as to the amount.
6. Recommendations involving the employment of additional personnel, and the reassignment of existing personnel, should include partial job descriptions of new positions or assignments.
7. Wherever feasible, the recommendation should include some statement of the time factor—when the recommendation should go into effect, for what period and when any change involved should be evaluated.

The Visiting Committee. The prospective visit of a group of educators from outside the school and, in some studies, from outside the district, is a focus of much planning, concern and even trepidation for the faculty of the school involved in self-study. The visit takes on such overriding importance that some educators would like to minimize or eliminate this aspect of the school evaluation. The review of a faculty's self-study by an external group is so characteristic, however, of evaluations of high schools, colleges and universities, and also of many elementary schools, that this review is likely here to stay. Furthermore, the review can be of major importance in school improvement if it is carefully planned, executed and followed up.

Local school districts usually have policies controlling the selection of visiting committee members. In our judgment, these policies should provide for selecting a committee of persons experienced in good middle school education, including at least one specialist in each area or section of the self-study schedule and also one or more generalists. It is also important to include persons with special interests in elementary and high school education to help in the troublesome problems of articulation of the middle school with the schools below and above. Otherwise usual criteria as to a balanced representation of the school population should assure an adequate committee.

The work of the visiting committee is detailed in the Manual Section of the *Evaluative Criteria,* and also well reflected in the reports of visiting committees available from exemplary middle schools. In general, regardless of the particular areas and sections under study, it is to be expected that the visiting committee will spend at least three days visiting the school, with some of this time devoted to meeting with school personnel and some to visiting classes and talking with students. Other time goes to meetings of the total committee and the various subcommittees, usually one for each major section of the self-study, and to the review of school materials and to the preparation of the committee report. Advance copies of the school self-study report and of various materials exhibiting the school program and operation are usually sent to the visiting committee members for study before the on-site visit.

The culmination of the visiting committee's work is the presentation of its report. In many instances, the visiting committee simply endorses or comments upon each section of the school self-study report and then adds other comments and/or recommendations; the report can be very brief if the endorsement-plus-comments route is followed. In other instances the visiting committee may produce a report almost as long as the original self-study report! In most instances there is some oral reporting to the administration and faculty of the school before the visit is concluded, with a written report following in due time.

Reports and Plans. For purposes of continuing evaluation and planning, it is essential that written reports be made at each stage of the self-study program. First, there is the report of the faculty self-study which should be and usually is the basis for the work of the visiting committee, and the follow-up locally by the school and district. We have found that these reports necessarily run into many pages if they follow the *Evaluative Criteria* or some other complete guide, as they should for local credibility and utility. This basic document becomes a very important part of the continuing archives and the plans of the school—available as a benchmark for comparison from time to time, and especially for subsequent self-studies, as required by districts every three, four or five years, and by accrediting agencies, usually for five years, with annual interim reports, or for ten years, with periodic interim reports.

Examination of many self-study reports leads us to recommend that the local school have a clear-cut organization for this report, not only by the major sections of the self-study but an internal organization of the sections that is easily followed by the writers and readers of the report. It is most disconcerting to read a self-study report that uses entirely different formats within its several sections. In general, the user of a self-study report wants to find in each section answers to these questions:

1. What is the role (or objectives) of this aspect of middle school education?
2. What evidence is available as to how well this role is being discharged (or these objectives realized)?
3. What factors seem to facilitate or hinder the achievement of this role (or these objectives)?
4. What plans or recommendations are made to improve the achievement of this role (or these objectives)?

As to the visiting committee report, we like the more succinct type that endorses or comments upon each self-study section and presents additional recommendations of the visiting committee. For example, a visiting committee report for the Amory, Mississippi, Middle School has for most sections of the self-study report these brief items: (A) commentary; (B) recommendations for school improvement; and (C) recommendations for meeting accreditation standards (generally none given since standards were met). A form used in the Jefferson County, Kentucky, middle school evaluations required for each section a rating, a listing of strengths and a statement of specific recommendations for further study by the visiting team.

Some districts publish multiple self-study and visiting team reports. For example, an evaluation report of the four middle schools of District 6/Weld County, Colorado, includes in one volume (166 mimeographed pages) data on the curriculum of the schools; a year-end summary by the principal and by the school advisory council; reports of opinion surveys of pupils, teachers and parents of the four middle schools; and also some data for the two junior high schools. In the Decatur, Alabama, Schools, studies were reported separately of the Oak Park and Brookhaven Middle Schools, but a general statement by the visiting committee covering both schools was included in each report.

Another written postevaluation report that may be prepared is the school's statement of recommendations or plans made as a result of the self-study and the visiting committee's evaluation. For example, the Alachua County, Florida, five-year review plan provides that the school respond within one month to each of the recommendations of the visiting committee, with a final document for each school evaluation to include: (1) the report of the school's self-study; (2) the visiting committee findings and recommendations; and (3) the school response. State and regional accreditation reports may include continued reports of progress made in compliance with recommendations of school evaluations, and plans for further improvement.

Long-Range Studies. A three-year study of the Brown Middle School in Hamilton County, Tennessee, is suggestive of studies with a longer range than the usual one-year self-study. A report of this study published by Middle Tennessee State University gives detailed information as to the hypotheses tested, the data gathered and the conclusions and recommendations made in the course of this study, which was supported by a Title III, ESEA, grant.[9] Aspects of this study included: teacher attendance, attitudes and turnover; student attendance, discipline, attitudes and achievement; report card/student progress changes; parent evaluation; dissemination of program information; use of consultants; curriculum development activities; and others.

A progress report of the Webster Transitional School of Cedarburg, Wisconsin, also includes data for three years.[10] This report includes descriptive material regarding the development of the instructional program including school and instructional organization, instruction and curriculum, supporting services and student effects in these categories: basic skills and academic concepts, independent learning, social skills and cultural understanding, self-discipline and responsibility, self-understanding and acceptance and opinion polls of students, visitors to the school, parents and teachers. Such reports should be of value not only to the schools and districts involved but to other middle schools interested in comprehensive evaluations as guides for continuing improvement.

Evaluation as Hypothesis Testing

In a section entitled as this one, eighteen hypotheses about middle school education were proposed in the evaluation chapter of *The Emergent Middle School* as some of the possible bases for significant studies of middle schools:

1. *Pupils in the middle school will become more self-directed learners than pupils in the control schools.*
2. *Pupils in the middle school will have fewer and/or less intense social and psychological problems than pupils in conventional schools.*
3. *Achievement of middle school pupils on standardized tests will equal or exceed that of pupils in conventional schools.*
4. *Middle school pupils will equal or exceed pupils in conventional schools on standard measures of physical fitness and health.*
5. *Pupils in the middle school will have more favorable attitudes toward school than will pupils in conventional schools.*
6. *Middle school pupils will hold more adequate "self concepts" than will pupils in the conventional schools.*
7. *Social acceptance among middle school pupils will be higher than among those in conventional schools.*
8. *The average daily attendance of middle school pupils will exceed the attendance of pupils in conventional schools.*
9. *Measures of creativity among middle school pupils will show an increase rather than a decrease during middle school years.*
10. *Middle school graduates will compile better academic records in ninth grade than will ninth-graders from the control schools.*
11. *Middle school graduates will drop out of senior high school less frequently than pupils who follow the traditional pattern.*
12. *Middle school teachers will more often use practices which experts generally recommend as superior.*

13. *Teachers in the middle school will experience a higher degree of professional ful-fillment and self-satisfaction than teachers in conventional schools.*
14. *Teachers in the middle school will utilize a greater variety of learning media than will teachers in conventional schools.*
15. *Teacher turnover will be lower in the middle school than in conventional schools.*
16. *Teachers in the middle school will be more open to change.*
17. *Patrons of the middle school will hold more positive attitudes toward objectives and procedures of the school than patrons of conventional schools.*
18. *Principals of experimental and control schools will have similar operating patterns within each school system.*[11]

To our knowledge, no school district has attempted to test all of these hypotheses, nor did the authors of *The Emergent Middle School* suggest such a large-scale evaluation in a single district. Note this suggestion, which seems still a very useful one school districts and state and regional, even national, groups might utilize:

Obviously, a thorough evaluation in which even the hypotheses to be listed in this section were tested would strain or be beyond the resources of most school systems. However, with state or federal help, a single system could give evidence on many or most of the hypotheses. It would be better, however, from the standpoints of both economy and sound research if a number of systems were to cooperate in testing these and perhaps additional hypotheses. If a dozen schools were involved, and if there were eighteen major hypotheses to be tested, then each school might test six of the eighteen. In this way, the opportunity to generalize results would be greatly increased, for each hypothesis would be tested four times in different schools.[12]

Many of these hypotheses have been at least partially tested singly or in some combination as self-studies, while other evaluations have collected and analyzed data relevant to the hypotheses. Some doctoral dissertations have used certain hypotheses for researching the effects of middle schools. The three-year study of the Brown School cited earlier in this chapter investigated many of the aspects concerned; the following hypotheses were posed and data collected and analyzed regarding them in this study:

1. *That teacher attendance will be equal to or greater than attendance in a junior high school.*
2. *That average daily attendance of middle school pupils will be equal to or greater than attendance of junior high school students.*
3. *That student discipline cases will be equal to or less than pupil discipline cases in a junior high school.*
4. *That parent attitudes will be equal to or move favorable than parent attitudes toward a junior high school.*
5. *That student attitudes will be equal to or more favorable than student attitudes in a junior high school.*
6. *That student achievement on standardized test scores will be equal to or better than student achievement test scores in a junior high school.*
7. *That former middle school student grade point averages in the first semester of high school will be equal to or better than grade point averages of students from junior high school.*

8. *That materials, activities, course and program development will be equal to or greater than that of a junior high school.*
9. *That program and school communications with the community, parents, feeder and receiver schools will be equal to or greater than that of a junior high school.*
10. *That teacher attitudes toward school organizational design, programs, and students will be equal to or more favorable than teacher attitudes in a junior high school.*
11. *That curriculum expansion and flexibility will allow equal or greater individual student choices in the learning process than student choices in the junior high schools.*[13]

Although statistical data were inadequate for generalization on some hypotheses, the comparisons of the Brown Middle School over the three-year period with the predecessor junior high school were favorable toward the middle school. The design of this study should be of interest not only to school districts wishing comprehensive, longitudinal evaluations but to research agencies and directors interested in comprehensive evaluations of the middle school.

Other Approaches to Middle School Evaluation

Several other approaches to evaluating a middle school that are recurrent in evaluation literature are briefly noted in this section.

Needs Assessment. Any needs assessment is a type of evaluation, and indeed any evaluation of a school yields needs assessments. The term is currently most frequently used to denote the process of identifying the discrepancy between where the program or program element under study is, and where the persons responsible wanted it to be. Thus a repeated needs assessment, identifying the discrepancy at successive periods, evaluates progress or lack thereof on the element(s) studied. Any of the evaluation approaches discussed or combinations thereof could be used in the needs assessment process. A needs assessment is in effect a diagnostic evaluation; repeated needs assessments yield formative evaluation data; and various needs assessments can constitute a summative evaluation, as these terms were defined earlier in this chapter.

This useful listing of steps in needs assessment efforts was published in the *Practitioner:*

Decide on which level to plan initially (class, grade, school district).
Select good instruments and processes.
Determine where you are at present.
Determine where you want to be.
Reconcile differences among participants involved in planning.
Identify priorities and select those on which action will be taken.[14]

This publication also described an interesting application of needs assessment processes:

The School Bonanza Game is another tool. It can be administered to students (Grades 4–12), parents, boards of education, and laymen, as well as school staff and faculty. Basically, each participant is given a hypothetical sum of money to invest in various school programs, such as the three R's or social studies. Players are forced to choose how their money is to be spent and then must rate the school (ranging from poor to great) on how well it is doing in each category. This process leads to a discussion of priorities among the participants. The game has been used inexpensively in many schools.[15]

Shadow Studies. A 1964 report of the Association for Supervision and Curriculum Development on *The Junior High School We Saw: One Day in the Eighth Grade* was influential in revealing the inadequacies of the junior high school program at that time and also a significant application of the shadow study technique. Skilled curriculum workers followed ("shadowed") for one day 102 eighth-grade students in 98 schools in 26 states, recording at ten-minute intervals the situation in which each student was working. Such observations can now be more systematically made with observational procedures more recently developed. For evaluation of a particular school it is of course important to have the shadowing done on a valid sampling basis and by trained observers using relatively identical procedures. This procedure can be used alone for a specific program element evaluation, or in combination with other procedures for comprehensive evaluation purposes. Use of the technique for more generalizable purposes requires district, state or national samples, along the ASCD 1964 lines.[16]

Employment of Evaluators. Consultants are frequently employed from other school districts, universities, professional and/or commercial organizations to assist in various phases of evaluation involving local school and district personnel, and sometimes unpaid personnel from outside. They may also be employed to do the total evaluation job for particular purposes.[17] The objectivity of the outside evaluator as well as the expertise presumably available support this practice, although there is the significant problem of how well school personnel will accept results and implement changes indicated from evaluations in which they have not been involved. We ourselves feel that internal evaluations, aided by consultants and other participants from outside, are most likely to effect continuing improvement.

Follow-Up Studies. Follow-up studies of high school and college graduates have been very valuable evaluation processes. Although generally somewhat more casual, follow-up conferences and reports of former middle school students' progress and behavior in the high schools are also used, and could be used more effectively for school evaluation and especially in planning for improved continuity of educational progress. For example, detailed data from the ninth grade as to former middle school students' status in continued learning skills such as use of library tools could influence instruction in these skills in both the middle and high school. Repeated assessment can yield information as to the results of changes made. Experimental studies using experimental and control groups from different schools or having different instructional systems can be very helpful in providing data for evaluating curriculum and instructional practices.

Annual Reports. The annual report is not an evaluation, of course, but it is an effective way of reporting evaluative data to the public. For example, an annual report of the Spring Hill Middle School in High Springs, Florida, reported for 1977–78 mental and achievement test score percentages within broad ranges: achievement of fifth- and eighth-grade students by percentages on each minimum performance standard, on the Florida Statewide Assessment Test; student attitude toward school from a statewide test; review team findings and recommendations in the self-study program; and the school enrollment and school budget. Other annual reports examined include similar data as available, and also results of opinion polls, and general statements as to school achievements, problems and plans.

Comprehensive Evaluations. Earlier citations of long-term evaluation studies illustrated the use of combination procedures to yield continuing formative data as well as a summative profile on an individual school. Most efforts at significant school evaluations do use combination procedures including feedback of various types, opinion polls, self-study programs, student progress tests and others. For example, a report from the Alief, Texas, Independent School District for 1978–79, on Management Objectives included detailed objectives for the total school district and included a wide variety of data for the elementary, middle and high school levels on many objectives. Note an excerpt from the report on the objective that the "Student will feel a more personalized relationship with teachers and other employees:"

1. 75% of High School students, 80% of Middle School students, and 90% of the Elementary students will indicate that most teachers take an interest in them (1977–78: H.S. 74%; M.S. 74%; Elem. 92%)
2. 70% of High School students, 75% of the Middle School students, and 90% of the Elementary School students will indicate that they can talk with at least one teacher on a personal basis, (1977–78: H.S. 68%; M.S. 72%; Elem. 87%)
3. 85% of High School students, 85% of Middle School Students, and 90% of the Elementary School students will indicate that teachers and support staff are courteous, friendly, and respectful to them. (1977–78: H.S. 67%; M.S. 70%; Elem. 88%.)

This report also includes data regarding students' attitudes toward themselves and school, and toward other students and student decision making and behavior, the provision of reports of student achievement and progress and plans for evaluation and reports thereof for all aspects of the school program and support elements.

Evaluating the Middle School Movement

Although statements are frequently made in journals and speeches about the success or failure of the middle school movement, there really are few comprehensive data available to support such statements. As we noted in chapter 1, it is equally impossible and unwise to make any categorical assessment of the junior high school. Indeed we know of no comprehensive study justifying categorical statements as to the efficacy of any one pattern of school unit organization, elementary, secondary or otherwise. For one reason, it is very difficult if not impossible to control the other variables in experimental comparisons of different school organizations. Nevertheless the middle school movement is a sufficient departure from the prior 8-4 and 6-3-3 school organizations as to need such critical examination if possible.

Several types of studies are possible, and a few have been attempted. Comparisons of the status of middle schools with regard to practices relevant to the goals of the movement can be made at different periods. We reviewed in chapter 1 the several surveys that showed the numerical growth of middle schools, and through two of them (Alexander, 1967–68, and Brooks, 1977–78) using some identical questions, giving some comparative data regarding program and organizational features of the middle schools.[18] In addition to such repeated benchmark surveys, national collection and publication of local research studies and school evaluations can help to provide "state of the art" information and perhaps stimulate additional studies in neglected and critical areas.[19] Also, statewide studies sponsored by leagues of middle schools or state agencies are useful as surveys and also comparisons of different school organizations in the state.[20] It also seems desirable for networks or other organizations of middle schools to design, with appropriate consultant and financial help, large-scale studies seeking to control variables sufficiently to secure valid answers as to the relative effectiveness of middle school and other grade-age organizations serving the population of children moving from childhood to adolescence. Even more desirable, we believe, are studies minimizing the competitive nature of such organizations and maximizing the significant questions of what program and other features of their schools produce most effectively the results sought in student learning and behavior.[21] When and if basic research or full school evaluations can tell us how best to organize a school and provide a program therein that will tend to produce students with the most interests and skills in continued learning, then we can have full confidence in such a school. Our own guess is that such comprehensive and conclusive research studies and findings are unlikely, and that we had best work for careful evaluations in every middle school, with as much attention through states, districts and organizations as possible to the broader publications and approaches herein discussed.

ADDITIONAL SUGGESTIONS FOR FURTHER STUDY

A. Books
Association for Supervision and Curriculum Development, *The Middle School We Need*. Washington, D.C.: The Association, 1975.
Glasser, William, *Schools Without Failure*. New York: Harper and Row, 1969.

Popper, Samuel H., *The American Middle School, An Organizational Analysis.* Waltham, Massachusetts: Blaisdell Publishing Company, 1967.

B. Periodicals

"Competency in Education," *The High School Journal,* 62, 157–204 (January 1979, entire issue).

Gatewood, Thomas E., "What Research Says About the Junior High Versus the Middle School," *North Central Association Quarterly,* 46, 264–276 (Fall 1971).

Georgiady, Nicholas P. and Romano, Louis G., "Do You Have a Middle School?" *Educational Leadership,* 31, 238–41 (December 1973).

Scarborough, Gerald E., "Middle School Students Respond," *Middle School Journal,* 8, 10–1, 15 (November 1977).

Stewart, William J., "What Causes a Middle School to be Ineffective," *Clearing House,* 49, 23–5 (September 1975).

Vars, Gordon F., "Student Evaluation in the Middle School: A Second Report," *Clearing House,* 49, 244–5 (February 1976).

Wiles, Jon, "The Emerging Design of Middle School Evaluation," *Middle School Journal,* 9, 3, 18–9 (February 1978).

Wilson, Laval S., "Can An Open Space Middle School Meet the Educational Needs of Minority Youngsters?" *The Journal of Negro Education,* 44, 368–76 (Summer 1975).

C. ERIC

McAndrews, J. Briggs, "Middle School Evaluation: Format, Case History and Perspective," a Paper Presented at the Annual Meeting of the American Educational Research Association. New York, New York, Bethlehem Central School District, Delmar, New York, 1977. (ERIC No. ED 138 615)

D. Dissertations and Dissertation Abstracts

Blake, Michael F., "An Assessment of Practices for the Implementation of the Individualization Function in Connecticut Middle Schools," *Dissertation Abstracts,* 36 (January 1976) 4138-A.

Canning, John Aloysius, "A Comparative Study of Selected Growth Objectives of Sixth Graders in a New Middle School with Sixth Graders in Elementary Self-Contained Classrooms," *Dissertation Abstracts,* 34 (May 1974) 6862-A.

Case, David A., "A Comparative Study of Fifth Graders in a New Middle School with Fifth Graders in Elementary Self-Contained Classrooms," Unpublished doctoral dissertation, The University of Florida, 1970.

Mooney, Patrick F., "A Comparative Study of Achievement and Attendance of 10–14 Year Olds in a Middle School and in Other School Organizations," Unpublished doctoral dissertation, The University of Florida, 1970.

Powell, William Walter, "The Development of Evaluative Criteria for a Middle School," *Dissertation Abstracts,* 35 (March 1975) 5743-A.

Raymer, Joe Tate, "A Study to Identify Middle Schools and to Determine the Current Level of Implementation of Eighteen Basic Middle School Characteristics in Selected United States and Michigan Schools," *Dissertation Abstracts,* 35 (March 1975) 5801-A.

Rosenau, Alan E., "A Comparative Study of Middle School Practices Recommended in Current Literature and in Practices of Selected Middle Schools," *Dissertation Abstracts,* 36 (November 1975) 2690-A.

Swezig, Grover Wayne, "Middle School Certification: A Rationale and Justification," *Dissertation Abstracts,* 37 (November 1976) 2800-A.

Trauschke, Edward M., Jr., "An Evaluation of a Middle School by a Comparison of the Achievement, Attitudes and Self-Concept of Students in a Middle School with Students in Other School Organizations," Unpublished doctoral dissertation, The University of Florida, 1970.

Vance, Paul Lawrence, "Factors Related to Successful Educational Innovation in Selected Middle Schools in Philadelphia, Pennsylvania," *Dissertation Abstracts,* 36 (July 1975) 86-A.

White, James William, Sr., "Differences Between Open and Traditional Elementary Students on Selected Characteristics and Changes in Same Characteristics After Six Months in a Middle School," *Dissertation Abstracts,* 34 (April 1974) 6526-A.

Williams, Edward Michael, "An Assessment of the 'Junior High School/Middle School Evaluative Criteria,'" *Dissertation Abstracts,* 37 (February 1977) 5023-A.

FOOTNOTES

1. See Benjamin S. Bloom, J. Thomas Hastings, and George F. Madaus, *Handbook on Formative and Summative Evaluation of Student Learning* (New York: McGraw-Hill Book Company, Inc., 1971), especially Chapters 4–6, for extended treatment of these types.

2. See J. Galen Saylor, William M. Alexander, and Arthur J. Lewis, *Curriculum Planning: For Better Teaching and Learning* (New York: Holt, Rinehart & Winston, Inc., 1981), Chapter 7. For detailed descriptions of the three newer models, also see: (1) Decision Making Model—Phi Delta Kappa National Study Committee on Evaluation, Daniel Stufflebeam, chairman, *Educational Evaluation and Decision Making* (Itasca, Ill.: R. E. Peacock Publishers, Inc., 1971); (2) Goal-Free Evaluation Model—David Hamilton, David Jenkins, Christine King, Barry MacDonald, and Malcolm Parlett (eds.), *Beyond the Numbers Game: A Reader in Educational Evaluation* (London: Macmillan Education Limited, 1977), pp. 123–142; and (3) Responsive Model—Robert Stake, "Language, Rationality and Assessment," in Walcott H. Beatty (ed), *Improving Educational Assessment and an Inventory of Measures of Affective Behavior* (Washington, D.C.: Association for Supervision and Curriculum Development, 1969).

3. Hollis L. Caswell, "Persistent Curriculum Problems," *Educational Forum,* 43, 100–101 (November 1978).

4. Eugene J. Webb, Donald T. Campbell, Richard D. Schwartz, and Lee Sechrest, *Unobtrusive Measures: Nonreactive Research in the Social Sciences* (Skokie, Ill.: Rand McNally and Company, 1966).

5. Webb, Campbell, Schwartz, and Sechrest, p. 1.

6. William C. Miller, "Unobtrusive Measures Can Help in Assessing Growth," *Educational Leadership,* 35, 264–269 (January 1978).

7. School Board of Alachua County, *Five-Year Review: Self-Study Packet for Elementary and Middle Schools,* 1979–80 (Gainesville, Florida: The Board, 1979.)

8. National Study of School Evaluation, *Junior High School/Middle School Evaluative Criteria: A Guide for School Improvement* (Arlington, Virginia: The Study, 1979.)

9. Jerry C. McGee, Robert Krajewski, and Earl E. Keese, *A Three-Year Study of Brown Middle School, 1974–77* (Murfreesboro, Tennessee: Middle Tennessee State University, Faculty Research Committee, November 1977). Also see for

a brief summary of this study, Jerry C. McGee and Robert J. Krajewski, "Middle School Effectiveness: A Three Year Study," *Middle School Journal*, 10, 16–17 (November 1979).

10. Cedarburg School District, *Webster Transitional School: Three Year Progress Report* (Cedarburg, Wisconsin: The District, June 1977).

11. William M. Alexander, Emmett L. Williams, Mary Compton, Vynce A. Hines, Dan Prescott, and Ronald Kealy, *The Emergent Middle School*, 2nd, enl. ed. (New York: Holt, Rinehart & Winston, Inc., 1969), pp. 139–145.

12. *The Emergent Middle School*, p. 139.

13. McGee, Krajewski, and Keese, p. 2.

14. National Association of Secondary School Principals, "Taking a New Look at Needs Assessment," *The Practitioner*, 4, 3 (December 1977).

15. National Association of Secondary School Principals, p. 5. Further information about the Bonanza Game can be secured from Professor David Mullen, College of Education, University of Georgia, Athens, Georgia, 30602.

16. See John H. Lounsbury and Jean V. Marani, *The Junior High School We Saw: One Day in the Eighth Grade* (Washington, D.C.: Association for Supervision and Curriculum Development, 1964).

17. See National Association of Secondary School Principals, "Program Evaluation . . . Survival of, by, and for the Fittest," *The Practitioner*, 6, 4–6 (December 1979) for a discussion of the qualifications and schedule of activities of evaluators. This bulletin also discussed models and examples of program evaluation.

18. See William M. Alexander, "How Fares the Middle School Movement?" *Middle School Journal*, 9, 3 and 19–21 (August 1978), for an analysis of these surveys and a commentary on the title question.

19. See, for an example, Heather Sidor Doob, *Summary of Research on Middle Schools, Research Brief* (Arlington, Virginia: Educational Research Service, Inc., 1975). This report summarizes nineteen studies, with their findings organized in sections on student achievement and attendance, student self-concept and attitude, teacher and parent attitude, and administration, curriculum, staffing and facilities.

20. See, for example, Paul S. George and Thomas Erb, *A Comparative Study of Middle Schools and Junior High Schools in the State of Florida* (Gainesville, Florida: Florida League of Middle Schools, Spring 1975).

21. See Carol Kehr Tittle, "Evaluative Studies," Chapter XVI in Mauritz Johnson, Ed., *Toward Adolescence: The Middle School Years*, Seventy-Ninth Yearbook of the National Society for the Study of Education, Part I (Chicago: University of Chicago Press, 1980), for a classification and review of various types of evaluative studies that can be useful in decision making about middle school programs.

Epilogue

The crystal ball in which the authors gaze as *The Exemplary Middle School* goes to press shows the middle school as depicted in this book a very significant and influential unit of schooling in the twenty-first century. In 1960, one of the authors was searching for an educational unit and program in the middle of the school ladder that would bring about the badly needed continuity of education that previous units had not provided. Our dream of a widely provided, student-focused bridge school that would effectively tie together our best elementary and secondary education units has become a reality in the exemplary middle school. For at least twenty years now educators have been working to develop this school, and for fifty years earlier the junior high school had been developed in part for the same purpose. The middle school is now widely provided, and we believe it is becoming more student focused than its predecessor units. We believe the new school in the middle will be an increasingly effective unit in the learning society of the future seen in our crystal ball.

For despite all the problems that beset our society and our schools in the 1980's, there is much reason to believe that this and future decades will be characterized by ever growing demands for education. Whether schools will continue to be the major providers of education is challenged by current criticisms of schooling and its costs, and by the potential educative uses of modern technology. We ourselves cannot see a really functioning learning society, one in which all individuals are interested in continuing their education, that does not use schools at various connected levels to teach the skills of continued learning and to develop the interests in education that fuel lifelong learning. In this society learning is lifewide as well as lifelong, since the media, the home, the community and its institutions must all work together in providing educational opportunities.

The school in the middle, connecting elementary and secondary education and, more importantly, childhood and adolescence, is the most critical unit in the educational design for continuous educational progress. The middle school can help its students move as smoothly and uninterruptedly as possible through the trauma of puberty, and from the relatively protected environment of the elementary school to the sophisticated and regimented high school setting. It must deal with a very heterogeneous population including some who do not experience puberty as early or perhaps as late as the middle school, and including children whose home and elementary education backgrounds vary widely. This school in the middle has the potential of turning on or off the interests in learning which help students become self-directed. It also has great opportunity to influence the development of valuing processes and moral reasoning sorely needed to deal with the conflicts and tensions to which the emerging adolescent will be increasingly subjected.

We believe that the educators and citizens who have brought about the widespread movement since 1960 toward the middle school organization will help it succeed. Already there are the exemplary middle schools which we have cited very frequently in this book. We now know that it is possible to put into practice the essential characteristics that are associated with fundamental goals of middle school education. We now have consensus on what these characteristics are, and all middle schools, not just the exemplary ones, must implement them more widely and fully.

In this book the authors have fully identified these characteristics of exemplary middle schools. We stated them in chapter 1 and in each successive chapter we have described and illustrated in detail how one or more of the twelve characteristics could be and indeed have been put into practice. We left to this Eiplogue comprehensive suggestions for implementation of the final characteristic: "Participation with other schools and with community groups in the continuing study of the middle school population and of society as a whole, to be responsive to changing needs and conditions of the future." Our suggestions on this point are summarized in the following paragraphs.

Maintain Vertical and Horizontal Articulation of Educational Programs

Although somewhat out of usage now, the terms "horizontal" and "vertical articulation" are quite descriptive, we think, of the joining together of educational units and agencies essential to maintenance of the continuity, flexibility and scope educational opportunities must demonstrate in the learning society ahead. We embrace the predictions that learning will become the major characteristic of our society with its constant change and need for adaptation, and that lifelong learning needs will dictate the many programs of education offered by communities, industries, government and other major social elements. But with the burgeoning number of educational programs, and the continuing interest and activities of home, school, church and community in the whole educational enterprise, the classification, relationship, financing, social approval, availability and cooperation of all these programs and units become exceedingly important social agenda.

As we see it, such relatively informal structures as we describe in the next section should suffice for the horizontal articulation of educational agencies and units and programs aimed toward the same or similar populations. The vertical articulation of units serving different levels of education requires clear-cut organizations for curriculum planning and other purposes described in chapter 3 and summarized later here.

The middle school is a key unit in both types of articulation. Serving as it does the population in transition from childhood to adolescence, the middle school is in a critical position related to home, church, social agencies and community forces in general concerned with such urgent problems of growing up as valuing processes, moral responsibility, sexual awareness and behavior, teen-age pregnancies, teen-age vandalism and violence and others. The middle school faculty and parents may be the pivotal group to organize and maintain a continuing study of the characteristics and needs of this population of middle school age children, and to bring about community action programs for children and youth. As to vertical articulation, the middle school is in the middle and thus able to connect with programs both below and above, and to ensure continuous educational progess. More than any other level the middle school simply cannot work effectively at its own level only, for middle school personnel must be aware of prior and subsequent programs that condition the present and future learning of their students.

Organize Community-Wide Planning of Education

Coordination and cooperation of the large number of agencies providing education in a community is a Herculean challenge. Who can bring together representatives of home, schools, churches, social agencies, community museums, libraries, parks, media, youth organizations, business and industry to plan and execute educational programs that will complement and not conflict? Undoubtedly the answer will not be the same in each community. We ourselves would like to think that the school organization could be the force that first brings together these groups, but we have to recognize that some school organizations lack the leadership and/or the power to get the job done.

Initially the task may be to identify and explore needs for cooperative educational programs. Reading, for example, is an area in which home, the media and schools can and do cooperate. Vocational education has been a conspicuous example of cooperation of business, industry, government and schools. Critical problems in today's and probably tomorrow's society that could be greatly helped by united, articulated programs of education include these; sex education, law enforcement, parenting, leisure time activities, economic education, energy conservation, aesthetic appreciation, political responsibilities. As any of these or other problems and needs appear significant in the local community, middle school or other school people may well take the lead in interesting influential members of the community to organize study and planning groups. Ultimately from such study and planning should come action program suggestions for all concerned educational units, with some proposals as to a continuing organization for guiding and monitoring the program.

Maintain Vertical Planning of School Programs

The basic purpose of the middle school as a transitional unit is vitiated when its program is planned in isolation from the units the middle school precedes and follows. Although vertical curriculum planning is essential in the school districts for all levels, the middle school curriculum is unhinged at both ends when it is not planned in relation to the elementary and high school curriculum. We do not mean that the curriculum plan should be so fixed and complete that teachers are unable to fit plans to their students; we do mean that the alternatives envisioned in the curriculum plan are sufficient to help teachers find and adapt plans that will recognize past plans and be relevant to their students now and also to the needs of these students as they continue their educational careers.

We have illustrated in this text, especially in chapters 2 and 3, several planning organizations designed to provide vertical articulation. We would especially emphasize here the necessity, first, of an organization in the public school district which brings together on a continuing basis representatives of elementary, middle and high schools to assess common needs, and develop related proposals and plans. Second, there is need in the district for vertical curriculum planning of the curriculum areas which extend over more than one level, for example, all of the major areas of language arts, mathematics, science, social studies and health and physical education. Third, current problem areas such as energy conservation need study for development and placement of appropriate units of instruction in the curriculum plan, and this may require the designation of special task forces for the specific problems involved.

Study Education, Society and the Future

Various individuals and organizations have developed impressive studies of the future, both in general and in education, in recent years.[1] We can hope that such studies and reports will continue, and that they are widely used as sources for local studies and planning operations. The need for considered attention to alternative futures and to the educational implications of knowledge and predictions about the future, suggests that our professional organizations and state and national educational organizations should give major emphasis to future planning and education. Middle school personnel may well press their National Middle School Association, the state leagues and other organizations, and other professional organizations to push forward with such studies. One excellent source of this type is the 1980 Yearbook (Part I) of the National Society for the Study of Education, *Toward Adolescence: The Middle School Years*. This volume presents much pertinent data regarding children in the middle school years and the forces which affect their development. It examines present efforts to intervene in their lives and the needs for continued research. The concluding statement of the editor is very pertinent to this Epilogue:

> The school has its distinctive functions and problems, but both are intertwined with those of other agencies. Teachers, counselors, and administrators in middle and junior high schools should take the lead in creating in every locality in the country a mechanism for coordinated community action in behalf of their clientele. By the year 2000, we should not only have learned more and acted wisely, but have found a way of working together.[2]

Make Self-Directed Learning the Central Goal

We believe that the fulfillment of hopes for an effective school in the middle can come only as the goals for this school are clearly defined and their achievement closely monitored. A goal we see as paramount for the future learning society is the development of the self-directed learner truly capable of and interested in lifelong learning. As stressed by the 1979 Yearbook of the Association for Supervision and Curriculum Development, the curriculum plan for lifelong learning must be deliberate: "A lifelong curriculum needs to be imbued with intentionality well beyond anything ever undertaken by the traditional public school. . . . If the public schools are to be vehicles for lifelong learning, then they must be radically reconceptualized."[3]

As we have already noted, the school in the middle is in a highly critical position for the teaching of skills and development of attitudes for continued learning. It is in these years that many learners simply lose interest in school learning and indeed in learning outside school that requires serious intellectual effort. We believe our concept of a school in the middle is the reconceptualization called for in the foregoing quotation (the omitted sentences questioned very critically the potential of the public school), but we must emphasize that the traditional program in the three Rs is not enough to develop the lifelong learners needed today and tomorrow. Learning processes must be made more exciting, more rewarding, more central. Independent study must be introduced as early as possible, with ever widening possibilities to invite and hold the interested student. The awards for middle schoolers should increasingly be for the demonstration of learning skill and interest rather than just athletic and other performance skills and interests of limited lifelong use.

Utilize Educational Resources Fully

In many school districts schools in the middle have developed effective programs of utilizing community and technological resources. By virtue of their position in the middle they have been able to affect practice above and below. But the learning society we anticipate in the future will require far more widespread use of the almost unlimited resources available in our communities. People constitute the primary resource, and the ability of school leaders to inventory and utilize the specialized resources of people in their communities becomes a major qualification for school leadership. With increased leisure time and increased specialization of workers, a great variety of abilities and interests are available to be tapped for resource leaders, volunteer teachers, field trip conductors and so forth.

Audiovisual resources have been utilized widely in their post-World War II heyday, and we can and should expect to see their continued and wiser use. As we noted earlier, television is an area for study and expansion. Current knowledge about its widespread use in the home by school children is much more common than information about its use in school and about effective usage of out-of-school viewing for school-related learning. We have here a tremendous educational aid that we do not use deliberately for educational purposes. It is generally expected that the computer will also come into much wider use for educational purposes; we have already emphasized the possibilities of community planning for the use of this and other major educational resources.

And so, we believe that the second twenty years of the middle school movement, roughly 1980 to 2000, will see a continuing expansion of this school unit with much greater effort in local communities to make the middle unit an effective, dynamic link for continuous educational progress. We hope that in these years, unlike the half century, 1910 to 1960, which saw the expansion of the junior high school to a dominant position, public education below the college will become a unitary program successfully seeking the general and full development of lifelong learners. If this millenium comes, the search for an effective school in the middle will have ended. Let us hope!

FOOTNOTES

1. See as significant examples: Alvin Toffler, *Future Shock* (New York: Bantam Books, 1970); Alvin Toffler, ed., *Learning for Tomorrow: The Role of the Future in Education* (New York: Vintage Books, 1974); Andrew A. Spekke, ed., *The Next 25 Years: Crisis and Opportunity* (Washington, D.C.: World Future Society, 1975); Harold G. Shane, *Curriculum Change Toward the 21st Century* (Washington, D.C.: National Education Association, 1977); Louis Rubin, ed., *Education Reform for a Changing Society: Anticipating Tomorrow's Schools*

(Boston: Allyn and Bacon, Inc., 1978); Peter H. Wagschal, ed., *Learning Tomor-rows: Commentaries on the Future of Education* (New York: Praeger Special Studies, 1979).

2. Mauritz Johnson, "Tasks for the School in the Middle," Chapter XVII in Maur-tiz Johnson, ed. *Toward Adolescence: The Middle School Years*. Seventy-ninth Yearbook of the National Society for the Study of Education, Part I, (Chicago: University of Chicago Press, 1980), p. 318.

3. Norman V. Overly, Chairman and Editor, *Lifelong Learning: A Human Agenda*, 1979 Yearbook of the Association for Supervision and Curriculum Development (Alexandria, Va.: The Association, 1979), p. 55.

Basic Information about Selected Exemplary Middle Schools

The schools listed in this Appendix are those providing the authors materials cited in the text, and later also responding to our request in early 1980 for the specific information summarized in this Appendix. Since some schools cited did not supply the latter information, the authors were unable, regrettably, to include them in this list.

School Name/Address	Grades	Enrollment	Principal
Brookhaven Middle 1300 Fifth Ave., S.W. Decatur, AL 35601	6-8	1055	Wade Webster

Interdisciplinary teams, daily homebase, three subschools, open space, student council each subschool, intramurals.

Oak Park Middle 16th Ave., S.E. Decatur, AL 35601	6-8	925	Nell Clem

Interdisciplinary teams, homebase, open space, flexible schedule, principal's advisory council shares in decision making, minicourses.

Beverlye Middle 427 S. Beverlye Rd. Dothan, AL 36301	6-8	630	James Daniels

Three-teacher teams; advisor/advisee program emphasizing values clarification; flexible schedule including rotating time for team planning; student forum for student involvement in school policy.

Carver Middle School 801 E. North St. Dothan, AL 36303	6-8	570	Phillip C. Hardy

Carver Middle School was built as a high school in 1965. It was changed to a junior high school in 1968 and then to a middle school in 1978. Six interdisciplinary teams; grade level school within a school; advisor/advisee program; flexible block schedule; team planning time; approved for accreditation by Southern Association of Colleges and Schools.

Girard Middle School 600 Girard Ave. Dothan, AL 36303	6-8	593	John B. Roland

Six interdisciplinary teams; grade level school within a school; advisor/advisee program; flexible block schedule; team planning time; approved for accreditation by Southern Association of Colleges and Schools.

School Name/Address	Grades	Enrollment	Principal
Honeysuckle Middle School 1407 Honeysuckle Rd. Dothan, AL 36301	6-8	620	Ronald Cox

Six interdisciplinary teams; grade level school-within-a-school; advisor/advisee program; flexible block schedule; team planning time; approved for accreditation by Southern Association of Colleges and Schools.

Montgomery Middle 1570 Melody Lane El Cajon, CA 92021	6-8	934	Leo E. Tuck

Grade 6 students have three periods daily with one teacher, grades 7 and 8 two; same homeroom teacher three years; flexible space; reading and math labs; mainstreaming.

Twin Peaks Middle 14640 Tierra Bonita Rd. Toway, CA 92064	6-8	1160	E. Robert Flood

Grade 6 students in basic elementary pattern, with grade 7 and 8 double-period block; reading priority with twenty minutes daily for all; extensive parent involvement.

Aurora West Middle 10100 E. 13th Ave. Aurora, CO 80010	6-8	533	Cecil A. Matthews

Interdisciplinary team teaching; advisor/advisee system with daily advisory group meetings; annual surveys of opinion of parents, teachers and students.

Brentwood Middle 2600 24th Ave. Greeley, CO 80631	6-7	400	Larry A. Irwin

Team teaching; multiage grouping; class meeting format for group counseling; annual opinion polls of parents, students, teachers.

Goddard Junior High School 3800 W. Berry Ave. Littleton, CO 80123	7-9	680	William E. Stradley

Three-teacher teams of at least three teachers and aids, flexible scheduling (continuous progress), students moved from level to level (up or down) as performance merits, ungraded classes (basic through honors), CAYC (Community As Your Classroom)—a regularly scheduled class, use of parents as resource instructors.

School Name/Address	Grades	Enrollment	Principal
Mebane Middle Rt. 1, Box 4 Alachua, FL 32615	5-8	519	Crystal Compton

Interdisciplinary teaming with multiage grouping; daily thirty-minute period for advisor-advisee activities; annual comprehensive planning with parent opinion polls and reports to parents.

North Marion Middle Rt. 1, Box 192 Citra, FL 32627	6-8	1065	William Caton

Two-teacher teams, grade 6, and four-teacher, grades 7 and 8; career education emphasis; small group guidance program operated by special scheduling of physical education.

Lincoln Middle 1001 S.E. 12th St. Gainesville, FL 32601	6-8	930	John P. Spindler

Interdisciplinary team organization with multiage grouping; extensive, changing list of exploratories; advisor/advisee groups meeting twenty-five minutes daily; adaptation of older building; annual evaluation activities; extensive use in policy making of Program Improvement Council, School Advisory Council, and Student Advisory Council.

Fort Clarke Middle 9301 N.W. 23rd Ave. Gainesville, FL 32605	6-8	950	William Cake

Grade level interdisciplinary teams; team budgeting; open space; well-designed flexible master schedule.

Spring Hill Middle Box 907 High Springs, FL 32643	5-8	325	Thomas Diedeman

Extensive interdisciplinary team organization; developmental age grouping; block schedule; advisory group program in which all instructional personnel participate; extensive use of Instructional Improvement Committee (IIC), Student-Faculty Planning Committee, Meeters and Greeters Group, and a Citizens Advisory Group.

Hobbs Middle 309 Glover Lane Milton, FL 32570	6-8	518	Billy W. Helms

Interdisciplinary grade level teams, within which smaller teams function by subject areas; daily team planning time; activity committee plans a special activity every month; active student council.

School Name/Address	Grades	Enrollment	Principal
Azalea Middle 7855 22nd Ave. N. St. Petersburg, FL 33710	6-8	900	Scotty East

Five-teacher teams in the sixth grade, separate reading and language arts; four-teacher teams in seventh and eighth grades; teams grouped homogeneously by ability in reading and math; homebase time; modular schedule with twenty-six mods; special interest period every other day; extensive evaluation of their first three years; house concept assignment for guidance and administrators.

Stuart Middle 575 Georgia Ave. Stuart, FL 33494	6-8	1097	W.E. George

Each grade divided into teams; language arts-social studies, and science-math; partially open space, part conventional; eight-period day, a two-period block for math-science, and a three-period block for language arts-social studies.

Griffin Middle 4010 King Springs Rd. Smyrna, GA 30080	6-8	1000	Bill Hood

Teachers organized in three-teacher teams, three teams per grade level in academics; exploratory team includes art, business, home economics, industrial arts, music (general and instrumental), physical education and speech-drama; each team has 100 minutes of planning time per day; teams schedule everything but planning time and lunch; flexible open-pod style plant; commons area for each pod serves as minicafeteria for grade level lunch.

Tipton Middle 400 E. 6th St. Tipton, IA 52772	5-8	325	Gerald Ferguson

Grades 5 and 6 are only partially self-contained with students spending half of the day with their homeroom teachers; homebase guidance; seven-period day; five-year plan for curriculum evaluation stressing a different area of the curriculum each year; student community projects.

Noe Middle 121 W. Lee St. Louisville, KY 40200	6-8	950	Terry Brooks

Interdisciplinary teams; multiage grouping adopted one team at a time over three-year period; exploratory minicourses offered as part of academic team; twenty-five minute advisor-advisee class daily, done as a part of the team schedule; open space; closed circuit television station; community

School Name/Address	Grades	Enrollment	Principal

education program from 2:00 until 10:00 daily; part of the University of Louisville Educational Park.

| White Brook Middle
200 Park St.
Easthampton, MA 01027 | 5-8 | 815 | Michael J. McNamara |

Open classroom design with two-, three- and four-person team teaching.

| Aberdeen Middle
111 Mt. Royal Ave.
Aberdeen, MD 21001 | 6-8 | 1117 | Shirley J. Rose |

Large teams of 200 students served by six language arts-social studies teachers, three mathematics, three science, one language arts special studies, one language arts/math resource teacher, a reading specialist and appropriate unified arts and physical education teachers; curriculum features daily period devoted to "functional enrichment skills" including logic, budgeting, map skills, drug education, etc.; semiopen space; Team Council and School Curriculum Committee.

| Owen Brown Middle
6700 Cradlerock Way
Columbia, MD 21055 | 6-8 | 549 | Donald J. Bell |

Interdisciplinary team organization; heterogeneous grouping of students; French; student tutor/aide program; seven-period day; monthly newsletter to parents; Town Council student government organized through social studies.

| Esperanza Middle
201 Maple Rd.
Lexington Park, MD 20653 | 6-8 | 603 | George Kirby, III |

Interdisciplinary team organization; common planning time; grade level teams grouped by teams according to determined needs of students; gifted and talented reading seminar; independent study; every student has one half hour of supervised study, activity or intramural period each day.

| MacDonald Middle
1601 Burcham Dr.
E. Lansing, MI 48823 | 6-8 | 540 | Sal diFranco |

Interdisciplinary team by grade level; one multigraded 6 to 8 bilingual team; intramural sports, no interscholastic; school-community coordinator to maintain communication between less affluent homes and the school; folding walls; swimming pool; learning assistance team helps teachers with low achieving students.

School Name/Address	Grades	Enrollment	Principal
Graveraet Middle 611 N. Front St. Marquette, MI 49855	6-8	430	John Tuttle

Interdisciplinary team organization by grade level; exceptionally diverse exploratory program; noon-hour intramural program; advisory-advisee program in teams; block schedule; "flex" program allows all the students to elect a special interest area three times every two weeks; regular parent-teacher conferences.

Marshall Middle 100 E. Green St. Marshall, MI 49068	5-8	865	Brad Haines

Interdisciplinary team organization by grade level; grades 5 and 6 designed as two-year programs; alternative open classroom open to seventh graders; ability grouping in reading; old high school in four separate buildings; block schedule.

Marshall Middle 207 N. 4th St. Marshall, MN 56258	6-8	429	Norman Olson

Interdisciplinary team organization combined with subject area specialization; each teacher has a multiaged group of sixteen to eighteen advisees who stay with the advisor for three years; most students have one period of independent study daily; active parent council.

Amory Middle Box 426 Amory, MS 38821	5-8	595	Dexter Montgomery

Cooperative teaching in departmentalized grade level groups; ability grouping separately for each subject; advisor-advisee program; six-period day.

Nipher Middle 700 S. Kirkwood Rd. Kirkwood, MO 63122	6-8	601	Tom Moeller

Interdisciplinary team organization; sizes of teams vary with grade level; one multiage team; all teams heterogeneously grouped with options for grouping within the team; homebase through team structure; block schedule in fifteen mods; old building; gifted program.

C.L. Jones Middle 520 W. 3rd St. Minden, NE 68959	4-8	364	Charles Featherstone

In grades 4 to 6 every teacher teaches language arts, and one other area; extensive exploratory program.

School Name/Address	Grades	Enrollment	Principal
Westbrook Junior High 1312 Robertson Dr. Omaha, NB 68100	7-9	400	Les Sladek

Interdisciplinary team organization in grade levels; heterogeneous grouping on grade levels; extensive exploratory program; teacher-advisor program; three-way conferences (student-teacher-parent) at the end of each quarter; block schedule; "Writing is Thinking" program; "Responsibility Pass Club."

Beck Middle Cropwell Rd. Cherry Hill, NJ 08003	7-8	800	Tracy L. Miller

Interdisciplinary team organization on grade levels; flexible block time schedule; teachers make up weekly schedules.

Glen Ridge Middle 235 Ridgewood Ave. Glen Ridge, NJ 07028	5-8	510	David Maltman

Five academic interdisciplinary teams, each multiaged by two grades; five teachers on a team; related arts team of eleven teachers who also teach multigraded classes; strong intramural program; each team has an advisor-advisee program; varied schedule provides for a multitude of possibilities; six-day related arts schedule; Program Improvement Council.

Alton U. Farnsworth Middle Guilderland Central School State Farm Rd. Guilderland, NY 12084	5-8	1423	Kenneth R. Kimball, Jr.

School-within-a-school format; self-contained for fifth graders to four-teacher teams for eighth graders; longtime commitment to mainstreaming; modular schedule; eighty electives; planetarium; closed circuit TV; graphics; participatory management.

Jamesville-DeWitt Middle Randall Rd. Jamesville, NY 13078	6-8	785	John Baker

School-within-a-school program; each house has three grade level teams with five teachers in an interdisciplinary organization; teams meet daily with house counselor; all students take foreign language-culture elective (French, Spanish, German); extensive exploratory program includes survival training, water sports, etc.; advisor-advisee; block schedule; pod-style building.

School Name/Address	Grades	Enrollment	Principal
Trotwood-Madison Junior High 3594 N. Snyder Rd. Trotwood, OH 45426	7-8	800	Charles Ott

Five interdisciplinary teams called learning communities; each team is multiage grouped; all classes are multiaged; advisor-advisee program; advisors meet monthly to discuss student needs; six-period day; open space; associated with League of IGE Schools; site for a Teacher Corps project.

Oaklea Middle 1515 Rose St. Junction City, OR 97448	5-8	620	Ted Hayes

Four cross-graded schools within a school, staffed by four interdisciplinary teams, students go to separate speciality teams for physical education (cross-graded, coed, ability grouped), music; Resource Rooms for remedial and gifted, and Occupational Versatility (art, home arts and industrial arts team—very unique forty-five learning stations in these three areas, students self-paced). Advisor/advisee (cross graded with same teacher for four years), 100 percent noontime intramurals, guaranteed participation interscholastic athletics; ability grouped and cross-graded in reading, language arts, mathematics, physical education and occupational versatility. A model middle school for the State of Oregon.

Stroudsburg Middle Chipperfield Dr. Stroudsburg, PA 18360	5-8	1069	Paul Harakal

Interdisciplinary team organization in a school-within-a-school; two houses, 5 to 8; open space; advisor-advisee program; basic skills center; television studio; block schedule; lunch hour special program in music, intramurals, special interests.

Boyce Middle 1500 Boyce Rd. Upper St. Clair, PA 15241	6-8	560	James R. Welsh

Four-teacher team—advisor-advisee-flexible block scheduling. Abundance of planning time; five-teacher expressive arts team, two health and growth counselors, student forum.

Fort Couch Middle 515 Fort Couch Rd. Upper St. Clair, PA 15241	6-8	523	John L. Wasson

Interdisciplinary teaming, advisor-advisee program, flexible block schedule, special interest program, unique counseling program, Townhall student organization.

School Name/Address	Grades	Enrollment	Principal
Brookings Middle 601 4th St. Brookings, SD 51006	6-8	557	H.A. Johnson

Departmentalized teaching teams at grade levels; extensive exploratory program; A and B day schedule; advisor-advisee program; eight periods; old building extensively remodeled; teacher advisory council.

Andrews Middle School 405 N.W. 3rd St. Andrews, TX 79714	7-8	450	Forest Scott

Multigrade grouping—minicourses in language arts, science, math lab, planetarium use for all courses, learning center with materials for level 4 through 12 in addition to the library.

Wayside Middle Box 79160 Ft. Worth, TX 76179	6-8	780	Truett Absher

Partially self-contained in grade 6, two-period block for social studies and language arts in grade 7, separate subjects in grade 8; seven-period day; five-year rotating evaluation plan.

Olle Middle 9200 Boone Rd. Alief, TX 77099	6-8	1325	Robert Schumacker

Interdisciplinary team organization in a school-within-a-school plan; strong exploratory emphasis produces seventy different activities each day; reading time one period twice weekly for twenty-five minutes; advisor-advisee period weekly for twenty-five minutes; open pods; each house elects a house president, and the three house presidents rotate leadership of the student coucil during the year.

Rusk Middle 411 N. Mound St. Nacogdoches, TX 75961	6-8	1187	Baker Denman

Interdisciplinary team organization on grade levels; five-teacher teams; two multiage blocks of students 6-7 and 7-8 are available as options; thorough advisor-advisee program featuring one-to-one relationships and parent conferences; seven-period day; old high school building.

Lawton Intermediate Essex, Junction, VT 05452	6-8	405	Stanley Knapp

Departmental organization; home base program; extensive student aide program; five-year accreditation program; eight-period day.

School Name/Address	Grades	Enrollment	Principal
Shelburne Middle Shelburne, VT 05482	5-8	530	John Winton

Interdisciplinary team organization at grade levels; block schedule; open space; one multiage team (5 to 8) open to anyone as an option; pilot school for development of "Evaluative Criteria for Middle School/Junior High School."

School Name/Address	Grades	Enrollment	Principal
Webster Transitional W75-N642 Wauwatosa Rd. Cedarsburg, WI 53012	6-8	700	Thomas Pautsch

Eight interdisciplinary teams on grade levels in eighth grade, five multiage 6-7 teams; team leaders elected by teams; block schedule; advisor-advisee program; three-way conferences at the end of the first and third quarters; semiopen space pods; three advisory committees: faculty, parent, student; minicourses; outdoor education program.

School Name/Address	Grades	Enrollment	Principal
Steuben Middle 2360 N. 52nd St. Milwaukee, WI 53210	6-8	930	Donald Leubke

Modified self-contained in sixth grade, two-teacher teams for 6-7, four-teacher teams 6-8, all options; extensive exploratory program offers over fifty courses each six weeks; additional fine art subjects; home base program; extensive evaluation program conducted by University of Wisconsin; School Coordination Committee sets policy; computer assisted instruction program.

School Name/Address	Grades	Enrollment	Principal
Oregon Middle 300 Soden Dr. Oregon, WI 53575	4-6	530	Ed Guziewski

Interdisciplinary team organization in multiage groups; extensive implementation of IGE; open space; gifted and talented program.

School Name/Address	Grades	Enrollment	Principal
Stoughton Middle 220 N. St. Soughton, WI 53589	6-8	725	Kenneth Peth

Interdisciplinary team organization in multiage groups, four 6-7 and two grade 8 groups; advisor-advisee program; eight-period day; Instructional Improvement Committee.

Index of Middle Schools

Schools are alphabetized by states and individual schools by cities. See the Appendix for further information provided by most of the schools.

Name Index

Subject Index